PEAK JAPAN

PEAK JAPAN

The End of Great Ambitions

Brad Glosserman

Georgetown University Press / Washington, DC

The publisher is not responsible for third-party websites or their content. URL links were active at time of publication.

Library of Congress Cataloging-in-Publication Data

Names: Glosserman, Brad, author.
Title: Peak Japan : The End of Great Ambitions / Brad Glosserman.
Description: Washington, DC : Georgetown University Press, 2019. | Includes
   bibliographical references and index.
Identifiers: LCCN 2018025058 (print) | LCCN 2018032310 (ebook) |
   ISBN 9781626166707 (ebook) | ISBN 9781626166684 (hardcover : alk. paper)
Subjects: LCSH: Japan—Politics and government—1989– | Japan—Economic
   conditions—1989– | Japan—Economic policy—1989– | Japan—Foreign
   relations—1989– | National security—Japan.
Classification: LCC DS891 (ebook) | LCC DS891 .G56 2019 (print) | DDC 952.05—dc23
LC record available at https://lccn.loc.gov/2018025058

20 19   9 8 7 6 5 4 3 2   First printing

Printed in the United States of America.

Jacket design: Martyn Schmoll
Cover image: iStockphoto

CONTENTS

ACKNOWLEDGMENTS

This book has been a long time in the making. It is the fruit of twenty-seven years (and counting) of living in Japan and working on Japan-related issues. Many people have contributed to its birth and the analysis it contains. What follows is only a partial list and my apologies to anyone who is left out.

First, thanks go to Allan Song of the Smith Richardson Foundation, who first approached me with the idea to explore the impact of the March 11, 2011, "triple catastrophe" in Japan. As always, Allan was forward leaning and sensitive to the significance of this moment for Japan and, by extension, for the United States. I will always be grateful for his support, his vision, and his patience as this project took shape. Thanks too go to Don Jacobs at Georgetown University Press, who gave the book a home and helped turn my musings into something marketable. Also at the press, Glenn Saltzman shepherded it through the production process, and Natalie McGartland did her best to ensure it got noticed in the real world. Vicki Chamlee fine-tuned the manuscript. The Australia Strategic Policy Institute gets a shout for publishing the first kernel of this study when it put out the special report "Peak Japan" in March 2016.

A long list of individuals gave generously of their time and thoughts about Japan, its future, and its role in the world. They include students, business professionals, academics, analysts, politicians, and government officials. Most of them are identified in the book, but a considerable number in that last group—government officials—cannot be identified for understandable reasons. Many of the comments I received did not make this final version of the manuscript, but all the people I talked to were insightful, and their thoughts helped shape my analysis.

In addition, several folks have played outsize roles in my thinking about Japan and its place in the world. Topping this list are Scott Snyder, Gordon Flake, Victor Cha, Satoh Haruko, Michael Urena, Ken Kaihara, Richard Jerram, Robert Madsen, and Christopher Sigur. They have all provided insight and, more important, advice and friendship.

At the Pacific Forum, where most of the work for this book was done, thanks go to virtually everyone. Ralph Cossa—president, mentor, and friend—made all this possible when he offered me the chance to join him at the forum in 2001 and help transform that organization. Georgette Almeida and Brooke Mizuno helped make my writings presentable. Japanese members of the Pacific Forum Young Leaders program, along with Japanese fellows whom the Pacific Forum hosted, provided invaluable observations on the thinking of the next generation of Japanese. I profited from the help of interns and research assistants, among them Yomon Chisato, Yoshida Takashi, Chris Ota, Eric Jacobson, and Jacob Merkle. Finally, there is Carl Baker, a close friend who has never failed me with guidance and advice. Carl always demanded that I think harder, more rigorously structure my analysis, and challenge the conventional wisdom. He has frustrated and pushed me—and almost invariably has been right. This book is much better for his wisdom and patience.

At Tama University I owe a special thanks to Igata Akira, a colleague who also put up with me when he was a visiting fellow at the Pacific Forum CSIS and as a Young Leader. He has provided great insight into Japan and lots of help throughout the book's gestation. Thanks too go to Kokubun Toshifumi, the director of the Center for Rule-making Strategies, for his leap of faith in bringing me on board. The Utagawas—Reizo, Eiko, and Daisuke—got me to Japan in the first place. None of this would have been possible without their support and guidance.

Finally, a very special thanks go to my wife, Fan Li. She may well be the real Japan expert in our family. She has provided many of the most important insights into the ways that Japan works and the thinking of the Japanese, expanding my perspective far beyond the political and policy worlds where I am most comfortable. She has been instrumental in helping me see the totality of the country and in helping me take note of and understand things often right in front of me that I had missed. And she has put up with my working on a book that has taken far longer than anticipated.

INTRODUCTION

J apan is understudied, undervalued, and underappreciated in the analysis and
conduct of international relations. One reason for this sad state of affairs
is the rise of China and the fundamental questions that it poses for the international order. Its stunning success has profound implications for international
security and the conduct of foreign policy worldwide, as do its business practices
and its internet and media policies. The rise of a peer competitor to the United
States, one threatening US preeminence in Asia while simultaneously being a key
US partner on many issues, has attracted—if not demanded—the attention of
analysts and policymakers. It has overshadowed Japan (along with other US allies
and partners) and has frequently cast Japan's relationship with the United States
as a mere adjunct to a larger set of concerns.

A second reason for the neglect of Japan is that the country lost its way after
the end of the Cold War. Once anticipated to overtake the United States (much
as China is today), Japan stumbled repeatedly, producing a decline "as spectacular and as confounding as its rise during the preceding decades."[1] As the former
world-beating economy stagnated, its political system seemed hopelessly decrepit
and ossified; internationally, Japan was eclipsed by neighbors and rivals. The
government proved unable to muster the resolve needed to respond to external
crises, and Japan's businesses lost their competitiveness. By 2009 the operating
profit of the Republic of Korea's conglomerate Samsung Electronics was more
than twice the amount of the combined operating profit of Japan's nine largest
electronic companies. In 2012 South Korea's credit rating surpassed that of Japan
for the first time in history.[2] When China overtook Japan officially to become the

1

world's second-largest economy in 2010, it marked the end of an era. Since 2008 and the election of Barack Obama, Tokyo has feared a condominium developing with Washington and Beijing. This notion has horrified the Japanese on several levels—not least because it threatened a partnership with the United States that had been the cornerstone of Japanese national defense and foreign policy for more than half a century.[3] From just about every angle, the nation's confidence had been shattered, and Japan is struggling to find its place in a rapidly changing world.

This stagnation and loss of direction are perplexing. Japan has demonstrated a capacity to formulate national goals and to mobilize the country in pursuit of their realization. Twice in its modern history, those efforts demanded striking reversals in national policy and objectives. At other moments, the Japanese people banded together in a display of unity and purpose that prompted speculations of a unique culture and social order. Yet since the end of the Cold War, Japan has drifted despite both ample analysis of the country's problems and widespread consensus on their causes and their cures. Political, business, and social leaders have sounded the alarm about the country's future if its current trajectory continues, and many of those warnings have proven prescient. The public has not hesitated to announce its dissatisfaction with current circumstances or its worries about future prospects. Yet the national trajectory remains largely unaltered.

As I write, Japan is enjoying one of its most prosperous and stable periods in more than two decades. Against long odds, Abe Shinzo has proven to be a visionary and energetic leader who has striven to realize his goal of "A Beautiful Country," a prosperous and secure nation that is a force for peace, order, and international stability. Abe has done far more than many thought was possible, and his term is not yet finished. The thesis of this book, however, is that the Abe era is the apogee of Japanese power and that a combination of structural and attitudinal constraints will limit Japan's ability to adapt to current and future challenges. This is "Peak Japan."

This thesis is not popular. For realists, conservatives, and traditionalists in Japan, diminished ambitions and a more inward-oriented focus are a rejection of core principles. For Japan's allies and partners, Peak Japan undercuts fundamental assumptions about order in Asia and the wider Asia-Pacific region. Anyone with an interest in Asian regional dynamics should be concerned about a gap between expectations of Japan and what the country can and will deliver. Unfulfilled expectations could lead to rupture in a crisis. Non-Japanese must therefore understand what Japan is doing and why so that they can make informed choices about their own options.

This project has been a long time in the making. It officially began in the aftermath of the triple catastrophe—earthquake, tsunami, and nuclear accident—on March 11, 2011, that resulted in nearly twenty thousand deaths, losses estimated to exceed $350 billion (about 5 percent of GDP and the worst disaster in economic terms in human history), and searing questions about Japanese identity in the twenty-first century. March 11 was an extraordinary moment: I was in San Francisco on the evening of March 10, preparing for a program the next day at the Japan Society of Northern California that was going to assess developments in Japan. In the hotel lobby, a big-screen TV was broadcasting in real time the unfolding disaster. It was a spellbinding experience. When my wife and I finally tore ourselves from the monitor, we retreated to our room, where we watched the news on Japan's national public broadcasting station NHK till early in the morning. Allan Song of the Smith Richardson Foundation, an old friend, contacted me soon afterward and asked if I would dig into the impact of this moment for Japan. Specifically, he wondered—like many others—if the incident might prove to be another "Meiji moment" that would snap Japan out of its complacency and its slump. In fact, that shock did not galvanize the public and bring about significant change, though for a while the response did not seem ordained. (In retrospect, it probably was.) As March 11 receded in history and memory, it became clear that crisis was part of a larger narrative: The physical shocks of that day were merely the latest in a series of powerful jolts Japan had experienced over several years, but none had proved capable of ending its lethargy.

This book attempts to explain why. I draw on twenty-seven years of living in Japan, of working on related materials, and of working with the Japanese. I have been privileged since I arrived in Japan in 1991 to have a unique vantage point to observe the country. I was invited by Utagawa Reizo, a former *Mainichi Shimbun* journalist who had extraordinary contacts throughout the business and political worlds and who not only took me under his wing but also welcomed me to live with him and his wife Eiko until I found my feet. He introduced me to Ogasawara Toshiaki, publisher of the *Japan Times*, who overestimated my knowledge and worth and who generously offered me a job on the editorial staff. Once there I was determined to learn everything I could about Japan, reading everything I could get my hands on and meeting as many people as possible. It was a great experience. While in Tokyo, I met Ralph Cossa, an international security specialist at the Pacific Forum CSIS, a think tank in Hawaii. We developed a friendship over his many trips to Tokyo, and when he became president of the Pacific Forum in 2001, I became the director of research there and soon after became the executive director. For the next seventeen years, I continued to study and analyze Japan, returning five or six times a year, and gained a keen appreciation of regional security, economic, and political dynamics with my near-constant travels throughout the Asia-Pacific region. That experience provides the foundation of this book.

The analysis here reflects not only extensive research and interviews but also day-to-day experiences engaging Japanese friends and colleagues in a variety of policy-related endeavors. It has drawn on a decade of reporting and seventeen years of work for the Pacific Forum: conferences, lectures, writings, and blather. For the book, I talked to a wide range of individuals who represented just about every age group, economic class, and point on the political spectrum. While canvasing "the usual suspects"—bureaucrats, politicians, academics, and think tank types—I also reached out to individuals and groups: students, artists, civil society activists, business people, and ordinary citizens across the country from Sapporo to Okinawa. Some of the most fascinating, enlightening, and encouraging conversations were with students at universities in Tokyo, Kyoto, and Osaka. We chatted in classrooms and on commutes, in coffee shops and in clubs, atop high-rise office buildings and in basement cafeterias, in high-class Japanese restaurants (*ryotei*) and salaryman bars. I've been as opportunistic as possible, seizing every chance to collect data and solicit opinions.

It's critical to talk to as broad a swath of Japanese people as possible. I suspect that some of the confusion about Japan may reflect that most researchers who produce studies go to the same experts in a particular field, when the answers to "big questions" demand a wider range of interviewees. In other words, questions about Japan's future demand answers from all Japanese—not just politicians, bureaucrats, and analysts—because all Japanese at some point participate in the decision-making process.

My analysis proceeds as follows. Chapter 1 lays out the dominant narrative of contemporary Japan, charting the country's evolution since the arrival of Commodore Matthew Perry in the 1850s, the opening of Japan that followed, and the subsequent successes and tragedies. It explains the system that emerged after World War II, how it worked, and how it broke down when the Cold War ended. There are two versions of the last piece of this story. The first, the majority view, is that Japan has experienced two "lost decades" and that big changes are required to move the country forward. A second, minority view concludes that Japan is in better shape than most believe, that its losses are exaggerated, and that only minor adjustments—if any—are needed for the country to resume its previous upward trajectory. Yet even if Japan's performance was not as bad as it seemed, most Japanese have been dissatisfied with their country's political and economic performance. This chapter explains why they felt that way and the scale of the challenges the country faced in 2008.

In the next four chapters, a series of "shocks" is used to explore Japan's "failure" in various policy arenas. As I mentioned, the genesis of the book was the March 11 triple catastrophe, but it was quickly apparent that those events were merely one in a series of jolts that had shaken Japan and challenged its fundamental assumptions and operating principles. In chapter 2, the global financial crisis and the Lehman shock provide a window on economic policy. In chapter 3, the rise to power of the Democratic Party of Japan after nearly a half century of Liberal Democratic Party rule is the vehicle to examine problems in national politics. Chapter 4 turns to foreign policy, using the 2010 crisis between Japan and China over the disputed Senkaku Islands (the Daioyu Islands to the Chinese) as a prism for exploring Japan's relationship with its neighbors and its security policy. Central to this analysis are the Meiji-era choice to go "out of Asia" and the enduring legacies of that decision. Chapter 5 looks at the events of March 11, 2011, and focuses on their impact on the conceptions of national identity that are revealed through the faith of the Japanese in technology and the ability of political, bureaucratic, and corporate institutions to manage crises.

The narrative of chapters 2 through 5 concludes at the end of 2012 and the collapse of the Democratic Party of Japan government. Chapter 6 takes up the Liberal Democratic Party's return to power under Abe Shinzo and assesses its (and his) economic policy, political performance, and foreign policy as well as how that government has addressed issues associated with identity politics.

Finally, chapter 7 summarizes the changes in each of the policy arenas and explains why the important reforms that many have demanded for Japan have not occurred. It reconciles the two seemingly inconsistent threads that dominate Japanese thinking about their country—the dissatisfaction they feel when assessing their country and the reluctance they have to embrace sweeping change. To be clear, Japan is not unchanging—no society is trapped in amber—but the sense of alarm, even with trigger events such as the four shocks, is not sufficient to move the Japanese people out of their comfort zone and to change direction from business as usual. Japan will adapt—it always does, even if more slowly than many outsiders expect—and may well surprise the world in how it evolves and what it can contribute to a world that seems in many ways to be passing it by. But the pace of change is insufficient to overcome the larger forces at work, and as a result, Japan can no longer harbor grand ambitions.

This is not an invitation to write off Japan. The country may be "shrinking"—home to just under 127 million people in 2017, its population is slated to drop to fewer than 100 million in a few decades—but it is still the world's third-largest economy and the tenth largest in terms of population. It shares the same values and interests of Western readers and is in a unique position to advance them. It can contribute in important ways to finding solutions to many of the most pressing challenges of the twenty-first century. Indeed, Japan is already tackling issues that all industrialized democracies will eventually face; thus, it is a potentially valuable laboratory to find answers. Americans in particular should be rooting for the success of an ally and partner that has been a cornerstone of their foreign policy and engagement with Asia, the most dynamic region in the world. Just as important would be the consequences of Japan's failure to surmount these challenges.

Japan matters. Since the end of World War II, the country has been unrivaled in its contributions to regional and global peace. It has been the second-largest financial contributor to the United Nations, it was for many years the world's largest source of overseas development aid, and its constitution renounced the use of war as an instrument of state policy. As of this writing, the Japanese government is reassessing fundamentals of postwar security and foreign policy, and the effects of that discussion are already being felt. Some worry about the potential for destabilizing East Asia and unbalancing a regional order that has provided the foundation of regional peace and security. An accurate understanding of Japan and its future will help us properly respond to changes that are occurring and ensure that Asia's dynamism continues.

Notes

1. Hahm Chaibong, "Preface," in *Japan in Crisis: What Will It Take for Japan to Rise Again?*, ed. Bong Youngshik and T. J. Pempel (Seoul: The Asan Institute of Policy Studies, 2012), 8.
2. Ibid.
3. The trade frictions that dominate the US-China relationship at the time of this writing—the spring of 2018—have reduced Japanese fears to some extent, but policymakers in Tokyo remain wary of the Donald Trump administration and worry that the deal maker in the White House who continually touts his personal relationship with Chinese president Xi Jinping could find common ground with Beijing on a range of issues that would jeopardize Japanese national interests.

1

THE UNHAPPY COUNTRY

The study of history is in many cases the plotting of national trajectories that soar and eventually collapse back into themselves. Few countries have experienced this wrenching dislocation as acutely as Japan has. No country in the last 150 years has enjoyed as many highs nor plummeted to such lows. Kawashima Yutaka, a diplomat who capped a distinguished career as number 2 in his country's Foreign Ministry, believes that "the 'ups and downs' of Japan is the biggest event" of the twentieth century.[1]

Those swings began in July 1853, when Commodore Matthew Perry arrived in Edo (now Tokyo) Bay and demanded that Japan open its doors to trade with the United States. Perry sought to end the *sakoku* (closed country), or isolation, policy that had been in place since 1633 and had strictly regulated Japanese commerce and foreign policy. Officially, no foreigner could enter Japan, nor could a Japanese leave, under pain of death. In truth, the country was not completely closed. It conducted some commerce with foreign nations through treaty ports but routinely denied other countries' demands for access to Japanese markets. On balance it was easy to conclude that "Japan wasn't part of the world in the 1870s and 1880s."[2] After being stiff-armed on that first visit, Perry returned less than a year later with a flotilla twice the size of his earlier force and obliged Japan—with a little help from the big guns on his ships—to sign the Convention of Kanagawa, which effectively ended sakoku.[3] That experience has been burned into the Japanese consciousness. A century and half later, "black ships"—referencing those of Commodore Perry—still symbolize any foreign force that shoulders its way into Japan.

Perry's guns made a big impression. His demands unleashed a political whirlwind in Japan, one that resulted in the overthrow of the established order. The shogun, a military leader who since 1192 was de facto ruler of the country (despite being appointed by the emperor), was defeated and forced from power by an alliance of Japanese regional leaders who recognized the need for national renewal. The then fifteen-year-old Meiji emperor replaced him.

While Japan may have been forced to join a new Western-dominated international order in East Asia,[4] the country embraced reform with a ruthless efficiency and sense of purpose. During the Meiji period, the government scoured the world for learning, technologies, and know-how that would facilitate its modernization of the country and ensure that it was never again at the mercy of larger, more powerful forces.[5] As historian E. H. Norman explained,

> The makers of Japanese policy saw that if they were to escape the fate of China or Egypt, they must adopt the political methods and economic policy of those powers who had been responsible for Japan's rude awakening and for the partial colonization of China. History is a relentless task master and all its lessons warned the Meiji statesmen that there was to be no halfway house between the status of a subject nation and that of a growing, victorious empire.[6]

The payoff was spectacular. Within three decades, Japan's GDP per capita had grown by 70 percent. (It would double by 1913 and double again by 1938.)[7] The country translated that economic success into international stature. By 1895 the Japanese army had defeated China and in the Treaty of Shimonoseki was awarded Formosa (Taiwan), the Pescadores Islands, and the Liaodong Peninsula. The same treaty also liberated Korea from Chinese domination, a move that opened the door to Japan's control of the peninsula. Less than a decade later, Japan challenged a Western power, Russia—which Tokyo saw as a check on Japanese ambitions in Northeast Asia—and won. Japanese forces inflicted a disastrous military defeat on the Russian Pacific Fleet in Port Arthur. In the Treaty of Portsmouth, negotiated by US president Theodore Roosevelt and signed in 1905, Japan was awarded southern Manchuria, the key cities of Port Arthur and Dalian, and southern Sakhalin. Moscow was also forced to accept Japan's "paramount interest in Korea," essentially rendering that country a Japanese protectorate. Korea was fully annexed in 1910. By then, notes historian Warren Cohen, Japan had become a world power.

> Japan . . . forced Korea to open its doors and came to dominate that country before the end of the century. It was Japan that became China's greatest tormentor. And it was Japan that rose to challenge the West's design for East

Asia, repelling the Russian thrust into Korea and Manchuria in the early years of the twentieth century. . . . [T]he Japanese created a state powerful enough not only to stop the Russians, but also to win an alliance with Great Britain and to threaten the interests of the United States in the Pacific.[8]

Also, and significantly from today's vantage point, "Japan had moved from being the victim of Western imperialism to [the] victimizer of its neighbors."[9]

Significant though those events were, they were only midpoints in Japan's rise. Tokyo had won revision of the unequal treaties—agreements forced on Asian countries by Western governments that awarded extraterritorial rights to those foreigners (among other things)—in 1899 and regained complete tariff autonomy, a vital symbol of sovereignty, in 1911. Throughout the second decade of the twentieth century, as Japan consolidated its empire in Asia, it was aided by two factors: the terms of the Treaty of Versailles, whose negotiation Japan joined as one of the "Big Five" victors, and the fact that Western powers were distracted by other events and unwilling to defend Chinese sovereignty.

In 1932 Japan created the puppet state of Manchuko in Manchuria to give its rule there a veneer of legitimacy and to then drive deeper into China. It simultaneously expanded its empire to Southeast Asia, eventually announcing the establishment of the Greater East Asia Co-prosperity Sphere in August 1940. That project sought to establish a new order in Southeast Asia, "a self-sufficient block of Asian nations free from Western powers led by Japan."[10] War with the United States followed within sixteen months, but that bold gamble ended in ruin: Japan's empire was lost and the homeland laid waste. Japan is reckoned to have lost between 2.6 million and 3.1 million people in the war, the equivalent of 3.67–4.37 percent of its 1939 population.[11] Perhaps more significant than the numbers were the ways that Japan was attacked: The firebombings of Tokyo and the atomic bombings of Hiroshima and Nagasaki unleashed destruction that was beyond the imagination.

"Japan as Number 1"

In 1945 Japan was devastated. Historian John Dower has reckoned that around a quarter of the nation's wealth was destroyed in the Pacific War.[12] Not only was it utterly defeated and occupied but also the country had no national resources other than the determination of its population and was politically, diplomatically, and economically isolated after a brutal and savage conflict. Yet from the rubble of defeat it constructed "the miracle," a bold and ultimately successful plan to rebuild the nation that propelled it into the leading ranks of nations and even prompted a reconsideration of development models. Japan's "development state" became the template for success in other Asian countries. That extraordinary record helped Japan overcome the brutal legacy of World War II and reestablish its position in Asia.

A single-minded bureaucracy working hand in hand with an ambitious political class and determined business sector fused a largely homogeneous society with an ancient culture to rewrite the rules of capitalism. Once famously derided as a nation of transistor salesmen, Japan focused on building a powerful export sector, created manufacturing conglomerates that set world standards, and crushed the competition. Companies such as Sony, Toyota, and Panasonic dominated their industries to become household must haves; even Japanese companies that were not as well known rose to the heights of their respective industries, emerging seemingly from nowhere and using their wealth to gobble up competitors. In 1988 Japan accounted for more than 16 percent of global wealth[13]—an impressive share for a small, resource-poor country—and this statistic helped validate the characterization of Japan's postwar economic trajectory as a miracle. Of the ten largest companies in the world in 1989, according to market capitalization, seven were Japanese. The value of NTT Corporation, Japan's telephone giant, which was privatized during the boom, exceeded the value of AT&T, IBM, Exxon, General Electric, and General Motors combined. By 1990 the world's five largest banks, measured by total assets, were Japanese.[14]

Living standards were steadily rising. In a fantastic display of its potential, a plan to double national incomes in a decade (from 1960 to 1970) was declared a success in just eight years as Japan recorded 10 percent annual growth.[15] Incredibly this growth was well distributed. Japan managed to sidestep the growing pains and social disparities that characterized most other industrialized economies. Routinely 90 percent of the Japanese—in some cases, even more—when surveyed labeled themselves middle class.[16] To commemorate their climb to international preeminence, Japanese companies bought up trophy properties around the world, with Pebble Beach golf courses and Rockefeller Center among them. Japanese tourists traveled in ever-growing numbers, flooding fashion boutiques and Michelin three-star restaurants while enjoying the newfound wealth that followed the near doubling in the value of the yen in 1985 after the Plaza Accord. Tokyo became the world's largest aid donor, the second-largest contributor to the United Nations (UN), and the only Asian nation to have a seat among the Group of Seven leading industrialized nations. In their essay, "The Japan That Can Say 'No,'" nationalist writer (and later Tokyo governor) Ishihara Shintaro and Sony founder Morita Akio argued that Japan had the economic and technological strengths to reshape the global balance of power—and should not hesitate to use that power accordingly.[17]

As the Japanese enjoyed their hard-earned success, others celebrated it. In 1976 the Brookings Institution published *Asia's New Giant*, a backbreaking nine-hundred-plus-page analysis by a team of US and Japanese social scientists that explained Japan's extraordinary economic performance over the previous twenty-five years.[18] In 1979 Harvard sociologist Ezra Vogel authored *Japan as Number 1*, a pathbreaking study that explored and applauded Japan's record. As Vogel explained, "The more I observed Japan's success in a variety of fields, the more I became convinced that given its limited resources, Japan has dealt more successfully with more of the basic problems of post-industrial society than any other country."[19]

Others were not so sanguine. Clyde Prestowitz, a former US trade negotiator, warned that "the power behind the Japanese juggernaut is much greater than most Americans suspect, and the juggernaut cannot stop of its own volition, for Japan has created a kind of automatic wealth machine, perhaps the first since King Midas."[20] He worried that within the span of a decade—the 1980s—Japan and the United States had traded places as the protégé surpassed its protector and mentor. A then little-known New York real estate developer with political aspirations named Donald Trump took out full-page advertisements in several national newspapers warning that Japan (along with other US allies) was "taking advantage of the United States" and that it was imposing significant costs on the United States in terms of the economy, the deficit, and taxes. Trump asked, "Why are these nations not paying the United States for the human lives and billions of dollars we are losing to protect their interests? . . . The world is laughing at America's politicians as we protect ships we don't own, carrying oil we don't need, destined for allies who won't help."[21] Edith Cresson, a briefly tenured French prime minister in 1991–92, was even more alarmist, likening Japanese to "yellow ants" trying to take over the world.[22] Dark speculations reached their apogee in *The Coming War with Japan*, a book by George Friedman and Meredith Lebard, whose title pretty much reflects its take on Japan's meteoric rise.[23] Only in comparison could Chalmers Johnson, the man who provided the intellectual framework to understand Japan's success in his classic study *MITI* [the Ministry of International Trade and Industry] *and the Japanese Miracle*, look restrained. He likened Japan to Venice, calling it "La Serenissima of the East." By the early 1990s, Johnson had concluded that "the Cold War is over and Japan won."[24]

Not everyone in Japan was celebrating that "victory." Some Japanese worried that in the aftermath of the collapse of the Soviet Union, the United States' "psychological need for a rival" would put their country in the crosshairs.[25] Those worries were validated when Gallup polls showed 77 percent of Americans viewed Japan as an economic threat.[26] A rising strain of anti-Japanese sentiment was encapsulated by James Fallows's seminal article "Containing Japan," in which he argued that Japan was engaged in a "one-sided and destructive expansion of its economic power."[27] If the United States did not recognize, acknowledge, and ultimately minimize the destructive consequences of Japan's economic model, then there was a risk not only that the United States (and other Westerners) would "one day be the noncommissioned officers in Japan's economic army" but also that Japan would do great damage to US national interests. Fallows was blunt: "Unless Japan is contained, therefore, several things that matter to America will be jeopardized: America's own authority to carry out its foreign policy and advance its ideals, American citizens' future prospects within the world's most powerful business firms, and also the very system of free trade that America has helped sustain since the Second World War."[28]

Yet, for many Japanese, and a considerable number of others, Japan was thought to have rewritten the rules of capitalism as it fashioned a new cultural, economic, and political model that overcame many of the challenges and limitations of the prevailing paradigm. It seemed poised to continue its awesome trajectory in a post–Cold War world. Indeed, many Japanese thought—and others feared—that Japan might be uniquely capable of thriving in that world.

The Bubble Bursts

Then the dream collapsed. The economic engine had already begun to show signs of strain and fatigue. The country's export machine, by the 1980s, was generating massive trade surpluses. The doubling of the value of the yen in 1985, launching the surge in Japanese buying around the world, was an attempt to restore some balance to the global economy (and undercut protectionist pressures in the United States), but it didn't have the intended impact on Japan's surpluses. Credit the extraordinary prowess of Japanese companies, which managed to squeeze productivity and maintain profitability at the new exchange rates. The Bank of Japan, the country's central bank, lent a hand in February 1987 by cutting interest rates in half—from 5 percent to 2.5 percent—to limit yen appreciation and to cushion the blow to the Japanese economy.[29] The move worked, but it goosed the growth in money supply, which expanded 9–12 percent in the three remaining years of the decade.[30]

The currency revaluation and the interest rate cuts resulted in a flood of capital washing over Japan. Unfortunately, there weren't sufficient productive places to invest that money. In some cases, that newfound wealth found its way outside Japan and was used to purchase those trophy properties. In more cases, however, the result was intense speculation in Japan's real estate and stock markets, which inflated extraordinary bubbles. The country's Nikkei stock index hit its all-time high on the last day of trading in 1989, reaching 38,957.44 before closing down slightly at 38,915.87; that number was more than three times the Nikkei's value at the time of the Plaza Accord. At that peak, Japanese stocks had a total market value of about $4 trillion, or around one and a half times the value of all US equities (even though Japanese GDP was less than half of US GDP at the time) and close to 45 percent of the world's equity market capitalization.[31]

Determined to give ostentation a whole new meaning, clients—never customers—drank sake sprinkled with gold flakes or nibbled sushi at over $100 a slice in Tokyo's most exclusive clubs. The world's best-known luxury brands reaped the lion's share of their sales in Japan. Real estate values also skyrocketed. In the Ginza district in Tokyo, a shopping and dining area best known for obscenely priced drinking establishments and equally expensive drinking companions, prime properties went for more than ¥30 million (approximately $215,000) per square meter (or about $20,000 per square foot). At one point, experts reckoned the value of the imperial palace in the heart of Tokyo—a piece of land a mere 3.4 square kilometers in size—was equivalent in value to all the land in the state of California. One economist in 1990 estimated that the aggregate value of all the land in Japan was 50 percent greater than the value of all land in the rest of the world. And no one blinked as banks used those valuations to lend money. Looking back, economists have calculated that the combined capital gains on stocks and land were 452 percent of nominal GDP for the 1986–89 period—a stunning expansion in just three years.[32]

Some recognized the danger signs. Officials at the Ministry of Finance and the Bank of Japan were responsible for long-term economic stability. While inflation remained under control, by 1989 they had concluded that the bubbles in real estate and stock prices were unsustainable. Determined to restore some sanity to prices, interest rates were sharply increased from 2.5 percent in May 1989 to 6 percent by August 1990. Shock therapy worked. Equity prices began to fall almost immediately; the Nikkei declined by 46 percent within a year. The interest rate spike was accompanied by new guidelines from the Ministry of Finance that restricted bank lending to the real estate sector. Together those two measures not only capped the explosion in property values but also lowered them by more than 30 percent.[33]

Unfortunately, real estate had served as collateral for extensive borrowing by both businesses and individuals. Bank regulations permitted borrowing of up to 90 percent of the value of real estate collateral, a policy that made sense in the go-go years of the 1980s and in a world in which property prices never declined. But the slowdown that followed the sharp increase in interest rates also strained business balance sheets at the very time the collateral that underpinned borrowing was losing its value. Banks suddenly found they had large volumes of nonperforming loans and little chance of making them whole. Worse, the excesses had infected the entire financial system; not only banks but also insurance companies and brokerages were overleveraged. Fortunately for them, Japanese bankers were a forgiving lot. For reasons of culture, politics, and business practice, bankers were reluctant to call in loans, foreclose on deadbeat debtors, or write off assets. The economy suffered, however, as a mountain of bad debt remained on the books, suppressing the ability of banks to loan money to viable businesses.[34]

In the real economy, aggregate supply exceeded demand by orders of magnitude. In other words, too many companies were making too many products (and employing too many people) for the market to absorb. Companies that should have gone bankrupt stayed in business. These "zombie companies" generated enough business to service their loans—ensuring that bank balance sheets remained healthy—but not enough to become viable and profitable. In some cases, banks loaned a customer just enough money to make a payment and avoid default. While this practice staved off bankruptcy, it also ensured that markets did not clear; companies that should have gone out of business did not, dragging down healthier companies. One study concluded that 37 percent of the decline in aggregate productivity growth due to inefficient labor reallocation in Japan in the 1990s can be blamed on "zombie lending."[35] As supply continued to outpace demand, prices fell and the economy deflated.

Then the miracle ran aground. After expanding 9.38 percent annually on average from 1946 to 1960 and registering 8.26 percent annual growth from 1960 to 1975 (and slowing to a still respectable 4.12 percent from 1975 to 1990),[36] Japan crawled through the 1990s. It marked real GDP growth of just 1 percent per year on average—the worst of all countries in the Organization for Economic Cooperation and Development (OECD)—and struggled through three recessions. Nominal GDP (economic output not adjusted for price levels) fared even worse: The level of nominal GDP in 2001 was approximately the same as in 1995, meaning the country had not grown at all.[37] It should come as no surprise then that the 1990s are usually referred to as Japan's "lost decade."

Crises, Domestic and Foreign

The darkening mood that had taken root in Japan reflected more than concern about the country's economic prospects. Two striking failures of crisis management contributed to the national malaise. In January 1995 the Great Hanshin Earthquake rocked the city of Kobe in southern Japan and, in the process, shattered Japanese confidence in the superior construction standards that had been created as a result of near-daily experience with temblors. Some sixty-four hundred people died in the quake. Twenty-two percent of the buildings in the Kobe central business district were left unusable; more than half the houses in the area were deemed unfit for occupation.[38] The iconic image from the earthquake was a collapsed one-kilometer section of the Hanshin Expressway, a column of rubble running through the city center.

The inadequacy of construction standards was only part of a larger perceived failure by the Japanese government. Assuming naively that their region was not susceptible to large tremors, Kobe city authorities were not ready for a disaster of this magnitude. Neither they nor the Tokyo government had crisis management procedures and mechanisms in place; at that time, no central government authority similar to the US Federal Emergency Management Agency existed to deal with a crisis.[39] The result was a confused response from the authorities and the eventual privatization of relief efforts, with private companies, organizations, and individuals taking the lead. The yakuza (organized crime groups) and the *uyoku* (right-wing activists) were among the most visible and effective in opening soup kitchens and distributing aid and relief supplies.[40]

The government's failure to anticipate and plan for a crisis of this magnitude was felt again just weeks later, in mid-March 1995, when the Aum Shinrikyo millennial terrorist group launched a sarin gas attack on the subway system that ran under Tokyo. That assault killed thirteen people, severely injured dozens more, and hurt nearly a thousand people. Aum is an especially dark and ugly chapter in modern Japanese history, but two elements of the story are particularly troubling. First, Aum members were not crazed youths on the margins of society; many of them were thirty- and forty-year-olds who were products of Japan's finest universities. That they could fall under the spell of a madman and launch a terrorist attack against innocent bystanders during the morning rush hour said something ominous about Japan in the mid-1990s. Second, subsequent revelations about what the government knew (or suspected) about the group make its lack of preparation for an attack even more astounding. Once again the Japanese people felt their government had betrayed them, amplifying and magnifying their uncertainty about the future.

That unease grew as the Japanese contemplated the world beyond their borders. Japan began the 1990s buoyed not only by its economic successes but also by the belief that the world was evolving in ways that Japan was uniquely able to exploit. The international coalition US president George H. W. Bush marshaled to confront and defeat the Iraqis' aggression against Kuwait promised "a new world order," one based on international law and institutions. This initiative delighted many Japanese, who envisioned a post–Cold War world in which the rule of law would prevail over brute force and in which Japan, with a constitution that abjured the use of force as an instrument of state power, would be singularly positioned to make a case for global leadership. Instead, Japan was rudely awakened to the limits of this new world order and of Tokyo's power and influence in it. Despite making the largest financial contribution to the coalition that defeated Saddam Hussein's army—$13 billion, courtesy of a specially imposed corporate tax—Japan was dismissed as a free rider and a practitioner of "checkbook diplomacy" that was unwilling to put its forces in harm's way, even when it was a leading beneficiary of such action.[41] When the government of Kuwait took out advertisements in leading newspapers around the world to thank nations that assisted in its liberation, it left Japan off the list.

More crises followed. In 1992 North Korea's nuclear ambitions became clear for the first time, prompting a near conflict between it and the United States the following year. The crisis was averted only by the intervention of former president Jimmy Carter and a US–North Korean agreement that worked for nearly a decade before collapsing under the weight of its overly optimistic assumptions. Nor was a rogue state the only nuclear concern. China conducted a nuclear test in 1995 as the rest of the world debated a comprehensive test ban treaty, and India and Pakistan entered the nuclear weapons club in 1998 with their own back-to-back tests. For Japan, a nation with a particularly sensitive nuclear history, the spread of nuclear weapons was especially alarming.

China's adoption of economic reforms in 1992 sparked blistering growth, which facilitated double-digit expansion of its national defense budget. Beijing's increasingly formidable military shifted perceptions of—and the response to—tensions between China and Taiwan, a Cold War hot spot that outlived the Cold War. A crisis flared in 1995 when Taiwan's president, Lee Teng-hui, an avowed supporter of Taiwan's independence, visited Cornell University, his alma mater, to give a speech titled "Taiwan's Democratization Experience." China warned the Bill Clinton administration that giving Lee a visa would create problems for the US-China relationship. While Secretary of State Warren Christopher assured his Chinese counterpart, Foreign Minister Qian Qichen, that no visa would be granted, the Republican-controlled Congress passed resolutions calling for allowing Lee to visit. The State Department reversed course, causing Qian to lose face and infuriating China. In 1996 China held missile exercises designed to intimidate Taiwanese voters, but the tactic failed: Lee won another term as president, and the United States responded by dispatching an aircraft carrier battle group through the Taiwan Strait. Japanese security analysts warned about "the rise of China as an aggressive power." They pointed to Beijing's readiness to use force to enhance its position in Asia; its democratic deficit, which could trigger internal instability; and its demand for greater international status as its economic strength grew.[42]

Unwilling to be overshadowed, North Korea continued sending signals of its own. In 1998 it launched a Taepodong missile that overflew Japan, awakening the Japanese (and the world) to the belligerent and bellicose nation's newly acquired ability to reach out and touch a longtime enemy. North Korean spy boats played cat and mouse with Japanese maritime forces as the former smuggled drugs and people into Japan. This is why "Japanese defense policy-makers have long identified North Korea's military capabilities as a potentially explosive cause of instability in Northeast Asia. . . . Official Japanese concern about North Korea has also been illustrated by the JDA's [Japan Defense Agency's] defence white papers, which since 1994 and for the first time have chosen to place North Korea ahead of Russia or China as the principal source of military instability in Northeast Asia."[43]

The Japanese people's unease was compounded by mounting concern about their relationship with the United States. A partnership that was famously described as "the most important bilateral relationship in the world, bar none!" was under severe strain.[44] Japan's economic success prompted critics (such as Donald Trump) to denounce Tokyo as a free rider that "tricked" the United States into paying defense bills that its ally was supposedly shirking. (Those critics overlooked both the substantial sums of host nation support that Tokyo provided for the US force presence and the benefits that the United States obtained from having that forward presence.) Trade tensions bubbled up, but they were largely contained by bilateral efforts such as the Structural Impediments Initiative. More worrisome was the prospect of a rupture in the security relationship. That possibility became alarmingly real in September 1995, when three American servicemen rented a van and kidnapped and raped a twelve-year-old Okinawan girl. The horrific event prompted soul-searching throughout Japan about the price of the US military's presence and prompted an intense dialogue between the two governments that changed the status of forces agreement that governed how American service personnel would be treated when they broke the law. Ultimately, they reached a new agreement on the terms of the US-Japan security partnership.[45] The goodwill and confidence that effort generated lasted two years, until US president Clinton made a two-week trip to China in 1998 and neglected to visit Japan on either leg. "Japan bashing" had given way to "Japan passing," prompting the Japanese to fear that they had been marginalized in US strategic thinking because of their economic woes and political weakness.

As the decade drew to a close, the Japanese surveyed their place in the world with resignation and some trepidation. In the Cabinet Office's annual survey of the thinking and outlook of Japanese citizens, the December 1999 poll showed just 3.3 percent of respondents said that life had improved over the previous year; 67 percent thought life was much the same, while more than 28 percent thought things were getting worse. Nine percent thought things would get better, 64 percent said life would stay the same, and 24.5 percent expected things to get worse.[46] As the new century rang in, the *Japan Times* lamented in its New Year's editorial that "the final ten years of the twentieth century have been called 'a lost decade' for Japan, which continues to suffer woes from the burst of the late-1980s bubble-economy. Japan's comeback as a globally competitive economic powerhouse will require fundamental reforms not only in the industrial and financial sectors but also in government administration, politics and social systems, including education, the judiciary and immigration."[47]

Days after the new millennium began, a special commission tabled its assessment of "the desirable future direction of Japan." The Prime Minister's Commission on Japan's Goals in the 21st Century, often referred to as the Kawai Commission, was established in March 1999 to set forth "the new ideals and organizational principles with which Japan should equip itself for the twenty-first century."[48] It concluded that the country was at "a historical turning point"—"a third great transition" akin to that of the Meiji Restoration and the country's defeat in World War II—as a result of globalization, global literacy, the information technology revolution, scientific advances, and demographic change (chap. 3, 2). It worried that the economic travails of the 1980s and 1990s "had undermined not only the economy but also the political order and society—even the value system and ethical norms at the very core of the nation" (chap. 1, 1). (This crucial theme is taken up in more detail later.) It acknowledged that a central mission for Japan is rewriting its social contract and redefining the relationship between individuals and society; nothing less is needed than "the creation of a new public space" (chap. 1, 7). The authors conceded that theirs is "a grand theme, one normally too sweeping to contemplate" (chap. 1, 19). Significantly, the commission's sixteen members felt that such drastic reform was a must, noting that "we share a sense of urgency. We fear that as things stand Japan is heading for decline" (chap. 1, 1).

Koizumi Junichiro to the Rescue

Those warnings had little effect. GDP contracted in the first quarter of 2001, unemployment rose to 5.5 percent, industrial production hit thirteen-year lows, and Japanese government debt was rated Aa2, the worst among all industrialized countries.[49] Economic planners decried the inexorable pace at which companies were moving facilities overseas, "hollowing out" domestic industries. "In 2001 alone, 69 major Japanese firms shut down 120 factories in Japan and 70 percent of these were moved to China."[50] Japanese foreign direct investment (FDI) in

China went from 5 percent of the total FDI in Asia in 1990 to 48.6 percent in 2004. "In 2002 the Fuji Research Institute estimated that between 2002 and 2010, domestic production would fall by ¥8.8 trillion (roughly $73 billion), GDP would fall by 1.7 percent and employment by a further 1.25 million. . . . [A] government council warned, not entirely tongue in cheek, that if the current rate of overseas FDI by Japanese firms were to continue, no manufacturing plants would be left in Japan by 2018."[51]

Still more disturbing for many Japanese was the social crisis engendered by a faltering economy. For a society that largely saw itself as homogenous and for which the fruits of success and prosperity were shared—remember, routinely 90 percent of Japanese considered themselves to be middle class—the personal dimensions of stagnation were appalling. By the early 2000s, many indicators of social distress had hit record highs: unemployment, bankruptcies by small firms, homelessness, crime, divorce rates, child abuse, and suicides. There was "a rapid exacerbation of private suffering . . . directly related to economic hardship."[52] According to the 2000 survey of the OECD, Japan's child poverty rate was 14.3 percent, which was 2.2 percentage points higher than the OECD average.[53] This was a stunning fall for a country that in the mid-1980s had a Gini coefficient (a measure of income inequality) of 27.8, which was below the OECD average. By 2000, it was above the OECD average (31.4), and inequality was growing twice as fast as the OECD average rate.[54] Ironically these disturbing developments were the product of Japan's previous economic success: As long as corporate Japan was booming, government-funded social safety programs were reduced in importance.

Meanwhile, and ominously for a country that watched as the security environment steadily deteriorated, questions were mounting in Washington about Tokyo's "ability to focus or reciprocate US efforts to strengthen the alliance."[55] Much of the worry reflected doubts about Japanese leadership: Prime ministers slipped in and out of office with dismaying regularity, and the honors system that rewarded loyalty and longevity in service to the Liberal Democratic Party (LDP) was no guarantor of competence. Bureaucrats could keep the alliance on course, but devising strategies and policies that would respond to a dynamic security environment demanded political leadership, which was in short supply in Tokyo.

That leadership vacuum was filled by an unlikely politician. A little-heralded third-generation politician, Koizumi Junichiro moved into the prime minister's office in 2001 (after prevailing in a party leadership election) and settled in for a remarkable five-year stay. Koizumi had previously served as minister of posts and telecommunications for eight months in 1992–93 and as health and welfare minister twice, serving for less than a year in the late 1980s and again seven years later. Koizumi was thought to be too young (he was "only" fifty-nine), too idiosyncratic (he was known for his leonine hairstyle and his love of Elvis Presley), and too reformist in his policy.

Despite those low expectations, Koizumi set new standards for Japanese leadership, instilling a new energy and dynamism in the Kantei (the building where the prime minister lives and works, the Japanese equivalent of the White House), transforming international perceptions of Japan, and kindling renewed interest in politics and possibilities in Japan. He was a telegenic politician who was cool, assertive, and media savvy. His personal popularity soared to an unheard-of 80 percent as he promised there would be no sacred cows in his pursuit of the revitalization of Japan and that he was ready to take on his own party to get it done—a promise he took up with relish as he encountered opposition to his reform plans.[56]

Koizumi's extended tenure as prime minister provided much-needed stability at the highest level of the Japanese government—a critical condition if the country was to regain its footing. In foreign policy Koizumi instantly made his mark by standing with US president George W. Bush after the September 11, 2001, terror attacks and declared—in English no less—that Japan would support the United States in its hour of need. His instinctive and forward-leading leadership style appealed to Bush, who saw many of his own best qualities mirrored in Koizumi. (It helped that many of the most senior foreign policy officials in the Bush administration were eager to move the US-Japan alliance forward and espied in Koizumi the much-needed partner for alliance modernization.) During their time together, Bush and Koizumi forged the "George-Jun relationship," which rivaled the "Ron-Yasu" partnership struck by President Ronald Reagan and Japanese prime minister Nakasone Yasuhiro during the late 1980s and was considered to be the high-water mark for the two countries' relations. Koizumi argued that Japan, as one of the chief beneficiaries of the liberal international order, needed to do more to sustain that order. Significantly, he made that claim not because Japan owed duties to the United States as an alliance partner but because Japan incurred obligations and responsibilities as a result of its success. In keeping with that mind-set, the Koizumi government pushed for a historical deployment of Japanese Self-Defense Forces both to Iraq to assist in Operation Iraqi Freedom and to help refuel coalition warships taking part in interdiction operations against terrorists in the Indian Ocean from 2001 to 2008.[57] By the end of Koizumi's tenure, a nation that had been derided as a free rider that was willing to cut checks and let other governments secure its defense was being touted as "the UK of Asia" and the possessor of a "special relationship" with the United States, one that matched that of the Anglo-American alliance.[58]

Relations with the United States got a jolt when Koizumi made the stunning announcement that he would travel to Pyongyang on September 17, 2002, to meet Kim Jong-il, the reclusive leader of North Korea. During that quick visit, Kim made the remarkable admission that over the years agents of his country had kidnapped more than a dozen Japanese citizens. Conservatives in Japan had leveled the charge for some time, but it had been denied by the North Korean government and its sympathizers in Japan. Kim may have thought that confessing would allow the two countries to wipe the slate clean and let them forge a productive bilateral relationship; instead, it created an issue that poisons bilateral relations to this day.[59] Questions continue to swirl around the abductees—how many were taken, and are they still alive?—and to block any rapprochement between Tokyo and Pyongyang.

Hopes that relations with North Korea would improve were fatally wounded weeks later when the United States accused Pyongyang of cheating on the 1994 Agreed Framework and pursuing a clandestine nuclear weapons program. That crisis has endured ever since, despite years of multilateral dialogue (trilateral US-China–North Korea talks, which soon became the Six-Party Talks), with North Korea conducting six nuclear weapons tests and launching dozens of missiles of all ranges—all in defiance of the international community and explicit UN Security Council resolutions. North Korea's gradual expansion of its nuclear capabilities prompted concern in Japan—a Cabinet Office survey early in Koizumi's tenure showed 92 percent of the Japanese were anxious about the North Korean threat—and raised questions about the credibility of Japan's alliance with the United States and the need to acquire indigenous nuclear capabilities.[60] Given Japan's history, a sensitivity to nuclear diplomacy is natural. The country's reliance on the United States for its defense, and the extended US nuclear deterrent in particular, makes the nuclear weapons questions even more elemental, however.[61] By the end of Koizumi's tenure, the Japan Defense Agency's annual white paper would decry North Korea's "developing, deploying and proliferating weapons of mass destruction (WMDs) and ballistic missiles and . . . maintaining large-scale special operations forces. . . . North Korea increases military tension over the Korean Peninsula, and its behavior constitutes a serious destabilizing factor for the entire East Asian region, including Japan."[62]

While North Korea posed an immediate concern, the Japanese were also made uneasy by the rise of China, a longtime rival for regional power and primacy. China is a big country with a robust and expanding economy, a burning set of grievances, and a readiness to right historical wrongs, some of the most painful of which were inflicted by Japan. For the past fifty years, Japan has dealt with China through adroit diplomacy and economic largesse buttressed by the knowledge that Tokyo's security alliance with the United States would protect Japanese national interests. But in the twenty-first century, China has appeared to be challenging even the United States for regional preeminence. This development has fed the concern that Washington would write off Japan and cut a deal with Beijing to form a condominium, which would effectively divide the Pacific in half.

Koizumi's relations with China were complex. As was noted, Japanese companies were increasingly reliant on China to provide cheap labor and sustain their competitive advantage, but as economic integration progressed—and profits swelled—political difficulties mounted. A quiet yet confident nationalist, Koizumi had pledged that he would visit the Yasukuni Shrine every year to pay homage to Japan's war dead. (All the souls of individuals who fought in war on behalf of Japan are "enshrined" at Yasukuni. The inclusion of fourteen executed class A war criminals has made the officials' visits a source of controversy, prompting complaints by liberals in Japan and by the governments of China and South Korea that honoring the dead demonstrated support for the militarist, expansionist government that waged the Pacific War.) Koizumi made six visits to the shrine during his tenure as prime minister and was the first officeholder to do so since 1985. When asked about the visits, Koizumi made no apologies but noted they were reminders of the horrors of war and the need to ensure peace. His determination to honor that campaign pledge was the source of difficulties in Japan's relations with China—it produced the era of "hot economics, cold politics"—but, fortunately, they did not prevent the two governments from working together on critical issues and dealing with crises when they emerged.

Similar forces were at work on Japan's relationship with South Korea. South Koreans were as angered as the Chinese were by Koizumi's visits to the Yasukuni Shrine, but a shared sense of threat from North Korea drove Tokyo and Seoul— together with Washington—to work closely together in the Trilateral Cooperation and Oversight Group, a group of the three governments that ensured they presented coordinated diplomatic and military responses to North Korean provocations. In addition, Japan and South Korea cohosted the 2002 FIFA World Cup, and the need for both countries to do a spectacular job holding that competition—especially to ensure that one host did not outshine the other—helped overcome the frictions generated by domestic politics. Unlike their relationship with China, however, economics was not a lubricant in these bilateral relations. Because of their industrial structures, the Japanese and South Korean economies saw less integration, as businesses in each country tended to see competitors from the other as chief rivals for international markets.

Domestically, Koizumi pushed a neoliberal economic reform program that was intended to open Japanese markets and promote competition in the economy. He pledged to maintain a relentless focus and tackle the coddled interests and sacred cows that sustained his own party's success. By many measures, he succeeded. Three years into his term, Japan enjoyed five consecutive quarters of growth and managed to almost reach 3 percent growth by the fourth quarter of 2003. Just after he left office, Japan marked fifty-seven straight months of growth, surpassing the "Izanagi boom" of 1965–70.[63] Between 2002 and 2007, Japan's listed companies posted consecutive record-high pretax profits, with a commensurate 100 percent rise in the Nikkei stock index between early 2003 and 2006.[64] As of January 2006, employment had recovered from the recession, with unemployment falling from a peak of 5.7 percent in 2002 to 4.6 percent.[65]

Nevertheless, Koizumi's record is mixed. For all the talk of a radical break, sharp-eyed observers note that "his administration continued, rather than initiated, a broad array of more technical reforms that have given Japanese businesses new options for restructuring."[66] Moreover, his commitment to a reform agenda ran hot and cold. While he showed no reluctance to take on opposition to liberalization within his own party—and cultivated the image of a rebel to great success—Koizumi's readiness to follow through on many reform proposals is still debated. Australia's Aurelia George Mulgan, one of the keenest observers of Japanese domestic politics, noted that "where Koizumi did take on special interest politicians and bureaucrats to advance his pet projects, he ended up compromising quite substantially on his original goals and left office with many reforms incomplete."[67] Tokyo University's Greg Noble is more forgiving, concluding that "the significant reforms that have occurred, including regulatory liberalization, drastic shrinkage of the fiscal investment and loan program, and reduction of *amakudari* [descent from heaven] posts [or private-sector jobs for former government officials], as well as the improved economic performance to which these changes have contributed, deserve recognition."[68] Ultimately, Koizumi's economic record was not stellar. Real GDP growth during his five years in office was just 1.3 percent, which was respectable (especially after ten years of stagnation) but nothing compared to the go-go years of the 1980s.[69]

Still, Koizumi changed the mood in Japan. The Japanese felt they had a leader who represented a revitalized administration and nation and one who could hold his own on the international stage. Pew Research Center opinion data showed a veritable explosion in the number of Japanese who considered themselves satisfied with the country's direction, going from just 12 percent of respondents in 2002 to 27 percent in 2006.[70] A similar wave washed over assessments of the country's economic situation. The number of respondents who felt Japan's economic situation was good went from a miserable 6 percent in 2002 to 28 percent in 2007.[71] The goodwill extended to Koizumi's Liberal Democratic Party too. In the 2005 parliamentary elections, the LDP won a landslide victory, picking up 85 seats to hold a commanding 296-seat majority in the 480-member lower house (House of Representatives). Adding the 31 seats of its coalition partner, the New Komeito (or Komei Party), Koizumi and the LDP held more than two-thirds of the seats in that chamber.

Old, Bad Habits Return

Koizumi left office in 2006, and while the economy managed to keep on track, politics quickly returned to a familiar pattern with a new prime minister in the Kantei every year. Abe Shinzo succeeded Koizumi as prime minister, and while dealt a favorable hand, his administration was plagued by missteps. On foreign policy, for example, Abe benefited from the tensions that marked Koizumi's relations with China and South Korea. By promising not to visit Yasukuni as his successor had done, Abe got an immediate boost in relations with Beijing and Seoul. North Korea tested a nuclear weapon shortly after Abe took office, helping him make the case for a hard-line national security agenda. In addition, he pushed an expansive foreign policy agenda and reached out to new partners, around the world but especially in Asia, to promote a "values-oriented diplomacy" that would differentiate Tokyo and like-minded countries from other capitals—read: Beijing—and provide a foundation for a higher international profile for Japan. During a visit to the headquarters of the North Atlantic Treaty Organization (NATO) in Brussels—the first Japanese prime minister to make that trip—Abe explained, "Japan and NATO are partners. We have in common such fundamental values as freedom, democracy, human rights and the rule of law. It is only natural that we cooperate in protecting and promoting those values. My government is committed to reinforcing the stability and prosperity of the world based on the fundamental values I have just mentioned."[72]

But while Abe was a conservative like Koizumi, he lacked the idiosyncrasies that softened Koizumi's nationalism. Abe was the grandson of Kishi Nobusuke, who was arrested and held for three years after World War II on suspicion of being a class A war criminal but still rose to serve two terms as prime minister. Thus, Abe's nationalist agenda—he was determined to promote "a beautiful country," to instill a sense of patriotism, and to overcome what he and other right-wing politicians considered the legacy of shame that marked Japan's postwar era—had a sharper edge and was, some feared, an attempt to rehabilitate Imperial Japan.[73] One of his first-term legislative achievements was the revision of a law concerning education goals to include nurturing a "love of country" and a respect for tradition and culture. That focus fed a perception among voters that the new prime minister's nationalist agenda took precedence over economic issues.

Negative feelings toward the prime minister intensified when he allowed eleven former LDP members to return to the party after Koizumi had kicked them out because they had opposed his reform legislation. Abe was generally seen as capitulating to the old order in the LDP, triggering a fall in public support for his cabinet. In another troubling indication of the reassertion of bad old habits, four cabinet ministers were forced to resign during Abe's year in office, and another committed suicide after being embroiled in a financial scandal. Finally, in May 2007, it was revealed that 50 million pension records had been lost, and the premiums that had been paid could not be linked to particular individuals. Abe abruptly left office after a shellacking in an upper house (formally known as the House of Councilors) election that cost the LDP control of the chamber for the first time in over fifty years. He resigned days after the new parliamentary session began, claiming that his unpopularity was hindering passage of important national security legislation (although it was also rumored—and subsequently confirmed—that ill health played a key role in his decision).

Abe was followed by Fukuda Yasuo, a more centrist politician with another distinguished pedigree: His father was Japan's sixty-seventh prime minister. Fukuda himself had also been Japan's longest-serving chief cabinet secretary, the individual in many ways responsible for the day-to-day administration of government and the second most powerful person in the cabinet. Fukuda's selection as prime minister promised both competence (after the series of scandals that scuttled the Abe administration) and moderation in both domestic and foreign policy, and it raised hopes among Japan's neighbors and partners of less friction in regional relations. His refusal to visit the Yasukuni Shrine mollified neighbors, and after he dropped Abe's talk of "a coalition of democracies," concerns eased that Tokyo was trying to draw a line through Asia that would force countries to choose between Japan and China.

Those hopes were quickly dashed, however. For all his experience, Fukuda was aloof and unable to connect with voters, who were increasingly frustrated by politicians who seemed indifferent to their concerns.[74] Although discovery of the missing 50 million pension records occurred during his predecessor's term, while Fukuda was in charge it was revealed that employers had changed or forged another nearly 70,000 pension records with the government's approval. Pensions are touchy political issues at the best of times, but they are electrifying when economies are struggling. Fukuda was especially vulnerable as he had been forced to step down as chief cabinet secretary in 2004 when he admitted that he had not made monthly payments into the national pension system over a three-year period.

The biggest blow to the Fukuda administration, however, was the divided National Diet in which the opposition controlled the upper house of the legislature and used that power to frustrate many government initiatives. The Democratic Party of Japan (DPJ), which led the opposition, smelled blood and did its best to block the Fukuda administration at every turn; the degree to which the DPJ pursued opposition for opposition's sake, rather than pursue the national interest, is still debated. At the very least, it set a precedent for obstruction that the LDP would then hone and practice to devastating effect in a few years (and is detailed in chapter 3). The DPJ opposition hampered the Fukuda administration's efforts to reauthorize Japan's participation in Indian Ocean naval refueling of coalition supply ships that were helping prosecute the war in Afghanistan. While the special measures law eventually passed, its terms were altered, and the delays frustrated Japan's supporters in the United States who were beginning to see Tokyo as again constrained by ineffectual politicians.[75]

Fukuda abruptly stepped down two days short of a year in office. He called a press conference with only ten minutes' notice to announce he would retire, explaining that internecine fights in the National Diet had crippled his effectiveness and that a new government with a new mandate was needed to overcome the stalemate. He was succeeded by Aso Taro, the foreign minister under Abe whose political career was marked by gaffes and controversial statements. He too served less than a year and will likely be remembered as the LDP politician who presided over the historical loss to the Democratic Party of Japan in 2009, the first time that the LDP lost control of the government in an election.

An Anxious Country

Plainly the Japanese in 2008 had good reason to feel that things were not right. The economic recovery that began during the Koizumi years may have been the longest in Japan's postwar era, but close examination provided ample reasons for concern. By 2006 Japan had the fourth-highest poverty rate among the thirty OECD countries.[76] While unemployment had fallen, many of the new jobs were temporary and contract positions that did not offer the stability and long-term prospects of regular employment. Nonregular workers more than doubled from 15 percent in 1984 to 34 percent in 2006. Especially hard hit were self-employed and family workers, who dropped from 18 percent of the total labor force in 1995 (about 11.8 million people) to 8.3 percent (or 5.3 million) in 2002.[77] The very fabric of society was being torn. "The number of households below the minimum income threshold had jumped from 780,000 in 2001 to 1,040,000 in 2005. . . . [T]he Gini coefficient had again risen during Koizumi's term in office and it is estimated that 10 million workers were among the 'working poor.' A *Yomiuri Shimbun* poll found that 81 percent of income and other disparities were increasing; 56 percent believed that Koizumi's structural reforms were to blame."[78]

For a nation that had prided itself on a sense of homogeneity and common purpose, the declining percentage of respondents who identified themselves as middle class while the number who considered themselves as lower middle class or poor had grown was a blow to Japanese national identity. While Pew data noted earlier showed a stunning increase in the number of Japanese respondents who thought at the end of the Koizumi administration that the economy was improving (jumping from 6 percent to 28 percent), by 2008 that figure had dropped to 13 percent, and those who considered the economic situation to be bad had soared to 85 percent and would hit 90 percent the following year.[79] The Bank of Japan's own survey data showed that in June 2008, 79.9 percent of respondents deemed the current economic conditions to be unfavorable or somewhat unfavorable, 36.9 percent thought that they would remain the same over the next year, and 60.5 percent thought they would deteriorate.[80] When asked about their present household circumstances, just 3.4 percent said things had become somewhat better, while 96.5 percent felt it was either difficult to say (34.9 percent) or had become somewhat worse (61.6 percent).[81]

When their attention turned to the world around them, the Japanese had still more reason to be unsettled. The 2007 *Diplomatic Blue Book* surveyed regional developments and concluded that there were "incidents constituting a serious threat to Japan's peace and security."[82] It highlighted Pyongyang's missile and nuclear tests as well as its continuing nuclear program, the growth and modernization of Chinese military forces, energy security, and pandemic diseases. The *Defense of Japan 2007* white paper identified the same threats while adding terrorism, the rising military expenditures throughout the Asia-Pacific region, the proliferation of WMDs, and the increasing uncertainty in the relationships of major powers. Significantly, it noted that "the most characteristic features of today's security environment are increasing diversity and complexity of threats and difficulty of accurately estimating emergence of such threats. This requires each country to develop new approaches to them."[83]

That last sentence is critical. It underscored the importance of leadership at the very moment that the Japanese had concluded that not only were their politicians feckless, self-absorbed, and incompetent but also that their political system was unstable and unable to correct its flaws. Bureaucrats kept the ship of state afloat, but real leadership was absent; and that vacuum, at a time of geopolitical churn, was a growing threat to Japan's security and prosperity. Again, Pew data is revealing. While the number of Japanese who expressed satisfaction with the country's direction had leaped from 12 percent in 2002 to 27 percent in 2006, that number had fallen back to 22 percent a year later. More worrisome was the 74 percent of Japanese who were dissatisfied with their country's direction in 2008.[84]

Economic and geopolitical anxieties intensified the Japanese people's sense that their country had lost its way on a more fundamental level, perhaps even because of its remarkable economic success. As the country commemorated the sixtieth anniversary of the end of World War II in 2006, the Institute for International Policy Studies (IIPS)—a think tank closely associated with former prime minister Nakasone and now officially known as the Nakasone Yasuhiro Peace Institute—released "A Vision of Japan in the 21st Century." That "vision" started with two foundational premises: First, the country, and the world, was "at the dawn of a new era"; and, second, there was confusion in "the national consciousness, consequently blurring national goals and leading to a loss of national dignity."[85] After applauding Japan's economic success during the Cold War, the report noted that the relative stability of the superpower standoff had "given way to a time of confusion, instability, and unrest." China's own economic success and its rising military capabilities threatened not only regional stability but also the actual balance of power. North Korea's expanding capabilities were equally alarming, and the authors urged Tokyo to keep a wary eye on other countries such as India that could also disturb the regional order.

This uncertain environment demanded nothing less than "a break with the outdated existing order within the country, and for a more assertive and strategic approach in diplomacy." Not surprising for a conservative institution, its report endorsed a new constitution and educational reform as well as changes in finance, social security, population, and foreign and security policies. Make no mistake: This conservative critique of Japan focused on realist ideas of national power.

Significantly, however, the IIPS included a second, equally important cultural critique, framing the challenge for Japan as one of national identity. Consequently, the first component of the vision is to "rebuild our national identity and convey a unique Japanese message." The report explains that "Japan must rediscover and reappraise the value of its history, tradition, and culture and reconstruct its national identity. Japanese culture, with a deep spirituality characterized by a reverence for peace and harmony and living compatibly with nature, has been underpinned by cultural plurality supported by open-mindedness toward international cultures." (Readers who reflexively consider this a reactionary nationalist mind-set should pay particular attention to that last phrase and the explicit renunciation of "narrow-minded nationalism" that follows.)

This sense of drift is not new. Ozawa Ichiro, an LDP strong man who was instrumental in creating opposition parties since the early 1990s and sought to forge political competition that would make Japan "a normal country," complained in 1994 that the concept of identity in Japan "was overly biased towards Japan's economic status."[86] The Kawai Commission's report also expresses similar unease about the degree to which economic activity has overshadowed all other elements of engagement and expression in Japan, and it calls for greater freedom for individuals to express the values and lifestyles that they would prioritize.[87]

The IIPS report decries "the shift away from the traditional concept of the community . . . to a society in which profit is the prevailing measure of success."[88] While some critics insist that any mention of "culture" or "community" is code for a reanimated communitarian ethos that yearns to re-create the organization and hierarchy of Imperial Japan, in fact most—but not all—such visions acknowledge the need to empower individuals and give them the freedom to pursue their own lifestyles and life choices. This perspective is evident in the IIPS's vision, the Kawai Commission's report, and *Japan 2025* by Keidanren, the powerful Japan Business Federation. The latter's proposal calls for "respect for diverse values" and more opportunities for individuals to live according to their personal values and interests rather than those of the companies for which they work.[89]

Significantly, the Right has no monopoly on this fear that Japanese society is crumbling from within. Despite two very different political endpoints, this view dovetails nicely with traditional Marxist-leftist criticism that Japan has been dominated by capitalist institutions that dehumanize society and put corporate interests ahead of those of individuals and more organic groupings. In some cases, the Left's perspective results in a "small Japan" or "beautiful island" mentality that turns its back on *homo economicus* (economic man). This strain of thought has a long and distinguished pedigree in Japan, having first been articulated by Ishibashi Tanzan in the 1920s. While it is tempting to dismiss this view as a holdover from the 1970s, it has some surprising sympathizers. Murata Daisuke, the president of a multibillion-dollar, Kyoto-based multinational company, confided that "we have to shrink. We are a small island. It's not right for us to have 20 percent of the world economy."[90] That thinking struck a chord with Iwase Sachiko, a senior adviser for the Japan International Cooperation Agency. She believes many others agree. "Most Japanese have accepted that it is time to go down, to slow down a bit. From the top, there is no way but down."[91]

While originally articulated by Ishibashi and other like-minded thinkers as a strategy that endorsed the abandonment of overseas possessions, today this thinking also encompasses quality of life concerns and rejects the rush to acquire both goods and power. Proponents insist that the full-throated embrace of modern capitalism has alienated the Japanese from nature and community, two components of their essence. They urge a reconsideration of national goals and ambitions to reshape Japanese society to better suit Japanese national identity and its current circumstances. Some backers of the leftist approach use history to validate their thinking, arguing that Japan's embrace of Western notions of modernization and power in the first decades of the twentieth century led to excesses and abuses that culminated in military imperialism, colonialism, war, and eventual defeat. They want to stave off any such temptation in the future.[92]

This is by no means a majority opinion, however. Many Japanese consider the "small Japan" school of thought silly. Funabashi Yoichi, former editor in chief of the *Asahi Shimbun* and one of the country's foremost international analysts, is dismissive of such thinking. "Japan can no longer afford the delusions of 'graceful decline' or small island beautiful . . . our choice is rebirth or ruin."[93]

Whatever one thinks about his conclusion, Funabashi's word choice— "rebirth"—is revealing. The Japanese people's unease about their country and its place in the world has focused not just on policy shifts but also on adjustments that raise fundamental questions about national identity and purpose. Language of transformation or revolution (or rebirth) evokes similar transitional moments in Japanese history and is evident in the Kawai Commission, the IIPS report, and other strategies, plans, and visions that are discussed in later chapters. Yet a decade and a half of stagnation, confusion, and loss of position, prestige, and status were not enough to spur change in Japan in the first decade of the new millennium. What would? The next four chapters detail a series of "shocks" that could constitute such a trigger. One such shock was already at work on the world and Japan during the hapless struggles of the Aso government in 2008.

Notes

1. Roundtable Discussion: "Looking back at the 20th Century: The Cycles of Modern Japan's Rise and Fall," *Gaiko Forum*, Summer 2000, 21.
2. Ibid., 23.
3. The efforts by other countries to open Japan are detailed in E. H. Norman, *Japan's Emergence as a Modern State*, 60th anniv. ed. (Vancouver: University of British Columbia Press, 2000), 35–40.
4. Warren I. Cohen, *East Asia at the Center: Four Thousand Years of Engagement with the World* (New York: Columbia University Press, 2000), 263.
5. Historian Najita Tetsuo insists that the very nomenclature—that of a mere "restoration"—sells short the transformation Japan experienced. "Historians and commentators of the immediate post-Ishin era did not use the term 'restoration.' Liberal historian Takekoshi Yosaburo . . . characterized the Ishin as 'revolution'

and as 'anarchical revolution' [20]. . . . We need to teach the Ishin as a real break and not a restoration." Najita Tetsuo, "Japan's Industrial Revolution in Historical Perspective," in *Japan in the World*, ed. Masao Miyoshi and H. D. Harootunian (Durham, NC: Duke University Press, 1993), 20–22.

6. Norman, *Japan's Emergence*, 198.

7. Takeda Yoko, "Will the Sun Also Rise? Five Growth Strategies for Japan," *Strategic Japan Working Papers 2015*, Center for Strategic and International Studies (CSIS) Japan Chair (Washington, DC: CSIS, 2015), https://www.csis.org/programs/japan -chair/strategic-japan-working-papers.

8. Cohen, *East Asia*, 273.

9. Ibid., 302.

10. Wakamiya Yoshibumi, *The Postwar Conservative View of Asia*, selection no. 8 (Tokyo: LTCB International Library Foundation, 1998), 271.

11. Yulanda Lawson, *The Impact of World War II*, rev. ed. (New York: Research World, 2016), http://ebooks.wtbooks.com/static/wtbooks/ebooks/9781283496124/978 1283496124.pdf.

12. John Dower, "The Myth of Change-Resistant Japan," in *Reimagining Japan: The Quest for a Future That Works*, ed. Clay Chandler, Heang Chhor, and Brian Salsberg (San Francisco: VIZ Media, 2011), 64.

13. "Japan: Percent of World GDP," TheGlobalEconomy.com, accessed August 6, 2018, https://www.theglobaleconomy.com/Japan/gdp_share/.

14. Shahin Kamalodin, "Asset Bubbles, Financial Crises and the Role of Human Behavior," *Rabobank Economic Research Department* (Utrecht), January 2011, 11–12, https://economics.rabobank.com/Documents/2011/Januari/Asset_bubbles _financial_crises_and_the_role_of_human_behaviour.pdf.

15. Godo Yoshihisa and Hayami Yujiro, "The Human Capital Basis of the Japanese Miracle: A Historical Perspective," Paper presented at Workshop on State, Community, and Market in Development, National Graduate Institute for Policy Studies, Tokyo, February 27, 2009, 2, http://www3.grips.ac.jp/~otsuka/Workshop2009 /paper/S5%20Godo.pdf.

16. Susan Pharr, "Officials' Misconduct and Public Distrust: Japan and the Trilateral Countries," in *Disaffected Democracies: What's Troubling the Trilateral Countries?*, ed. Susan Pharr and Robert Putnam (Princeton, NJ: Princeton University Press, 2000), 178.

17. Ishihara Shintaro, *The Japan That Can Say No: Why Japan Will Be First among Equals* (New York: Simon & Shuster, 1991); and Morita Akio and Ishihara Shintaro, *"No" to ieru nihon: Shin nichibei kankei no housaku* (Tokyo: Koubunsha, 1989). By the time the essay became a book, Morita had disassociated himself from the project.

18. Hugh Patrick and Henry Rosovsky, eds., *Asia's New Giant: How the Japanese Economy Works* (Washington, DC: Brookings Institution Press, 1976).

19. Ezra Vogel, *Japan as Number One: Lessons for America* (New York: HarperCollins, 1979), viii–ix.
20. Clyde Prestowitz, *Trading Places: How We Are Giving Our Future to Japan and How to Reclaim It* (New York: Basic Books, 1988), 72.
21. John Shanahan, "Trump: US Should Stop Paying to Defend Countries That Can Protect Selves," Associated Press (AP) News Archive, September 1, 1987, http://www.apnewsarchive.com/1987/Trump-U-S-Should-Stop-Paying-To-Defend-Countries-that-Can-Protect-Selves/id-05133dbe63ace98766527ec7d16ede08.
22. Cited among other places by Yamaguchi Mari, "Cabinet Spokesman Retaliates for French Premier's Remarks," AP News Archive, July 18, 1991, http://www.apnewsarchive.com/1991/Cabinet-Spokesman-Retaliates-For-French-Premier-s-Remarks/id-236b5ee30b7631c806e6300fb41c792c.
23. George Friedman and Meredith Lebard, *The Coming War with Japan* (New York: St. Martin's Press, 1991).
24. While this comment is usually sourced to his book *Japan: Who Governs? The Rise of the Developmental State* (New York: W. W. Norton, 1995, 9), Chalmers Johnson was saying this as early as 1991. See, for example, his appearance in "Losing the War with Japan," *Frontline*, Public Broadcasting Service, season 9, episode 20, November 19, 1991. Transcript available at http://ftp.monash.edu.au/pub/nihongo/losewar.pbs.
25. David Sanger, "After the Cold War—Views from Japan: Tokyo in the New Epoch, Heady Future, with Fear," *New York Times*, May 5, 1992, http://www.nytimes.com/1992/05/05/world/after-cold-war-views-japan-tokyo-new-epoch-heady-future-with-fear.html?pagewanted=all.
26. Art Swift, "Fewer in U.S. See Japan as an Economic Threat," Gallup, December 7, 2016, http://www.gallup.com/poll/199115/fewer-japan-economic-threat.aspx. It should be noted, however, that even in 1992, 47 percent of respondents had "neutral" feelings toward Japan, topping the 43 percent who had "friendly" feelings toward the country. Favorable ratings would steadily increase from that year, surpassing those who were neutral the very next year, and reached 64 percent in 2016. Those who called themselves "unfriendly" never topped 9 percent, and that number steadily declined to 2 percent in 2016.
27. James Fallows, "Containing Japan," *The Atlantic* 263, no. 5 (May 1989): 41.
28. Ibid., 53.
29. Jinushi Toshiki, Kuroki Yoshihiro, and Miyao Ryuzo, "Monetary Policy in Japan since the Late 1980s: Delayed Policy Actions and Some Explanations," in *Japan's Financial Crisis and Its Parallels to U.S. Experience*, ed. Ryoichi Mikitani and Adam S. Posen (Washington, DC: Institute for International Economics, September 2000), 124.
30. See, for example, Okina Kunio, Shirakawa Masaaki, and Shiratsuka Shigenori, "The Asset Price Bubble and Monetary Policy: Japan's Experience in the Late 1980s

and the Lessons," Discussion Paper No. 2000-E-12 (Tokyo: Institute for Monetary and Economic Studies, Bank of Japan, February 2001), https://www.imes.boj.or.jp /research/papers/english/me19-s1-14.pdf.
31. Kamalodin, "Asset Bubbles," 11.
32. Kunio, Masaaki, and Shigenori, "Asset Price Bubble," 4.
33. Kenneth Kuttner, Iwaisako Tokuo, and Adam Posen, "Monetary and Fiscal Policies during the Lost Decades," in *Examining Japan's Lost Decades*, ed. Funabashi Yoichi and Barak Kushner (London: Routledge, 2015), 19.
34. Corruption is an important part of this story. A raft of scandals involving financial institutions throughout the 1990s were equal parts entertaining and alarming. Both the scale of the malfeasance and the players—some of the country's most important decision makers (including top politicians and bureaucrats) were tainted—meant that cleaning up the scandals would take time, which dragged out the tumult and delayed recovery. Jake Adelstein tells parts of this story well in *Tokyo Vice: An American Reporter on the Police Beat in Japan* (New York: Pantheon Books, 2009). I heard versions of some of his stories during my time in Japan, and rumors of others were even worse.
35. Hyeog Ug Kwon, Narita Futoshi, and Narita Machiko, "Resource Reallocation and Zombie Lending in Japan in the '90s," Discussion Paper Series 09-E-052 (Tokyo: Research Institute of Economy, Trade, and Industry, 2009), https://www.rieti.go.jp /jp/publications/dp/09e052.pdf. For more, see Alan Ahearne and Shinada Naoki, "Zombie Firms and Economic Stagnation in Japan," *International Economics and Economic Policy* 2, no. 4 (December 2005): 363–81, doi.org/10.1007/s10368-005 -0041-1.
36. Ito Takatoshi, "Japan and the Asian Economies: A 'Miracle' in Transition," *Brookings Papers in Economic Activity* 2 (1996): 209, www.brookings.edu/~/media/files /programs/es/bpea/1996_2_bpea_papers/1996b_bpea_ito_weinstein.pdf.
37. Tim Callen and Jonathan Ostry, eds., *Japan's Lost Decade: Policies for Economic Revival* (Washington, DC: International Monetary Fund, 2003), 1.
38. Lydia Smith, "Kobe Earthquake 20th Anniversary: Facts about the Devastating 1995 Great Hanshin Earthquake," *International Business Times*, January 16, 2015, https://www.ibtimes.co.uk/kobe-earthquake-20th-anniversary-facts-about -devastating-1995-great-hanshin-earthquake-1483786.
39. Glen Fukushima provides a detailed critique in "The Great Hanshin Earthquake," Japan Policy Research Institute (JPRI) Occasional Paper No. 2 (Cardiff, CA: JPRI, March 1995), http://www.jpri.org/publications/occasionalpapers/op2.html.
40. See, for example, Robert Orr, "The Relief Effort Seen by a Participant," JPRI Occasional Paper No. 2 (Cardiff, CA: JPRI, March 1995).
41. Tim Kelly and Kubo Nobuhiro, "Gulf War Trauma Began Japan's Retreat from Pacifism," Reuters, December 20, 2015, https://www.reuters.com/article/us-japan

-military-history-insight/gulf-war-trauma-began-japans-retreat-from-pacifism
-idUSKBN0U300D20151220.

42. Michishita Narushige, "Security Arrangements after Peace in Korea," in *The Japan-U.S. Alliance: New Challenges for the 21st Century*, ed. Nishihara Masashi (Tokyo: Japan Center for International Exchange, 2000), 50–51.

43. Christopher W. Hughes, *Japan's Economic Power and Security: Japan and North Korea* (New York: Routledge, 1999), 88–89. The National Defense Program Outline of 1997, the document that lays out the framework for Japan's defense policy, highlighted "continued tensions on the Korean Peninsula." Ministry of Foreign Affairs of Japan, "National Defense Program Outline in and after FY 1996," 2014, http://www.mofa.go.jp/region/n-america/us/q&a/ref/6a.html.

44. Ambassador Mike Mansfield's comment became boilerplate for any US official and de rigueur for any US ambassador to Japan. See Mike Mansfield, "The Indispensable Relationship: Southeast U.S./Japan Association," September 17, 1982, Mike Mansfield Papers, 1902–1990, Mss 065, series 32: Ambassador: Speeches, 1976–1988, Montana Memory Project, Helena, http://mtmemory.org/cdm/ref/collection/p16013coll41/id/1549.

45. Ministry of Foreign Affairs, "Japan-U.S. Joint Declaration on Security Alliance for the 21st Century," April 17, 1996, http://www.mofa.go.jp/region/n-america/us/security/security.html.

46. Cabinet Office, Government of Japan, "Survey," December 1999.

47. "Carrying Out Reform Is Only the Beginning for Politicians," *Japan Times*, January 1, 2001, https://www.japantimes.co.jp/news/2001/01/01/national/carrying-out-reform-is-only-the-beginning-for-politicians/#.Um3hVZGorwI.

48. This and all subsequent quotes are from the Prime Minister's Commission on Japan's Goals in the 21st Century, *The Frontier Within: Individual Empowerment and Better Governance in the New Millennium*, January 2000, http://www.kantei.go.jp/jp/21century/report/pdfs.

49. Brad Glosserman, "US-Japan Relations: Making History the Hard Way," *Comparative Connections* 3, no. 1 (2001).

50. Ulrike Schaede, *Choose and Focus: Japanese Business Strategies for the 21st Century* (Ithaca, NY: Cornell University Press, 2008), 144.

51. Ibid.

52. Ibid., 22.

53. David Arase, "Japan in 2008: A Prelude to Change?," *Asian Survey* 49, no. 1 (January/February 2009): 116.

54. Ibid.

55. Michael Green, "US-Japan Relations: Small but Important Steps," *Comparative Connections* 2, no. 3 (October 2000).

56. Ilene Prusher, "Koizumi's Popularity Rubs Off," *Christian Science Monitor*, June 26, 2001, https://www.csmonitor.com/2001/0626/p6s1.html; and Bill Clifford, "Japan's

Man with a Mandate," *Market Watch*, July 31, 2001, https://www.marketwatch.com /story/comment-koizumi-must-show-the-beef-in-no-sacred-cows.

57. Cited in Brad Glosserman, "US-Japan Relations: Dream of a Quarter," *Comparative Connections* 8, no. 3 (July 2006).

58. Jonathan Beale, "Koizumi in US for Sayonara Summit," BBC News, June 29, 2006, http://news.bbc.co.uk/1/hi/world/asia-pacific/5127360.stm.

59. One Japanese politician in particular, Abe Shinzo, would make the abductees' cause a foundational element of his political career. Pyongyang's subsequent intransigence on the issue would undermine Abe's image as a leader who was able to secure important national interests.

60. Brad Glosserman, "US-Japan Relations: How High Is Up?," *Comparative Connections* 5, no. 1 (April 2003).

61. Japan's nuclear diplomacy defies simple characterization. While Japan has been a vocal supporter of disarmament, that objective is tempered by its historical reliance on the US nuclear arsenal for its security. Nothing worried Japanese strategists more than the prospect that President Barack Obama was serious when he said he wanted a world free of nuclear weapons (even though he said it is unlikely in his lifetime). Serious Japanese strategists admit that their high-minded diplomacy—the three nonnuclear principles that Prime Minister Sato Eisaku won a Nobel Peace Prize for—depends on the US nuclear umbrella. For more on this subject, see Ralph Cossa and Brad Glosserman, "Extended Deterrence and Disarmament: Japan and the New US Nuclear Posture Review," *Nonproliferation Review* 18, no. 1 (March 2011): 125–45.

62. Ministry of Defense, *Defense of Japan 2006* (Tokyo: Japan Ministry of Defense, 2006), 29, http://www.mod.go.jp/e/publ/w_paper/2006.html.

63. Gene Park and Steven Vogel, "Japan in 2006: A Political Transition," *Asian Survey* 47, no. 1: 26.

64. Schaede, *Choose and Focus*, 2.

65. Ibid., 179.

66. Park and Vogel, "Japan in 2006," 23.

67. Aurelia George Mulgan, "Agriculture and Political Reform in Japan: The Koizumi Legacy," Pacific Economic Paper No. 360 (Canberra: Australia-Japan Research Centre, 2006), 2.

68. Gregory W. Noble, "Koizumi and Neo-liberal Economic Reform," *Social Science Japan* 34 (March 2006): 9, http://newslet.iss.u-tokyo.ac.jp/ssj34/ssj34.pdf.

69. Takao Komine, "How Did Koizumi Cabinet Change Japan?," *Japan Spotlight* (May/June 2007), 7, https://www.jef.or.jp/journal/pdf/153cover%20story01.pdf.

70. Pew Research Center, "Global Indicators Database: Satisfaction with Country's Direction, Japan, 2002–14," *Global Attitudes and Trends*, http://www.pewglobal.org/database/indicator/3/country/109/.

71. Pew Research Center, "Global Indicators Database: Country's Economic Situation, Japan, 2002–17," *Global Attitudes and Trends,* http://www.pewglobal.org/database /indicator/5/country/109/.

72. Prime Minister Shinzo Abe, Ministry of Foreign Affairs of Japan, "Speech at the North Atlantic Council: 'Japan and NATO: Toward Further Collaboration,'" January 12, 2007, http://www.mofa.go.jp/region/europe/pmv0701/nato.html.

73. Abe's cri de coeur for Japan was titled *Utsukushii Kuni e* [Toward a beautiful country] (Tokyo: Bunshun Shinso, Bungei Shunju, 2006).

74. Arase, "Japan in 2008," 109.

75. Kristi Govella and Steven Vogel, "Japan in 2007: A Prelude to Change?," *Asian Survey* 48, no. 1 (January/February 2008): 103–4.

76. Arase, "Japan in 2008," 109.

77. Schaede, *Choose and Focus,* 179.

78. Park and Vogel, "Japan in 2006," 24. See also Arase, "Japan in 2008," 116.

79. Pew Research Center, "Country's Economic Situation, Japan."

80. Public Relations Department, Bank of Japan, "Results of the 34th Opinion Survey on the General Public's Views and Behavior," August 4, 2008, questions 1, 3, and 4, https://www.boj.or.jp/en/research/o_survey/ishiki0808.pdf.

81. Ibid., question 6.

82. Ministry of Foreign Affairs, *Japan Diplomatic Blue Book 2007: "Arc of Freedom and Prosperity: Japan's Expanding Diplomatic Horizons"* (Tokyo: Ministry of Foreign Affairs, March 2007), http://www.mofa.go.jp/policy/other/bluebook/2007/html /index.html.

83. Ministry of Defense, "Part I: Security Environment Surrounding Japan," *Defense of Japan 2007* (Tokyo: Japan Ministry of Defense, 2007), 3, http://www.mod.go.jp/e /publ/w_paper/pdf/2007/06Part1_overview.pdf.

84. Pew Research Center, "Satisfaction with Country's Direction."

85. Institute for International Policy Studies, "A Vision of Japan in the 21st Century," September 5, 2006, http://www.iips.org/en/research/data/NationalVision.pdf. This and all subsequent quotes are from the report.

86. Kitaoka Shinichi, "III. Japan's Identity and What It Means," in *Japan's Identity: Neither the West nor the East,* ed. Ito Kenichi et al. (Tokyo: Japan Forum on International Relations, n.d.), http://www.jfir.or.jp/e/special_study/seminar1/conver _3.htm. An additional takeaway here is that the concept of Japan as "a normal nation"—the key theme of Ozawa Ichiro's important book *Blueprint for a New Japan: The Rethinking of a Nation* (Tokyo: Kodansha International, 1994)—focuses on political processes rather than on specific outcomes. Most discussion of "a normal Japan" addresses its foreign and security policy instead, however.

87. Prime Minister's Commission on Japan's Goals in the 21st Century, *Frontier Within.*

88. IIPS, "Vision of Japan."

89. Nippon Keidanren (Japan Business Federation), *Japan 2025: Envisioning a Vibrant, Attractive Nation in the Twenty-First Century* (Tokyo: Nippon Keidanren, 2003), http://www.keidanren.or.jp/english/policy/vision2025.pdf.

90. Author interview, Kyoto, November 9, 2012.

91. Author interview, Nago, Okinawa, August 9, 2012.

92. This interpretation betrays a surprising lack of faith in Japanese democracy as it implies that the nation will be seduced by international power and unable to avoid the mistakes and miscalculations that previously led it to war.

93. Funabashi Yoichi, "March 11—Japan's Zero Hour," in Chandler, Chhor, and Salsberg, *Reimagining Japan*, 8.

2

THE LEHMAN SHOCK

Koizumi Junichiro left Japan two valuable legacies when he stepped down as prime minister in 2006: political stability and an economic recovery. His successors—Abe Shinzo, Fukuda Yasuo, and Aso Taro—squandered the first as they reverted to traditional governing principles and practices of the Liberal Democratic Party, were enmeshed in scandals, and proved unable to navigate an increasingly partisan political terrain as their party's power diminished. The causes and consequences of those political failures are explored in chapter 3.

It is hard to blame Koizumi's three successors, however, for the economic calamity that hit Japan soon after his departure. For sure, their political priorities differed from his, and when they did address economic issues, none was as committed as Koizumi was to reform (even though some question his bona fides). While more may have been required to stimulate growth or to insulate the economy from dislocations, a foundation had been laid and Japan had resumed a growth trajectory, albeit considerably slower than that of the go-go years of the 1970s and 1980s. To say that Japan was blindsided by the global financial crisis (GFC) that erupted in 2007–8 is unfair, as hardly anyone anywhere expected that crisis. In fact, most observers credit Japan with protecting its economy from the first-order effects of the GFC. Japan's economy was not directly affected by the crisis that followed the collapse of the US subprime mortgage market, but it was hammered when global demand shrank after credit and liquidity evaporated. At that point, Japan sustained more severe damage than almost every other country in the world did.

This chapter uses the global financial crisis to explain Japan's economic travails. It examines the impact of that event on Japan and the reactions of its government and business community. This analysis focuses on the structural causes of Japan's economic problems and the failure of purported remedies to have any enduring effect. The global financial crisis was a body blow to the Japanese economy, yet even as experts and officials evoked the worst possible futures for Japan, the GFC was unable to galvanize policymakers and prompt them to make changes that would alter Japan's course and trajectory.

From a Whisper to a Scream

The debate over the causes of the global financial crisis has only intensified in the decade since it occurred. While diagnoses are frequently as much the product of political outlook as they are of economic insight, the time line of what occurred and how the crisis unfolded is much less controversial.[1] There is general agreement that the first tangible sign of the crash to come was on August 9, 2007, when the French investment bank BNP Paribas decided to freeze three of its hedge funds because it could not value the assets in them, owing to a "complete evaporation of liquidity" in the market. A month later Northern Rock, a British bank, appealed to the Bank of England for an emergency loan after liquidity dried up and it could no longer finance the mortgages on its books. The British government was forced to step in to avert the first run on a British bank in over 150 years. In October major banks and investment companies around the world announced severe losses attributable to mortgage-related lending; top management was forced to resign. By the end of the year, central bankers had engaged in unprecedented coordination to inject hundreds of billions of dollars of liquidity into world markets.

In January 2008 the World Bank warned of a global slowdown as liquidity shortages intensified, and central bankers pushed through historical cuts in interest rates to offset shrinking demand. In February Northern Rock was nationalized; a month later, Bear Stearns, Wall Street's fifth-largest bank, was sold to J. P. Morgan Chase for just 7 percent of its value in 2007. In September the US government was forced to bail out mortgage lenders Fannie Mae and Freddie Mac, which accounted for nearly half the outstanding mortgages in the country. A week later Lehman Brothers, an investment firm that had been founded in 1850, filed for bankruptcy days after posting a $3.9 billion loss for the previous quarter.

This "Lehman shock" knocked down the remaining dominoes. It triggered a series of bank failures and takeovers, prompting governments around the world to take aggressive action to shore up their national and international financial institutions. Governments passed banking rescue packages—in some cases after several tries—and central banks made emergency rate cuts to keep markets from seizing. On December 1 the United States was officially declared to be in a recession; however, economists noted the contraction actually began a year earlier. By January 2009, millions of jobs had been lost around the world, economies were imploding, and governments were struggling to find ideas and resources to reverse course.

For Japan the financial crisis was first a worrisome blip on the horizon. Japanese banks had limited exposure to the radioactive securities "because they neither invested directly in subprime-related products nor conducted the 'originate-and-distribute'-business with structured financial products, such as credit default swaps, on a large scale." Subprime-related losses were just ¥1.038 trillion by September 2010—or less than 2.2 percent of Japanese banking tier-1 capital (or the reserves that banks are required to hold so they can protect against insolvency in the event of a run)—and were covered by capital requirements.[2] Sato Takafumi, a former commissioner of the Financial Services Agency, reckoned cumulative realized losses between April 2007 and July 2009 were about $25 billion, and the valuation losses were about $5 billion.[3] If he is right, those losses were an order of magnitude smaller than those of their US and European counterparts.[4]

The Lehman shock transformed the crisis from a distant danger to an actual threat to Japan. Japan was battered for three reasons, all resulting from its increasing integration into the global economy. First, Japanese financial institutions were vulnerable because of their greater reliance on foreign capital flows. Japan had enjoyed net capital inflows as its economy recovered and as foreigners returned to Tokyo in search of investment opportunities. When the rest of the world reeled from liquidity shortages, those investors withdrew funds to meet needs at home. Foreign investors and hedge funds, in particular, became net sellers on Japanese stock markets, and net foreign purchases of Japanese equities became negative. This shift was a huge blow as foreign holdings of Japanese stocks accounted for a quarter of market capitalization, and foreigners were responsible for nearly two-thirds of market turnover.[5] Not surprising, the Nikkei stock index plummeted from 18,000 in July 2007 to 7,000 in March 2009. This drop, in turn, bludgeoned Japanese banks, whose stock holdings constituted a major part of their tier-1 capital. Those losses manifested in the real economy as banks became reluctant to write loans to medium- and small-size companies with less than stellar credit; and as bank credit dried up, commercial paper and commercial bonds became increasingly expensive for those same companies.[6] (Big companies generally had less difficulty maintaining their lines of credit.)

While painful, that contraction would have been bearable had not the rest of the world plunged into recession—it was called the *global* financial crisis for a reason—and crushed demand for the export goods that were central to the Japanese economy. Since over 90 percent of Japanese exports were highly income-elastic industrial supplies, capital goods, and consumer durables, the collapse of US and European markets "exerted a severe negative influence on Japanese exports." In the fourth quarter of 2008, Japan began to experience "a severe economic contraction" as exports fell 12.5 percent in comparison with the previous year. The plunge accelerated in the first quarter of 2009, with exports dropping by more than a third (36.8 percent). Industrial production fell in tandem, declining by 15.0 percent, 34.0 percent, and 27.6 percent (year on year) in the fourth quarter of 2008 and the first and second quarters of 2009, respectively.[7]

If those two blows weren't sufficient, Japanese exporters were then punished by a sharp appreciation in the value of the yen. The International Monetary Fund (IMF) reckons that the yen appreciated in real terms by more than 20 percent during the GFC.[8] When the dust settled, Japan's real GDP shrank 1.2 percent in 2008 and 6.3 percent in 2009, constituting one of the largest falls in real output among major OECD countries.[9] More alarming, Japan did not recover as quickly as those economies directly affected by the GFC did. Nominal US GDP returned to its precrisis peak in about two years, and real GDP managed it in three. Japan's real GDP had not completely recovered by the fourth quarter of 2013, and nominal GDP remained flat.[10] The IMF concluded that "the contraction experienced during the recent [global financial] crisis reduced real output in 2010 to its 2005 level (in nominal terms, to its 1995 level)."[11]

A Crisis Long in the Making

Japanese businesses and officials had no illusions about the scale of the problem. During Abe Shinzo's first term as prime minister (2006–7), even as Japan's economy had regained its feet, alarm bells were ringing. His administration developed the Asian Gateway Initiative, a comprehensive package of reforms that was based on the following premise:

> While Japan is experiencing substantial economic recovery, it is also facing various challenges such as declining population and aging society. In order for Japan to continue stable economic growth and become an attractive "venue" to the rest of the world, it is critically important to incorporate the growth and vitality of the world, in particular Asia's growth. . . . [I]t is essential for Japan to establish an open economy and society which promotes freer exchange of people, goods capital, culture and information.[12]

In other words, even at a time of "substantial economic recovery," policymakers worried about demographic problems and the need to make Japan relevant and "attractive" to the world, and they sought to link Japan to the outside world, Asia in particular. They recognized that "the 21st century is the century of Asia" and that Japan had to find its place in the region. The initiative's authors worried that "it is Japan, [more] than any other Asian country, that is likely to be left out. . . . [T]here are a number of fields where Japan's competitiveness is weakening due to delayed measures to cope with globalization."[13]

A year later the GFC would descend, and in March 2009, Keidanren, the supreme association of the country's business groups, warned that "Japan faces an economic crisis unlike anything it has experienced in the past. The impact of the world financial crisis has spread to the real economy and set off a global recession. Japan . . . has been dealt a particularly severe blow."[14] The group called for a "Japanese New Deal . . . to ensure employment security, create jobs, and enhance Japan's growth potential."[15]

The continued deterioration of the economy prompted experts and officials to endorse ever more aggressive responses. At the end of 2009, Keidanren released a "New Growth Strategy" for the postcrisis period.[16] This document began by warning that Japan had been "more heavily impacted by the global recession than any major industrialized economy," had suffered "from inadequate growth capacity in domestic demand and population decline," was being weakened by the hollowing out of its corporate production bases, and was finding it difficult "to secure manpower necessary to maintain social and economic systems." Six months later, the Ministry of Economy, Trade, and Industry (METI, the successor to the Ministry of International Trade and Industry) released its "Industrial Structure Vision 2010," which also warned that Japanese industries were "deadlocked" and, "lagged behind the world's major players and market changes."[17]

Significantly, both initiatives started from the premise that Japan's problems predated the global financial crisis, as the nominal rate of economic growth between 2000 and 2008 had averaged 0.2 percent annually, or "almost zero." This was a stark contrast to the OECD average (excluding Japan) of 5.8 percent. The outline for the METI vision also acknowledged that Japan's problems were evident long before the GFC and even blamed "the success mythology built on growth in the postwar era." It highlighted Japan's shrinking share of global GDP, dropping from 14.3 percent in 1990 to 8.9 percent in 2008; its change in the International Institute for Management Development's World Competitiveness Ranking, plunging from first in 1990 to twenty-second in 2008; and the drop in global ranking of per capita GDP, falling from third in 2000 to twenty-third in 2008. Worse, METI noted, the situation was deteriorating as the yen appreciated, the economy deflated, public finances worsened, and rising costs undermined Japan's competitive advantage. The profitability of Japanese companies was less than half that of their overseas competitors. The former's share of the global market in technologies such as dynamic random-access memory, liquid crystal panels, and solar power generation panels, to name just three, had plummeted. And China had supplanted Japan as the hub of the regional economy, with the mainland becoming the preferred destination for corporate R&D centers, back offices, and integrated bases in Asia. METI pulled no punches in its conclusion: "Japan has rapidly lost competitiveness in all functions as the central stronghold of Asia."

The proportion of Japanese companies in the Fortune Global 500's total revenues shrank from 35 percent in 1995 to 13 percent in 2009. Japan's share of the value of global electronic goods exports was cut in half, going from 30 percent in 1990 to 15 percent in 2011.[18] Among all high-technology industries, the global market share of Japanese companies was anticipated to plummet another 20 percent from 2008 to 2013.[19] According to economist Vaclav Smil, Japan's share of global value added by manufacturing fell at a faster rate than that of the United States, plunging from 18 percent in 1990 to 11 percent in 2010 (during which the US share went from 23 percent to 19 percent).[20] He underscored Japan's shrinking share of the global economic product, which fell from 9.2 percent in 1991 to 5.8 percent in 2010—a 37 percent dip—and contrasts with a 31 percent drop in Germany and an 11.5 percent fall by the United States. It was increasingly clear to sharp-eyed observers that "the challenge that the Japanese economy faces is comparable in magnitude to those at past historical turning points, including the opening of the country in the mid-19th century, the turmoil in the 1920s, and the devastation after World War II."[21]

"Why Did Japan Stop Growing?"

The literature that purports to explain Japan's lackluster performance fills bookshelves. One of the most accessible and most accurate reports is titled, simply enough, "Why Did Japan Stop Growing?"[22] In it economists Hoshi Takeo and Anil Kashyap argue that Japan failed to adapt to three critical changes in circumstances after its extraordinary growth. First, it had closed the economic gap with its competitors, meaning that easy, catch-up growth was exhausted. New opportunities had to be identified and exploited. Second, the postwar system of global financial management (often called the Bretton Woods system) ended, forcing rapid changes in exchange rates; thus, Japan could no longer rely on an undervalued yen to boost exports. Third, Japan's demographic profile had transformed, and its rapidly aging workforce made productivity gains more difficult.

Decision makers in Tokyo fumbled the response when they tried to address these challenges. They made macroeconomic policy mistakes, such as failing to grasp the scale of financial problems in the 1990s, the spiraling public debt, and the tight-money monetary policy in the early and mid-1990s that mistakenly focused on inflation when Japan's real problem was overcapacity. Regulatory policy discouraged innovation by coddling old industries, and regulations and cultural norms hindered the development of labor mobility. Politicians and bureaucrats tinkered on the margins of the economy, waiting for the pendulum to swing back (as it invariably had), and they failed to recognize the global shifts that had been triggered by the collapse of the Soviet Union, the subsequent expansion of markets and market economies, and the information technology revolution.

Today diagnosing the problems that stall Japanese growth is easy. First, it has a massive debt overhang. Japan's total public debt exceeded 190 percent of GDP in 2008, but that sum would swell to 244 percent, or a record ¥1.0086 quadrillion ($10.46 trillion), on June 30, 2013, an amount that was larger than the economies of France, Germany, and the United Kingdom combined.[23] Once the poster child for the "economic miracle," economists now honor Japan as having the worst indebtedness among all developed nations. Debt service alone is reckoned to cost $257 billion, or larger than the economy of Singapore.[24] That deficit is the outgrowth of two Japanese government policies. The first is an enduring commitment to fiscal stimulus measures. While the government changed every year throughout the 1990s, all administrations embraced fiscal stimulus measures to goose the sputtering economy and make up for falling demand.[25] That strategy worked, at least until 1997 when a triple whammy—the government cut spending, increased the consumption tax from 3 percent to 5 percent, and let an income tax break expire—plunged the economy into recession. The second contributing policy is its European level of social spending despite US levels of taxation.[26]

To get its books in order, Japan has to raise revenues and/or halt expenditures. If the current government is serious about reaching a primary budget balance by 2020, in which government revenue equals outlays excluding debt-service costs on existing liabilities, then it will have to increase the consumption tax to 19 percent. (The tax was increased from 5 percent to 8 percent in 2014, with predictable consequences: The economy plunged into recession. A second increase to 10 percent was scheduled for October 2015, but the government pushed it back eighteen months so the economy could recover, then quailed again when that deadline approached, postponing it until October 2019.[27]) A substantial part of the total debt is the government deficit, which reached 10.3 percent of GDP in 2013, increasing from 9.9 percent in 2012. Some 83 percent of the ¥1 quadrillion in debt is from government bonds.[28] That is a mighty headwind as the economy attempts to pick up its pace.

Second, the country's grim demographic profile also hinders Japan's growth. Japan is already the "grayest" country in the world, with a median age of forty-five years. The 24.1 percent of the population (30.79 million people) aged sixty-five or older is set to grow to 38.8 percent by 2050. In 2013 the number of people fourteen and younger fell to a record low of 13 percent.[29] The country's population is not only aging but also shrinking in size. Japan's population is projected to decrease from 127 million in 2012 to about 106 million in 2040 and about 1 percent a year annually after that. An aging and shrinking population has a rising "dependency ratio"—that is, the number of retirees supported by current workers. This ratio is critical to the viability of pension plans. With pensions adjusted for inflation, retirees invariably take out more benefits than they put into a pension plan. As a result, there have to be more workers paying into the system than there are pensioners withdrawing funds if such schemes are to survive. According to the World Bank, Japan's dependency ratio in 2011 was 57.9 percent,[30] but with the working-age population projected to decrease about 2 percent annually, the OECD forecasts that by 2050 the ratio will exceed 100 percent (in contrast to the OECD average of about 89 percent).[31]

A third problem is excess capacity. The government's determination to avoid economic instability means that companies are actively discouraged from going bankrupt (and social mores contributed to avoiding that option). Policymakers have worried about spiraling unemployment rates in a country that believes in lifetime employment, but if Japanese markets aren't allowed to clear, then too many products chase too few consumers. These zombie companies—unproductive and unprofitable firms that should exit the market but stay in business courtesy of aid from creditors or the government—undermine the health of profitable companies.[32] Equally, if not more, worrisome is the feared impact of mass bankruptcy on financial institutions that hold essentially worthless debt. If the companies go under, then the banks too will be threatened.

Persistent deflation is a fourth obstacle. Prices have been falling in Japan since the mid-1990s, leading economists to conclude that the country has been experiencing "chronic deflation."[33] Economist Milton Friedman called deflation a scourge and with good reason: It wreaks havoc on an economy. While falling prices sound good in the abstract and maybe even in small doses, in practice they suppress demand, which in turn reduces production. Deflation reduces the value of large assets—such as real estate, which is the primary source of household wealth—and increases debt service costs. Falling asset values and diminished consumption then cut tax revenue. Companies cannot raise prices as demand falls, so they hold workers' pay steady and put hiring on hold. That creates more uncertainty and more reasons to hold tightly onto money instead of spending it, and so on. It is a downward spiral, one that Japan knows well.

The price squeeze has given Japanese companies even more incentive to move overseas. In the 1980s they made their first forays into Southeast Asia to escape the ballooning labor costs that followed the yen revaluation after the Plaza Accord. New competition from South Korea and China intensified the need to control production costs, and labor is invariably the place to start. More recently a growing middle class in Asia and the desire to source production closer to final markets had compounded the inclination to build facilities overseas. This "hollowing out" is a fifth economic obstacle, and it is getting worse. In 2010, 17.9 percent of production by companies in the Japanese manufacturing industry occurred overseas; that number is expected to climb to 22.4 percent in 2016.[34] Over the same period overseas production is expected to jump from 24.8 percent to 31.3 percent in processing industries and from 14.9 percent to 19.2 percent in materials industries.[35]

Put it all together and it is hard to avoid the conclusion that Japan's problems are neither cyclical nor the result of a global crisis in which Japan happened to get ensnared. Japan's grim performance is the product of structural problems that the country's leadership has noticed but not addressed. A straight-line projection of Japan's GDP that uses data from the 1980s, for instance, produces numbers 40–50 percent higher than the size of the economy in 2012. *Washington Post* correspondent Chico Harlan summed up the prevailing sentiment in a bleak portrait in October 2012: A nation once touted "as a global model for how to attain prosperity and power" was now "not just in a prolonged slump but in an inescapable decline."[36]

Surveying the national landscape, Tamamoto Masaru—a research associate in the faculty of Asian and Middle Eastern studies at the University of Cambridge and a senior fellow at World Policy Institute—despaired for his country. He concluded,

> For Japanese under the age of 40, the quality of adult life is under constant threat from deflation, which exacts a tremendous psychological toll. Rising suicide rates across all age groups are a clear sign the old narrative has gone awry. There are many others: rising unemployment and underemployment, the spread of contract hiring over permanent employment, declining income levels, and an insolvent social security system. Feelings of pessimism, envy and resentment now permeate all aspects of modern Japanese life. Japan's future is no longer certain—and to the extent that the future is knowable, it is bleak.[37]

A "Disappointing" Response

As soon as the bubble burst in the early 1990s, perceptive observers could see the scale of Japan's problems and the time required to fix them. In 1992 journalist Christopher Wood warned that the Japanese would spend the first half of the 1990s working off the speculative excesses of the 1980s, "a painful, contractional, time-consuming process that will inevitably reduce their country's capacity for economic growth. Recession in the form of slow or even negative economic growth now threatens the stability of Japan's post-1945 political order."[38] Sony chairman Morita Akio agreed. When he surveyed his country's business environment, he called for a new "paradigm" of competitiveness.[39] Two years later Wood wrote that "the Bubble's bursting has affected everyone in Japan," and he anticipated the situation would deteriorate as Japan faced a combination of "excess production capacity, failing demand and a rampantly high yen." As Japan struggled through the "most severe economic crisis since the American occupation," the country had to face up to the need for fundamental changes in the way "Japan Inc." did its business. "The message of the symbolic collapse of the Bubble Economy is that that form of economic development has now reached its practical limits and beyond."[40]

Wood was prescient, but even his harsh forecast proved too timid. Japan's great recession, "an era pregnant with both economic stagnation and political instability," extended from 1990 to 2003.[41] In one of its assessments of the 1990s, the IMF characterized Japanese economic performance more laconically, calling it "disappointing, both relative to its own history and relative to the record of other industrialized countries."[42] When Jeff Kingston—an academic who lived through the "lost decade" at ground zero (Tokyo's Temple University)—toted up the losses, his tally included "mountains of money, a sense of security, stable families, and the credibility of the nation's leadership."[43]

Prolonged and painful stagnation is perplexing, especially in Japan, a country that has repeatedly proven able to rise to challenges and overcome them. Every Japanese prime minister since 1991 bemoaned the country's economic ills and called for reform. In 1994 Prime Minister Hata Tsutomu lamented, "The Japanese economy has experienced sufferings previously unknown and has even gone to the point of shaking our confidence about future prospects."[44] Seven years on, then prime minister Koizumi Junichiro could only report inaction. "Since the outset of the 1990s, however, the Japanese economy has been unable to break free from long-term stagnation as trust in the political leadership has been eroded and our society has become enveloped with disillusionment. It is now apparent that the structures that hitherto served us so well may not be appropriate for our society in the 21st century."[45] Seven years and another four prime ministers later, then prime minister Aso Taro would insist that "rebuilding the Japanese economy is an issue of utmost urgency."[46] Prime Minister Noda Yoshihiko in 2012 still urged the Japanese to "break out of the deflationary economy and the excessive appreciation of the yen, which generate a chain of anxieties about the future."[47] And to get a bit ahead of the story, Prime Minister Abe would concede in 2016 that "we are only halfway to the exit from deflation."[48]

This chorus of complaint is even more remarkable given the proposals, programs, and initiatives that were in circulation and were implemented in several cases. Beginning in 1996, for example, Prime Minister Hashimoto Ryutaro oversaw "big bang" reforms that deregulated the financial sector. That project included dozens of proposals that sought to make Japan's banking sector "free, fair and global"; to revitalize the economy by ensuring the more effective use of capital; and to turn Tokyo into a world-class financial center on par with New York or London.[49] The introduction of a more transparent, rules-based, market-oriented system was an important modernization of the country's financial sector, but it wasn't sufficient to get Japan back on track. Later, during Prime Minister Koizumi's term, the government set up special zones for structural reform, but they too failed to do the trick.

All the while, businesses and bureaucracy were advancing their own ideas. In 2003 Keidanren developed *Japan 2025* (mentioned in chapter 1), an initiative whose starting premise is that the country's "economic strength has faltered and confidence is on the wane domestically and internationally."[50] Six years later, after the global economic crisis, Keidanren developed a "New Growth Strategy Envisioned for the Post-Economic Crisis Period,"[51] and METI produced its "Industrial Structure Vision 2010." Keidanren piled on again in 2012 with its "Call for Growth Strategy Implementation," in which it concluded that "Japan's global presence will steadily diminish if deflation continues and the enormous fiscal deficit remains unaddressed amid ongoing political indecision. . . . Japan's per capita nominal GDP ranking fell from 10th in the world in 1990 to 25th in 2011. Japan's economic status is steadily declining."[52]

What is most impressive about these documents is not their uniformity but the language they use to make their case. Keidanren and METI are sober, buttoned-up institutions that represent the apex of the Japanese state and society. They don't indulge in hyperbole or hysterics. When they indict the system, they are, indirectly, indicting themselves; yet both describe a country that is losing strength and status, as its industries are "deadlocked" and becoming less competitive. Both paint a dire picture of the future if the ship of state does not change course. Naoshima Masayuki, the then head of METI, explained that a comprehensive plan was needed "to shake off the sense of stagnation among the people."[53]

The Lehman shock did not end that complacency. Chapters 3–5 take up similar moments—in politics, foreign policy, and domestic affairs, respectively—that could have, in theory, served up the impetus for change. In particular, there was hope that the March 11, 2011, triple catastrophe of the earthquake, tsunami, and nuclear accident that walloped the country (and is discussed in more detail in chapter 5) would awaken the leaders, the elites, and the public to the severity of their country's situation—"that Japan has almost completely lost its way"[54]—and spark bold collective action to transform the nation. Ohde Takashi, the former general manager for Hitachi in the United States, spoke for many Japanese when he called March 11 "the biggest crisis for Japan since World War II" and "beyond the scope of our expectation."[55] Economists Hoshi and Kashyap warned, "Absent better long-run growth policies, the economy will likely lapse back into the stagnant state that prevailed just before the 2011 tragedy."[56]

Seizing the Moment

To its credit, the government in Tokyo, then headed by the Democratic Party of Japan, recognized the opportunity and tried to use the March 11 tragedy to drive a radical policy shift. Nine months after the triple disaster, the cabinet of then prime minister Noda adopted the "Strategy for Rebirth of Japan," a startling document whose very name signaled the government's willingness to embrace the notion that the events of March 11 could and should serve as a catalyst for instituting transformational change in Japan. This government was not going to let the crisis go to waste.

The Council on National Strategy and Policy, which is sometimes called the National Policy Unit (NPU), produced the strategy and pulled no punches in its report. The tone is set in the first line: "Japan is now facing a great crisis." Japan, having "delayed in transforming its industrial structure to address [a] new era of a matured society, . . . is facing the . . . 'lost two decades' as well as a lot of unprecedented serious difficulties, such as the Great East Japan Earthquake, nuclear power plant accident, yen appreciation, and worldwide volatilities in financial markets. . . . Japan is truly in the midst of 'historical crisis.'"[57]

The case for change—or, to be more precise, "rebirth"—is made in the thirty-five pages that follow. The diagnosis is familiar: Japan's woes began two decades earlier with the collapse of the bubble, and its problems intensified as a result of its subsequently sluggish economy, decreased growth potential, appreciating yen, fiscal imbalances, and demographic constraints. Internal difficulties were compounded by the transformation of the global economy—in particular Asia's rise, globalization, and Europe's economic travails. Rising inequality, widening poverty, and deteriorating conditions for small- and medium-size enterprises increased anxiety in Japan and uncertainty about the future. The report warns that "without a sound, broad middle class, Japan should have no future" (2). For a country where 95 percent of the population self-identified as middle class, that is an ominous note.

In the NPU's strategy, recovery begins with the reconstruction of the battered Tohoku region, but that effort is part of a broader agenda that addresses economic fundamentals, such as ending deflation and halting the appreciation of the yen that hammered Japan's export powerhouses. The package includes reforming social security to ease the impact of Japan's demographic plight, promoting innovation through regulatory reform, and unleashing the power of the country's small- and medium-size enterprises. Other efforts such as the Cool Japan project, which seeks to capitalize on the global appeal of Japanese culture and creativity, would "strengthen elements of non-price competitive edge of Japan" (8). The goal is an average nominal GDP growth of about 3 percent and a real growth rate of about 2 percent until 2020.[58] The rebirth strategy also frames economic recovery within the context of "a society of participation and mutual support"—a vague formulation that translates as more communitarian and has echoes of the traditional Japanese social ethos—and a country that makes international contributions. A key element of the new strategy is to demonstrate "a new growth model to the world and make a contribution by being a leader in solving pressing issues on the global agenda, including those related to disaster risk reduction, aging society, the declining birth rate and environmental problems."[59]

But how would Japan achieve these goals? Here, the NPU's strategy came up short. Its ideas made sense, but details were missing. Japan should support the adoption of renewable energies and enhance R&D hubs; promote innovation; expand markets by "overcoming problems, such as declining birthrate, aging society, and energy/environmental constraints"; strengthen small- and medium-size enterprises and management capabilities; cultivate sustainable and robust agriculture; realize a new system for children and child care; and so on (11). In many cases, the solution looks as though it is wishing away the problem.

Cognizant of those shortcomings, the National Policy Unit set up the Frontier Subcommittee, a top-level advisory group that met with Prime Minister Noda throughout the first half of 2012 before laying out its "vision for Japan's ideal future in 2050 for becoming a 'country of hope and pride.'" It sought "to present a roadmap for resolving the various challenges which Japan faces (to present a pioneering national model which Japan, a country 'developed' in terms of the many serious challenges it confronts, should pave the way for others to follow)."[60] If the title of the report—"Toward 'a Country of Co-Creation,' Promoting a Society with Extensive Supports for Those in the Frontline of the Turning Point"—does not captivate, then its four supporting pillars will: wisdom, prosperity, happiness, and peace.

The Frontier Subcommittee's report echoes many of the sentiments of the NPU's rebirth strategy. The former also sought to create "a country of hope and pride" and saw the realization of that ambition would make Japan a model for other countries to follow. It agreed that the country's current course is unsustainable and should seek to avoid a future with the "extension of the freefall of Japan" (1). It asserted that the stakes at risk are not only the country's economic interests but also its "core national interests" as the loss of the Japanese people's identity is threatened. The solution is to create high value-added industries and make Japan a regional hub, one that exploits all its resources—natural and human—and actively participates in international rule-making and the provision of international public goods. The Frontier Subcommittee acknowledged that change is required at the most element level: The Japanese people must change their very way of thinking and take more initiative. The political process must "exercise leadership" in this effort (6). Ultimately, a national dialogue on the national vision is required.

The NPU's "Strategy for Rebirth of Japan" and the Frontier Subcommittee's report are intriguing documents for several reasons. First, there is the tone. The National Policy Unit states, "Japan stands at a crossroads: Will it develop as a vigorous nation, or will it decline?" (1). It is hard to imagine any other country serving up such a bleak and blunt assessment as official policy. Typically, those questions are asked by outsiders and answered with resounding affirmation by the Japanese government.[61] Moreover, in the case of the "Strategy for Rebirth of Japan," it sounds as if the outcome isn't predetermined. The strategy acknowledges that there is another plausible alternative—"stoically allowing the economy to balance in a smaller size"—before rejecting it and concluding instead that "Japan must turn the current crisis into an opportunity by creating new industries and adding new value to push ahead with economic expansion" (8).

Significantly, the choice that Japan must make is not just a political or economic decision but also one that is intimately connected to Japanese identity. The strategy is not only about what is good for the country but ultimately about what it means to be Japanese. Responding will not simply put the nation on the right path but will "restore hope and pride to Japan" as well (1). That seems to root national policy in a very personal and individual level. Or as the report explains, "True revitalization of Japan means restoring hope and pride so that

Japanese citizens will feel, 'I'm glad I was born in this nation'" (1). It is hard to imagine an official US government report that reaches out to the individual citizen and frames policy on that level.

Note, too, that re-instilling that hope and pride requires radical measures. "A strong sense of crisis" is "absolutely necessary," and the nation must be ready for "drastic policy actions on high-priority matters" (1). That is shocking language and suggests that the NPU and its strategists recognized that Japan was confronting a "Meiji moment," one that demanded the bravery, insight, and readiness to jettison the past in the hope of building a better tomorrow. As the report continues, "It is necessary to recognize that there is greater risk in doing nothing than there is embarking on something new. Japan must get ready to take actions" (8).

Another important feature of the documents is the way that they root Japan's future within the larger international environment. The rebirth strategy explicitly links the nation's future to that of the outside world: "Japan's rebirth cannot come about without international development" (18). While that may seem obvious to most outsiders, the idea clashes with a national image that has been historically insular, one that seeks to define Japan on its own terms. The strategy acknowledges as much, pushing for Japan "to break away from [the] inward-oriented mind in the past" (18). The role that Japan will play in this new world is that of problem solver. Tokyo (or, more appropriately, "the entire country") will turn the many dimensions of the March 11 crisis into opportunity, becoming a pacesetter in efforts to address and solve many of the problems that postindustrial societies will face: building resilient, disaster-resistant communities, developing environmentally sustainable economic models, and constructing urban spaces that better accommodate the needs of aging populations. The rebirth strategy is clear: "Japan will lead the way in finding appropriate solutions" and will use those successes to reassert itself as a leader in the community of nations (18).

A final notable component of the two documents is their embrace of government-led efforts to lead change. Some argue that Tokyo should establish a framework for economic growth, especially after March 11, and then get out of the way, letting entrepreneurs take the lead. That runs counter to the Japanese penchant for top-down planning, a system that not only centralizes control but also has actually made change easier. The government creates a vision, and the people work to make it real. Sacrifices are demanded of every citizen, allowing everyone to get involved in and identify with the national goal and purpose. The incremental changes that are implemented in daily life are tangible goals that offer every Japanese an opportunity to participate and innovate in helping realize the attainment of those objectives. Ironically, then, for all its talk of change, the rebirth strategy was in a crucial way very consistent with traditional Japanese thinking. In every field of endeavor and priority area identified in the document, the central government had critical roles to play, whether laying out strategies and visions, setting up councils, establishing partnerships, or providing subsidies. In this sense, the "Strategy for the Rebirth of Japan" and the Frontier Subcommittee's report aren't as radical as they seem.

The fate of the rebirth strategy, whatever its merits, was sealed the day the LDP retook power in December 2012. Despite being adopted by Prime Minister Noda's cabinet on December 24, 2011, the strategy was repudiated along with its creator, the National Policy Unit, almost immediately after Abe Shinzo became prime minister. The NPU website vanished, and almost no trace of its work is available. There are several explanations for the scrubbing of the NPU and its handiwork. One of them is that many of the politicians (and some bureaucrats) in the upper reaches of the Japanese government had an anti–anything-by-Minshuto (Democratic Party) mentality. For this group, the three years of DPJ rule were a dark and preferably forgotten interregnum and a reminder of how Japan can lose its way when amateurs are in charge. A second explanation is that the ruling party believes Japan needs change but not the radical approach promoted by the rebirth strategy. For party stalwarts, plenty of better-designed—that is, LDP-created—initiatives and strategies will get Japan back on track. Indeed, one attempt to trace the genealogy of the rebirth strategy linked it to "Innovation 25," a program developed by the first Abe government in 2007.[62] Finally, the argument is that if Japan needs a course adjustment, then the LDP should generate its own new proposal. That plan—"Abenomics"—was articulated shortly after Abe's return to power and is discussed in chapter 6.

It's Hard to Do Things That Are Not Easy

There are many reasons that reform efforts failed to put Japan's economy on a permanent growth track. The simplest explanation is the most unsatisfying: The scale of change required to remedy Japan's ills is very large—indeed, structural—and thus demands wide-ranging mobilization and exceptional efforts by all citizens. Altering a country's demographic trajectory, for example, especially after trends have been set for a generation or two, is a monumental task. The provision of child or elderly care centers, similar to instituting tax reform to lessen the penalty for second family incomes, will help on the margins, but success ultimately depends on changing values and lifestyles, which are rooted in conceptions of the appropriate family size and structure and which will only shift over time. Altering that mentality is a far more challenging assignment than tweaking a tax code.

A second "mundane" problem with reform efforts rests with vested interests. Typically, these interests are created by the nexus of corporate and political actors who seek to protect privileged access to government resources, either funding or regulatory protection. T. J. Pempel, a shrewd observer of Japan's political economy, pulled no punches when he noted that "Japan has always had its share of well-institutionalized feeders at the public trough, but over the last decade or so, the country has become even more dominated by mutually beneficial back-scratching among powerfully entrenched LDP politicians, individual bureaucratic agencies, and domestically oriented economic sectors such as agriculture, construction, distribution, financial services, air transport, road freight, food agriculture and small business generally."[63] One of the more interesting cases of entrenched interests is the nuclear power industry, which is explored in chapter 5.

Significantly these interests are not just pecuniary. Equally debilitating are the ways that political and bureaucratic actors become entrenched and empowered by a particular regulatory structure and are captured by the ensuing status and authority. As Professor R. Taggart Murphy argues, the most effective steps to promote reform are obvious, but they "would threaten current power alignments." Change would "involve a form of suicide by Japan's entrenched elites, and elites do not commit suicide."[64]

A third factor in stymieing reform efforts is the country's political morass. Instability in the upper reaches of government deprives Japan of many elements that are critical to successful reform: leadership, which is essential to forge the consensus needed to implement difficult and wide-reaching change; consistency in policy to prevent backsliding (or reversals); and the courage to overcome setbacks and make hard (and sometimes unpopular) decisions. Bureaucrats can implement programs and keep them on course, but it takes political leadership to make change happen. The revolving door in the prime minister's office and the routine shuffling of cabinets deny Japan those prerequisites to reform.

A fourth factor is national pride in the creation of a distinctive model of capitalism, one that corresponds to Japan's particular culture, psychology, and history. The Japanese entertain many ideas that support the notion that they have evolved into a unique and superior social organization: 95 percent of Japanese are middle class, they can manage competition to support a broader national interest, and their culture is homogenous and thus immune to many defects that afflict other capitalist societies. (Whether these beliefs are factually correct is irrelevant; that the Japanese believe them makes them formidable.) But a justifiable pride in the society the Japanese have made also serves as a powerful obstacle to reform. Their belief was often used in the 1990s to fend off calls for liberalization: If the country's woes were cyclical in nature, as many assumed, why pursue root and branch reform? Why give up a system that had worked so well for so long when the pendulum will inevitably swing and Japan will come roaring back as it had in the past? This thinking is also evident in variations of the "small Japan" school of thought identified in chapter 1: Adherents believe their country should reject reform and accept a smaller place in the world if change would compromise or subvert important elements of national identity.

A fifth obstacle combines national pride and vested interests but is a distinct variant nevertheless. Independent of their personal (or institutional) interests and the national identity tropes, many Japanese believe that the model they have adopted is the best way to organize an economy. In other words, the system worked and thus should be retained. This normative logic animates Murphy's analysis. He doesn't believe all Japanese actors are venal or self-interested (although some may be); rather, the system that they have constructed and in which they operate is rational and self-evidently optimal for all parties. For example, he argues that Japanese banks and regulators perceive their role in the economy as fundamentally different from that of bankers in the West. They "conceive of banks as utilities, serving the general interest,"[65] rather than as just another sector of the economy (albeit frequently privileged) as in the West.

This mentality also girds the work of Hoshi and Kashyap, who conclude that "policy actions undertaken by the government have worked to thwart restructuring."[66] In the response to the Japanese financial crisis of the late 1990s, they note that "instead of recognizing that major structural adjustments were needed, much of the policy response was calibrated under the assumption that Japan faced a simple cyclical problem that could be addressed with indiscriminate fiscal stimulus."[67] In other work, they highlight the inclination to keep zombie firms alive as one indication of this predilection.[68] Steven Vogel acknowledges this thinking in his appraisal of Japan's failure to maintain "its edge in areas of its greatest economic strength"—namely, electronics, including information and communications technology hardware. He concludes that the Japanese government and corporations "have favored incremental reforms designed to reinforce valued institutions rather than to generate new sources of competitive strength. Specifically, Japanese firms have preferred strategies to preserve long-term relationships with workers, banks, suppliers, and other business partners and to leverage the benefits of those relationships when possible. And these firms have lobbied the government to enact incremental reforms to facilitate corporate restructuring without undermining the traditional basis of their competitive advantage."[69] And the government has accepted that approach.

The case of postal reform illustrates the obstacles to reform. Prime Minister Koizumi made postal reform a top priority during his tenure. This is anything but an anodyne proposal: Japan's post offices are central to the country's financial architecture, and breaking them up or transferring ownership would transform the Japanese financial system. Postal service banks hold savings deposits of about ¥176 trillion, or roughly one-fifth of Japan's total cash and deposits. They offer depositors higher interest rates than do banks, and that is one way the government procures funds for public works programs. The insurance arm of the postal service banks is also a huge holder of Japanese government bonds, and that helps suppress interest rates, which are a vital concern to bureaucrats managing the country's ever-expanding sovereign debt. Post offices are also critical nodes in the patronage system, serving as sources of jobs and political power. The Japan Postal Group Union is the country's largest union, and the postal service employs more than 200,000 people.[70]

Koizumi's postal reform plan was so controversial that it split his party. In the 2005 general election he actually ran his own slate of candidates—popularly referred to as assassins—against those members of his own party who opposed his reforms. Members of the Liberal Democratic Party who defied him were kicked out of the party. After Koizumi stepped down, Abe, his successor, welcomed the holdouts back into the party, a factor that contributed to the LDP's defeat in the 2007 upper house election. Meanwhile, the Democratic Party's position shifted. It originally backed reform, but smelling the opportunity afforded by disaffected postmasters and the union, it reversed course. When the DPJ took office in 2009, it tabled legislation to undo the Koizumi changes. That bill didn't become law but continues to command some support. Another bill that would also undo many of the changes in the Koizumi legislation also circulated.[71] Finally, in November 2015 the government moved forward, with the Japan Post Holdings Company and its two financial units each selling about 10 percent of their shares to the public. The government plans to raise about ¥4 trillion ($35 billion) through additional stake sales in the Japan Post group to fund reconstruction in areas devastated by the 2011 earthquake and tsunami.[72]

This brief recitation of the fate of postal reform reveals many of the obstacles to real change. There is no single explanation. Instead, there is a fatal mix of vested interests, political weakness and opportunism, shifting policies and some outright reversals, and, beneath it all, a belief that the system has merits and works for the greater good. In the face of those hurdles, achieving any change— and there have been some—is an impressive feat.

Ultimately, significant change did not occur, because key constituencies in Japan felt there was no need. For all the problems detailed in this chapter and in chapter 1—rising levels of poverty, unemployment, and inequality; structural challenges like demographics; and declining competitiveness—the Japanese have opted for the status quo. This bias has many causes, and they are examined in the chapters to come.

Visit Tokyo, See the Future

One of the most remarkable claims is that the situation in Japan isn't so bad. The Japan bulls generally concede that the 1990s were a horrific decade, but they insist that the aughts are another story. For them Japan is not only in better shape than its detractors declare but also better positioned to exploit the changes that are taking place in the region and the world.

First, the revisionists argue that the slowdown of the 1990s is exaggerated. Yes, total GDP growth was virtually stagnant, but per capita growth was only 0.5 percentage points lower than that of the United States (1.5 percent in Japan vs. 2.0 percent in the States).[73] While mistakes were made in the 1990s, economic policy had adjusted by the turn of the century, and a strong and sustainable recovery was in place. The 2002–8 recovery, writes Adam Posen, president of the Peterson Institute of International Economics, was "the longest unbridled expansion in Japan's postwar history." And when corrected for its falling population, a much-lamented productivity gap disappeared as well. From 2003 to 2008, Japan's growth in economic output outpaced that of the United States on a per worker basis. Japan had the highest annual GDP growth per worker and the largest annual growth in total factor productivity.[74] From 1991 to 2012, "Japan's real GDP per unit of the labor force approximately kept pace with that of the United States and Germany."[75]

Unemployment had increased—it more than doubled from the 1990 rate of 2.1 percent—but it peaked at 5.7 percent in 2002 and has dropped to levels that spark envy in other developed economies. Economist Noah Smith points out, "During the worst years of the 'Lost Decade,' Japanese unemployment was only 3 percent higher than at the peak of the bubble." He conceded there may have been policy mistakes during the 1990s, but the slowdown that followed was merely the end of "catch-up growth" and "inevitable." More significant, Smith adds that per capita GDP (in nominal terms) in 2001 was $45,900, making Japan richer per person than any comparable country (meaning a developed nation with a population between 50 million and 150 million people).[76]

More important, Japan is poised to exploit the future. Klaus Schwab, founder of the World Economic Forum, noted that "Japan excels in the most sophisticated areas that drive competitiveness." It is the world leader in business sophistication, as defined by the forum; fourth in innovation; ninth in the quality of its health care and primary education; and eleventh in infrastructure. To ensure that

businesses are ready to build the future, Japan's total spending on R&D continues to grow and has reached 3.8 percent of GDP, or the fifth-highest level in the
world, outpacing the United States, Germany, and the OECD average.[77] Consistent with that investment, Japan continues to register increasing numbers of
patents. It now produces 20 percent of patent applications—an increase from 10
percent over the first decade of the century—while claiming a 21 percent share of
US patent registrations for inventions, a percentage equal to the share of Germany,
South Korea, Taiwan, Canada, the United Kingdom, France, and China combined.[78] In the thirty-five technical areas in which the World Intellectual Property
Organization classifies patents, Japan is first in twenty-six areas, second to the
United States in eight others, and third behind the United States and China in the
remaining category.[79] This commitment to pushing the R&D horizon has yielded
some 200–250 "hidden champions," or companies that have less than $4 billion
in annual sales, enjoy preeminent local and large global market shares in their
businesses, and are little known to the general public or investment community.[80]

Even for "high-growth startup companies"—companies formed after 1997,
were public by 2007, and had at least 50 percent annual revenue growth from
2005 to 2007—Japan holds its own, ranking fourth behind China, India, and
the United States. Despite being half the size of the United States in terms of
GDP, Japan had about half as many high-growth start-ups.[81] It is hard, given
these rankings, to take seriously the charge that Japan's best days are behind it.
Concluded Noah Smith: "'Lost decade' or no, Japan in 2012 is right where . . .
it should be."[82]

The most dogged defender of "the myth of Japan's lost decades" is writer
Eamonn Fingleton, who predicted the collapse of the Japanese stock market at the
end of the 1980s. Fingleton is a contrarian who uses both hard facts and observa-
tion of daily life in Japan to dismiss the naysayers. He notes that for all its troubles,
Japan's trade surplus increased more than fivefold—from $36 billion in 1990 to
$194 billion—from 1991 to 2011. Meanwhile, the value of the yen at one point
had risen 65 percent against the dollar for the strongest rise of any major currency
during that time.[83] The economy may be expanding at an anemic 1 percent a
year, but the Japanese are living longer; driving bigger, newer, more expensive, and
better-equipped cars; using some of the world's most advanced cell phones; and
possessing the biggest and best high-definition TVs. The secret of Japan's success,
argues Fingleton, is that while many of the world's goods are made in China, "the
highly capital-intensive and knowhow-intensive manufacturers in Japan have qui-
etly done much of the most technologically demanding work."[84]

Certainly, visitors to Tokyo would not recognize the portrait of a country in ter-
minal decline. The city continues to throw up massive new buildings that redefine

the skyline. Between 1991 and 2006, Japan built 94 buildings 150 meters or taller.[85] Another 121 were built between 2006 and 2017.[86] The stodgy central Marunouchi business district, once a virtual stockade of gray-brown brick buildings that housed financial institutions, has been remade into an upscale shopping and dining district with museums, brand boutiques, cafés, and restaurants that are swamped on evenings and weekends alike by shoppers and families. Omotesando continues to captivate tourists and locals; the street once charitably likened to the Champs Elysées now rivals its Parisian namesake with crowds that are just as big and the prices as stunning. Tokyo's restaurants have more Michelin stars than any other city in the world and have topped that list for eleven consecutive years.

The Roppongi club district was run down in the 1990s and had developed a reputation for ludicrously priced after-hours excesses. But the area has been transformed by the Roppongi Mori complex, a $4 billion project that sprawls over twenty-three acres and includes a fifty-four-story office tower, apartments, shops, restaurants, cafés, movie theaters, a museum, a hotel, a major TV studio, an outdoor amphitheater, and a few parks. Seventeen years in the works, Roppongi Hills opened in 2003 and rejuvenated a once-quiet corner of the city. Less than half a mile away, Tokyo Midtown—a 6.1 million square foot, $3 billion project on the grounds of the old Defense Agency—opened in 2007. Every weekend and most weeknights, each site is overrun with shoppers and sightseers. New gleaming developments such as Shiodome (a fifty-four-acre site that was formerly a railway yard and now features, among other things, Japan's tallest condominium tower) have arisen on once-neglected train stops on the Yamanote Line that rings Tokyo. Japan's architecture can match anything in Pudong, whose skyscraper silhouette is the symbol of China's rise in the twenty-first century. Author William Gibson, the éminence grise of cyber fiction, spoke for many when he said, "When I want to see the future I go and spend a week in Tokyo."[87]

Shaken, Not Stirred

Gibson's optimism could reflect the fact that he spends only a week in Tokyo; longer stays might reveal a fuller, darker picture. Similarly, "hidden champions" in the Japanese economy don't preclude a more general economic stagnation or decline. What is incontrovertible is the dissatisfaction that a large majority of the Japanese felt when they assessed their prospects; recall the three-quarters of Pew respondents who believed their country was going in the wrong direction. While the elites might have shrugged off the Lehman shock, ordinary citizens did not. Japanese voters went to the polls as the effects of that crisis washed over their country, and they delivered a stunning rebuke to the established order. That shock is the subject of chapter 3.

Notes

1. This summary is from "Timeline: Credit Crunch to Downturn," BBC News, August 7, 2009, http://news.bbc.co.uk/1/hi/business/7521250.stm; Patrick Kingsley, "Financial Crisis: Timeline," *The Guardian,* August 6, 2012, https://www .theguardian.com/business/2012/aug/07/credit-crunch-boom-bust-timeline; and Federal Reserve Bank of St. Louis, "The Financial Crisis: Full Timeline," accessed August 14, 2018, https://www.stlouisfed.org/financial-crisis/full-timeline.
2. Uwe Vollmer and Ralf Bebenroth, "The Financial Crisis in Japan: Causes and Policy Reactions by the Bank of Japan," *European Journal of Comparative Economics* 9, no. 1 (2012): 58.
3. Sato Takafumi, "Global Financial Crisis—Japan's Experience and Policy Response," presentation at Asia Economic Policy Conference, Federal Reserve Bank of San Francisco, Santa Barbara, October 20, 2009, 5–6, http://www.frbsf.org/economic -research/files/09_Sato.pdf.
4. Economists also credit Japanese reforms in the late 1990s for insulating Japan from the first shocks of the GFC.
5. Vollmer and Bebenroth, "Financial Crisis in Japan," 61.
6. Ibid., 62.
7. All figures and quotes from Masahiro Kawai and Shinji Takagi, "Why Was Japan Hit So Hard by the Global Financial Crisis?," Working Paper Series No. 153 (Tokyo: Asian Development Bank Institute, October 2009), 2.
8. Dennis Botman, Irineu de Carvalho Filho, and W. Raphael Lam, "The Curious Case of the Yen as a Safe Haven Currency: A Forensic Analysis," Working Paper WP/13/228 (Washington, DC: International Monetary Fund, November 2013), 3, https://www.imf.org/external/pubs/ft/wp/2013/wp13228.pdf. The idea that the yen is considered a safe haven may be a bit ironic given the discussion that follows.
9. Vollmer and Bebenroth, "Financial Crisis in Japan," 63.
10. Jun Saito, "Recovery from a Crisis: US and Japan" (Tokyo: Japan Center for Economic Research, May 7, 2014), 2, https://www.jcer.or.jp/eng/research/pdf /saito20140507.pdf.
11. Group of Twenty, "Japan Sustainability Report 2011" (Washington, DC: International Monetary Fund, 2011), 7, https://www.imf.org/external/np/country/2011 /mapjapanpdf.pdf.
12. Prime Minister of Japan and His Cabinet, List of Councils and Headquarters, "Council for the Asian Gateway Initiative," May 16, 2007, www.kantei.go.jp /foreign/gateway/index_e.html. Again note the initiative cautioned that as it

pursued opening, "Japan needs to reassess its valuable resources in areas such as nature, history, culture and tradition."

13. Council for the Asian Gateway Initiative, "Asian Gateway Initiative" (Tokyo: Council for the Asian Gateway Initiative, May 16, 2007), 2, http://japan.kantei.go .jp/gateway/kettei/070516doc.pdf.

14. Nippon Keidanren, "Urgent Proposal for Emerging from the Economic Crisis: Calling for the Prompt Implementation of a Supplementary Budget for Fiscal 2009," March 9, 2009, http://www.keidanren.or.jp/english/policy/2009/019.html.

15. Nippon Keidanren, "A Call for a Japanese New Deal: Promoting National Projects to Ensure Employment Security, Create Jobs, and Enhance Japan's Growth Potential," February 9, 2009, http://www.keidanren.or.jp/english/policy/2009/009.html. The language of this proposal is worth flagging for later consideration: "The business environment is harsher than it ever has been in the past. Amid these conditions, companies must make every effort to maintain employment. . . . Fully recognizing that stabilizing employment is a Corporate Social Responsibility, companies must eliminate the public's anxiety by actively promoting these kinds of measures on an ongoing basis. Companies must also make every effort to provide living assistance, including offering displaced workers a place to live, as an emergency measure."

16. Nippon Keidanren, "New Growth Strategy Envisaged for the Post-Economic Crisis Period: Five Fields of Expected New Demand, and Three Pillars of Policy to Support Sustained Growth," December 15, 2009, http://www.keidanren.or.jp /english/policy/2009/109.html.

17. Ministry of Economy, Trade, and Industry, "Industrial Structure Vision 2010," 2, accessed October 15, 2017. Available at Centre for Science, Technology & Innovation Policy (University of Cambridge), Manufacturing Policy Portal, access date August 22, 2018, https://www.manufacturing-policy.eng.cam.ac.uk/documents -folder/policies/japan-the-industrial-structure-vision-2010-outline-meti/view. All quotes in this paragraph and all statistics in the next are from the METI presentation.

18. Gordon Orr, Brian Salzberg, and Naoyuki Iwatani, "Japan's Globalization Imperative," in Chandler, Chhor, and Salsberg, *Reimagining Japan*, 151 (see chap. 1, n. 12).

19. Ingo Beyer von Morgenstern, Peter Kenevan, and Ulrich Naeher, "Rebooting Japan's High-Tech Sector," in ibid., 297. Per the Japan Electronics and Information Technology Industries Association ("2017 Production Forecasts for the Global Electronics and Information Technology Industries," December 21, 2016, 2, https://www.jeita.or.jp/japanese/topics/2016/1222/Jpfget_en.pdf), the fall was even greater.

20. Vaclav Smil, "Japan's Economy in 2012: Multiple Challenges," *Asia-Pacific Journal* 10, no. 24 (June 11, 2012), http://www.japanfocus.org/-Vaclav-Smil/3768#sthash .knOoSfPS.dpuf.

21. Hoshi Takeo and Anil Kashyap, "Why Did Japan Stop Growing?" (Tokyo: National Institute for Research Advancement Report, January 21, 2011), 3–4.

22. Ibid.

23. Otsuma Mayumi, "Japan's Debt Exceeds 1 Quadrillion Yen as Abe Mulls Tax Rise," Bloomberg, August 9, 2013, http://www.bloomberg.com/news/2013-08-09/japan -s-debt-surpasses-1-quadrillion-yen-as-abe-weighs-tax-rise.html.

24. Yamaguchi Takaya, "Japan's Debt-Funding Costs to Hit $257 Billion Next Year: Document," Reuters, August 27, 2013, http://www.reuters.com/article/2013/08 /27/us-japan-economy-debt-idUSBRE97Q05H20130827.

25. See, for example, Murtaza Syed, Kenneth Kang, and Tokuoka Kiichi, "'Lost Decade' in Translation: What Japan's Crisis Could Portend about Recovery from Great Recession," Working Paper 09/282 (Washington, DC: International Monetary Fund, December 2009), 10–12. Hoshi Takeo and Anil Kashyap note that "Japan's budget position over the last 20 years has moved from amongst the best of the developed countries to the worst" ("Why Did Japan?," 23).

26. Noah Smith, "Japan Had One Lost Decade, but Not Two," *Noahpinion* (blog), January 10, 2012, http://noahpinionblog.blogspot.com/2012/01/japan-had-one -lost-decade-but-not-two.html.

27. Brian Bremner, "US Debt Mess Could Be Epically Worse. Just Ask Japan," *Bloomberg/Businessweek*, October 8, 2013, www.businessweek.com/articles/2013-10-08 /u-dot-s-dot-debt-mess-could-be-epically-worse-dot-just-ask-japan; and "Japan Delays Sales Tax Rise to 2019," BBC News, June 1, 2016, http://www.bbc.com /news/business-36423218.

28. Mayumi, "Japan's Debt Exceeds."

29. Kyodo News, "Japan's Population Falls by Record Level," *Japan Times*, April 17, 2013, http://www.japantimes.co.jp/news/2013/04/17/national/japans-population -falls-by-record-level/#.Um2w6ZGorwI. In 2016 the percentage of the population aged sixty-five and older was 25.56 percent—a 1.5 percentage point climb in two years is testimony to the seriousness of Japan's problem—while the number for the percentage of the population younger than fourteen years of age was just less than 13 percent (12.936 percent). See World Bank, "Population Ages 65 and Above (% of Total), 1960 and 2016" (Washington, DC: World Bank, 2018), https://data .worldbank.org/indicator/SP.POP.65UP.TO.ZS?locations=JP; and World Bank, "Population Ages 0–14 (% of Total), 1960–2016" (Washington, DC: World Bank, 2017), https://data.worldbank.org/indicator/SP.POP.0014.TO.ZS?locations=JP& view=chart.

30. "Japan—Age Dependency Ratio (% of Working-Age Population)," *Trading Economics*, accessed October 28, 2013, http://www.tradingeconomics.com/japan/age -dependency-ratio-percent-of-working-age-population-wb-data.html. In 2016 the number had risen to 65.29 percent; see World Bank, "Age Dependency Ratio (%

of Working-Age Population), 1960–2016" (Washington, DC: World Bank, 2016), https://data.worldbank.org/indicator/SP.POP.DPND?locations=JP.

31. For Organization for Economic Cooperation and Development's numbers, see OECD, "Age-Dependency Ratios," *Society at a Glance 2006: OECD Social Indicators* (Paris: OECD Publishing, 2007), 42, http://dx.doi.org/10.1787/soc_glance -2006-4-en.

32. John Plender, "Japan Counts 'Zombie' Cost of Easy Money," *Financial Times*, November 6, 2012.

33. Nishizaki Kenji et al., "Chronic Deflation in Japan" (Basel: Bank for International Settlements, 2012), https://www.bis.org/publ/bppdf/bispap70c.pdf.

34. Research Division, Japan Bank for International Cooperation, "Survey Report on Overseas Business Operations by Japanese Manufacturing Companies," March 2017, 1, https://www.jbic.go.jp/wp-content/uploads/reference_en/2017/03/54456 /20170316_spot.pdf.

35. Sugiura Tetsuro, "Future Scenarios of the Japanese Economy: Withdrawal and Dissipation vs. Competition and Globalization" (Tokyo: Mizuho Research Institute, April 23, 2012), 5.

36. Chico Harlan, "A Declining Japan Loses Its Once Hopeful Champions," *Washington Post*, October 27, 2012.

37. Tamamoto Masaru, "People of Japan, Disorganize!," in Chandler, Chhor, and Salsberg, *Reimagining Japan*, 389.

38. Christopher Wood, *The Bubble Economy: The Japanese Economic Collapse* (London: Sidgwick & Jackson, 1992), 2.

39. Cited in ibid.

40. Christopher Wood, *The End of Japan Inc. and How the New Japan Will Look* (London: Simon & Schuster, 1994), 16–17.

41. Funabashi Yoichi, "Introduction," in Funabashi and Kushner, *Examining Japan's Lost Decades*, xx (see chap. 1, n. 33).

42. Tim Callen and Jonathan Ostry, *Japan's Lost Decade: Policies for Economic Revival* (Washington, DC: International Monetary Fund, 2003), 1.

43. Jeff Kingston, *Japan's Quiet Transformation: Social Change and Civil Society in the Twenty-First Century* (Abingdon: Routledge, 2004), 1.

44. "Prime Minister Hata's First Policy Address," C-SPAN Video Library, May 10, 1994, http://www.c-spanvideo.org/program/Hatas&showFullAbstract=1.

45. "Policy Speech by Prime Minister Junichiro Koizumi to the 151st Session of the Diet" (Tokyo: Ministry of Foreign Affairs of Japan, May 7, 2001), http://www .mofa.go.jp/announce/pm/koizumi/speech0105.html.

46. "Policy Speech by Prime Minister Taro Aso to the 170th Session of the Diet" (Tokyo: Prime Minister of Japan and His Cabinet, September 29, 2008), http:// www.kantei.go.jp/foreign/asospeech/2008/09/29housin_e.html.

47. "Policy Speech by Prime Minister Yoshihiko Noda to the 181st Session of the Diet" (Tokyo: Prime Minister of Japan and His Cabinet, October 29, 2012), http://www .kantei.go.jp/foreign/noda/statement/201210/29syosin_e.html.

48. Cited in Bloomberg, "Want to Speed Up Japan's Exit from Deflation: PM Shinzo Abe," *Economic Times*, July 13, 2016, http://economictimes.indiatimes.com/news /international/world-news/want-to-speed-up-japans-exit-from-deflation-pm -shinzo-abe/articleshow/53188131.cms.

49. Valentine V. Craig, "Financial Deregulation in Japan," *FDIC Banking Review* 11, no. 3 (1998): 1–12, https://www.fdic.gov/bank/analytical/banking/9811.pdf.

50. Nippon Keidanren, *Japan 2025*, 3 (see chap. 1, n. 89).

51. Nippon Keidanren, "New Growth Strategy."

52. Nippon Keidanren, "Call for Growth Strategy Implementation and Decisive Action for Fiscal Reconstruction—Leading Japan out of the Present Crisis" (Tokyo: Nippon Keidanren, May 15, 2012), https://www.keidanren.or.jp/en/policy/2012/030 _outline.pdf.

53. Japan External Trade Organization, "Japanese Fundamentals Drive Adoption of New Industrial Structure Vision," *Focus Newsletter*, October 2010, 2, http://www .jetro.go.jp/en/reports/survey/pdf/2010_07_other.pdf.

54. Funabashi, "Introduction," in Funabashi and Kushner, *Examining Japan's Lost Decades*, xxv.

55. Author interview, Washington, DC, September 25, 2012.

56. Hoshi Takeo and Anil Kashyap, "Policy Options for Japan's Revival," Working Paper (Tokyo: Nippon Institute for Research Advancement, June 2012), 2, http:// www.nira.or.jp/pdf/1202english_report.pdf.

57. Council on National Strategy and Policy, "Strategy for Rebirth of Japan: Overcoming Crises and Embarking on New Frontiers" (Tokyo: Council on National Strategy and Policy, December 24, 2011), 1. All subsequent quotes, unless otherwise identified, are from this report.

58. These targets have been embraced by almost every Japanese government for the last decade.

59. National Policy Unit, Cabinet Secretariat, "Overcoming Crises and Embarking on New Frontiers," press release, December 22, 2011.

60. Secretariat of the Frontier Subcommittee, "Toward a 'Country of Co-Creation' which Generates New Value by Manifesting and Creatively Linking Various Strengths" (Tentative Translation), July 6, 2012, www.cas.go.jp/jp/seisaku/npu /policy04/pdf/20120706/en_hokoku_gaiyo1.pdf. Forgive the clunky language; it *is* a tentative translation. More to the point are the vision's scope and ambition, which are striking.

61. That is what Prime Minister Abe said in his February 2013 speech in Washington as he responded to questions posed by a US think tank when its members

pondered Japan's future: "Japan is back." Center for Strategic and International Studies, "Statesmen's Forum: Shinzo Abe, Prime Minister of Japan," Washington, DC, February 22, 2013, http://csis.org/files/attachments/132202_PM_Abe_TS.pdf; and Abe Shinzo, "Japan Is Back," Policy speech at the Center for Strategic and International Studies, Washington, DC, February 22, 2013, http://www.mofa.go.jp/announce/pm/abe/us_20130222en.html. The questions were posed in Richard Armitage and Joseph Nye, *The US-Japan Alliance: Anchoring Stability in Asia* (Washington, DC: CSIS, August 15, 2012).

62. Sean Connell, "Innovation and Growth Policies in Japan-US Economic Relations: Considering Areas for New Engagement," Discussion Paper Series 12-P-018 (Tokyo: Research Institute of Economy, Trade, and Industry, October 2012), 20–21.

63. T. J. Pempel, "Review of 'Japan's Failed Revolution,'" *Journal of Japanese Studies* 30, no. 1 (Winter 2004): 243.

64. R. Taggart Murphy, "Rethinking Japan's Deflation Trap: On the Failure to Reach Kuroda Haruhiko's 2% Inflation Target," *Asia-Pacific Journal* 14, no. 3 (2016): 14.

65. Ibid., 5.

66. Hoshi Takeo and Anil Kashyap, "Japan's Financial Crisis and Economic Stagnation," *Journal of Economic Perspectives* 18, no. 1 (Winter 2004): 9.

67. Hoshi Takeo and Anil Kashyap, "Will the US and Europe Avoid a Lost Decade? Lessons from Japan's Postcrisis Experience," *IMF Economic Review* 63, no. 1 (2016): 111.

68. This is no judgment about whether this approach is correct. The Japanese have made choices about the appropriate costs to be incurred and how they are distributed within their society, and they appear to have privileged stability over the disruptions that come. Crudely put, the Japanese prefer high employment to high growth. Distributing losses is the essence of the zombie company problem. Given the inequality that has arisen in the United States, which has chosen another set of priorities, it is by no means clear which model is correct.

69. Steven Vogel, "Japan's Information Technology Challenge," in *The Third Globalization: Can Wealthy Nations Stay Wealthy?*, ed. Dan Breznitz and John Zysman (Oxford: Oxford University Press, 2013), 380.

70. Fujita Junko, "Japan Govt Plans to List Japan Post in Three Years," Reuters, October 25, 2012, https://www.reuters.com/article/us-japanpost-ipo/japan-govt-aims-to-list-japan-post-in-three-years-idUSBRE89P03420121026.

71. Aurelia George Mulgan told the story of resistance to postal reform in "Reversing Reform: How Special Interests Rule Japan," *East Asia Forum*, April 12, 2010, http://www.eastasiaforum.org/2010/04/12/reversing-reform-how-special-interests-rule-in-japan/; and Gary Hufbauer and Julia Muir do as well in "Japan Post: Retreat or Advance?," *Policy Briefs in International Economics,* Peterson Institute for International Economics 12, no. 2 (January 2012).

72. William Mallard, "Government to Name Underwriters for Further Japan Post Share Sale," Reuters, January 16, 2017, http://www.reuters.com/article/us-japan -post-listing/government-to-name-underwriters-for-further-japan-post-share-sale -idUSKBN1501K0.

73. Robert E. Scott, "On Balance, Japan's So-called 'Lost Decade' Not So Bad," *Economic Policy Institute*, April 19, 2004, http://www.epi.org/publication/webfeatures _snapshots_04192004/.

74. Adam Posen, "Send in the Samurai," in Chandler, Chhor, and Salsberg, *Reimagining Japan,* 104.

75. William Cline, "Japanese Optical Illusion: The 'Lost Decades' Theory Is a Myth," *International Economy*, Spring 2013, 57.

76. Noah Smith, "What Happened to Japan?" *Noahpinion* (blog), August 3, 2012, http://noahpinionblog.blogspot.com/2012/08/what-happened-to-japan.html. Smith also compares GDP in purchasing power parity (PPP) terms, of which he is suspicious: "PPP does not take into account quality differences between similar products across countries. Japanese consumers have a famous preference for quality." And Japan's performance falters, dropping below that of Germany, the United Kingdom, and France.

77. Klaus Schwab, "Is Japan Past Its Competitive Prime?," in Chandler, Chhor, and Salsberg, *Reimagining Japan,* 122.

78. Ibid., 122–23.

79. Allen Miner, "The Next Challenge for Japan's Entrepreneurs," in Chandler, Chhor, and Salsberg, *Reimagining Japan,* 313.

80. R. Taggart Murphy, *Japan and the Shackles of the Past* (Oxford: Oxford University Press, 2014), 230. Theodore Levitt and Hermann Simon coined the term "hidden champions" in 1990. Unlike those of other countries, the majority of Japan's hidden champions are in manufacturing.

81. Miner, "Next Challenge," in Chandler, Chhor, and Salsberg, *Reimagining Japan,* 315.

82. Smith, "What Happened to Japan?"

83. It has since retreated, deliberately, to help Japan's stumbling exporters. A more detailed discussion is in the assessment of Abenomics in chapter 6.

84. Eamonn Fingleton, "The Myth of Japan's Lost Decades," *The Atlantic*, February 26, 2011, http://www.theatlantic.com/international/archive/2011/02/the-myth -of-japans-lost-decades/71741/.

85. Data from the Global Tall Building Database of the Council on Tall Buildings and Urban Habitat, "Timeline: Japan, All Companies, 150m+, 1991–2006," accessed August 14, 2018, http://www.skyscrapercenter.com/compare-data /submit?type%5B%5D=building&status%5B%5D=COM&status%5B%5D= STO&base_region=0&base_country=82&base_city=0&base_height_range=3&

base_company=All&base_min_year=1991&base_max_year=2006&comp_region
=0&comp_country=0&comp_city=0&comp_height_range=3&comp_company=
All&comp_min_year=0&comp_max_year=9999&skip_comparison=on&output
%5B%5D=list&output%5B%5D=timeline&dataSubmit=Show+Results.

86. Data from the Global Tall Building Database of the Council on Tall Buildings
and Urban Habitat, "Timeline: Japan, All Companies, 150m+, 1991–2017,"
accessed August 14, 2018, http://www.skyscrapercenter.com/compare-data
/submit?type%5B%5D=building&status%5B%5D=COM&status%5B%5D=
STO&base_region=0&base_country=82&base_city=0&base_height_range=3&
base_company=All&base_min_year=1991&base_max_year=2017&comp_region
=0&comp_country=0&comp_city=0&comp_height_range=3&comp_company=
All&comp_min_year=0&comp_max_year=9999&skip_comparison=on&output
%5B%5D=list&output%5B%5D=timeline&dataSubmit=Show+Results.

87. Cited in Ayesha Khanna and Parag Khanna, "Japan: Hybrid Civilization of the
Future," *Newsweek Japan*, May 2011, https://www.paragkhanna.com/home/japan
-hybrid-civilization-of-the-future.

3

THE SEIJI SHOKKU

If politicians and policymakers were sanguine about the need for change, Japanese voters were not. Their discontent was bubbling over. In the July 2007 upper house elections, the Liberal Democratic Party lost control of that chamber for the first time since 1989, inaugurating what became known as the "twisted Diet."[1] The inability of the party either to mend its ways or to get Japan to change course—two interrelated phenomena—prompted voters to do the unthinkable in the July 2009 lower house election and hand control of government over to the Democratic Party of Japan.[2] The DPJ victory marked the first time that voters had thrown the LDP out of office since the party's formation in 1955. Ultimately the DPJ's inexperience and the LDP's ruthless "take no prisoners" opposition proved a fatal combination to hopes of political change in Japan. This chapter explores the causes and consequences of that tumultuous period in Japanese politics, focusing on larger, enduring issues that predated and outlived the DPJ's stormy time in power.

From the "1955 Order" to Twenty-First-Century Chaos

The Liberal Democratic Party was formed in 1955 by a merger of Japan's Liberal and Democratic Parties, occupants of the conservative half of the political spectrum. The party proved a formidable political machine, crushing the opposition and ruling Japan virtually uninterrupted since 1955. As noted previously, the LDP has surrendered the prime minister's office only twice. The first instance occurred in 1993, when the party lost power for eleven months after reformers within the LDP, sensing decay and paralysis within their own party, bolted to form the Japan Renewal Party. Emerging as the core of a credible alternative to LDP rule, the reformers then forged a governing majority with several center-left groups.

During that brief interregnum, the new government passed an electoral reform bill that put an end to the multi-seat electoral districts that had been a hallmark of Japanese politics and moved to a system that mixed single-seat constituencies and proportional representation. (In such a system, voters cast two ballots: one for a candidate in their district—one of three hundred nationally—and a second for a party. Then 180 seats were apportioned from a second master list of candidates based on national support.) The electoral reform marked a crucial change in Japanese politics. In a multi-seat system, candidates do not have to win a majority of seats to take office; instead, they merely have to capture a significant percentage of the vote. This system had several important implications. First, multiple candidates from the same party could contest—and win—seats in a given district. Second, a politician only needed to maintain a sufficiently large core of supporters, and that number was considerably lower than that needed to prevail in a head-to-head contest. A candidate only had to be "good enough," not the best. Third, and as a result of the first two factors, candidates were not forced to debate ideas and offer alternatives to voters; elections tested popularity instead. The result was LDP dominance and a permanent opposition as Kitaoka Shinichi, a professor of political science at Tokyo University, has explained. Until 1993 the leading Japanese opposition party, the Japan Socialist Party, "generally managed to secure one seat out of three or more, and before long it had grown content with this slice of the pie and abandoned any idea of seizing the reins of power."[3] Representation, not ruling, was the opposition's goal. It succeeded.

The 1993 reforms ended that cozy arrangement. They were intended to create a direct clash of ideas and push Japan toward a (largely) two-party system in which power would alternate between ideologies contesting at the ballot box.[4] Unfortunately, the new government proved unstable, and in 1994, the LDP did the unthinkable, aligning with its former adversary, the Japan Socialist Party—now called the Social Democratic Party—and returned to power. This time, however, the coalition featured a former socialist as prime minister. This move seemed inexplicable until it became clear that putting a leftist in the prime minister's office obliged the occupant to reject key principles of the progressive platform (in particular the opposition to the armed forces). This was a crushing blow to the spirit of many supporters of the Left and proved that their leaders were just as opportunistic as the conservatives they had so forcefully denounced for years.

Two and a half decades later, whether the Left has recovered from that body blow is still uncertain.

The Social Democratic Party prime minister, Murayama Tomiichi, lasted only eighteen months before surrendering the office to the LDP. With the Left's defenestration complete, the LDP ruled without challenge for two more years until a credible alternative emerged from the primordial stew of Japan's splinter parties—the Democratic Party of Japan. The DPJ slowly gathered strength, merging with other parties that objected to LDP policies. Unfortunately for them, at this time the LDP was headed by Koizumi Junichiro, one of the few genuinely charismatic leaders that Japan has had in the last few decades. Unlike most of his predecessors, Koizumi appealed to the Japanese public rather than to fellow politicians; indeed, one of the sources of his popular appeal was his readiness to take on the core constituencies of the LDP, promising to pursue "structural reforms without sacred cows."[5] He even pledged to "destroy the LDP."[6] That was no idle threat. As noted in chapter 1, in the 2005 general election, Koizumi assembled a slate of "assassins" that he ran against politicians from his *own party* who did not support his reform agenda. No wonder the opposition party foundered during this time; the real opposition was running the LDP!

Koizumi won a landslide victory in the 2005 general election, but after serving two full terms as the party's president, he stepped down in 2006. He was followed by Abe Shinzo in his first stint as prime minister, but Abe's tenure was wracked by scandals and health problems. In July 2007, less than a year into his term, the LDP lost its majority in the House of Councilors, or the upper house of the National Diet, to the opposition, thus creating the twisted Diet. That mattered because, as Kitaoka explained,

> few if any other bicameral parliamentary democracies today have an upper house with such powers. Under the Constitution of Japan, any legislation passed by the House of Representatives—with the exception of the budget bill—can be blocked by the upper house, unless the House of Representatives passes the bill again by a two-thirds majority. . . . This means that for a party to govern effectively, it must either control both chambers of the Diet or control a two-thirds majority in the lower house.[7]

The DPJ used its majority to frustrate the LDP at every turn, paralyzing the legislature. With the upper house focused relentlessly on LDP mistakes and ineptitude, and doing everything possible to block legislation, the LDP appeared both amateurish and incapable of governing.

The image of a spent party was magnified by its comparison with the dynamism of the Koizumi years. Abe served exactly one year before resigning unexpectedly, declaring that he had become an obstacle to his government's agenda; in fact, his cabinet's plummeting approval rating—a product of scandals (one cabinet minister committed suicide) and a misguided policy agenda—and his health were the real motivating factors. His replacement, Fukuda Yasuo, served exactly 363 days before he too resigned. The onset of the global financial crisis made the need for a functioning government even more acute, yet the Diet remained gridlocked and the revolving door in the prime minister's office continued to swing. Aso Taro, another LDP politician, succeeded Fukuda, making the tally four prime ministers in four years.

After a decade spent with their noses pressed against the window, the DPJ got its chance to govern in 2009 when voters finally gave up on the LDP. In the July ballot, the DPJ claimed a landslide victory, taking 221 of the 300 electoral districts and 42.4 percent of the proportional block votes, yielding another 87 seats. In the new 480-seat legislature, the DPJ held 308 seats to the LDP's 119, a turnaround that not only constituted the worst drubbing of a sitting government in Japan's modern history but also followed the second-biggest election victory in LDP history four years earlier. The results were "widely heralded as Japan's most significant political transformation since the LDP's formation and assumption of power in 1955."[8]

Most daily newspapers in Japan had anticipated the LDP's loss. As one observer explained, "The Japanese people deserted the LDP because of the sense that it had failed at addressing the marked decline in the quality of life of the Japanese people over the past two decades, especially the past decade."[9] More ominously, one assessment concluded, "something deeper may be afoot. . . . There are signs of what some call 'a collective identity crisis' in Japan. Income disparity, growing numbers of impoverished pensioners and child poverty clash with a view of their society that the Japanese cherish. Likewise, they look outside their borders and see their country being eclipsed by China, which is enjoying just the sort of boom Japan did from the 1950s to the 1980s."[10]

The DPJ promptly threw that victory away. The party virtually self-destructed, first by installing Hatoyama Yukio as prime minister. Despite Hatoyama's impressive pedigree—his family is sometimes called the Japanese equivalent of the Kennedys as one grandfather served as prime minister, his father was foreign minister, and his mother's family founded the Bridgestone Tire Company—he proved to be a flighty prime minister, proposing and abandoning policies with indifference. Hatoyama was out of office in a little less than nine months and was replaced by

Kan Naoto in June 2010. He too struggled with the reins of government. His task became immensely more difficult a month later when the LDP regained control of the upper house in another election swing and embarked on a campaign of obstruction that made the previous DPJ effort look amateurish. At a lunch shortly after that vote, a senior LDP politician smirked as he confessed that his party was preparing to be "a little irresponsible" in the opposition.

The events of the March 2011 triple catastrophe (taken up in chapter 5) would have overwhelmed any government, but given that the DPJ had so little experience and was struggling, Kan's government was doomed. He tried to take control of the situation and largely failed. He served as prime minister for over a year, but he too was forced from office in September 2011 (primarily because of policy gridlock, leavened with a dollop of responsibility for the handling of the March crisis) and was replaced by Noda Yoshihiko, also from the DPJ. Noda performed well, restoring stability and a veneer of competence to the prime minister's office. Unfortunately for the DPJ, Noda's instincts were conservative, and the policies of his government were virtually indistinguishable from those of the LDP. While many in the LDP were infuriated that Noda was implementing—read: stealing—their policies on defense and tax reform, left-leaning members of the DPJ felt that the party had abandoned them. Confusion and incoherence took their toll. When fifty lawmakers left the party in July 2012 in a dispute over tax policy, the DPJ's fate was sealed. In the fall of 2012, Noda faced a vote of confidence. To prevail, he struck a deal with the LDP in which it backed his government in exchange for his agreement to call an election soon.

The particulars of this no-confidence vote illustrate how "twisted" Japanese politics had become. Several small opposition parties in the lower and upper houses called the vote to protest the government's decision to increase the consumption tax, a policy that the LDP supported and had even voted for. Yet when the lower house voted on the no-confidence motion in early August, the LDP abstained. In the upper house vote, taken a few weeks later, the party actually backed the no-confidence motion; in other words, the LDP voted against the government for pursuing a policy the party supported.

True to his word, Noda called a general election for late December 2012, and in that ballot his party took an even worse beating than it had administered to the LDP just three years earlier. When the dust settled, the LDP held 294 seats. Adding those of its ally the Komeito (or Komei Party), the two-party coalition claimed 325 seats; thus, with more than a two-thirds majority in the lower house, it could overrule the House of Councilors. The DPJ fell from 230 seats to 57. Noda resigned, and Abe Shinzo returned, triumphant, to the prime minister's office.[11]

A Victim of the System and Self-Inflicted Wounds

The postmortems on the Democratic Party of Japan's rule were grim. Typical was the critic who lashed the party for "mind-boggling ineptitude,"[12] a criticism that would appear justified by the DPJ's flip-flops. Machidori Satoshi, a professor at Kyoto University's School of Law, concluded that "in the end, the Democrats failed to deliver on many of the policies they had trumpeted as planks in their election platform. Even when they were able to partially implement their key proposals . . . they ended up backtracking on nearly all of the progress made."[13] Another postmortem analysis went further: "The DPJ lost public support and fell from power in much the same way the LDP had only three years earlier—a ruling party beset with infighting, widely perceived as out of touch with the general public, and unable to implement meaningful reform."[14]

Many of the problems the DPJ faced were not of its own making. It inherited a government that was exhausted and immobile. Whoever was in charge had to wrestle with the corpse of a system that had worked spectacularly well for half a century. Success created its own obstacles to reform, and stagnation had been the norm in Japanese politics for nearly two decades. "It would be inappropriate," Machidori acknowledged, "to place the blame solely on the DPJ's inexperience or lack of preparation or on the lack of leadership shown by Prime Ministers Hatoyama and Kan. Dysfunction in Japanese politics was evident even before the Democrats took power, in the waning days of LDP leadership."[15]

While most observers agree that the DPJ wasn't ready to take the reins of power, it is doubtful if the party would have ever been ready given the half century of the Liberal Democratic Party's domination of Japanese politics. The DPJ, just as any opposition party, had only a rudimentary understanding of the policy process and the fundamentals of governing. Throughout the long period of the LDP's control of government, ruling and opposition parties had worked out Diet procedures that ensured the eventual passage of legislation while allowing sufficient time for questions and interpellation so that it didn't look as though bills were being rammed through the Diet via "the tyranny of numbers."[16]

There wasn't much real discussion of issues, however. Objections were ideologically grounded, with little attention paid to the substance of policy. The government (more precisely, the LDP) traditionally monopolized expertise either by drawing experts into the party or through relationships with the bureaucracy. Bureaucrats were no more inclined to bring the opposition up to speed on policy matters. There was no institutionalized mechanism to inform opposition politicians of the substance of policies, and why bother if they were permanently consigned to the wilderness? In fact, there was a disincentive to do so: The ruling party, which preferred an uninformed opposition (it looked better in comparison), punished bureaucrats who reached out to the minority. DPJ Diet member Izumi Kenta observed that most party officials have neither the ability to gather information nor the authority to do so in the field. Compared to bureaucrats, elected officials are "relatively unseasoned and unprepared for taking part in the policy process." Gaining access to those bureaucrats is critical to successful governing, but, Izumi complained, the quantity of information that bureaucrats provide to the ruling and opposition parties differs, producing striking gaps in policymaking and other organizational abilities.[17] Understandably, then, when the DPJ took power in 2009, its learning curve was steep.

Unfortunately, the DPJ made a bad situation worse. An integral part of the DPJ program was "politician-run politics." Throughout the 2009 campaign, the party argued that real power in Japan resided in the hands of bureaucrats; the LDP merely steered the ship of state while officials made important decisions and kept the ship afloat. Japan's bureaucrats have the data and the grasp of technical details that afford them the biggest role in policymaking. By one count, the bureaucracy drafted about 90 percent of all legislation that the Diet passed since 1955. In addition, bureaucrats have other ways to supplement or sidestep the legislative process. They can create and interpret ordinances and regulations either directly through ministries or through the cabinet, where bureaucrats also have outsize influence. The ministries frequently refer to deliberative or advisory councils that include critical constituencies and experts. In theory, these bodies are sources of outside expertise; in reality, bureaucrats set their agendas, identify participants, and write all reports. Such "independent" stamps of approval are often fig leaves for bureaucratic manipulation.[18]

Koda Yoji, a gruff former commander of the Japan Self-Defense Fleet, summarized the prevailing view of his country's political system: "We don't have leaders. Instead, Japanese politics are driven by old-fashioned, behind the curtain, invisible control by bureaucrats. The Diet is a political mechanism to approve the role of the bureaucracy."[19] He calls this system a "Japocracy." Koda believes this system leaves the country ill-prepared to deal with crises. "When classroom logic is more important than reality, that develops a culture of bureaucrats. . . . They demand a rationale for everything, rather than focusing on reality and being prepared for anything."

That logic parallels a long-standing critique of Japanese politics. In the 1990s, as Japan was going through prime ministers and cabinets with breathtaking (and alarming) regularity, political scientist Inoguchi Takashi decided that his country was in the thrall of "karaoke democracy."[20] Just as any amateur could show off his or her singing skills while belting out favorites as long as a song sheet was available, so too could any politician assume a cabinet position (with the requisite seniority). All he or she had to do was read the lyrics and follow the prerecorded music. The system ensured its own survival, no matter who was in charge.

Okumura Jun, a former Ministry of International Trade and Industry official, laughed at the notion of an all-controlling, omniscient army of bureaucrats and pointed to changes that make the regulatory process more transparent, permitting outsiders to track decision making and watch it unfold. "The meetings are even open," he snorted. Okumura faulted bureaucrats for perpetuating myths about their influence: "The bureaucracy probably claimed too much credit. We never really denied Chalmers Johnson's book [*MITI and the Japanese Miracle*, the Rosetta stone for arguments about the bureaucrats' power in the developmental state]."[21] The assertion that this process operated independently of politicians was an exaggeration. Politicians intervened to protect their interests and those of their constituents. If bureaucrats did the legwork, drafting legislation and ensuring that procedures were followed, politicians had an equally critical role in mustering support among their colleagues and communicating policies to the public. Popular support is a sine qua non in a democracy. Nevertheless, there is no denying that bureaucrats play a large role.

A DPJ administration, its supporters promised, would reassert the preeminence of politicians and, by extension, better reflect the will of the people. Of course, that could go too far, as when cabinet ministers were criticized for reading notes or briefing papers prepared by staff. And wrestling power from the bureaucracy was one thing; bad-mouthing a needed partner in governing was another. Shortly after the DPJ took office, I visited a friend in the Foreign Ministry. Most Japanese bureaucrats are rumpled and often sleep deprived, for they put in long hours preparing for Diet testimony and doing the essential work that bureaucrats do. In a marked departure from previous visits, my friend looked rested and even sported a tan. When I pointed that out, he smiled almost ruefully and said that he was getting more time at home with his family and working in the garden. Such were the benefits of politician-run politics. Meanwhile, the government's foreign policy was in disarray. Those bureaucrats took no delight in seeing their country humbled or humiliated, but they had little compunction about seeing politicians cut down to size who had bashed the experts and rejected the bureaucrats' assistance.

This antagonism had practical consequences: The DPJ government was unable to bring about policy changes. Despite winning control of both chambers of the Diet, there was no notable increase in the legislation proposed and enacted, even in comparison to the lethargy and gridlock of the late LDP years. Only after the March 11 earthquake was there an uptick in activity, and that proved temporary.[22] "Under LDP rule, about 70 to 100 percent of legislation submitted by the Cabinet was passed. Under the DPJ, this rate fell to a low of 55 percent in 2010 and averaged 66 percent," which was "astonishing."[23] With but one month to go in the DPJ interregnum, an authoritative assessment concluded that "only 30 percent of the DPJ's 170 original proposals had been implemented."[24]

The DPJ was hampered by a basic feature of its identity: The party was more an assortment of individuals and groups opposed to LDP rule than a coherent party. Political parties in Japan have traditionally been organized by personality rather than by policy. Yet even by Japanese standards, the DPJ was an odd mix. Its organizing principle was a desire to break the LDP's grip on Japanese politics. Thus, in early summer 2010, a senior political appointee in the Foreign Ministry could not articulate his government's foreign policy strategy, explaining that it was not yet clear because the party's most important goal was defeating the LDP in the upcoming upper house elections. Only after that ballot would the government focus on policy objectives.[25] That approach might have made sense for an opposition party, but the DPJ had been in office for ten months at that point. Focusing on politics rather than on policy—especially in the Foreign Ministry—was irresponsible.

Nakabayashi Mieko, a DPJ Diet member who rode the party's 2009 tidal wave into office, provided the context for that Foreign Ministry official's silence. She explained that her party was "not a united party but existed to reform Japan and the system that the LDP had built." Thus, the bonds between party members were weak and easily stretched when crises hit. "The party is very fragile," said Nakabayashi. "It is very easy to be broken."[26] Nakabayashi shared her thoughts as a political mess was brewing: Power broker and backroom manipulator par excellence Ozawa Ichiro had been indicted once again, this time for falsifying funding reports. Few individuals have been as central to or as influential in Japanese politics over the last twenty-five years as Ozawa has. He was the primary mover behind the split in the LDP in 1993 that forced it from power, as well as the master tactician behind the DPJ's election wins in 2007 and 2009. All the while, the "shadow shogun" has been a scandal magnet, and his troubles tarnished the DPJ in the public's eyes, made a mockery of the claim that the party represented a new era in Japanese politics, and divided the party into pro- and anti-Ozawa factions.[27] He was eventually acquitted of the last charges against him, but his troubles proved fatal to the DPJ. When he and forty-nine other lawmakers left the party in July 2012 in a dispute over the consumption tax, Nakabayashi was proven right. Being prescient did her little good, though. Nakabayashi was swept from office when the tide shifted in the 2012 LDP counterrevolution.

The absence of a hard core of beliefs to unite party members meant that the DPJ was flexible to the point of being spineless when making policy. Political science professor Yamaguchi Jiro, an adviser to the DPJ, described the party well just before it self-destructed: "The DPJ is a patchwork party resulting from the single-seat electorate system and it is blindingly obvious that to look to it for ideology is like climbing a tree to look for fish."[28] Without bedrock principles, discipline among members was hard to enforce. Lacking inspiration, direction, or a benchmark, policy drifted. In some cases, shifts reflected a politician's idiosyncrasies; in others, it was opportunism. As another observer noted, "Close scrutiny of the DPJ record has clearly shown that its stances on structural reform are driven by vote-seeking, not economic reform principles."[29]

This problem was compounded by personalities who rose to top positions in the DPJ administrations. Hatoyama's reversal on relocating the US Marine Corps's air station in Okinawa Prefecture fatally undermined confidence in him. Ozawa's penchant for closely held and seemingly arbitrary decisions—invariably tied to calculations on a political chessboard that only he could see—further confused voters. The public was unable to tell what the party believed in amid abrupt policy shifts or modifications. So, for example, Prime Minister Kan could suddenly announce that Japan would become nuclear energy free in the aftermath of March 11 (3.11)—"a blatant and populist approach to saving his job" that was the political equivalent of a Hail Mary pass.[30] Or, under Prime Minister Noda, the DPJ's policy on the consumption tax (raise it to balance the books), the US-Japan alliance (reaffirm it as a critical pillar of Japanese security policy), and the Trans-Pacific Partnership (join it) became indistinguishable from that of the LDP. Voters and party members alike were unclear about what the DPJ stood for and what, if anything, distinguished it from the much-despised LDP. The need to focus on reconstruction after the triple catastrophe further narrowed the scope for policy innovation or the departure from more traditional policies. One political analysis concluded, "The devastation of 3.11 narrows Japan's policy options and further converges the position of Japan's two major political parties." The authors decried the "reluctant consensus" that delays "much needed changes and reform in Japan."[31]

This policy convergence intensified the competition between the two main parties. Japanese politics became a blood sport, with both parties committed to embarrassing and frustrating their opponents. The machinations behind the 2012 no-confidence votes are the most egregious examples, but they are only differences of degree, not of kind. Tactics have dominated political calculations, with little if any attention given to broader national interests. Satoh Haruko, an assistant professor at the School of International Public Policy at Osaka University, charged that "members of the Japanese parliament (Diet) are perceived only to be concerned with the *seikyoku* [insulated] game of political survival in

Tokyo, as if existing in a parallel universe from the rest of Japan besieged by the worst national catastrophe since World War II."[32] LDP member Kono Taro agreed. Kono is a third-generation LDP politician who has held various cabinet portfolios and whose bluntness and candor are refreshing, although they have likely undermined his credibility with his colleagues. In the summer of 2012, he confessed that politics had not reacted to the events of March 11. Even as the crisis unfolded, politics went on as usual. "We could have worked with the DPJ and quit the political bickering for a while. . . . But there was no sense of urgency among politicians."[33] The DPJ's Nakabayashi reached the same conclusion from her vantage point on the other side of the aisle. "I thought March 11 would have a huge impact on bipartisan cooperation. We used to think that it would take a crisis to get parties and officials to put party interests aside and do something for the nation. But it didn't happen. That was the biggest surprise for me."[34]

In July 2012 Kono was reconciled to the fact that the triple catastrophe had failed to bring about change in Japan. He recounted the mood in his party after the 2009 general election, when the LDP was forced from office. Kono had then sensed change was in the air. "I thought the DPJ would rule for ten years, and they would do the reform the LDP couldn't do and that would be good for Japan." He paused. "But they failed miserably. They couldn't do worse." The sense of crisis in the LDP receded as the DPJ stumbled from one problem to another. "We picked up seats in the 2010 election and the sense of urgency receded." As the end of DPJ rule approached that summer, Kono, like many others, could not see much difference between the two main parties. "The DPJ is becoming a lot like the LDP." And the promise of a new political order that would end the stagnation and instill a new sense of purpose in Japan evaporated. "The 2009 vote created a big mess, but it is an old mess. It's not something new. Was I surprised? I guess not."[35]

Once again, the DPJ's Nakabayashi proved prophetic. She worried in the summer of 2012 that "as long as the LDP remains united, it will be impossible to realign Japanese politics." She predicted that the country was "very likely to go back to politics before 2009."[36] The December 2012 election and the LDP's landslide win proved her right.

The DPJ's defeat was inevitable given both the party's performance while in power and the public's outsize expectations. A poll taken the day after the 2009 vote showed that 69 percent of voters applauded the change of government; that number included 46 percent of people who had voted for the LDP. The same survey revealed that 81 percent of respondents thought that the DPJ's victory reflected a desire for a change of government; just 38 percent credited the party's policies.[37] It is more than a coincidence that a survey taken after the December

2012 shellacking showed 81 percent of voters identified "disappointment in the DPJ government" as the reason for the election results, and only 7 percent pointed to the LDP's policies.[38] Disappointment was especially high because the DPJ had not only overpromised in its 2009 campaign but also performed virtually identically to how the LDP had. As one assessment concluded, "The DPJ did not implement policies significantly different from that of its predecessor. The government appeared rudderless and internally divided, repeatedly modifying or abandoning core campaign pledges that were seemingly at the heart of the party's electoral strategy."[39]

If the DPJ's defeat reflected those particular failings, the scale of its loss was the product of structural factors in Japan's political system. One analysis of the 2012 vote noted that the LDP won just 31.7 percent of seats and 27.6 percent of votes in the proportional representation constituencies, or "practically the same" results as in the last lower house election (30.6 percent of seats and 27.6 percent of proportional representation constituencies); yet 2009 was labeled "a crushing defeat."[40] Other number crunchers highlighted the 10 million abstentions as key in the scale of the LDP's win. The LDP won more seats in single-member districts despite collecting 2 million fewer votes in the second election.[41] Nevertheless, the LDP claimed a mandate for its politicians and their policies, and it wiped the policy slate clean.

"The Easiest Thing to Do Is Wait"

The dismal experience of DPJ rule confirmed to the Japanese public that the problems that plagued their political system (and their country) were not the result of one-party rule, LDP rule, or Duverger's law. Japan was hobbled by political personalities ill fitted to the needs of the moment, poorly designed and executed policies, a political-economic structure that is remarkably resilient and resistant to change, a conservative culture and national psychology that effectively muted reform efforts, and bad luck. Events, both domestic and foreign, repeatedly intervened, distracting policymakers and voters, reordering priorities, and transforming the environment in which decisions were made and implemented.

For many Japanese, the solution lies in a single word—leadership. Since the country lost its way when the bubble burst, the public has had a powerful desire for true leadership and not just political gamesmanship. In a 2012 editorial, the *Mainichi Shimbun* captured the growing public anger and disgust at the country's political class: "Political parties are supposed to share an ideal vision for the country, map out policy measures to achieve it, elect their leaders with the aim of implementing their policies and ask the public for support in elections. Political parties exist to implement the policy measures they pursue, to govern."[42] It excoriated both the DPJ and the LDP for failing in that task. Hayashi Yoshimasa, an LDP grandee who is likely to reside in the Kantei one day, argued that "it's very difficult, but top leaders must decide, must take risks and take responsibility." But after serving in several cabinet and party posts, he conceded that "the easiest thing to do is wait."[43] One political insider, who requested anonymity, admitted that "there are few visionaries" among leading politicians. Most "don't care at all about the direction of Japan. They just have a three-month time horizon. They don't think about a real vision and future trajectory of the country. They don't have strategic vision."[44] Nakanishi Hiroshi, a professor of international studies at Kyoto University's School of Law, explained the public's yearning for a leader: "We want to have our [own Barack] Obama, someone whose leadership shows us choices in a different way."[45] Some see their ideal type in Koizumi Junichiro; some look still further back. Writer and commentator Tamamoto Masaru argued that "we are waiting for [a Mikhail] Gorbachev, someone who has the guts to betray the system and act out what he really believes."[46]

One sign of that hunger was evident in 2010 (ominously, it would turn out) during the first year of DPJ rule, as Japan experienced a "Ryoma boom," or a flowering of remembrances for Sakamoto Ryoma. He was one of the most outsize personalities of the Meiji Restoration, the period in the nineteenth century when Japan abandoned isolation and embraced breakneck modernization. Often referred to as "the renaissance samurai," Ryoma is a seminal figure in the overthrow of the Tokugawa shogunate and the country's decision to enter the modern world. His personal history is a fascinating story, one that mirrors in important ways that of Japan itself.

Born in 1835 in Kochi, in the southern part of the southern island of Shikoku, Ryoma was the youngest son of a *goshi* samurai. While the goshi were the lowest-ranking samurai, his family came from relatively successful merchants. They had enough money to send him to private school, but Ryoma showed little academic aptitude. He did, however, demonstrate an ability at *kenjutsu* (a form of fencing). At the age of eighteen, Ryoma moved to Edo (now Tokyo) to hone those skills and become a master swordsman. That allowed him to see the black ships that Commodore Matthew Perry sailed into Uraga Harbor in 1853 and from which Perry demanded that Japan open its doors to foreign commerce.

Outgunned, the shogunate bowed to superior force. But as the shogunate made one concession after another to the foreigners, Ryoma, as with many other Japanese of his status and age, became increasingly radicalized. He united with like-minded Japanese under the slogan of *Sonno-joi* (Revere the emperor, expel the barbarians); while adhering to the obvious pillars of its philosophy (supporting the emperor and kicking out the foreigners), the movement led to the assassination of those Japanese officials who were considered traitors. One such official was Katsu Kaishu, a ranking official in the shogunate and a student of Western learning who, among other crimes, had been a member of the first Japanese Embassy to the United States in 1860. His advocacy for opening Japan to the rest of the world was one more element in his indictment and made him a target for killing.

According to one of his collaborators, when Ryoma entered Katsu's house to murder him in December 1862, the intended victim first asked Ryoma and his accomplice to let him explain and justify his actions. After hearing him out, Ryoma was so impressed that he not only abandoned his mission but also became a disciple of Katsu, even going so far as to call him "the greatest man in Japan." Two years later, Ryoma was forced to flee to Kagoshima amid the shogunate's crackdown against dissent. (While the government backed opening to the West, Katsu and Ryoma went much further than the shogunate was prepared to go.) In Kagoshima, Ryoma brokered the alliance between the Satsuma and Choshu Provinces, two historical enemies whose entente proved fatal to the old order in Japan. Most historians believe that Ryoma's status as a neutral was the key to their reaching an agreement.

Ryoma is also credited with helping establish the Imperial Japanese Navy as a result of his efforts to build a maritime force that would protect the young rebel alliance against the shogunate's formidable navy. He founded the first modern company in Japan, the Kameyama Shachu, a private shipping firm that was used to transport guns and matériel for the anti-shogun forces. (Kameyama Shachu later became the Kaientai, or Ocean Support Fleet.) After returning to Tosa, he played a key role in negotiations that resulted in the resignation of Shogun Tokugawa Yoshinobu in 1867, the final step that launched the Meiji Restoration. Ryoma was himself assassinated in 1867, allegedly by pro-shogunate groups. His death at the age of thirty-two deprived Japan of a charismatic and calculating leader who demonstrated time and time again an ability to move the nation.

Few historical figures have so captivated generations of Japanese. Some liken his status to that of Lord Byron, a romantic "man of action." His preference for samurai dress and Western boots captured the ease with which he mixed Japanese culture with the trappings of modernism, blending tradition and pragmatism. A man of ideas, Ryoma produced the *Senchu Hassaku* (Eight Point Plan), which spelled out the prerequisites for a stable government. They included the vesting of ultimate authority in the emperor, a bicameral legislature, new rules and legal codes while discarding feudal counterparts, the establishment of a navy, and several other features. Ultimately, his work provided the basis for the new Meiji emperor's Charter Oath.

Ryoma's popularity has only grown in recent years. The airport in his hometown of Kochi now bears his name, and his image graces everything from commemorative coins to toilet paper. The logo of the information technology giant SoftBank is based on that of Ryoma's company, Kaientai, and his biography is a ready reference volume for younger Japanese, whose elders urge them to emulate his determination to remake their country or, as he once put it in a letter to his sister, "to cleanse Japan once again." When the *Asahi Shimbun* asked executives of two hundred Japanese companies which figure from the last thousand years of world history would best help Japan overcome its current malaise, Ryoma got the nod. By 2010 Ryoma had inspired seven television dramas, six novels, seven manga (graphic novels), and five films.[47] That year Japan's state broadcaster NHK aired a *taiga* drama—an annual yearlong historical fiction TV series—based on Ryoma's life.

Ryoma is not just another historical figure. He wrestled with and fashioned responses to the most pressing issues that Japan faced in his day. Many of those same questions—Japan's place between East and West, its readiness to abandon a comfortable order and adapt to new circumstances, its willingness to reach out to the world—dominate Japan's agenda today. In asking—and, more important, answering—those questions, Ryoma became a heroic figure in the true sense of the word; he personified the spirit of a society and its ambitions. The intensity of hero worship is directly proportional to the perceived absence of the values he represents. Ryoma matters to modern-day Japan precisely because no Ryoma-like figure exists in Japan today. The former prime minister's son Koizumi Shinjiro, who won the Diet seat his father formerly held upon his father's retirement in 2008, sees the continuing relevance of Ryoma and his colleagues. "People are frustrated and disappointed at the state of politics. The international community is looking at us and wondering if Japan can change. . . . In twenty or thirty years, we will be judged on whether we made the decision to change or not when we should have done so." For inspiration, he too looks back to the Meiji era.

> Ryoma Sakamoto, Takamori Saigo—these young people once staked their lives to change the country. Even though we don't get to know them personally, we all recognize their names and what they did. . . . because they faced problems at that time, made every effort to tackle them and staked their lives. This era offers a golden opportunity for the Japanese people . . . because we have many problems. I believe those Japanese who live in this era can be like them. In one hundred years, we can be seen as twenty-first century Meiji patriots.[48]

"They Are Still Hoping for a Hero"

The absence of leadership at the national level has prompted some observers (and voters) to look to prefectural and local governments for dynamism and policy entrepreneurs. Traditionally, Japanese prefectural governors were competent, phlegmatic former bureaucrats who focused on administration over politics. But the growing discontent with national politics in the 1990s was also felt at the prefectural level, and several iconoclastic politicians rode that wave of disaffection to challenge and defeat incumbents or LDP-supported opponents. The first sign of a shift in public attitudes occurred in April 1995, when celebrities Aoshima Yukio (an actor, screenwriter, and producer) and Yamada Isamu—the comedian who is better known by his stage name, Knock Yokoyama—were elected governors of Tokyo and Osaka, respectively.[49] Both victories shocked the political establishment, sparking denunciations of voters by some and self-reflection by others.[50] Yamada was a popular governor who was reelected to a second term but resigned after losing a civil lawsuit in which a campaign worker alleged he had sexually harassed her. After one largely unsuccessful term, Aoshima was followed as governor of Tokyo by conservative nationalist Ishihara Shintaro.

Ishihara is one of Japan's best-known and most controversial politicians. He won the prestigious Akutagawa Prize while still a university student. That launched—and was likely the peak of—his literary career. Ishihara shared the intense nationalism of his close friend Mishima Yukio, the world-famous writer who committed suicide in 1970, and continues to espouse nationalist causes. As noted previously, he coauthored "The Japan That Can Say 'No'" with Morita Akio, the late founder of Sony, and misses no opportunity to tweak Japan's neighbors or its ally the United States. Ishihara was first elected to the Diet in 1968 and, after one term in the upper house, served in the lower house for eight consecutive terms. He left the Diet after a failed bid for the LDP's presidency in 1995. He bummed around the world, writing and painting. In 1999 the political itch returned, and Ishihara ran for and was elected governor of Tokyo. Running as an independent, he won four consecutive terms as governor of Japan's largest prefecture, a city that rivals many countries in size and influence. His tenure was punctuated by scandal, however, and his acerbic comments offended many. Sometimes called Japan's (Jean-Marie) Le Pen, Ishihara's nationalist politics were probably more important than his policies; his readiness to pick a fight with China contributed to the undoing of the DPJ government (as is explained in chapter 4).

A fourth political outsider was Tanaka Yasuo, a novelist who served as governor of Nagano Prefecture from 2000 to 2006. Tanaka was the only one of these four politicians to articulate a coherent and focused platform. He was an environmentalist who sought to halt dam building and other wasteful and destructive public works projects, and he pledged to promote transparency (literally) by working in a glass office and by terminating the press club that traditionally handled media relations. He was removed from office after a vote of no confidence in the local assembly but was reelected to a second term.

In more recent years, two other politicians have used governorships to try to create a national political platform. The first is Hashimoto Toru, a telegenic lawyer turned politician. Hashimoto used the visibility afforded by his frequent appearances on national television shows (where he offered legal advice) to launch a campaign for governor of Osaka in 2008. The cornerstone of his bid was the argument that Osaka's economic woes—an industrial center, the city had been hammered for two decades—had been intensified by a political and economic system that put Tokyo at the center of national decision making. Local problems demanded local solutions, but politicians and bureaucrats in Tokyo were too far away and too blinkered in their thinking to find appropriate answers to Osaka's ills. He won but soon realized that his ambitions demanded a political machine. In 2010 Hashimoto established Osaka Ishin no Kai (Osaka Restoration Society), which promptly swept local assembly and city municipal elections. As the DPJ government imploded in Tokyo, Hashimoto was being touted as a national political figure. Opinion polls in early 2012 showed majorities throughout Japan hoped that Hashimoto would step up to the national stage.[51]

The second governor with eyes on the national stage is Koike Yuriko, governor of Tokyo since 2016. She is neither a political neophyte nor an outsider, having served in the Diet (1993–2016); having held three cabinet posts, including a brief stint as minister of defense in the first Abe Shinzo cabinet; and having served as a national security adviser. A conservative nationalist, she was a member of the LDP for most of her time in the Diet, although she left the party to run for governor. She was extremely successful in her first year as governor and rapidly became one of the most visible and popular politicians in Japan. Her job as a presenter on *World Business Satellite*, a national TV news show that she turned into a hit, helped hone her image and her instincts. "She understands business, particularly entrepreneurs, better than a lot of politicians," said one acquaintance from that time. She has "decisiveness and guts," said Kiuchi Takatane, a Diet member from the DPJ.[52]

In each case, however, personal popularity was insufficient to generate the change that these politicians sought. Ambition demanded the creation of national political parties to advance their causes. In 2005 Tanaka founded New Party Nippon with four other reformers, but by 2012 all had lost their seats in the Diet. Ishihara had more success: He left the Tokyo governor's office in 2012 to form the

Sunrise Party (named after his award-winning book), which months later merged with Nippon Ishin no Kai (Japan Restoration Party, or JRA), the national version of Hashimoto's Osaka party. The JRA won fifty-four seats in the December 2012 ballot, establishing itself as a third force in Japanese politics. That was the JRA's high-water mark, however; afterward, the party imploded. Hashimoto made a series of ill-considered remarks that damaged his popularity.[53] A merger with another party was called off, and Hashimoto and Ishihara split after disappointing results in the May 2014 election. The December 2014 snap election proved fatal to both men's national ambitions. Ishihara lost his seat in the election and retired from politics. The JRA merged with another party, but after another underwhelming performance in that ballot—the party lost one seat overall—Hashimoto declared that he would step down from his national party post and focus on Osaka politics. The final nail in his political coffin came when voters defeated his cherished plan to create an Osaka "metropolis" similar to that of Tokyo. Following that loss, Hashimoto announced he would not run again for office.

Hashimoto's fortunes have dimmed, but those of Governor Koike have brightened. Her first year in office was marked by a public spat with the national government over cost-sharing plans for the 2020 Summer Olympics, which Tokyo will host, and by the humiliation of Ishihara following the discovery that the land to which his administration had decided to move the world-famous Tsukiji fish market was contaminated.[54] Koike's popularity soared as a result. In the first real test of her political capital, Tomin First no Kai (Tokyoites First)—the party she formed just before the summer 2017 Tokyo local assembly elections—won a landslide victory and took 55 seats in the 127-seat assembly. After forming a coalition with Komeito (the Komei Party, which partners with the LDP nationally and often in local assemblies too), Tomin First supplanted the LDP as the ruling party in the Tokyo Metropolitan Assembly. In September 2017 Koike announced the launch of Kibo no To (Party of Hope) to contest the October 2017 snap national election. In one clear sign of the winds behind her, the Democratic Party of Japan—the official opposition and the second-largest party in the Diet—said it would not run candidates and would let its members run as representatives of the new party.[55] This action fueled speculation that this is the end of the Democratic Party.[56]

Although short lived, the JRA deserves more than a cursory mention among the ever-lengthening list of Japan's political parties. The party embraced a transformational agenda that was designed to break Tokyo's iron grip on local affairs and devolve authority to regional and city governments.[57] Its key concept was *jiritsu*, which can be translated as "independent" or "self-reliant." The party's name, Nippon Ishin no Kai, explicitly evoked the first transformative period in modern Japanese history, the Meiji Restoration. (The Japanese word for "restoration" is *ishin*.) If that historical reference were not enough, the JRA also adopted an eight-point plan, *Ishin Hassaku* (the Eight Policies for Restoration), which provided the foundation for what Hashimoto called "the great reset." Here, too, the JRA echoed Ryoma's own *Senchu Hassaku*.

That evocation of the past reinforces a key element of Hashimoto's appeal—his image as a man of action. As mayor he had no compunction about taking on powerful opponents—the Osaka teachers' unions, for example—and ingrained and encrusted bureaucracies. He has big ideas—such as closing one of Osaka's local airports—and even when they are rejected, he gets credit for the effort. Osakans consider him someone with the ideas and the energy to break Japan's political gridlock. In almost every conversation, the same words are used to describe Hashimoto: smart, charismatic, media savvy, populist. They starkly contrast with the image of mainstream national politicians who cannot get things done.

As he surveyed the hard-charging Hashimoto in 2012, Kiyoto Tsuji, a young LDP Diet member, identified the core of his appeal. "Hashimoto reflects the same thing as the DPJ election three years ago. . . . The Japanese want 100 percent change very fast. . . . They believe someone else—'someone smarter than me'— can help solve these problems."[58] The DPJ's Nakabayashi agreed. Hashimoto "represents the people's sentiment in looking for strong leaders. They are still hoping for a hero who can make everything possible and realize whatever people want." Nakabayashi paused and added, "After 2009, people should have learned. They should know that change is impossible even if he wins big."[59] Nakanishi Hiroshi was prepared to go further, arguing that Hashimoto responded to a *need* the Japanese have. "People want strong leadership to deal with issues and create solutions out of divided society. But they're also frustrated by politics and want a savior outside the system. This may be dreamlike or fantasy, but people need that sort of imagination because things have been tough. This is the status of the Japanese psyche."[60]

Finding that person is a struggle. As Tamamoto Masaru explained, any person "who can change Japan . . . has to rise through the system, and the system is designed to weed out such people. . . . When they reach positions of power, they have learned to suppress their mind or changed their thinking. That is the power of the organization." Even Koizumi—"an extraordinary personality" who rose to power at a special moment in Japanese politics and reached out to the people, something that "no Japanese prime minister does"—came up short. "He broke the LDP, but he couldn't break bureaucratic rule," said Tamamoto.[61]

The rigidity that girds the status quo reflects a powerful cultural bias and a deep-seated aversion to risk that many Japanese have. Said Tamamoto, "If you take a risk, then you are doing something others aren't. . . . But in Japan, you should only take risks whenever everyone takes it. Everyone fails or succeeds together. Watch *The Seven Samurai*. It's not about the samurai, but about the peasants. There is no nobility in Japan. This is a peasant society run by peasants calling themselves bureaucrats."[62] There are echoes of Tamamoto's criticism in more conventional analyses of Japan's political problems. For example, in their assessment of the political impact of March 11, Miura Lully and Joshua Walker blamed "a lack of leadership and the tendency to escape responsibility by 'respecting' the formality of 'due process'" for blocking implementation of innovative solutions to the crisis.[63]

The dynastic nature of Japanese politics reinforces systemic bias. An estimated 30 percent of the 480 members of the House of Representatives are nisei (second-generation) members of the Diet, and 40 percent of the LDP Diet members are as well. Of the thirty postwar prime ministers, only three had no politicians among their family members, and most of the others were children or grandchildren of former prime ministers and ministers.[64] That presence is reinforced by an 80 percent victory rate among those nisei. Eight of the nineteen members of Abe's second cabinet also had relatives who were in the Diet or in local politics.[65] Children of politicians not only gain valuable insight and exposure into the inner workings of politics but also inherit habits, assumptions, and procedures. Especially valuable—and limiting—are the relationships that are an integral part of political success and are passed from one family member to another. These are embodied in the *koenkai* (political support groups) that are the cornerstone of Japanese politics as they lubricate the process and lock in relationships. Note that Hayashi, the Diet member who acknowledged that "the easiest thing to do is wait," is a fourth-generation politician.

The problem hasn't gone unrecognized, and there have been attempts to break the grip of dynastic politics. The 2009 DPJ manifesto said the party would "create a new political culture by bidding farewell to hereditary politics," and the party enforced bans on its hereditary candidates in the 2009 and 2012 elections. A law to institutionalize that practice across the country never gained traction (and would likely have been unconstitutional).

"This Isn't Syria!"

The Japanese are increasingly dismayed by the failure of Japan's politicians to meet current challenges. Yet some acknowledge that "systemic failures" on one level represent the voters' abdication of responsibility. Kanno Masaaki, managing director and chief economist of J. P. Morgan, insisted, "You ultimately have to blame voters. They won't listen to truth or hear the issues."[66] At the most rudimentary level, that means casting ballots. Incredibly, even after the appalling failures of March 11, voter turnout in the December 2012 election fell nearly 10 points from the 2009 vote, reaching new postwar lows of just under 60 percent.[67] This disturbing outcome—which has continued since that ballot, with turnout in the December 2014 national election hitting 52.6 percent—makes sense given the widespread belief among Japanese voters that the political system does not reflect their interests or preferences. In a 2012 Cabinet Office poll, more than 80 percent of respondents said they do not believe the will of the people is reflected in government policies. At 81.9 percent, that is an increase of 3.2 percent from the previous year and the highest level recorded since the government began asking the question in 1982.[68]

Plummeting turnout would seem to signal resignation. Some argue that this is to be expected because the Japanese were "given" democracy by the Occupation authorities; therefore, the people do not appreciate the commitment it demands of citizens.[69] That may be an incendiary argument, but even politicians such as Kono Taro are perplexed by their constituents' behavior. "What surprised me after [March 11] was people emailing me, asking *me* what they can do. Going to the ballot box isn't enough. They have to be heard by politicians, they have to pressure them." He paused. "This isn't Syria. They won't shoot you," he added with no small amount of exasperation.[70]

Inculcating a sense of responsibility among voters is only half the answer; there also have to be candidates who can take up the burden. Several schools have been established to diversify the pool of politicians. The most famous of these is the Matsushita Seikei Juku (Matsushita Institute of Government and Management). Founded in 1979 by Matsushita Konosuke, chairman of the Panasonic group, it aims "to combat the vanity and mediocrity of 20th century leadership through a long-term strategy, which entailed an innovative approach to education, designed to foster a more profound change for Japan and her relationship to the world."[71] The four-year graduate program is free, but admission is tough. As of 2016, the school claimed more than 260 graduates, 42 percent of whom have become politicians. Its most famous alumnus is former Prime Minister Noda.[72] Other notable alumni include Onodera Itsunori, who served as state minister for foreign affairs and as minister of defense; Maehara Seiji, former president of the DPJ and foreign minister; Murai Yoshihiro, governor of Miyagi Prefecture; and Sanae Takaichi, a senior LDP official who has held several cabinet portfolios and is on the short list of women who could become prime minister.

Inspired by his stay at Harvard's Kennedy School of Government, in 2010 the former Ministry of Economy, Trade, and Industry official Asahina Ichiro helped found the think tank, school, and consulting company Aoyama Shachu. Named after Ryoma's original trading company, Kameyama Shachu, the organization aims "to produce Japan's revival by bringing global competitiveness." Its website spells out its ambitious mission: "to fundamentally reshape Japan's national policy making process by effectively informing the policy options to the public and mobilizing key stakeholders in the government and the private sector." The school offers leadership training seminars and support for drafting election campaign platforms for candidates.[73]

Consistent with Ishin no Kai's goal to build a national party, it established its own training school for politicians as well. The Ishin Seiji Juku (Restoration Politics Academy) opened in March 2012 with over two thousand enrollees. Students came from all walks of life, paying tuition to attend twice-monthly training sessions and learn to talk about issues.[74] In speeches to the group, Hashimoto urged them to "become warriors. Let's fight together. Let's change Japan." By the summer, the number of students had been reduced to 888, 65 of whom were already low-level politicians.[75] They professed a desire to spread Hashimoto's message throughout Japan, but the school itself seemed uncertain about whether it was cultivating politicians or nurturing a grassroots movement.[76] Sixteen students won election to the Diet in the December 2012 election, but interest in the school has diminished with the dimming of Hashimoto's fortunes.

In keeping with her desire to cultivate a national following, Tokyo governor Koike also set up her own leadership academy, Kibo no Juku (Academy of Hope), in October 2016. More than forty-five hundred people from across the country applied to attend monthly seminars on a series of topics related to politics.[77] At the time, Koike was coy about using the school as a recruitment site for her own political party; but, as noted previously, she also launched Kibo no To in late September 2017, just prior to the October 22 snap election. Despite high hopes, the party disappointed at the polls, coming in third in terms of seats won.

"Creating a New Culture"

For some Japanese, the answer to their country's woes lies not in politics but in civic activism. This work is still in progress, having begun more than two decades ago with the Great Hanshin Earthquake that struck Kobe in January 1995. The quake prompted more than 1.3 million people across the country to volunteer to help the thousands of victims who lost family and friends and whose homes were destroyed. The official response to the temblor was appalling and drove home the point that civil society groups had to supplement governmental efforts. Among the most prompt and effective early responders were the yakuza groups, a fact of no small embarrassment to the government. The Great Hanshin Earthquake and its aftermath spurred a reexamination of the role that civil society could play in Japan—a role that the powers that be looked on with considerable suspicion—and resulted in 1998 in the Law Concerning the Promotion of Specific Non-Profit Organization Activities.[78] The government's relationship between civil society organizations and nonprofit organizations (NPOs) remains contentious, however. By definition, civil society groups challenge government priorities; they are created to empower the powerless and fill the gaps that emerge from the implementation of policy. In theory, they should complement each other; in reality, they often conflict. The NPO law institutionalized a relationship between those two groups and the resulting frictions. For example, ministries must officially approve nonprofits if they are to receive favorable tax treatment (so that donations are tax deductible), and the approval process has raised concern about its potential for compromising a group's independence. Nevertheless, this third sector continues to develop.

Kudo Yasushi founded Genron NPO, a think tank and an NPO, because he was skeptical about the ability of existing political parties to tackle Japan's problems. "These are just groups. They are not real political parties," he explained. "They aren't sufficiently united to solve problems. When they can't, they fracture."[79] The continuing failures of the political class were evident after the March 11 catastrophe. "People were expecting the government to help, but seeing the crisis in front of their eyes, people took action. They learned they had to act."

Asahina Ichiro, the former METI bureaucrat, envisions activism of a different sort. He sees a new entrepreneurism, one that threatens the old order, in which governments create a vision and bureaucrats implement it. The clearest evidence for him is that the bureaucracy no longer claims the best and the brightest of Japan's young people. "Today, the best students don't want to be bureaucrats. They want to be innovators."[80] Among the reasons for this change in thinking are the new vogue for neoliberalism and the smaller government it produces, the fiscal crunch that has limited bureaucrats' salaries and perks, and the image of government employees as crusty, cosseted, and unimaginative. Asahina saw a parallel between the current situation in Japan and that of the Meiji era and thinks young people must take action to change the country. He too believes that Ryoma is a compelling role model, as well as Steve Jobs.

While at METI, Asahina set up the Project K team with a plan to reorganize Japan's cumbersome administrative structures.[81] The group brought together current and former civil servants from throughout the central government and their counterparts from other administrations (local and prefectural) and the private sector to figure out how to streamline the bureaucracy. He left the ministry in 2010 after realizing that "it isn't just a government problem. Government reform isn't enough to bring about structural change." To do that, as noted previously, Asahina set up Aoyama Shachu to develop leaders. "We don't just need new politicians. We need leaders to change the system—in the bureaucracy, the private sector, civil society." His new academy offers classes that develop the skill set needed for leadership. "We're creating a new culture."

There is a third interpretation of the changes under way in Japan. Kuroda Kaori, a longtime civil society activist, believes that the thinking of ordinary Japanese has changed, so there is now a simple demand for action. Kuroda has labored for many years to build civil society in Japan, and there is no missing the fatigue in her voice as she traces her work over the last two decades. On the one hand, she sounds disillusioned with large-scale activism. "I'm not sure how the civil society sector and nonprofit organizations are relevant to individuals," she confessed.[82] "They can't necessarily respond to individual needs and hopes. Well-established nonprofits are very conservative these days. . . . NGOs [nongovernmental organizations] and NPOs [have] become bureaucratic." Yet if these institutions are failing the Japanese, opportunities still exist for individual action "in the gap between what organizations can do and what individuals want to see." As she surveyed the weekly Friday afternoon rallies in front of the prime minister's office that started after the March 11 crisis, she saw ordinary people "who just want to do something." They were not activists, nor were they necessarily part of some vast movement. "I'm not sure if it leads to big changes, but obviously, each individual has some kind of impact." Kuroda sounded a lot like Tsuda Daisuke, the mediaist (i.e., a commentator on evolving forms of social media in Japan) who argued that "people are doing activities but they are not interested in joining activities. These are leaderless revolutions."[83]

Not surprising, Kuroda was one of the few people who was ambivalent about the call for a new Ryoma. "It's a simple answer," she concluded. "Changes will happen from the bottom anyway. It's not a top-down process. . . . The communities I work with don't have a charismatic leader, but they do fine. We need politicians who are sensitive and see what is happening on the ground."

"To Fix Japan, Politics Should Be Fixed"

One such politician might be Koizumi Shinjiro. He is the son of Koizumi Junichiro, the radical who declared war on his own party while in office. Initially dismissed as a pretty boy for his youth and pop-star looks (and his family connections), Shinjiro has emerged not only as a popular figure in the LDP but also as an introspective and thoughtful politician. A fourth-generation politician who inherited his father's seat, he appears to be the embodiment of the old order. He is head of the party's Youth Division, where he sprinkled the Koizumi magic on the next generation of LDP parliamentarians. During the 2010 upper house elections, the LDP sent him out to drum up support for seventeen candidates, fourteen of whom won. While his poster-boy good looks do not hurt, most observers credit his hard work. Former METI official Okumura Jun overcame initial doubts to conclude that Koizumi is evolving into a real leader. "Koizumi has the same calm and easy stage presence and delivery that masked [Ronald] Reagan's killer instincts and enabled him to maintain a benign aura even when he launched savage attacks against opponents, 'welfare queens,' and other Republican targets."[84] He is not alone in that assessment. One poll of political reporters ranked Koizumi fourth among the nation's most effective politicians.[85]

An LDP stalwart, Koizumi Shinjiro acknowledges the reality that his party is now back in power. But it isn't enough to just be a member of the ruling party. "We need to ask how to make a new LDP and a new model for Japan's recovery."[86] Ultimately, that requires a functioning two-party system. Stability is good for politics, but too much stability breeds complacency and laziness. "To have better politics, we need a strong opposition party and a strong ruling party. They are a pair." When we talked in 2012, the DPJ had imploded, leaving no real counterweight to the LDP. Shinjiro believes that "people should challenge the LDP by pointing out that 'you are not changing, you are the old LDP.'" He took one of his frequent pauses before concluding, "We need to struggle and strive for change."

For Koziumi Shinjiro, as with many Japanese, the core of the nation's problem is a political superstructure that has been unable to adjust to a rapidly changing world. As he explained, "To fix Japan, politics should be fixed."

Notes

Seiji shokku means "political shock." I like the alliteration.

1. The LDP lost its majority in the July 1998 upper house election as well, but it remained the largest party in the chamber by far (with more than twice the number of seats of the closest opposition party, the Democrats). Soon it forged a coalition with the Liberal Party and Komeito to control that house.
2. The lower house is the more powerful of the two chambers in the legislature. The prime minister must be a member of the lower house.
3. Kitaoka Shinichi, "Breaking the Political Deadlock with Bold Reforms" (Tokyo: Tokyo Foundation for Policy Research, January 19, 2012), http://www.tokyofoundation.org/en/topics/politics-in-persepctive/bold-reforms.
4. There is debate in Japan about becoming a "normal nation." This is usually interpreted as referring to the "abnormality" of a country that does not have a real

military and whose constitution gives up the right to use force as an instrument of state policy, as articulated in Article 9. In fact, the first references to becoming a normal nation referred to the monopolization of power by one party. Normalcy means alternation in government and a genuine contest of ideas within politics.

5. "Koizumi Seeks Prudent Budget Requests," *Japan Times*, August 3, 2002, http://www.japantimes.co.jp/news/2002/08/03/business/koizumi-seeks-prudent-budget-requests/#.Ucuf76yuqLE.

6. Rebecca MacKinnon, "A Poll Where Anything Is Possible," CNN, July 28, 2001.

7. Kitaoka, "Breaking the Political Deadlock."

8. Kushida Kenji and Phillip Lipscy, "The Rise and Fall of the Democratic Party of Japan," in *Japan under the DPJ: The Politics of Transition and Governance*, ed. Kushida Kenji and Phillip Lipscy (Washington, DC: Brookings Institution Press, 2013), 3.

9. Tobias Harris, "How Will the DPJ Change Japan?," *Naval War College Review* 63, no. 1 (Winter 2010): 77–78.

10. "Japan's Election: Lost in Transition," *The Economist*, September 3, 2009.

11. A critical factor in that election was the increasingly fraught relationship with China. Noda, like his predecessors, was tested by Beijing; that situation underscored the need for experience and a steady hand on the ship of state amid foreign policy challenges. The China challenge is taken up in chapter 4.

12. Kitaoka, "Breaking the Political Deadlock."

13. Satoshi Machidori, "Behind Japan's Political Turmoil" (Tokyo: Nippon Foundation, July 25, 2012), http://www.nippon.com/en/simpleview/?post_id=1899.

14. Kenji and Lipscy, "Rise and Fall," 10.

15. Satoshi, "Behind Japan's Political Turmoil."

16. Using majorities to pass legislation causes real discomfort in Japan. Disregarding minority views is very poor form. There needs to be an appearance of consulting, discussing, and accommodating diverse opinions, even if outcomes are no different, and the only difference is the time spent in discussion. A key mechanism in this coordination process is the Diet Affairs Committee, at which leading members of the government and opposition parties reach agreements on legislative procedures to provide a veneer of fairness. It is not uncommon to lubricate the parliamentary process with money; the government provides funds to the opposition to win its acquiescence.

17. Aihara Kiyoshi, "The Bureaucratic Role and Party Governance (Symposium Report 3)" (Tokyo: Tokyo Foundation for Policy Research, November 5, 2008), http://www.tokyofoundation.org/en/articles/2008/the-bureaucratic-role-and-party-governance-symposium-report-3.

18. Editor's note, "Political Reform of the Japanese System of Government (Symposium Report 2)" (Tokyo: Tokyo Foundation for Policy Research, October 28,

2008), n. 1, http://www.tokyofoundation.org/en/articles/2008/political-reform-of -the-japanese-system-of-government-symposium-report-2#relatedarticles.

19. Author interview, Tokyo, July 10, 2012.

20. Purnendra Jain and Inoguchi Takashi, *Japanese Politics Today: Beyond Karaoke Democracy* (New York: St. Martin's Press, 1997).

21. Author interview, Tokyo, July 13, 2012.

22. Kenji and Lipscy, "Rise and Fall," 18.

23. Ibid., 20.

24. Ibid., 24.

25. Author conversation with senior Ministry of Foreign Affairs political appointee, Tokyo, July 2010.

26. Author interview, Tokyo, July 24, 2012.

27. Few figures loom larger than Ozawa in contemporary Japanese politics. Although it is a little dated, Jacob Schlesinger's *Shadow Shoguns: The Rise and Fall of Japan's Postwar Political Regime* (Stanford, CA: Stanford University Press, 1999) remains the best guide to Ozawa and his maneuverings.

28. Yamaguchi Jiro, "The End of the Democratic Experiment," *Asia-Pacific Journal* 10, no. 28 (July 9, 2012).

29. Aurelia George Mulgan, "Japan: Is the DPJ the Party of Economic Reform?," *East Asia Forum,* August 4, 2009; and Aurelia George Mulgan, "Agricultural Politics and Democratic Party of Japan," *Japanese Studies Online* (Australian National University) 2 (2011), http://japaninstitute.anu.edu.au/sites/default/files/u5/Japan _Agricultural_Politics_DPJ.pdf.

30. Miura Lully and Joshua Walker, "The Shifting Tectonics of Japan One Year after March 11, 2011" (Washington, DC: The German Marshall Fund of the United States, March 8, 2012), 4.

31. Ibid., 1.

32. Satoh Haruko, "Post-3.11 Japan: A Matter of Restoring Trust," Analysis No. 83 (Milan: Instituto per gli Studi di Politica Internazionale, December 2012), 2, https://www.ispionline.it/it/documents/Analysis_83_2011.pdf.

33. Author interview, Tokyo, July 17, 2012.

34. Author interview, Tokyo, July 24, 2012.

35. Author interview, Tokyo, July 17, 2012.

36. Author interview, Tokyo, July 24, 2012.

37. Michael Green, "Japan's Confused Revolution," *Washington Quarterly* 33, no. 1 (January 2010): 7.

38. "Asahi Poll: Voters Mixed on Abe, LDP Victory," *Asahi Shimbun*, December 19, 2012.

39. Phillip Lipscy and Ethan Scheiner, "Japan under the DPJ: The Paradox of Political Change without Policy Change," *Journal of East Asian Studies* 12 (2012): 313.

40. Miyano Masaru, "One Perspective on the Results of the 2012 Lower House Election," *Japan News*, January 15, 2013, http://www.yomiuri.co.jp/adv/chuo/dy/opinion/20130115.html.

41. Joshua Tucker, "The Japanese General Election of 2012: Sometimes, Lucky Is Better Than Popular," *Monkey Cage*, December 27, 2012, http://themonkeycage.org/2012/12/the-japanese-general-election-of-2012-sometimes-lucky-is-better-than-popular/.

42. "Political Parties Must Cultivate Leaders, Return to Core Values to Regain Public Trust," *Mainichi Shimbun*, April 30, 2012.

43. Author interview, Tokyo, July 18, 2012.

44. Author interview, Tokyo, July 18, 2012.

45. Author interview, Kyoto, November 9, 2012.

46. Author interview, Yokohama, July 22, 2012.

47. Hongo Jun, "Sakamoto: The Man and the Myth," *Japan Times*, April 27, 2010.

48. Author interview, Tokyo, July 10, 2012.

49. While the two men played up their image as newcomers, both had in fact served in the House of Councilors as independents: Aoshima for twenty-seven years and Yamada for twenty-four years.

50. Ioan Trifu, "Prefectural Governors and Populism in Japan (1990s–2010s)," *Acta Asiatica Varsoviensia* 26 (2013): 10.

51. Kamiya Matake, "Restoration: A Work in Progress?," *Japan Journal* (March 2012): 14–15.

52. Both quotes are from Leo Lewis and Robin Harding, "Yuriko Koike, Politician Taking on Japan's Grey Elite," *Financial Times*, September 29, 2017.

53. In the spring of 2013, Hashimoto made comments that seemed to justify the Imperial Japanese Army's brothel system and to dismiss the problem of the "comfort women" (women forced into sexual servitude during World War II). Yoshida Reiji, "As Hashimoto Self-Destructs, Party also Reels," *Japan Times*, May 23, 2013, https://www.japantimes.co.jp/news/2013/05/23/national/politics-diplomacy/as-hashimoto-self-destructs-party-also-reels/#.WyfufS2ZOf4.

54. For the latter tale, see Sarah Baird, "The Toxic Saga of the World's Greatest Fish Market," *Eater*, July 25, 2017, https://www.eater.com/2017/7/25/16019906/tokyo-tsukiji-toyosu-olympics-delay.

55. Linda Seig and Kiyoshi Takenaka, "Japan Calls Snap Election as New Party Roils Outlook," *Reuters*, September 27, 2017, http://www.reuters.com/article/us-japan-election/japan-calls-snap-election-as-new-party-roils-outlook-idUSKCN1C23AO.

56. Yoshida Reiji, "Democratic Party Effectively Disbands, Throwing Support behind Koike's Party for Lower House Poll," *Japan Times*, September 29, 2017, https://www.japantimes.co.jp/news/2017/09/28/national/politics-diplomacy/abe-dissolves-lower-house-opposition-bands-together/#.Wc2YTK2ZOHo.

57. While the initial referendum was rejected, the subsequent victory of the two Osaka Ishin no Kai candidates in the November 2015 "double election" (for mayor of Osaka City and governor of the prefecture) means that the plan has not yet died.

58. Author interview, Tokyo, August 13, 2012.

59. Author interview, Tokyo, July 24, 2012.

60. Author interview, Kyoto, November 9, 2012.

61. Author interview, Yokohama, July 24, 2012.

62. Author Interview, Yokohama, July 24, 2012.

63. Miura and Walker, "Shifting Tectonics of Japan," 2.

64. Cesare Scartozzi, "Hereditary Politics in Japan: A Family Business," *The Diplomat*, February 9, 2017, http://thediplomat.com/2017/02/hereditary-politics-in-japan-a -family-business/.

65. "Japanese Politics: To the District Born," *The Economist*, November 27, 2014, https://www.economist.com/news/asia/21635073-political-families-are-rise -district-born.

66. Author interview, Tokyo, July 11, 2012.

67. Kyodo News, "Voter Turnout Plummeted to a Record Postwar Low," *Japan Times*, December 18, 2012.

68. "Over 80% Say People's Will Not Reflected in Japan's Policies: Survey," Kyodo News, March 31, 2012.

69. See, for example, John Dower, *Embracing Defeat: Japan in the Wake of World War II* (New York: W. W. Norton, 1999), 71.

70. Author interview, Tokyo, July 17, 2012.

71. Robert D. Eldridge, "Translator's Preface," in *Backroom Politics: Factions in a Multiparty Era*, by Watanabe Tsuneo (Lanham, MD: Lexington Books, 2013), 57n152.

72. Matsushita Institute of Government and Management, "MIGM Graduates: Career Paths," http://www.mskj.or.jp/en/graduates/index.html.

73. Tai Makoto, "Young Bureaucrats Plugging Away at Kasumigaseki Reform," *Japan Times*, January 11, 2013, http://www.japantimes.co.jp/news/2013/01/11/national /young-bureaucrats-plugging-away-at-kasumigaseki-reform/#.UdEVJhbmK2w.

74. "Hashimoto Fires Up Class at School for Aspiring Politicians," *Japan Today*, June 24, 2012, http://www.japantoday.com/category/politics/view/hashimoto-fires-up -class-at-school-for-aspiring-politicians.

75. Eric Johnston, "Hashimoto Reeling after Students' Names Leaked," *Japan Times*, August 9, 2012, https://www.japantimes.co.jp/news/2012/08/09/news/hashimoto -reeling-after-students-names-leaked/#.W3LSZy2B2Ho.

76. Charles Weathers, "Reformer or Destroyer? Hashimoto Toru and Populist Neo-liberal Politics in Japan," *Social Science Japan Journal* 17, no. 1 (January 2014), https://doi.org/10.1093/ssjj/jyt029.

77. "Tokyo Gov. Koike's Political School Gearing Up, Raising Possibility of New Party," *The Mainichi*, October 29, 2016, http://mainichi.jp/english/articles/20161029/p2a/00m/0na/005000c.

78. See, for example, Yamamoto Tadashi, "The Recent Debate on the Role of NPOs in Japan and Private-Sector Responses," *Civil Society Monitor* 2 (Spring 1997).

79. All quotes from author interview, Tokyo, July 23, 2012.

80. All quotes from author interview, Tokyo, August 14, 2012.

81. Tai, "Young Bureaucrats."

82. All quotes from author interview, Tokyo, August 13, 2012.

83. Author interview, Tokyo, August 14, 2012.

84. Okumura Jun, "Things People Don't Talk About (5): How the Media Reported on the Seven LDP No-Confidence Vote Dissenters," *Global Talk 21*, August 12, 2012.

85. Okumura Jun, "Noda, Tanigaki, Hoshino, Koizumi, Ishiba-Okada-Kan—in That Order," *Global Talk 21*, December 17, 2012.

86. All quotes author interviews, Tokyo, July 10, 2012, and March 2013.

4

THE SENKAKU SHOKKU

opes that a political earthquake—the Democratic Party of Japan's ascension to government—would provide Japan the shock it needed to better address national problems were quickly crushed as the new government stumbled almost immediately and never again found its footing. The wounds that the DPJ received during its first year in office were largely self-inflicted. In 2010, however, the country experienced a third shock that could—and eventually did—produce a change in national tone and direction. This third jolt was, like the Lehman shock of 2008, external in origin, but this time Japan was the target, not an accidental victim. The 2010 shock was the result of a territorial dispute with China over unoccupied islands in the East China Sea. This long-standing source of tension between the two countries assumed greater significance as China emerged from its isolation after the death of Mao Zedong and began to reassert its claim to regional leadership. This chapter begins by examining the relationship—the rivalry—between Japan and China, and then explores Japanese foreign and security policies more generally, using the territorial dispute as a prism to examine Japan's relationships with the United States and Asia more broadly.

From a Golden Era to a Time of Reckoning

The central question for Japan in the modern era—since the arrival of Commodore Perry's ships in 1853—has been how the country situated itself in relation to Asia and the West. Did the Japanese stick with their geographic, historical, and cultural roots or shed those ties to join a modern and seemingly "advanced" group of countries with which it shared no discernible ties or features other than a hunger for progress? The Meiji leaders chose to "escape from Asia," a decision whose logic was laid out in a March 16, 1885, editorial ("Datsu-a ron") in the newspaper *Jiji Shimpo*. Its anonymous author—who is generally thought to be Fukuzawa Yukichi—argued that Japan had to transform if it was to maintain control of its destiny, and the process required a rejection of the Eastern civilizations that had defined its past and a closer alignment and involvement with the newly industrialized nations of the West.

That choice led first to stunning success but ultimately resulted in world war and ruin (as explained in chapter 1). Seventy-plus years after that defeat and another cycle of success and failure, Japan continues to straddle and grapple with that civilizational divide. Consistent with the Meiji-era framing, Japan still sees the West as standing for modernity and its accoutrements (good and bad); this perspective is reinforced by the country's reliance on the United States for security. But geography is constant, and Asia is catching up. Reconciling those tugs and strains is the preeminent foreign policy challenge for Japanese decision makers in the twenty-first century.

If Japan's positioning between Asia and the West is the context, its relationship with China is the key variable. Since the two countries became aware of each other, there has been a mutual wariness and competition. As June Teufel Dreyer explained in her magisterial study of Japan-China relations, the issues that create tensions between the two countries reflect an "underlying problem that stretches back to the beginning of relations between the two states: the unwillingness of either China or Japan to accept the other as an equal, and the refusal of the other to accept a position of inferiority to the other."[1] Until the mid-nineteenth century, China was the acknowledged hegemon—the Middle Kingdom—and Japan was the primary Asian challenger to that order. In the Meiji era, Japan replaced China as the preeminent regional power, and while never completely occupying and subjugating China, it did colonize and brutalize vast swaths of the country and Asia. Relations between the two were largely frozen after World War II. Whatever thoughts the Japanese leadership may have had about the victory of the Chinese Communist Party in 1949—and some felt that a productive relationship was possible—US hostility to the communists meant that Tokyo would have nothing to do with them. Yet as Japan's economy developed, business leaders and politicians looked hungrily toward China, sensing opportunities to extend influence, to reclaim some political and diplomatic autonomy, and to advance their business interests. US president Richard Nixon's opening to China—while coming as a genuine shock to the Japanese—was welcomed for the possibilities it offered Tokyo.

Japan seized them, inaugurating what some consider "the golden age of Sino-Japanese relations."[2] The two countries quickly agreed to normalize relations, although negotiations took six years to complete. Economic ties grew rapidly. The first trade agreement between the two countries was negotiated in 1978 and set a goal of $10 billion in exports from each country in the first decade. In fact, trade grew from $1.1 billion in 1972 to almost $20 billion in 1988 as Japanese companies raced to make inroads into China's vast market.[3] Official development assistance (ODA) began in 1979 and virtually exploded: Japan provided ¥331 billion in loans in 1979–84 and ¥540 billion in 1984–89, and the amount would reach 10–15 percent of Japan's total ODA by the 1990s.[4] Both governments sought to use the other to gain room for diplomatic maneuver and to develop their respective economies. Both leaderships also recognized the need to establish a solid foundation for the relationship and to create an enduring reconciliation between the two giants of Asia. Sheila Smith, in her penetrating study of Japan-China relations, concludes that "economic interdependence—and at that time the complementarities of the two economies—was seen as the salve that would heal the wounds of Japan's wartime invasion and subsequent defeat in 1945."[5]

For a while that logic prevailed. The volume of China-Japan trade grew more than tenfold from 1990 to 2005, and by the summer of 2008 China had replaced the United States as Japan's biggest export market.[6] When Japan's economy finally appeared to have escaped the stagnation of the lost decade—before prospects were crushed by the Lehman shock—China's role was pivotal. Former deputy minister for foreign affairs Tanaka Hitoshi noted, "It is now widely acknowledged in the Japanese business community that much of Japan's recent economic recovery can be attributed to China's rise—i.e., China's economic growth has 'pulled' the Japanese economy out of the doldrums."[7]

Total cumulative investment by Japanese firms in China had reached $83 billion by the end of 2011, making Japan the third-largest source of China's foreign direct investment.[8] China's Ministry of Commerce reported that by the end of 2012, 23,094 Japanese firms were doing business in China, and Japanese business investment in China totaled $7.4 billion, an 18 percent increase from the previous year.[9] A May 2012 survey by the Ministry of Economy, Trade, and Industry revealed that the total profit of Chinese-based subsidiaries of Japanese companies was ¥1.9 trillion (approximately $20 billion) in 2010, an increasingly weighty share of all operating profits. In the transportation equipment industry, to take one example, the proportion of profit generated in 2010 by China-based subsidiaries of Japanese companies accounted for 35.3 percent of the entire profit earned by all Japanese industry of that category.[10] Nor did benefits flow in just one direction. Japanese investments in China created 10 million jobs, transferred technology, and provided revenues for taxes, infrastructure, and social services.[11]

That positive economic relationship, however, was increasingly threatened by political irritants. From the outset of relations since World War II, China has complained about Japan's assessment of its wartime history, particularly its treatment in history textbooks; Japanese politicians' visits to the Yasukuni Shrine; and Japan's relationship with the Soviet Union (Beijing wanted Tokyo to take a more assertive stance against Moscow), with the government in Taiwan, and, when US-China relations deteriorated, with the United States. The Japanese, in turn, decried the Tiananmen Square massacre, the Chinese interference in Japanese domestic affairs (when it pressed Tokyo to be more aggressive against the Soviets), and their unfair trade practices.[12] Both countries complained about territorial disputes and the disregard the other government showed for its interests. During the Cold War, a shared concern about the Soviet Union outweighed those frictions. Once the Soviet Union collapsed, however, priorities changed in both countries, and contested issues assumed greater prominence and salience.[13] Yet economic self-interest continued to prevail—for a while. As political tensions rose, the economic relationship stayed on track, giving rise to the phrase "hot economics, cold politics" to describe the overall relationship. One commentator would claim that "hot economics, cold politics" made the Japan-China relationship "a poster child for the liberal thesis that economic interdependence is a source of peace."[14]

Paradoxically, the economics of the relationship were becoming a liability as well. A *People's Daily* comment noting that "Japan's economy lacks immunity to the Chinese economic measures" highlighted both growing Chinese confidence (if not arrogance) and mounting Japanese insecurities, which were triggered by Japan's increasing reliance on the Chinese market.[15] Mei Xinyi—a researcher at the Chinese Academy of International Trade and Economic Cooperation, a Ministry of Commerce think tank—was more explicit: "China has the ability to make Japan pay a heavy price in a trade war" in view of Japan's higher reliance on exports to China.[16] The Japanese were not only irritated by China's ingratitude for their country's contributions to China's development but also increasingly troubled by the thought that those contributions were spurring a military modernization effort that would threaten Japan.

Underlying and compounding these misgivings was the dramatic shift in the two countries' trajectories. Japan from 1991 was descending into economic stagnation, while China was enjoying an extended period of explosive double-digit growth. Both developments profoundly affected thinking in each country: The Japanese became increasingly insecure and anxious, worried about the growing power of China and their own diminishing influence, while Chinese became more confident and assertive. As Sheila Smith trenchantly observed, "Nothing focused [Japan's] leaders and its citizens on the country's national policy priorities more than the questions generated by China's rise."[17] The public and elites in both countries sensed a shift in the balance of power, and some hoped—and others feared—a reckoning with the past was imminent.

The Trawler Trigger

The territorial dispute over the Senkakus crystalized the two countries' differences. The Senkaku Islands consist of five uninhabited islets and three barren rocks, about 6 square kilometers in total size, located some 170 kilometers southwest of Okinawa—the same distance from the northern tip of Taiwan—and 380 kilometers from Wenzhou on the Chinese mainland. They first appear in Chinese records in the early fifteenth century, although it is thought that fishermen or travelers from Okinawa (then the Kingdom of the Ryukyus) knew them by different names. The Japanese government declared the Ryukyus a feudal domain in 1872, announced that it would annex the islands in 1879, and in January 1895 finally annexed the islands themselves as terra nullius.[18] It leased the islands to a Japanese businessman, who then built and ran a fish factory on one of them until 1940. Following Japan's surrender in World War II, they were placed under US administration (along with Okinawa and other Japanese islands) and returned to Japan in 1972. The Chinese counter that the islands were not terra nullius but were part of Chinese territory since the fifteenth century. Both Beijing and Taiwan insist that they should have been returned to the Chinese government at the end of World War II on the basis of the Cairo and Potsdam Declarations.

The dispute was of little significance until the late 1960s when UN-sponsored exploration discovered what appeared to be large oil reserves in the area.[19] During the normalization talks between Japan and China, China's then supreme leader Deng Xiaoping famously said that the dispute should be tabled for future, wiser generations to solve. That was an expedient gesture, one that ensured the dispute would persist. Since that time, there have been regular protests—including visits to the island and attempted flag planting—by nationalists in each country against the other's claim, regular incursions by Chinese and Taiwanese fishing boats into the waters, and periodic intrusions by research vessels as well.[20] Each government made repeated moves to reinforce its claim to the islands, although each also insisted when challenged that it had not changed its policy.

The room for fudging vanished in September 2010, when Zhan Qixiong, the captain of a Chinese trawler, resisted Japanese Coast Guard attempts to stop him from fishing in contested waters near the Senkaku Islands. Rather than reverse course, Zhan rammed the two vessels and ran, obliging the coast guard to give chase and arrest him. That triggered outrage in China since the traditional means of dealing with such incidents was to release the offenders without charge. When seven Chinese activists landed on the islands in March 2004, they had been detained for forty-eight hours and then deported to China. Japanese authorities countered that Zhan's resistance necessitated a different response. Their reply carried little weight in China, which believed the DPJ government was either unaware of protocols for handling such incidents or was trying to change them. Either way, Beijing sensed a disregard for Chinese equities and escalated the crisis to get Tokyo's attention.

First, China arrested four Japanese citizens who were in the country working for the Fujita Corporation on a project to reclaim chemical weapons left there after World War II. Then China canceled the meeting between Prime Minister Wen Jiabao and Prime Minister Kan Naoto that was scheduled to take place that week at the annual opening of the UN General Assembly. Third, Beijing canceled several cultural and exchange programs. Then, in perhaps the most alarming development, China began blocking the export of rare earths to Japan. Chinese officials offered various explanations: first, that there was no embargo; then, that any cutoff was the result of unofficial actions by patriotic, overzealous customs officials; and, finally, that China was cutting exports of rare earths to prevent overexploitation. Regardless of the reason, Japan's dependence on China for 90 percent of its supply of rare earths—which are critical to the production of high-quality electronics—meant that Beijing had essentially declared war by other means. Escalation succeeded. Within days, Japan decided to release Zhan because his detention was negatively affecting the bilateral relationship.

The DPJ government mishandled the crisis. While the decision to arrest the captain broke with procedure, the central government missed a chance to solve the problem by acknowledging from the start the political nature of the incident and by dealing with it accordingly. Instead, Tokyo first delegated authority to the Naha prosecutors and then overruled their judgments as the heat from Beijing intensified.

The impact of the crisis was severe. Respective views of the other country sunk to historical lows. A joint survey by the *Yomiuri Shimbun* and the *Xinhua News Agency* in late October 2010 showed a record 87 percent of Japanese respondents considered China to be untrustworthy, while 79 percent of Chinese respondents felt the same about Japan. A stunning 90 percent of the Japanese public and 81 percent of the Chinese public thought that bilateral relations were in bad shape. Those Japanese who felt "friendly toward China" dropped to a record low of 20 percent, down 18.5 percentage points from the previous survey in 2009.[21]

Significantly, this incident occurred only months after it was reported that China had surpassed Japan to become the world's second-largest economy, a position that Tokyo had held since 1968 when it overtook Germany. This news confirmed for many Japanese that the malaise they sensed was real. Anthropologist Anne Allison captured the resignation many Japanese felt in a lament by one of her friends:

> In terms of workmanship and quality of goods, China is nothing like Japan. . . . But the energy and optimism of the people! Well, we had that too, you know. In the '70s and '80s, when Japan was the cutting edge of the world. We all worked hard, had great ideas, and were globally dynamic. But now we've slowed down, gotten tired, retreated into our island country (*shimaguni*). The Chinese are marching forward and the Japanese? We've kind of died.[22]

There was another, more ominous dimension to this shift: China's new assertiveness was a sign of the very real consequences of the reversal of the two countries' fortunes, and observers worried that more dangerous moments would follow. Takahara Akio, one of Japan's foremost China watchers, traced China's new confidence back to the Lehman shock and the global financial crisis, noting that "China came out stronger, and even faster than expected" while the United States struggled. This experience led China to gain "greater self-confidence" and "directed it to take more assertive positions in international relations."[23]

A list of troubling indicators was easily compiled. Tanaka Hitoshi espied Beijing's "more confident, assertive approach . . . at the ASEAN [Association of Southeast Asian Nations] Regional Forum meeting in [2010] . . . as China attempted to keep territorial disputes in the South China Sea off the agenda. Ongoing tensions with Japan over the Senkaku Islands, the banning of fish imports from Norway in 2010 as retribution for awarding Chinese dissident Liu Xiaobo the Nobel Peace Prize, [etc.], . . . are also indicative of this trend."[24]

Chinese aggressiveness in the South China Sea was as worrisome to the Japanese as its muscle-flexing in the East China Sea. "The maritime highway along the Eurasian rim literally constitutes the lifeline of the Japanese economy," explained maritime specialist Kotani Tetsuo.[25] There, China was not only aggressively expanding its claims to waters throughout the sea—despite claims from several other littoral states—but also changing the status quo via a massive land reclamation project that has been turning reefs and rocks into military outposts. The declaration that the South China Sea was one of China's "core interests"—and thus nonnegotiable[26]—was particularly troubling for a trading nation that relied on seaborne shipping for 99.7 percent of its overall trade by volume and for which nearly 42 percent of its maritime trade and 19.1 percent of its total trade in goods passed through the South China Sea.[27] While China has insisted that it never threatened freedom of navigation or maritime trade, the Japanese nonetheless fear that China's control of the vital waterways could give Beijing a potential stranglehold over its rival.

China Ups the Ante

The Senkakus again provided the anvil on which the DPJ government would be hammered in 2012. This time, the instigator was a Japanese—Tokyo governor Ishihara Shintaro. Determined to tweak the DPJ government for what he considered a supine response to Chinese aggression, Ishihara announced that he had begun negotiations to purchase the three Senkaku Islands that were owned by Kurihara Kunioki and then launched a public campaign to raise the funds. Rightfully concerned about what Ishihara would do if he got the islands, DPJ prime minister Noda Yoshihiko announced that the central government would buy them instead. Noda assumed that the purchase was no big deal as the title would transfer from one Japanese citizen to a Japanese entity. He was wrong. China erupted, noting first the insult delivered when the announcement of the purchase took place on the seventy-fifth anniversary of the Marco Polo Bridge Incident (a day that marks the beginning of the war between Japan and China). The Chinese government also insisted that "nationalization" of the islands strengthened the Japanese government's control over them and would fundamentally change the status quo. When Noda tried to explain his decision at a meeting with Chinese president Hu Jintao in Vladivostok in September, Hu dismissed the arguments and called the purchase illegal and invalid.[28] Tokyo proceeded with the purchase anyway, and the apparent disregard for Chinese concerns rubbed yet more salt in Chinese wounds. The following week, tens of thousands of people protested the move in over a hundred Chinese cities.[29] Celebrations marking the fortieth anniversary of Japan-China relations were canceled, there were boycotts and violence against Japanese businesses, and bilateral trade and tourism sharply declined.

Another critical difference to China's response in this iteration of the confrontation was that it began to send its own maritime vessels into the Senkakus' waters. In September 2012 the State Oceanic Administration sent 81 ships into contiguous waters around the islands and another 13 into Japan's twelve-nautical-mile territorial waters; the next month another 122 entered contiguous waters and 19 in territorial waters; and in November the figures were 124 and 15 ships, respectively. (In the eight previous months of 2012, only 25 ships in total entered any of those zones.)[30] By December there were also encounters above the islands as China dispatched its air forces to monitor the situation and as Japan responded in kind to monitor those flights. The mere presence of these planes and vessels greatly magnified the possibility of an accident or miscalculation and made the prospect of a conflict much more real.

China's decision to up the ante had several important consequences. First, the response posed a direct challenge to Japan's claim of administrative control over the islands, undermining Japan's legal position in ways that a mere reiteration of China's own claim did not. Second, Chinese actions constituted a potential military challenge to Japan's territorial integrity, raising questions about the US-Japan security relationship and what steps Washington was prepared to take to defend those islands. Japanese officials asked for and received assurances that an attack on the islands would invoke Article 5 of the Treaty of Mutual Cooperation and Security.[31]

A third important consequence of this incident was that many Japanese recognized the deteriorating security environment in their region was real and that China played a role in its decline. In his ministry's annual assessment of the Asia-Pacific region, Minister of Defense Morimoto Satoshi in 2012 described that environment as "increasingly harsh."[32] The report highlighted North Korea's provocations and its nuclear weapons program; China's military modernization, its lack of transparency surrounding that effort, and its increasing number of incursions into Japanese waters; and the rising tempo of Russia's military activities in the Far East.[33] China posed a special concern, however. The 2012 Ministry of Defense's white paper noted that "the nominal size of China's announced national defense budget"—which, the report points out, is only part of the country's actual military expenditures—"has more than doubled in size over the past five years and has grown approximately 30-fold over the past 24 years."[34] The result was a force with rapidly expanding capabilities and a growing reach: The army was being modernized and professionalized, and its navy plied waters farther from China's shores and, while it couldn't be called blue water, it was well on its way. In the last decade, China also demonstrated a growing array of advanced technologies: It tested a satellite interceptor, had sea trials for its first aircraft carrier, and revealed a stealth fighter. These capabilities were especially alarming as tensions rose between the two countries. The Defense Ministry's white paper highlighted China's expanding and intensifying maritime activities in waters near Japan.[35]

As the white paper also noted, China is not the only direct threat to Japanese security. Japan also has a territorial dispute with Russia over the Northern Territories, four islands that the Soviet Union seized in the closing days of World War II and that Moscow continues to hold, angering Japanese nationalists and preventing the two countries from signing a peace treaty to officially end that conflict.[36] Russia and Japan have been close to a deal on several occasions but never managed to finalize an agreement. While their official positions seem irreconcilable, diplomats persevere. The outlines of a deal are easy to see, but it would require both sides to compromise, which neither seems willing to do.[37] Japanese sensitivities were inflamed in November 2010, just weeks after the Senkaku crisis, when Dmitri Medvedev made the first visit to the disputed islands by a Russian head of state. Japanese concerns were magnified because his visit followed a China-Russia summit in September at which the representatives denounced countries that tried to rewrite history, a formulation that policymakers in Tokyo believe was aimed at them.[38] Russia beefed up military activities on the islands the following year and increased its naval and air activities in the area. Japan sharply increased aircraft scrambles during that time and they have increased since then. Medvedev also made a second visit in July 2012 just before the second Senkaku crisis erupted.[39]

In Japanese eyes, even more troubling than Russia is the escalating North Korean threat. Pyongyang has long been a source of regional instability, and Japan assumed a special place in that regime's rhetoric as a target of its military capabilities. One of the greatest shocks to Japanese sensibilities was the overflight of their country in 1998 by a long-range North Korean missile. Chief Cabinet Secretary Nonaka Hiromu called the test "a very dangerous act," one that "will have a serious impact on the security of Northeast Asia."[40] In an analysis published as the DPJ took office, Christopher Hughes, one of Britain's leading Japan experts, noted that North Korea "loomed increasingly large in the determination of Japan's defense posture." It had "elbowed itself to the front of Japan's declared security anxieties, apparently relegating even China to a secondary position, and taking up a role as the primary Japanese security concern once occupied by the USSR."[41]

The annual Ministry of Defense white papers confirm that conclusion. The 2010 edition cataloged a long list of concerns about North Korea: its military forces (both conventional and special operations); its nuclear, chemical, and biological weapons; its missile capabilities; its abduction of Japanese citizens; its escalating of tensions on the Korean Peninsula; and its domestic instability. The Defense Ministry was blunt in its final assessment: "The fact that North Korea is carrying out nuclear testing [two tests had been held at that time] and strengthening its ballistic missile capabilities is a significant threat to the security of Japan. This cannot be accepted."[42] Potential dangers became real on March 26, 2010, when a North Korean submarine sank the South Korean military patrol vessel *Cheonan*, resulting in the deaths of forty-six seamen (another seaman died in the salvage operations).[43] Lives were lost again in November of that year, when North

Korean and South Korean forces exchanged artillery fire over Yeonpyeong Island. Four South Koreans died, while North Korea claimed to have sustained no casualties. The first words in the Ministry of Defense's 2012 white paper noted Kim Jong-un's ascension to power in Pyongyang and repeated the conclusions from 2010 about the "significant threat to the security of Japan."[44]

The persistence of the Senkakus dispute and its subsequent escalation, along with growing challenges from Moscow and Pyongyang, highlighted the importance of having a competent and capable government in Tokyo, but three years into its tenure, the DPJ continued to struggle. Much of the blame must be placed on the shoulders of the first DPJ prime minister, Hatoyama Yukio, who badly fumbled alliance issues (details of which follow). At a time of rising Chinese power and influence, doubts about the DPJ's commitment to the US-Japan alliance would prove fatal to his administration, and even though his successors worked assiduously to mend ties with Washington and rebuild confidence, those doubts persisted and tainted public perceptions of the DPJ. Paul Midford argued that the Senkakus dispute "helped reignite the discourse that DPJ inflicted damage to the US-Japan alliance was encouraging neighbors to challenge Japan's territorial claims. . . . Thus, the DPJ headed into the 2012 election with widespread public demands for stronger policy precisely where the party's brand had been most damaged: foreign and security policy."[45]

"A New Type of International Power"

An acute sense of vulnerability has shaped Japanese thinking about their place in the world. Kawashima Yutaka, a former vice foreign minister of Japan, believes that "an obsession about the scarcity of key natural resources in Japan seems to have deeply embedded in the national psyche."[46] Situated off the coast of a huge Asian land mass that could be dominated by a potentially hostile government, generations of Japanese decision makers have looked to that neighboring continent for resources and strategic depth. Japan's expansion in the first half of the twentieth century began with Korea and quickly spread to Manchuria, a region recognized as "Japan's bastion of national defense and economic development."[47] From there, Japanese interests broadened as resistance to the imperial army's presence demanded the establishment of buffer zones, which in turn required more resources to support that growing presence; the cycle proved unstoppable.[48] Over time, Japan changed its objectives from self-defense to the creation of the Greater East Asia Co-prosperity Sphere, "a self-sufficient bloc of Asian nations free of Western Powers led by Japan."[49] That venture ended badly in defeat, devastation, and occupation.

Determined to ensure that Japan would never again be a threat to the peace, the US Occupation authorities wrote a constitution that denied Tokyo the means to go to war.[50] The language could not have been clearer: Article 9 renounced war as a right of the nation, as well as the threat or the use of force to settle international disputes. To ensure there were no loopholes, the next sentence declared Japan would not acquire the land, naval, or air forces that it would need to fight.[51] In an anarchic world, that was quite a commitment. Fortunately for Japan, the United States as an occupying power was ready to defend Japanese interests if they were threatened.

That arrangement continued even after the end of Occupation in 1952 and Japan had regained its sovereignty. By then, US thinking had changed. The Korean War drove home to Washington the need to secure allies around the world as the Cold War intensified. With South Korea's being a frontline state and the communists seizing power in China in 1949, Japan seemed ever more vital both as a base for forward-deployed US forces in Asia and as a source of matériel in the superpower confrontation. Yet Japan by that time resisted US entreaties to rearm.

Japan's then prime minister, Yoshida Shigeru, was a shrewd leader who recognized that the US protective umbrella served Japanese national interests in more ways than one. US readiness to defend Japan meant that Tokyo could redirect monies toward more productive investments that would otherwise be used on a military. His focus on economic development helped shore up his political support and sidestepped the national debate that would inevitably follow once Japan decided to rearm. At a minimum, questions of civil-military relations, especially civilian control, would have to be addressed; at worst it could reopen the wounds of the Pacific War as Japan looked anew at culpability and responsibility. In a supreme irony, as the Cold War heated up, Yoshida used the restraints of Article 9 to parry US requests to assume a higher profile in regional security affairs. This was all part of the "Yoshida Doctrine," a policy by which Japan assumed a low-profile defense and security policy and instead focused on economic development.

The Yoshida Doctrine was not quite what it seemed, however. While some dismissed it as pacifism, Japanese leaders accepted that the world remained anarchic and that "hard power" would prove determinative in some situations. They merely insisted that Japan would not be a weight on that scale. Nor was the doctrine a repudiation of the realist outlook that dominates security policy thinking. Rather, the Yoshida Doctrine bought Japan time to get stronger and rearm on its own terms. Moreover, Japan's focus on economic development allowed it to engage other nations of Asia in ways that would not be seen as threatening or hostile. The alliance with the United States also provided cover for Japan's international ambitions; Washington served as "a cap on the bottle" to prevent the "bad" Japan from reemerging. Hosoya Yuichi, a professor of political science at Keio University, described the Yoshida Doctrine as "non-militarism to guide a nonaggressive, low-cost post-war Japanese security policy" based on US-Japan alliance diplomacy.[52]

More important, the Japanese public backed the Yoshida Doctrine. They accepted a national narrative that said they too had been victimized during the Pacific War by a military that had come unmoored from its civilian anchors. Better then to avoid such temptations and to focus instead on building an economically strong and developed nation. That was, after all, a national mission to which all Japanese could contribute. A powerful left-leaning teachers union reinforced the message that militarism was bad, inculcating a sentiment among many Japanese that seemed similar to pacifism. That tendency was evident in years of postwar opinion polls that showed strong support for Article 9, little respect for the Self-Defense Forces as an institution,[53] and periodic outbursts of anti-American sentiment, usually coinciding with US military action somewhere in the world.

The Yoshida Doctrine worked—at least until the 1990s. The world's second-largest economy emerged from the rubble of World War II with nary a national resource except for a hardworking public. Nestled under the US nuclear umbrella, Japan extended its business networks throughout Southeast Asia and, some insist, achieved through its corporations what its military could not half a century earlier—that is, gain the leading position in the region. In 1980 its GDP was $1.086 trillion, or nearly ten times larger than that of China and India, both of which had a GDP of about $189 billion at the time; no other Asian economy cracked the $100 billion mark.[54] Japan's outsize economy also meant that it played a large role in the economies of its regional partners. Japan absorbed 10 percent of ASEAN's exports and produced 18 percent of its imports; a decade later, the numbers were 12 percent and 13 percent, respectively. By 2004 and after an extended slump, Japan still took 13 percent of ASEAN exports and dispatched 15 percent of its imports to the region.[55] Japanese investments in Southeast Asia were also substantial, totaling $83.4 billion between 1951 and 2004, and nearly 90 percent of them occurred after 1981.[56] Japan's success and its identity as an Asian nation enhanced its attractiveness to other countries in the region. The appeal was demonstrated by Malaysian prime minister Mahathir Mohamad's Look East Policy, which launched in 1981 and used Japan as a model for his country's development.

Economic success also bankrolled the world's largest aid program (at least for several decades). Political economist Hugh Patrick found that "of the 10

Southeast Asian ASEAN members and East Timor, all but Brunei and Singapore have received significant ODA. Japan is by far the largest single donor to each of the countries, providing more than half of total ODA in every one but Cambodia, where the share is 45%."[57] Generous aid was part of a broader package of assistance—ideas, policies, programs—that helped foster the image of a country with a different approach to international security.

Strategists drew on Japan's own postwar experience to craft a distinctive foreign policy strategy. Professor Hosoya explained Japanese thinking:

> The logic of development dictated that since the roots of revolution lay in poverty, Asia ought to take the path of solid nation building and put emphasis on economic development. In this view, political measures such as class struggle or military containment of communism are less effective to solve the essential problems in Asia. . . . Japan itself is the archetype for nation building along these lines in postwar Asia and this logic of development would appear to be at the root of postwar Japan's engagement with Asia.[58]

Japanese officials and analysts call this "an East Asian perspective on development" in yet another way of linking Japan and the region that it aspired to lead.[59]

A third pillar of Japan's regional diplomacy has been its commitment to diplomacy and the peaceful resolution of disputes. This strategy is a natural consequence of the decision to abandon its own pursuit of hard power, but it also should be seen as an asset of its own. While one can easily fault Japanese foreign policy for being reactive and limited in scope and intention, it is important not to overlook its successes. Japan is viewed as a champion of international diplomacy and the rule of law. Tokyo has been a leading contributor to the United Nations; as the second-largest financial donor, it has provided a little over 10 percent of the UN budget.[60] Ever cognizant of its status as the world's only atom-bombed nation, Japan has been on the front lines of international nuclear diplomacy and lent momentum for the Global Zero movement, which pushes for disarmament. Japan has also been a moving force behind environmental protection; indeed, it is no coincidence that the first international convention to protect against climate change is called the Kyoto Protocol. Japan's history of tackling its own environmental mess in the 1960s gives it credibility when it offers to help other countries overcome similar problems. Japan has also furnished intellectual, political, and economic support for regional institutions such as ASEAN and the Asia-Pacific Economic Cooperation forum, the preeminent mechanism for dealing with trade, investment, and development issues across the Asia Pacific. Tokyo actually came up with the idea for the forum but let Australia lead in its creation.

It pushed for the establishment of the Asian Development Bank as well and has been one of its largest shareholders since it was set up in 1966.

Japan's positive relationship with Asia, and Southeast Asia in particular, was the product of hard work and statecraft. With few exceptions, regional perceptions of Japan's behavior during the Pacific War were negative. The Greater East Asia Co-prosperity Sphere, the name Tokyo affixed to its attempted empire, sought resources to fuel the Japanese military. Whatever the stated objectives of the effort—Japanese nationalists have done their best to make them as benign and positive as possible—the occupation forces were brutal and cruel, and they committed many atrocities.[61] That legacy endured throughout the Cold War and beyond, and whenever "Japan tried to assert itself in the region in the post-war years, Asian leaders constantly reminded Tokyo of its war crimes, repeatedly warned the public about Japan's new ambitions, and made references to Japan's perceived attempt to 'take a step toward becoming a military giant.'"[62] In a bon mot that captured the sentiments of his generation, Singapore's prime minister Lee Kuan Yew in 1991 opined that having Japan join international peacekeeping operations was "like giving liqueur chocolates to an alcoholic."[63]

Japan's leaders recognized that they had to overcome that bitter legacy and worked assiduously to court and cultivate Southeast Asian leaders and their publics. When Prime Minister Tanaka Kakuei's 1974 visit to Indonesia sparked some of the worst riots in that country's history, it served as a reminder that wartime memories remained fresh and that Japan had to do more to win Asians' hearts and minds. That lesson, along with fears of US disengagement from the region after the Vietnam War, prompted Tokyo to begin a concerted effort to reengage Southeast Asia. This evolved into the Fukuda Doctrine, a foreign policy strategy named after Prime Minister Fukuda Takeo that was launched in 1977. The Fukuda Doctrine had several key components: a deep engagement with ASEAN as an institution and recognition of its central role in Southeast Asian foreign policy; a broader definition of security to encompass a wider range of variables and instruments, opening the door to Japanese participation and involvement; and more extensive government assistance and business investment (led in no small measure by the appreciating value of the yen and Japanese businesses' search for lower-cost labor to retain competitiveness). Each helped tamp down enmity toward Japan and overcome resistance to Tokyo's more visible role in the region, one concentrated on making political and economic contributions to regional peace and well-being.

As the Cold War drew to a close, Japan's extraordinary economic success—coupled with its focus on cooperation with others in the pursuit of international objectives; its concentration on nonmilitary, primarily economic, means to secure

national goals; and its willingness to develop supranational structures to manage international issues—was heralded as the prototype of a "new type of international power."[64] Iwase Sachiko, a senior adviser for the Japan International
Cooperation Agency, the organization that funds and implements Japan's development assistance programs, is convinced that her work has been facilitated by
Japan's approach. "International politics is complicated, but our aid has no hidden
agenda." After a long career in the field, working throughout Southeast Asia, she
concluded that "people feel they can trust us. We try not to betray that trust."[65]

Japan's Presence Has Declined

The bursting of the bubble and the subsequent lost decade did as much damage to
Japanese foreign policy as it did to its economy—understandably, as the two were
inextricably linked. Japan's economic performance provided much of the foundation for its regional status while generating funds that bankrolled its investment,
development, and aid policies. The revolving door of prime ministers and cabinets
made it difficult for governments to focus on foreign policy; domestic political survival was the paramount concern. Finally, changes in the region—China's growth
and the subsequent expansion of its military capacity along with a readiness to
flex those muscles, in tandem with an increasingly bellicose and belligerent North
Korea—deflated the value of Japan's approach to security policy and underlined
the continuing importance of military power. The country's official development
assistance began shrinking; by 2007 it was 30 percent below its peak, ranking fifth
among foreign donors. Its military budget had been decreasing for five years and
remained below 1 percent of GDP. Japan was eighty-third among contributors
to UN peacekeeping operations.[66] By 2008 international conferences included
panels with titles such as "Has Japan Lost its Relevance?"

While the policymakers, the politicians, and the public understood that Japan's
resurgence on all levels began with a revitalized economy, the DPJ also had ideas
about the conduct of foreign policy that offered new opportunities to Tokyo.
In its election manifesto, the DPJ identified three key objectives: establishing
a more equal alliance partnership with the United States while maintaining the
centrality of the alliance in the country's security policy; deepening political and
economic ties with Asia, primarily through the development of a proposed East
Asian Community; and pursuing a more active UN-centric diplomatic agenda.[67]
"Armed with a mandate for change and a team of relatively like-minded cabinet officials and advisers, Prime Minister Hatoyama embarked on an attempt
to forge a new, post-LDP diplomacy, including a recalibrated strategic dynamic
with the United States."[68]

Some saw these changes as adjustments to Japanese foreign policy, but that restrained assessment was overshadowed by the more widespread concern that they signaled wholesale transformations designed to reorient Japanese diplomacy.[69] Those fears were amplified by Hatoyama's erratic behavior. Among other things, he promised during the election campaign to reexamine the 2006 agreement with the United States to move the Futenma Air Station to a location in northern Okinawa. (After saying that the base should be moved "out of the prefecture, if not out of Japan," he eventually concluded that the deal should remain as struck. This reversal was a key factor in his resignation as prime minister within the year.) The DPJ government's decision to end Japan's participation in refueling operations for coalition forces fighting in Afghanistan compounded concern, as did Hatoyama's promotion of an East Asian Community.

At first Hatoyama insisted that his Asia diplomacy would not come at the expense of the United States. "We have no intention of excluding the United Sates. To the contrary, we should begin by building an East Asian Community which should evolve into an Asia Pacific community."[70] But his position seemed to waver. A month later he told Chinese premier Wen Jiabao and South Korean president Lee Myung-bak, "Until now, we have tended to be too reliant on the United States. The Japan-US alliance remains important, but as a member of Asia, I would like to develop policies that focus more on Asia."[71] His criticism of the United States in explaining his political philosophy also seemed to distance him from the United States. He charged Washington with promoting a market fundamentalism that "results in people being treated not as an end but as a means" and endorsed the principle of *yuai* (fraternity), which "aims to adjust to the excesses of the current globalized brand of capitalism . . . to accommodate the local economic practices that have been fostered through our traditions."[72]

Others in his party compounded the sense of its policy confusion and drift. Speaking to the foreign media in Japan, then foreign minister Okada Katsuya pointedly excluded the United States from his East Asian grouping, noting that "Japan has its national interests and the US has its own."[73] DPJ secretary general Ozawa Ichiro's December 2009 visit to Beijing with a delegation of over six hundred lawmakers and businessmen raised eyebrows still higher.

Hatoyama was forced to step down within a year as his shifting positions, especially on Futenma; the scandals within his party; the loss of a coalition partner; and other domestic problems created a crisis of confidence in his cabinet. He was replaced by Kan Naoto, who devoted attention to mending ties with the United States and shifted his government's foreign policy onto a more traditional footing.

Nevertheless, dissatisfaction and concern continued to dominate Japan's foreign policy community. A 2011 assessment of its position in the world concluded that "Japan could in no sense be regarded as a major player in international politics. This has led to the perception that Japan's presence was of no particular import in the international politics of postwar Asia."[74] To remedy that perception, the Japan Institute of International Affairs, the official think tank of the Foreign Ministry, launched a project to articulate a diplomatic strategy and agenda for the next twenty years. It began from the following premise:

> Japan's international status during that [postwar] period was guaranteed by its economic capabilities, and that its political status was also proportional to its economic evaluation. Even today, ten years on from the end of the so-called "lost decade" that followed the bursting of the economic bubble, Japan remains unable to recover the economic strength that it formerly wielded. In proportion to this economic decline, Japan's political presence in the international community has likewise declined, and among the Japanese people today (and what is particularly troubling is that this is shared by young people), there is a tendency to accept this decline as an inevitable fact.[75]

At the very moment that the Japan Institute of International Affairs' report was being delivered (the conference announcing the report literally was forced to halt), Japan was hit by the devastating March 11 earthquake. The various dimensions of that crisis are taken up in chapter 5, but it should be noted here that the tragedy had important foreign policy implications for Japan. Immediately after the quake, fears arose that the size of the calamity would compound Japan's inward turn as the country focused on rebuilding. That danger was averted, however. In some ways, the tragedy helped internationalists make the case for greater engagement with the outside world. It forced the public to rethink the role of the Self-Defense Forces, garnered a new appreciation for the US-Japan alliance, and created possibilities for a different relationship between Japan and Asia. The LDP government that followed the DPJ was eager to seize those opportunities.

The Japanese Counterweight

Japanese attempts to secure a higher profile in East Asia can succeed only if countries in the region welcome those overtures. Here, Tokyo has benefited from the region's growing sense of unease toward China. Memories of Japanese militarism have receded; by the mid-1990s Southeast Asian nations were more concerned by Japan's immobilism than by its activism. They were especially worried by the country's poor economic performance and the drag it created on regional growth. While those governments had once looked to the US-Japan alliance to check renewed revanchist ambitions in Tokyo, when the Asian financial crisis rocked the region in 1997, the chief complaint from regional capitals was Tokyo's unwillingness to challenge the United States and do more to help the foundering economies of Southeast Asia. By the start of the new millennium, Singaporean analyst Bhubhindar Singh could conclude that "although not totally forgotten, the image of a militarist Japan has become less prevalent in the perceptions of ASEAN countries."[76]

Events in the first decade of the new century stimulated the Southeast Asian leaders' eagerness to see Japan step up. Their attitude toward Washington was schizophrenic: At times they worried that Washington would be distracted by its global war on terror; at others, they feared the United States would be too focused on Southeast Asia and would risk destabilizing the region when it turned its military-driven global war on terror on militant groups such as Indonesia's Jemaah Islamiya or the Philippines' Abu Sayyaf. Tokyo played two roles in this setting: It was a convenient hedge if the United States was distracted, and hopefully Tokyo could temper some of Washington's excesses if it became too involved in the region.

As noted, by the first decade of the twenty-first century, Southeast Asian nations were also worried about a rising China. While they were quick to benefit from China's economic dynamism (as they had with Japan's a decade or two earlier), regional governments were growing anxious about Beijing's new, more muscular foreign policy. In the 1990s Beijing won many friends with its "smile diplomacy," in which it applied former leader Deng Xiaoping's famous "24-character" guideline for Chinese foreign policy: "Observe calmly; secure our position; cope with affairs calmly; hide our capacities and bide our time; be good at maintaining a low profile; and never claim leadership."[77] That strategy paid off. In 1999 Aileen Baviera, a Philippine security analyst, concluded that "Southeast Asian countries . . . appear prepared to accept China's legitimate interests in the region. . . . Since 1993, all-around China-ASEAN relations have improved greatly through institutionalized bilateral and regional cooperation mechanisms. . . . Tensions over bilateral issues such as territorial disputes and treatment of ethnic Chinese, among others are nevertheless expected to periodically emerge as part of the normal state of relations."[78]

At the turn of the century, though, China seemed to tire of Deng's advice. Southeast Asians, like the Japanese, observed that Beijing was becoming more aggressive in disputes and showed no reluctance to stake a claim or assert a position. A standoff with the United States triggered by the April 2001 collision of a US reconnaissance aircraft and a Chinese fighter jet set alarm bells ringing. The

International Crisis Group observed that "China's ambiguous territorial claims and its refusal to clarify them publicly have raised concerns in the region that it is assuming a more assertive posture in the South China Sea, particularly when combined with its growing naval build-up and the aggressive actions of its maritime law enforcement agencies."[79] It then delineated those actions: making aggressive legal claims, harassing non-Chinese vessels in waters claimed by Beijing in the South China Sea, warning foreign oil companies of consequences for their business in China if they cooperated with rival claimants on energy exploration projects in the area, operating enhanced law enforcement patrols in contested waters, clashing with non-Chinese vessels in contested waters, and conducting People's Liberation Army exercises in the region.[80] Tensions ebbed and flowed until 2010, when the frictions over competing claims to the South China Sea boiled over. At a now infamous meeting of diplomats in Vietnam, Chinese foreign minister Yang Jiechi responded to challenges to those claims by noting that "China is a big country and other countries are small countries, and that's just a fact."[81]

Somewhat predictably, Southeast Asian nations began to hedge against Chinese dominance, reaching out in every direction both to balance China and to claim as many diplomatic opportunities as possible. Japan (along with Australia, the United States, India, and even Russia) is a key player in this effort. Philippine analyst Rommel Banlaoi has written that Southeast Asia "cautiously welcomes" Japanese efforts in this area as "a counterweight to China's growing influence in the region."[82] But Southeast Asia hasn't reached a definitive judgment on China. Views within the region, as well as within states, vary. Japan is one hedge against an aggressive China, and Southeast Asian governments are prepared to offer Tokyo a higher political and security profile within the region.

Relations with the Northeast Asian governments of China and South Korea have been more difficult. The relationship with China is troubled at its core. "China and Japan both view themselves as the victim and the other as the aggressor. Each party sees itself as peaceful, while the other state is aggressive and revisionist. Both also have bubbled conspiracy theories against the other, placing doubt on the other's intentions."[83] The competition that dominates the Japan-China relationship also frames the Japan–South Korea relationship, and the tensions that perspective introduces are heightened by the historical legacies of the twentieth century. Japanese nationalism has exacerbated the strains, with the conservatives' attempts to inculcate patriotism (by visiting the Yasukuni Shrine or by challenging the darker assessments of Japanese history) interpreted in Beijing and Seoul as "resentment at the international order after World War II."[84]

Relations with South Korea are especially challenging.[85] From a distance, the two countries would seem to be natural allies. Both are advanced industrial democracies that are dependent on freedom of navigation and secure sea lines of communication. Both have profited greatly from the existing international order and its institutions and would be well served by their consolidation and spread. Both are allies of the United States and are similarly situated geographically. In theory and when asked, their interests, concerns, and ambitions align. Yet deep reservoirs of ill will toward Japan have limited cooperation between the two countries on vital security matters. The potency of that poison was plain in 2012 when the plan to sign an agreement—known among bureaucrats as a general security of military information agreement—that would merely standardize the forms used to exchange defense information was twice derailed. The second occurred only hours before the signing ceremony because of popular displeasure with any security agreement with Japan. Its supporters were charged with "selling out the country" in a secret deal with Tokyo.[86]

The speed with which relations can reverse was evident after March 11. South Korea quickly responded to the disaster, dispatching a rescue team within days of the earthquake. Seoul sent fifty-three tons of boric acid to help control the Fukushima nuclear plants and a week later delivered a hundred tons of water and six thousand blankets for people in shelters. Within two weeks, the Korean Red Cross had raised over $19 million, the largest amount of voluntary donations for a natural disaster in or outside of Korea. Within three weeks, Korean donations had reportedly reached $46 million. Hope that this aid might constitute "a new milestone for upgrading Korea-Japan relations," "a paradigmatic shift in the Korean mindset," or a "turning point for breaking the vicious cycle of repeated controversies" was shattered at the end of the month when Japan's Ministry of Education approved new textbooks that repeated Japan's claims to disputed islands known as Dokdo to the Koreans, Takeshima to the Japanese, and the Liancourt Rocks to anyone who does not want to take a side.[87] In one case, the number of charitable donations for earthquake victims went from as many as 167,000 a day to 82; that number then dropped to 21 when the Japanese cabinet approved the 2011 *Diplomatic Bluebook*, which repeated the claim to the islets.[88]

Japan's assumption of a higher security profile in the region goes straight to the heart of Korean insecurities. A 2012 report by the Korea Research Institute for Strategy, a nonprofit research institute in Seoul, lays bare those fears. The title of the chapter on Japan says it all: "The Militarization of the so-called Peace-Creating Country."[89] The analysis rightly describes Japanese efforts to beef up its security capabilities and concludes it is doing so to "counter China's growing influence" in East Asia and "to promote Japan's stance in the international community through both economic and military means."[90] Yet the authors repeatedly note that this is a nationalist and conservative agenda, and they imply at least that Tokyo is thinking about doing more than countering China. Indeed, Japan's adoption of a conservative line toward the territorial dispute has led South Koreans to become "increasingly disheartened and distrustful about their relationship with Japan."[91] If Japan hopes to play a security role in the region, it must aggressively court South Korea and work with Seoul to assuage any concerns about Japanese behavior and intentions.

"The Japanese Era Is Finished"

Japan's foreign and security policies have always defied a short and simple description. The Yoshida Doctrine is a more complex array of policies and inclinations than its usual characterization as "one nation pacifism." Japan's rejection of the military as an instrument of state policy is foreign to American strategists; indeed, many view Japan as lacking strategic thought altogether in the postwar era.[92] But confusion and oversimplification increased when the DPJ took office in 2009. Part of the problem reflects the demands of political marketing—or the need to distinguish between parties—and the blood sport of politics. The DPJ promised a transformation in thinking about foreign policy. Misperception was abetted by the LDP, which sought to exaggerate the opposition's changes to bolster its claims that the DPJ was a party of amateurs whose ideas jeopardized Japanese national interests.

In fact, the DPJ's approach to Asia, representing the fundamental change in its foreign policy agenda, was not so much a revolution as a recalibration. Asia has always been a target of Japanese diplomacy, although its priority has shifted as the nature of the resulting relationship has changed over time. Japan has tried since the articulation of the Fukuda Doctrine in 1977 to build a more durable relationship with Southeast Asia.[93] An accurate assessment of the DPJ's intentions and objectives was complicated by the inconsistencies and reversals between and even within administrations that sought to implement the DPJ agenda. Yet, for all its rhetoric, the DPJ did not stray from postwar Japan's mainstream Asia policy.

While continuity has been the hallmark of Japanese foreign policy even during the DPJ interregnum, Tokyo is clearly under increasing pressure to forge a new relationship with Asia, one that is built on a genuine partnership rather than the hierarchy of the past. Since the Meiji era, Japan has assumed the role of regional leader—as an imperial-colonial power in the first half of the twentieth century and then as an economic hegemon in the 1980s and 1990s. Even though the "flying geese" model of regional economic development that was articulated in the 1930s envisioned all countries of a region advancing together, Japan always saw itself as the lead goose.

No longer. As one Tokyo bureaucrat dispatched to Fukuoka to advise local businesses explained, "Until 1990, Japan completely dominated the economy of the region and could influence political, economic, and development issues by using its economic powers."[94] But that was then. Today, "Japan is losing global power. . . . Japan was number one, but only for twenty years. The Japanese people have an illusion about the strength of the Japanese economy. The majority of Japanese people don't realize the power balance between Japan and China has changed. They believe Japan is still number one. This is a total misunderstanding and a dangerous misunderstanding." Now, he warned, "the Japanese era is finished."

For some, the end of an era is an opportunity. This group rejects the rigid hierarchy of the past and envisions a more balanced partnership between Japan and its neighbors. Japanese businesses have been quick to embrace this new relationship with Asia, and it is no surprise that the case for "Asian activism" is made most forcefully outside Tokyo. As the nation's capital, Tokyo has a 360-degree perspective, but the tug of the relationship with the United States is strongest in the capital. In other cities, especially those in the south and west such as Osaka, Kyoto, or Fukuoka, people are acutely aware of the proximity of Seoul, Busan, Shanghai, and Taipei. In other words, while a distinction between "Asia and the West" has neatly bifurcated Japanese strategic thinking since the start of the modern era, in practice the lines are not nearly that sharp. Japan may have "chosen" the West at critical junctures, but geography continues to shape Japan's destiny. Hosaka Masatake, general manager of an international hotel in Fukuoka, spoke for many in the business world when he observed, "Thirty percent of our business is Asian. It is critical that we be part of that community."[95] The Japan International Cooperation Agency's Iwase agreed: "ASEAN is very popular among chambers of commerce, and small- and medium-size businesses know they cannot survive in Japan but have to shift to Asia. Businesses feel that Asian countries are very important to their future, but not only as a market. They have to extend their manufacturing lines. This is a very different type of partnership. It's not just buying and selling."[96]

Supply-chain vulnerabilities exposed by March 11 added to Asia's growing weight in the strategic calculations of Japanese businesses. This reassessment has been facilitated by the rapid evolution of the regional labor market as skills develop, cost curves shift, and local workers become more confident in their abilities. Asia's rising middle class is a new source of demand, and Japanese companies will get as close as possible to reach those consumers and meet their needs. A shrinking Japanese market is the flip side of that dynamic. "A partnership is coming," said Yoneyama Nobuo, then general manager of the Washington offices of Mitsui and Company. But, he cautioned, while "business is promoting Asian integration . . . this is all about moving to Asia with the US. It isn't a choice between the West and Asia."[97]

The intuitive appeal of this partnership belies its difficulty. An executive at one of Japan's top international manufacturing companies, who requested anonymity, explained that "the countries surrounding Japan are growing faster and becoming more confident. They have a sense of accomplishment and a belief that they can outdo Japan. This will complicate Japan's management of relations with these countries. Japan has never negotiated these types of changes. It will struggle. The Japanese people will have to think hard about who they can trust."[98]

The greatest irony of the DPJ years is that a party that seemed to understand the changes required of Japanese foreign policy and seemed prepared to make them was undone by its most important potential partner in that endeavor—China. It is tempting to see the discrediting of the DPJ as discrediting the case for those foreign policy shifts as well. But the realities that shaped the DPJ's thinking survived the collapse of the party. In many ways, Asia is more important to Japan than before, making it more urgent than ever to bridge the two choices of the Meiji worldview.

Notes

The disputed islands are called the Senkakus in Japan and the Diaoyu in China (and the Dioayutai in Taiwan). Because this book is about Japan, they are referred to throughout as the Senkakus. Again, I like the alliteration.

1. June Teufel Dreyer, *Middle Kingdom & Empire of the Rising Sun: Sino-Japanese Relations, Past and Present* (Oxford: Oxford University Press, 2016), 3.
2. Ezra Vogel, Yuan Ming, and Tanaka Akihiko, eds., *The Golden Age of the U.S.-China-Japan Triangle, 1972–1989* (Cambridge MA: Harvard University Asia Center, 2002).
3. Tanaka Hitoshi, "Japan and China at a Crossroads," *East Asia Insights* 1, no. 2 (March 2006): 1.
4. Sheila Smith, *Intimate Rivals: Japanese Domestic Politics and a Rising China* (New York: Columbia University Press, 2016), 35. ODA would continue to expand, increasing ¥810 billion from 1990 to 1995 and another ¥970 billion from 1996 to 2000. From 1979 to 2011, Japan provided ¥3.65 trillion ($37.6 billion) in ODA to China.
5. Ibid., 33.
6. Richard Bush, *The Perils of Proximity: Japan-China Security Relations* (Washington, DC: Brookings Institution Press, 2010), 16.
7. Tanaka Hitoshi, "A Japanese Perspective on the China Question," *East Asia Insights* 3, no. 2 (May 2008): 2.

8. Wang Zhuoqiong, "China's Growth Fuels Investment from Japan," *People's Daily*, August 30, 2013, http://en.people.cn/102774/7929031.html.

9. The number of firms doing business in China is cited in Aoyama Rumi, "What's Pushing Japanese Firms out of China?," *East Asia Forum*, October 21, 2015, http:// www.eastasiaforum.org/2015/10/21/whats-pushing-japanese-firms-out-of-china/; and for Japanese business investment in China, see Junhua Wu, "Economics of the Territorial Disputes," in *Clash of National Identities: Japan, China and the East China Sea Territorial Dispute*, ed. Tatsushi Arai, Shihoko Goto, and Zheng Wang (Princeton, NJ: Woodrow Wilson International Center for Scholars, 2013), 71.

10. Junhua, "Economics," in Tatsushi, Shihoko, and Zheng, *Clash of National Identities*.

11. Christopher Herrick, Zheya Gai, and Surain Subramanian, *China's Peaceful Rise: Perceptions, Policy and Misperceptions* (Oxford: Oxford University Press, 2016). According to Japan's Ministry of Finance, Japanese companies directly or indirectly created about 9.2 million jobs for Chinese by 2005 and paid more than $5.9 billion annually in corporate taxes. Jun Hongo, "Japanese Companies Become Protest Targets in China," *Japan Times*, September 19, 2012, https://www.japantimes .co.jp/news/2012/09/19/business/japanese-companies-become-protest-targets-in -china/#.WdoCukyB2Ho.

12. Dreyer, *Middle Kingdom*, provides a depressing summary on pp. 166–87.

13. Smith, *Intimate Rivals*; Dreyer, *Middle Kingdom*; and Richard Bush, *The Perils of Proximity: Japan-China Security Relations* (Washington, DC: Brookings Institution Press, 2010) provide excellent analyses of these problems.

14. Amy King, "Japan and China: Warm Trade Ties Temper Political Tensions," *East Asia Forum*, October 22, 2012, http://www.eastasiaforum.org/2012/10/22/japan -and-china-warm-trade-ties-temper-political-tensions/.

15. "People's Daily Implies Economic Measures against Japan," *People's Daily*, September 18, 2012, http://en.people.cn/90883/7951384.html.

16. Cited in Wang Xinyuan, "Protests Hit Japanese Goods," *Global Times*, September 17, 2012, http://en.people.cn/90778/7950204.html.

17. Smith, *Intimate Rivals,* 250.

18. Daqing Yang speculates that Japan hesitated to take them along with the Ryukyus for fear of antagonizing the Chinese government. Daqing Yang, "History: From Dispute to Dialogue," in Arai, Goto, and Wang, *Clash of National Identities,* 22.

19. Ibid., 21.

20. Smith's summary, "A Shared Maritime Boundary," is extensive. See Smith, *Intimate Rivals,* 101–44.

21. Yimian Li, "Japan's Hedging Strategy and Its Implications for Regional Peace and Security," in *The United States and Japan in Global Context, 2011*, ed. Edwin Reischauer Center for East Asian Studies (Washington, DC: Edwin Reischauer Center for East Asian Studies, 2011), 53.

22. Anne Allison, *Precarious Japan* (Durham, NC: Duke University Press, 2013), 78.

23. Takahara Akio, "Putting the Senkaku Dispute into Pandora's Box: Toward a '2013 Consensus,'" in Arai, Goto, and Wang, *Clash of National Identities*, 77–78.

24. Tanaka Hitoshi, "The Future of East Asia: Four Risks to Long-Term Stability," *East Asia Insights* 8, no. 4 (December 2013): 1–2, http://www.jcie.org/researchpdfs/EAI /8-4.pdf.

25. Kotani Tetsuo, "Freedom of Navigation and the US-Japan Alliance: Addressing the Threat of Legal Warfare," US-Japan Papers (New York: Japan Center for International Exchange, December 2011), 2.

26. Michael Swaine, "China's Assertive Behavior—Part One: On 'Core Interests,'" *China Leadership Monitor*, November 15, 2010, 2.

27. For trade by volume, see Kotani, "Freedom of Navigation," 2. The other figures are for 2016 and from China Power Team, "How Much Trade Transits the South China Sea?," *China Power,* August 2, 2017, https://chinapower.csis.org/much-trade -transits-south-china-sea/. Swaine also concluded that it was not clear if China had actually declared the South China Sea to be a core interest. To some extent, that is irrelevant insofar as the Japanese believe that China was extending its sovereignty over those waters. Swaine, "China's Assertive Behavior," 8–11.

28. Shi Jiangtao, "Hu Warns Japan of Purchase of Diaoyu Islands," *South China Morning Post*, September 10, 2012, http://www.scmp.com/news/china/article/1033054 /hu-warns-japan-over-planned-purchase-diaoyu-islands.

29. Michael Green et al., *Countering Coercion in Maritime Asia: The Theory and Practice of Gray Zone Deterrence* (Washington, DC: Center for Strategic and International Studies, May 2017), 145; and M. Taylor Fravel, "Explaining China's Escalation over the Senkaku (Diaoyu) Islands," *Global Summitry* 2, no. 1 (2016): 33, https:// taylorfravel.com/documents/research/fravel.2016.GS.senkakus.escalation.pdf.

30. All figures from the Ministry of Land, Infrastructure, and Transport, cited in Smith, *Intimate Rivals,* 229.

31. The United States had made similar assurances after the 2010 incident and reiterated them in meetings with Chinese leaders. Then secretary of state Hillary Clinton was blunt in a joint press conference in 2010 with Japanese foreign minister Maehara Seiji: "Let me say clearly again, the Senkakus fall within the scope of Article 5 of the 1960 U.S.-Japan Treaty of Mutual Cooperation and Security." Hillary Rodham Clinton, "Joint Press Availability with Japanese Foreign Minister Seiji Maehara," Honolulu, October 27, 2012, https://2009-2017.state.gov/secretary /20092013clinton/rm/2010/10/150110.htm.

32. Morimoto Satoshi, "Foreword," in Ministry of Defense, *Defense of Japan 2012* (Tokyo: Ministry of Defense, 2012), http://www.mod.go.jp/e/publ/w_paper/e -book/2012/files/assets/downloads/publication.pdf.

33. Ibid.

34. Ministry of Defense, *Defense of Japan 2012*, 30.
35. Ibid., 35–38.
36. The four islands are called the Kurils in Russian and consist of Etorofu (Iturup), Kunashiri (Kunashir), Shikotan (same in Russian, Shikotan), and Habomai (Habomai Rocks).
37. Céline Pajon provides a good summary in "Japan-Russia: Toward a Strategic Partnership?," *Russia NEI Visions* 72 (September 2013): 15–17.
38. Russia-China ties are a constant concern in Tokyo. Japanese strategists invariably seek to offer Moscow an alternative partner in Asia to weaken those relations, but their success has been limited precisely because of the territorial dispute. Paradoxically, the Japanese hold out the prospect of a deal as enticement for Russia but then take a hard line in the negotiations.
39. Ministry of Defense, *Defense of Japan 2011* (Tokyo: Ministry of Defense, 2011), 101; and Ministry of Defense, *Defense of Japan 2012*, 54.
40. John Gittings, "North Korea Fires Missile over Japan," *The Guardian*, September 1, 1998.
41. Christopher W. Hughes, "Super-sizing the DPRK Threat: Japan's Evolving Military Posture and North Korea," *Asian Survey* 49, no. 2 (March/April 2009): 291–92.
42. Ministry of Defense, *Defense of Japan 2010* (Tokyo: Ministry of Defense, 2010), 4.
43. An international investigation concluded that the *Cheonan* was sunk by a torpedo fired by a North Korean midget submarine, a charge that Pyongyang denies. Joint Civilian-Military Investigation Group, "International Result on the Sinking of ROKS 'Cheonan,'" May 20, 2010, http://news.bbc.co.uk/nol/shared/bsp/hi/pdfs/20_05_10jigreport.pdf.
44. Ministry of Defense, *Defense of Japan 2012*, 3.
45. Paul Midford, "Foreign Policy as an Election Issue," in *Japan Decides 2012: The Japanese General Election*, ed. Robert Pekkanen, Steven Reed, and Ethan Scheiner (Basingstoke: Palgrave Macmillan, 2013), 189.
46. Kawashima Yutaka, *Japanese Foreign Policy at the Crossroads: Challenges and Options for the Twenty-First Century* (Washington, DC: Brookings Institution Press, 2003), 18.
47. Yomiuri Shimbun War Responsibility Reexamination Committee, *From Marco Polo Bridge to Pearl Harbor: Who Was Responsible?* (Tokyo: The Yomiuri Shimbun, 2006), 48.
48. Ibid.
49. Ibid.
50. The conventional wisdom holds the United States accountable for Article 9. Some scholars attribute the ideas, if not the language, to the Japanese. See, for example, James Auer, "Article Nine of Japan's Constitution: From Renunciation of Armed Force 'Forever' to the Third Largest Defense Budget in the World," *Law and Contemporary Problems* 53, no. 2 (Spring 1990): 173–74.

51. The text reads: "Article 9. Aspiring sincerely to an international peace based on justice and order, the Japanese people forever renounce war as a sovereign right of the nation and the threat or use of force as a means of settling international disputes. "In order to accomplish the aim of the preceding paragraph, land, sea and air forces, as well as other war potential, will never be maintained. The right of belligerency of the state will not be recognized." See Prime Minister of Japan and His Cabinet, "The Constitution of Japan," November 3, 1946, https://japan.kantei.go .jp/constitution_and_government_of_japan/constitution_e.html.

52. Hosoya Yuichi, "The Rise and Fall of Japan's Grand Strategy: The 'Arc of Freedom and Prosperity' and the Future Asian Order," *Asia-Pacific Review* 18, no. 1 (2011): 14.

53. That Japan still does not have an army, navy, or air force but does have Ground Self-Defense Forces, Maritime Self-Defense Forces, and Air Self-Defense Forces is another indication of this sentiment.

54. All figures from the World Bank, "GDP (current US$), 1960–2016," accessed August 15, 2018, http://data.worldbank.org/indicator/NY.GDP.MKTP.CD?page=6.

55. Hugh Patrick, "Legacies of Change: The Transformative Role of Japan's Official Development Assistance in Its Economic Partnership with Southeast Asia," APEC Study Center Discussion Paper No. 54 (New York: Columbia University, January 2008), 14.

56. Ibid.

57. Ibid., 10.

58. Yuichi, "Rise and Fall," 29–30.

59. Ohno Izumi, "The Strategic Environment Surrounding the Developing Countries and Japan's Development Cooperation: To Be a Global Civilian Power," in *The World and Japan's Foreign Policy in the Future: Prospects in 20 Years,* ed. Yamauchi Masayuki and Nakayama Toshihiro (Tokyo: Japan Institute of International Affairs, March 2011), 86.

60. Daily Yomiuri, "Contribution to U.N. Budget by Japan to Fall," *Jiji Press*, December 26, 2012, www.yomiuri.co.jp/dy/world/T121225001814.htm. While this is a big drop from the 20 percent of the budget Japan provided in 2000, Tokyo continues to hold the number two slot.

61. Bhubhindar Singh, "ASEAN'S Perceptions of Japan: Change and Continuity," *Asian Survey* 42, no. 2 (March/April 2002): 279–80.

62. Ibid., citing Funabashi Yoichi, ed., *Japan's International Agenda* (New York: New York University Press, 1994), 9.

63. Steven Erlanger, "The Search for a New Security Umbrella," *New York Times*, May 12, 1991, https://www.nytimes.com/1991/05/12/weekinreview/the-world-the -search-for-a-new-security-umbrella.html.

64. Hanns Maull, "Germany and Japan: The New Civilian Powers," *Foreign Affairs*, December 1, 1990.

65. Author interview, Nago City, August 7, 2012.
66. All numbers from Katahara Eiichi, "Has Japan Lost Its Relevance?," Paper for the 22nd Asia Pacific Roundtable, Institute of Strategic and International Studies Malaysia, June 4, 2008, Kuala Lumpur, http://www.isis.org.my/images/stories/isis/apr/22nd/22%20Eiichi%20Katahara.pdf. Those numbers didn't tell the whole story. Japan was still the world's second-largest economy, the largest source of regional investment, and one of the leading sources of technology and know-how. With a GDP per capita of $33,800, it ranked eighth overall and first among Asian nations in the UN Development Program's Human Development Index. The economy recorded four years of growth (exceeding 2 percent on average) and five years of export increases, and foreign exchange reserves were growing. It was the second-largest contributor to the UN budget, the World Food Program's fifth-largest donor, and the provider of 10 percent of UNICEF's budget and 20 percent of the UN peacekeeping budget, even if it wasn't providing bodies for peacekeeping efforts. Significantly, an annual BBC poll in 2012 showed Japan had "the most positive influence in the world" among the twenty-two countries surveyed, with twenty countries positive in their assessment of Japan and only two—China and South Korea—negative, and its position as number one has been steady. Globescan, "Views of Europe Slide Sharply in Global Poll, while Views of China Improve," May 10, 2012, http://www.globescan.com/news-and-analysis/press-releases/press-releases-2012/84-press-releases-2012/186-views-of-europe-slide-sharply-in-global-poll-while-views-of-china-improve.html.
67. The party's election manifestos from 2001 to 2009 outline these aims. Weston Konishi provides an excellent assessment of the DPJ's ideas and its ability to implement them in "From Rhetoric to Reality: Foreign-Policy Making under the Democratic Party of Japan" (Cambridge, MA: CreateSpace for Institute for Foreign Policy Analysis, April 2012), http://www.ifpa.org/pdf/fromRhetoricToReality.pdf.
68. Ibid., 23.
69. See, for example, Nakayama Toshihiro, "The United States and Japan-US Relations 20 Years Later: Ensuring the Alliance Is Not Cast Adrift," in Yamauchi and Nakayama, *World and Japan's Foreign Policy*, 57; John Pomfret, "U.S. Concerned about New Japanese Premier Hatoyama," *Washington Post*, December 29, 2009, http://www.washingtonpost.com/wp-dyn/content/article/2009/12/28/AR2009122802271.html?hpid%3Dtopnews&sub=AR; and Tobias Harris, "Japan's New Foreign Policy," *Newsweek*, October 2, 2009, http://www.newsweek.com/japans-new-foreign-policy-tobias-harris-81297.
70. Takahata Akio, "A Shaky Start for Hatoyama's *Yuai* Diplomacy" (Tokyo: Tokyo Foundation for Policy Research, November 13, 2009), http://www.tokyofoundation.org/en/articles/2009/a-shaky-start-for-hatoyamas-yuai-diplomacy.
71. Ibid.

72. Hatoyama Yukio, "My Political Philosophy," excerpted in the *Financial Times*, August 13, 2009.

73. Takahata, "Shaky Start."

74. Miyagi Taizo, "Post-War Asia and Japan—Moving beyond the Cold War: An Historical Perspective," *Asia-Pacific Review* 18, no. 1 (2011): 26.

75. Yamauchi Masayuki and Nakayama Toshihiro, "Why Do We Need to Possess a Vision of the World of 20 Years from Now?," in Yamauchi and Nakayama, *World and Japan's Foreign Policy*, 3, http://www2.jiia.or.jp/pdf/resarch/h22_kokusaijosei/all_en.pdf.

76. Singh, "ASEAN's Perceptions of Japan," 294.

77. Robert Gates, ed., "Military Power of the People's Republic of China 2008: Annual Report to Congress" (Washington, DC: US Department of Defense, 2008), 8.

78. Aileen S. P. Baviera, "China's Relations with Southeast Asia: Political-Security and Economic Interests," PASCN Discussion Paper No. 99-17 (Makati City: Philippine APEC Study Center Network, 1999), executive summary.

79. International Crisis Group, *Stirring up the South China Sea (1)*, Asia Report No. 223, April 23, 2012, 3, https://www.crisisgroup.org/asia/south-east-asia/south-china-sea/stirring-south-china-sea-i.

80. Ibid., 3–6.

81. Ibid., 5. Also, Robert Sutter and Chin-hao Huang trace the ups and downs of China's relations with Southeast Asia in *Comparative Connections*, an electronic journal on Asia-Pacific relationships that I coedit. Their analysis is available at http://cc.csis.org.

82. Rommel Banlaoi, "Southeast Asian Perspectives on the Rise of China: Regional Security after 9/11," *Parameters*, Summer 2003, 104.

83. Zheng Wang, "Perception Gaps, Identity Clashes," in Arai, Goto, and Wang, *Clash of National Identities*, 11.

84. "Resurgent Japanese Militarism a World Threat," *Xinhua*, September 29, 2012, http://www.china.org.cn/opinion/2012-09/29/content_26672419.htm.

85. Brad Glosserman and Scott Snyder, *The Japan–South Korea Identity Clash: East Asian Security and the United States* (New York: Columbia University Press, 2015).

86. For more on this sad tale, see Seongho Sheen and Jina Kim, "What Went Wrong with the ROK-Japan Military Pact?," *Asia Pacific Bulletin* (East-West Center, Washington, DC) 176, July 31, 2012. The two countries only overcame political objections and signed an agreement in November 2016.

87. Park Cheol Hee, "Post-Earthquake Japan-Korea Ties," *The Diplomat*, April 18, 2011, https://thediplomat.com/2011/04/post-earthquake-japan-korea-ties/.

88. Lee Hyo-sik, "Japan's Dokdo Claim Puts Brake on Quake Donation Drive," *Korea Times*, April 7, 2011, http://www.koreatimes.co.kr/www/news/nation/2011/04/117_84707.html.

89. Korea Research Institute for Security, *The Strategic Balance in Northeast Asia, 2012* (Seoul: Korea Research Institute for Security, December 2012).

90. Ibid., 147.

91. Ibid., 150.

92. This point is bitterly contested. Richard Samuels argues that Japan has demonstrated great acuity in preparing the conditions for its postwar revival in *Securing Japan: Tokyo's Grand Strategy and the Future of East Asia* (Ithaca, NY: Cornell University Press, 2009). In Gilbert Rozman, Kazuhiko Togo, and Joseph Ferguson, *Japanese Strategic Thought toward Asia* (Basingstoke: Palgrave MacMillan, 2007), the authors counter that Japan's foreign policy has foundered in recent years, lacking a strategic framework and direction.

93. Oba Mie, "Challenges to the New ASEAN-Japan Partnership in the Changing Regional Circumstances," *Discuss Japan* 20 (2014).

94. This and all subsequent quotes from author interview, Fukuoka, November 26, 2012.

95. Author interview, Fukuoka, November 26, 2012.

96. Author interview, Nago City, August 7, 2012.

97. Author interview, Washington, DC, September 25, 2012.

98. Author interview with executive with international manufacturing company, Washington, DC, September 25, 2012.

5

HIGASHI NIHON DAISHINSAI, OR THE "GREAT EAST JAPAN EARTHQUAKE"

On March 11, 2011, Japan was walloped by one of the worst disasters in its modern history. A 9.03-magnitude earthquake less than fifty miles off its eastern shore rattled the main island of Honshu. The quake unleashed a wall of water that smashed the Pacific coast, rolling miles inland and washing away entire villages and settlements. Nearly twenty thousand people were either killed or missing afterward. The tsunami also overwhelmed the defenses at the Fukushima Daiichi nuclear power facility, setting off one of the worst catastrophes of the nuclear era.

On March 10, 2011, the consensus view was that Japan had endured two lost decades, resulting in a decline "as spectacular and as confounding as its rise during the preceding decades."[1] A 2009 *Asahi Shimbun* poll that asked about prevailing impressions of prewar (1926–45), postwar (1945–89), and present-day (post–1989) Japan provided disturbing results. The most positive connotations were attached to postwar Japan, which was characterized as "vibrant" and "progressive." In contrast, prewar Japan was seen as "conservative" and "dark." Most disturbing were descriptions of contemporary Japan, which was considered "stagnant" and "dark." In other words, "life in contemporary Japan is perceived as harsher than that of the prewar period, characterized as it was by fascism and a military ideology."[2] The Bank of Japan offered an equally dismal picture of Japanese sentiment in the forty-fourth iteration of its "Opinion Survey on the

General Public's Views and Behavior," released January 14, 2011.[3] Just 3 percent of respondents thought economic conditions were improving, 41.5 percent said they were stagnant, and 54.7 percent believed they were worsening. More than 83 percent of respondents considered economic conditions to be either unfavorable or somewhat unfavorable, less than 15 percent opted for neither favorable nor unfavorable, and the remaining sliver, 1.4 percent, deemed them somewhat favorable. Looking ahead, 64.3 percent expected economic conditions to remain the same, while 30.5 percent assumed they would worsen.

The sequence of events that started on March 11 widened cracks in the Japanese psyche, forcing people to contemplate a series of failures that not only led them to question their government's capacity and competence but also challenged foundational elements of Japanese identity. The DPJ government was unable to manage the crisis, and the entire political class was tarnished by its failure to rise above partisan politics in a moment of dire national need. Neither the bureaucracy nor the business community could fill the leadership vacuum. All three—politicians, civil servants, and businesspeople—were revealed as being compromised when details of the nuclear infrastructure were exposed and scrutinized. The Japanese were confronted by the reality that all parties had colluded as "the myth of safety," which had been the rhetorical foundation of the nation's energy strategy, was exposed.

The psychic damage may have been more profound. The Japanese were forced to acknowledge that the notion of "one Japan," of a country whose people united in hardship to overcome obstacles and shared pain, was a myth. The rhetorical emphasis after the tragedy on "bonds" and "community" only underscored the divisions that had emerged in Japan and the pervasive sense of isolation in daily life. Finally, the events of March 11 forced many Japanese to confront the challenges of modernity. The failures at the Fukushima nuclear plant symbolized a larger failure of Japanese society in the twenty-first century, obliging citizens to ask if their ambition to be a great power with all that entailed—a capitalist economic model characterized by consumption and relentless growth—had alienated them from their fundamental nature and their "essence." Koda Yoji, former commander of the Japan Maritime Self-Defense Fleet, lamented that "March 11 took everything from Japan."[4]

Amid the tragedy, some Japanese nurtured hope that the crisis would jolt Japan out of its complacency and its slump. They saw parallels with the arrival of the black ships in Yokohama Harbor in 1853 or the imposition of a new political order by US Occupation authorities after World War II. Typical of this outlook was the conclusion by Vice Chairman Mikuriya Takashi of the Reconstruction Design Council, an advisory panel established for the prime minister after the triple catastrophe: "The events that day marked a turning point at which 'the postwar is over and the post-disaster has begun,' meaning that the disaster would present an opportunity for the Japanese people to overcome the inertia-of-modernization line and change fundamental thinking and behavioral patterns in the long run."[5] Wada Akira, a professor at the Tokyo University of Technology, was blunter still. He saw the crisis as a chance "to change our thinking, our civilization."[6]

"The Toughest and Most Difficult Crisis for Japan"

Japan's fourth shock in four years started as a physical jolt at 2:46 p.m. Japan standard time on March 11, 2011. At that moment, a 9.03-magnitude earthquake was triggered by subduction—the sliding of one tectonic plate under another— about 45 miles east of Japan's Pacific coast and some 20 miles beneath the ocean's surface. The quake was the largest known to have ever hit Japan and one of the five most powerful temblors felt around the world since 1900. The quake itself did considerable damage. The real devastation, however, was wrought by the tsunami that followed, producing wave heights reckoned to have reached 133 feet and to have traveled as far as 6 miles inland. That wall of water overwhelmed the Fukushima Daiichi Nuclear Power Plant located on the Pacific coast, setting off the worst nuclear disaster since the Chernobyl meltdown in 1986. Prime Minister Kan Naoto called the catastrophic chain of events the "toughest and most difficult crisis for Japan" since the end of World War II.[7]

The main quake lasted about six minutes and released surface energy of $1.9 \pm 0.5 \times 10^{17}$ joules, or nearly twice that of the devastating 2004 Boxing Day earthquake and tsunami that killed some 250,000 people along the Indian Ocean littoral and about 600 million times the energy of Little Boy, the atomic bomb dropped on Hiroshima in 1945. It was felt throughout the entire main island of Honshu. The earthquake changed the face of the Earth, moving parts of northeastern Japan nearly 8 feet closer to Alaska and dropping a 250-mile stretch of the Japanese coastline about 2 feet. Scientists reckon that the seabed at the site of the earthquake moved 150 feet east-southeast and rose more than 20 feet. The GPS station located nearest to the epicenter moved nearly 13 feet. The Earth's axis is estimated to have shifted between four and ten inches, and its rotation accelerated, shortening the length of the day by 1.8 microseconds.[8]

While the March 11 quake was historic in intensity, Japan was prepared. The country sits atop the Pacific Ring of Fire, a 25,000-mile-long horseshoe that follows the Pacific coast of the Americas, traverses the Arctic to Asia, and runs the length of Asia's Pacific coast, extending into Southeast Asia. More than 450 volcanoes, or more than 75 percent of the world's total, emerge from this crescent.

Japan is home to 10 percent of the world's active volcanoes. The same geologic forces that produce those volcanoes cause the earthquakes that rock Japan with alarming regularity. Minor tremors are felt somewhere in the country almost daily. As many as 1,500 earthquakes have been recorded in a single year.

Japan's history is dotted with large seismic events. One catalog details 486 major earthquakes between the years 400 and 1866; those of magnitude 8 and greater on the Richter scale occurred in years 684, 869, 1361, 1489, 1611, 1703, 1707, 1854, 1891, 1896, 1923, 1933, 1944, 1946, 1952, 1968, 2003, and 2011.[9] The 1923 Great Kanto Earthquake was a 7.9-magnitude temblor (some estimates of its intensity put it at 8.3) that devastated Tokyo, Yokohama, and surrounding areas. Estimates of casualties range from 100,000 to 142,000 deaths, with many having died in fires triggered by the lunchtime quake. Several thousand ethnic Koreans were killed after the quake in an orgy of violence sparked by rumors that they were looting and preparing to do worse in the confusion following the disaster. Most history books treat the incident as an ugly spasm of scapegoating an ethnic community that has a very uncomfortable history within Japan.

On January 17, 1995, the Great Hanshin Earthquake hit the southern part of Japan's main island, devastating the city of Kobe. It was smaller in length and intensity than the 1923 temblor. It was "just" a 6.8-magnitude quake that left "only" 6,434 people dead, another 30,000 injured, and 300,000 homeless. Causing some ¥10 trillion in damages (about $100 billion), equivalent to roughly 2.5 percent of Japan's GDP at the time,[10] the quake was also a body blow to Japanese confidence. The Japanese until that moment had been convinced of the superiority of their construction standards. The destruction wrought by the quake reminded the Japanese of their own frailty and, more significant, exposed the failure of their government to protect them against risk and insecurity. In retrospect, it was a warning and wakeup call for Japan.

Earthquakes are caused by shifts in the tectonic plates underneath the Earth's surface. Japan lies near the intersection of the Pacific Plate and the Okhotsk Plate. Where they meet, the Pacific Plate is pushed down and under the Okhotsk Plate at a rate of about 3.1–3.5 inches a year. The March 11 earthquake was caused when the Pacific Plate broke and the seabed then rose 15–24 feet, unleashing a massive tsunami on the Tohoku coast. The wave inundated 217 square miles of Japan, wiping away entire cities and towns.[11] The tsunami was huge, with reported heights varying across locations along the coast as well as by means of measurement. The Japan Meteorological Agency reported maximum readings ranging from 11 feet to 24 feet, the Port and Airport Research Institute concluded that wave heights ranged from 13 feet to 50 feet, and individual university researchers' calculations at specific sites produced estimates of waves as high as 133 feet.[12]

A Cascading Nuclear Disaster

The third and most enduring phase of the disaster began when the tsunami swell overwhelmed the 19-foot seawall protecting the Fukushima I Nuclear Power Plant.[13] The 864-acre facility houses six nuclear reactors that generate 4.7 gigawatts of electricity, making it one of the twenty-five largest nuclear power stations in the world. It is an old facility; while many internal systems have been updated, many structures were over four decades old. At the time of the earthquake, Reactor 4 had been defueled, and numbers 5 and 6 were in cold shutdown for scheduled maintenance.

The temblor triggered the plant's emergency systems, which automatically shut down the three working reactors.[14] Yet even as they shut down, power plants still need electricity to run critical systems such as monitoring and cooling; backup generators are on site for those purposes. Unfortunately, the Fukushima plant's backup generators were in the basement of the turbine buildings, below sea level, and thus susceptible to flooding. There was in place yet another safety measure—batteries for when or if the diesel generators failed—but the batteries could last only about eight hours.

The first tsunami—there were at least two waves—hit forty minutes after the quake, with the second just eight minutes behind; and Fukushima lost all generated backup power, leaving only emergency batteries for juice. (It was later discovered that Unit 1's batteries had been damaged—it was not clear when—and did not work.) Within three minutes, Tokyo Electric Power Company (TEPCO), which runs the plants, declared a "nuclear emergency situation" because it could not confirm that water was being injected into the emergency core cooling systems. Some twenty-five hours after the earthquake, an explosion occurred in the reactor building in Unit 1. Some radioactive material was released, and fears were that there might have been a partial meltdown of reactor fuel.[15] After considerable debate, seawater was injected into the reactor unit that evening to cool it off, a move that TEPCO had avoided since it would permanently destroy the reactor.

Unit 3's emergency systems worked for two days, but they failed on March 13 for reasons yet unknown. Just before noon on March 14, Unit 3 was also rocked by an explosion that was much larger than what had occurred in Unit 1 and was reportedly felt twenty-five miles away. Eleven people were injured in the blast, and radioactivity was released into the environment. TEPCO subsequently confirmed that Reactor 3 suffered a meltdown sixty hours after the earthquake.

The emergency cooling systems in Unit 2 worked better, operating for nearly a day and a half before shutting down for about twelve hours. Water levels continued to drop, however, and on the morning of March 15, an explosion occurred in Unit 2. Eventually TEPCO decided to use seawater to cool that reactor core too, but while that operation proved successful, it ruined the reactor. TEPCO has concluded that Reactor 2 suffered a meltdown about a hundred hours after the earthquake.

While Unit 4's reactor had been shut down and defueled before the accident, an explosion in the morning of March 15 damaged the fourth floor of that reactor building. Used fuel assemblies were stored there in cooling pools. Subsequent investigation showed little if any damage to those fuel rods.

Initially, Japanese officials assessed the accident as level 4 on the International Nuclear and Radiological Event Scale. They soon raised that rating to 5 and then to 7, the maximum. As noted previously, by every account and standard, the accident at Fukushima was the worst nuclear accident since the meltdown at the Chernobyl plant in the Ukraine in 1986. In addition to the damage sustained within the reactors themselves and to the radioactivity that was vented manually and by the explosions, the damage to the reactor buildings meant that much of the water used to cool the reactor units leaked out after it too was irradiated.

A Profoundly Manmade Disaster

The reaction to the events of March 11 was confused and chaotic.[16] That is to be expected given the scale of the earthquake, the tsunami, and the nuclear accident. Planners did not anticipate being forced to respond in an environment in which some combination of the three had occurred and that was so degraded and so hostile. To be sure, amid the chaos there were extraordinary incidents of heroism and sacrifice. Many of the individuals on site trying to combat the deteriorating situation at Fukushima did so at considerable risk to their own lives, and the analysis that follows is not intended to belittle their heroic efforts.

Nevertheless, any catalog of what transpired as the country attempted to deal with the Fukushima disaster is damning. The failures, mishaps, and mistakes that unfolded would be comic if the situation were not so severe and the results so tragic. For example, TEPCO's two top officials were unavailable and out of touch; their efforts to get back to headquarters were blocked by a series of bureaucratic and administrative obstacles. The chairman was in China, and despite the

Chinese government's offering him a private plane, he couldn't return home, as all airports in the Tokyo area were shut. The president was on vacation in Nara, and he too was unable to reach Tokyo until the next day, at which point he was stuck in Tokyo traffic for several hours. Neither got to company headquarters until twenty hours after the earthquake.

In Tokyo the government's response was hamstrung by a variety of factors, not least being the inability to get accurate and timely information from TEPCO about what was going on at the plant. This created friction between Prime Minister Kan Naoto and the company, tension that colored many interpretations of what transpired and why. Especially contentious was the prime minister's decision to visit the plant the day after the accident. Some observers believe he interfered with rescue operations; others insist he broke company-created paralysis. According to the Act of Special Measures Concerning Nuclear Emergency Preparedness, a nuclear accident of this scale triggered a meeting of the Nuclear Safety Commission, which would set up an emergency technical group to advise the prime minister. Unfortunately, that law did not anticipate a natural disaster occurring in Tokyo at the same time as a nuclear accident; as a result, the forty members of the commission could not overcome the Tokyo gridlock to convene. Later it was discovered that the underground emergency headquarters in the prime minister's office in the heart of Tokyo could not receive cell phone signals. It was decided to move the command center to the fifth floor, but the emergency phone and fax lines from agencies and ministries were hardwired to the underground facility and could not be rerouted. Messages were then manually conveyed from one floor to the other, and some reportedly got lost on the way.

At the plant, the situation was even more chaotic. Communications at Fukushima were poor since cellular towers were down, and sensors and indicators were not working without power. Emergency generators sent to the plant to provide backup power did not help, because the electrical panel board needed to reroute the power was flooded. While some of the newer backup generators for the reactors had been relocated to higher ground on the hillside to protect against flooding, switching stations that operated the generators were still in the basement, rendering them useless. Emergency power trucks were dispatched to the plant from other parts of Japan, but they were slowed by traffic conditions, much of that the product of road damage caused by the earthquake. When the trucks arrived, workers discovered that the voltage was incorrect and the plug sockets incompatible. Debris and damage made it difficult for those trucks that could operate to get close to the reactor buildings, and additional equipment, such as a 200-meter cable (which weighed one ton), was required. At one point, they used car batteries to supply the power needed to release a safety valve so fire trucks could access anti-fire foam stored at the plant. But it took so long to find and hook up the batteries that by the time the valve was opened, the fire trucks had run out of fuel, and no additional supplies were available.

As emergency workers tried to vent the pressure that was building up in the reactor units, TEPCO staff discovered that their design schematics did not indicate whether key valves could be operated manually. Workers had to venture into the operations room in the dark and risk being irradiated in their effort to find answers. And all this occurred as each of the reactors was heating up and risked exploding. As noted, some did eventually explode and damage emergency equipment working to cool other reactors, slowing other rescue efforts.

The investigations into what transpired at Fukushima reveal that the problems were not simply a result of the chaos that accompanies such catastrophes. Rather, there were systemic failures that were the product not only of political and regulatory structures that appear to have been hopelessly compromised but also of cultural dispositions that made planning impossible. Systemic failure is what makes the events of March 11 so important, as the postmortems indicate that the roots of the breakdown that day originated in the same beliefs and the same institutions that had propelled Japan to its greatness. In other words, a close look at the causes of March 11's problems demands that the Japanese people ask if the sources of their success contributed just as much to the catastrophic failures of that day.

The nuclear accident at the Fukushima plant produced four independent investigations: the Fukushima Nuclear Accident Independent Investigation Commission (NAIIC), the Investigation Committee on the Accident at Fukushima Nuclear Power Stations of Tokyo Electric Power Company, an internal investigation by TEPCO, and an independent assessment by the Rebuild Japan Initiative, a nonprofit think tank.[17] They provide valuable insight into the crisis; the concordance of their conclusions is remarkable and damning.

The Fukushima Nuclear Accident Independent Investigation Commission

Set up by the National Diet, the NAIIC was the first independent commission created in the sixty-six years of Japan's constitutional government.[18] Headed by Dr. Kurokawa Kiyoshi, a medical doctor and former president of the Science Council of Japan, the NAIIC made nine site visits to nuclear power plants, held more than nine hundred hours of hearings, and interviewed 1,167 people. All nineteen commission meetings, except for the first one, were open to the public and broadcast on the internet in Japanese and English; more than 800,000 people watched the proceedings. Its final 640-page report was published in June 2012.

The NAIIC decided Fukushima was "a 'manmade' disaster" whose root causes were the "organizational and regulatory systems that supported faulty rationales for decisions and actions" (16) but not any specific individual's competence. The accident was "the result of collusion between the government, the regulators and TEPCO, and the lack of governance" by them, and the report charged them with betraying "the nation's right to be safe from nuclear accidents" (16). It concluded that the direct causes of the accident were "foreseeable" by the operator, the regulators, and the government body promoting the nuclear power industry, but they "all failed to correctly develop the most basic safety requirements" (16). Regulators refused to force action on the operators and invariably checked with and seemingly deferred to TEPCO whenever new regulations were required. TEPCO's chief concern was interference with operations and the possibility of lawsuits, both of which threatened the company's bottom line. Thus, it invariably objected to changes or new restrictions. The report notes "a negative attitude" toward the adoption of "new advances in knowledge and technology from overseas" (16), and it faults TEPCO for inadequate "knowledge, training, and equipment inspection related to severe accidents" (17). It argues that TEPCO put profits over the potential risk to the public health and welfare.

The NAIIC also concluded that the prime minister's office and other responsible agencies did not function properly, lacking "preparation and the mindset to effectively operate an emergency response to an accident of this scope" (18). It faulted communications between TEPCO and the government, and lambasted TEPCO's mind-set, "which included a reluctance to take responsibility" (18). The report slammed nuclear regulators for being insufficiently expert to act independently of the nuclear industry and condemned "regulatory capture," dismissing their independence as "a mockery" (20). It concluded that "the safety of nuclear energy in Japan and the public cannot be assured unless the regulators go through an essential transformation process" (20). Here too the report clearly states regulations "are biased toward the promotion of a nuclear energy policy, and not to public safety, health and welfare" (20).

The NAIIC report makes for powerful reading. Even more colorful was the message from the chairman, Kurokawa Kiyoshi. He called the disaster "Made in Japan" because "its fundamental causes are to be found in the ingrained conventions of Japanese culture: our reflexive obedience; our reluctance to question authority; our devotion to sticking with the program; our groupism; and our insularity" (9). He noted that "at a time when Japan's self-confidence was soaring, a tightly knit elite with enormous financial resources had diminishing regard for anything 'not invented here.'" Reinforced by an organizational mind-set, bureaucrats "put organizational interests ahead of their paramount duty to protect public safety" (9).

Dr. Kurokawa's screed generated headlines around the world. Several commentators noted that his "Chairman's Message" wasn't included in the Japanese-language version and was only in the English translation. They complained that it pandered to stereotypes of Japanese uniqueness; indeed, the mind-set he describes and the problems he sees—whether regulatory capture or the "not invented here" syndrome—are common to many bureaucracies. Writing in the *Financial Times*, Gerald Curtis, one of the leading American experts on Japanese politics, countered, "To pin the blame on culture is the ultimate cop-out. If culture explains behavior, then no one has to take responsibility."[19] Kurokawa later conceded that his message was tailored for a global audience, but he insisted that the key points are elsewhere in the report. "This is about Japanese culture and values. There is nowhere else quite like that."[20]

The Investigation Committee on the Accident at Fukushima Nuclear Power Stations of Tokyo Electric Power Company

The Japanese Cabinet set up this committee to investigate and verify the causes of the accident and damage, and to make recommendations on ways to prevent similar accidents in the future.[21] Its report is a much more bureaucratic—and, frankly, turgid—document, but it too reaches harsh conclusions.

For example, it claimed that authority was never properly delegated among the nuclear agencies and that the chain of command was not clear. It noted that communications between the accident site and the government's emergency command posts were difficult, meaning that information was often lacking or incomplete. It condemned Prime Minister Kan for interfering in decisions that should have been made by the on-site authorities—noting, for example, his order to suspend the injection of seawater into the reactor.[22]

The committee acknowledged confusion regarding information released to the public, particularly concerning the possibility of a core meltdown. Lines of communication were blurred. In one case, officials from the Nuclear and Industrial Safety Agency (NISA) warned of a possible core meltdown. Other NISA members dismissed any such possibility, but they did not confirm whether they did so because they doubted the reliability of the reports or because they did not want to alarm the public or because the information had not first been cleared by the prime minister's office (and thus should not have been released). The subsequent decision that all critical information should first go through the prime minister's office provided a handy excuse for several parties, including TEPCO, not to release bad news. The commission concluded in its report that such centralization "is not necessarily appropriate" (17).

The commission also noted that accident management programs were inadequate, with no procedures to account for "external events such as earthquakes and tsunamis" (20). The recommendation was that "nuclear operators should conduct comprehensive risk analysis encompassing the characteristics of the natural environment including the external events, not only earthquakes and their accompanying events but also other events such as flooding, volcanic activities or fires, even if their probabilities of occurrence are not high" (20–21). This sounds like common sense, but the implication is that this analysis was not being done. The commission conceded that the nuclear safety administration was not doing its job, although the language is a bureaucrat's delight: "It is difficult to say that NISA has sufficiently fulfilled its role as the organization responsible for taking preventive measures against accidents as well as for responses to the accident" (22). It calls for more interaction with the international community and more consideration of international trends of safety regulations and nuclear security while also endorsing harmonization with international practices.

Turning to TEPCO, the report is scathing (in its bureaucratic fashion). It faulted TEPCO for having "not demonstrated sufficient enthusiasm in thoroughly clarifying the causes behind the accident" (22). It concluded that the power company was "not sufficiently prepared for such an accident"; indeed, it showed "insufficient capability in organizational crisis management; hierarchical organization structure being problematic in emergency responses; insufficient education and training assuming severe accident situations; and apparently no great enthusiasm for identifying accident causes" (25).

Stepping back, the commission acknowledged that the magnitude of the problems transcended any individual corporate culture. "A number of problems exist, which need highly specialized nuclear knowledge over a wide range for solving technical and nuclear engineering problems" (27). National as well as local governments "lack forethought" when dealing with complex disasters, and that finding "highlights the inadequacies of Japan's crisis management attitude" (27). Change in this policy arena requires a "humble" mind-set when thinking about natural threats and disasters, the adoption of a drastically different approach to risk reduction, and far greater attention to the concerns of victims rather than just those of the nuclear plant operator.

The TEPCO Fukushima Nuclear Accidents
Investigation Report

As the plant operator, TEPCO had to set up its own task force to study what transpired at Fukushima, review other investigations, and plot a course to improve safety and regain the public's confidence.[23] In early assessments, TEPCO was quick to blame political interference with the recovery effort. It admitted that it wasn't prepared for a disaster of this magnitude but applauded its workers for doing the best they could "amid unprecedented circumstances."[24] The reform plan blames the accident on "pride and overconfidence in the traditional safety culture and measures."[25] In echoes of the other investigations, it conceded that Japan should seek the opinions of experts both inside and outside Japan, and acknowledged the "immature probabilistic methods" that allowed it to discount the odds of a tsunami of the size that hit on March 11 (9).

TEPCO's explanation for why it was unprepared sounds very similar to that of the NAIIC report. TEPCO underestimated the probability of a severe accident, was concerned about litigation risks, feared that implementing severe accident measures would alarm local communities, was worried about economic losses as plants were shut down to implement accident measures, and had an organizational mind-set that discouraged the "ability to propose measures emphasizing quick execution" (10). Its assessment of the contributors to the inadequate accident response looks equally familiar: no planning for multiple disasters, insufficient training, a failure to update manuals, an ambiguous chain of command, and poor communications with the prime minister's office and regulators. This report also underscored the need to expect the unexpected.

The Independent Investigation Commission on
the Fukushima Daiichi Nuclear Accident

This last investigation was launched by the Rebuild Japan Initiative Foundation (RJIF).[26] Created after the March 11 events, it investigated the causes of the accident and then turned to the crisis concerning the "Lost 20 Years." It issued a report outlining the lessons learned and the ways to rebuild the country and its society.[27]

Its conclusion about the catastrophe is simple: The government and TEPCO were "astonishingly unprepared, at almost all levels, for the complex nuclear disaster that started with an earthquake and a tsunami."[28] It places the blame on individual actions—although it points out that workers were thrust into an emergency without benefit of training or instructions—and, as did the other reports, on systemic failures. TEPCO's failures reflected its management structure and culture. Government regulators had not anticipated an emergency that had to be handled despite a sustained power outage. The RJIF report also noted the poorly thought-out plans for the emergency response centers—front-line headquarters for nuclear disasters—that were inaccessible because of earthquake damage and that lacked basic equipment such as air-purifying filters. The greatest problem may well have been a lack of imagination. "Nothing like the Fukushima Daiichi catastrophe was possible—no tsunami of 45 feet could swamp a nuclear power station and knock out its emergency systems. No blackout could last for days. No triple meltdown could occur. Nothing like this could happen. Until it did."[29]

The three-hundred-page RJIF report blames the myth of "the absolute safety of nuclear power," a belief "that the nation's culture valued safety above everything—that nuclear power in Japan was somehow safer than in other countries and its nuclear reactor technologies were 'different.' . . . This perception prevented Japan from having science-based discussions and from pursuing thorough safe reform."[30] This shibboleth was "propagated by interest groups—the famed 'nuclear village'—to overcome the strong anti-nuclear sentiment connected to the atomic bombings of Hiroshima and Nagasaki."[31] This obliged authorities to play down anything that might stir up anxieties. It "forbids all doubts regarding the safety of nuclear power, replacing it with a certain logic leading inexorably to a predetermined and extreme conclusion: that nuclear power is simply safe."[32]

As with the other reports, the RJIF's analysis faulted Japanese regulators for being complacent about their own standards and dismissive of those from outside. It slammed the lack of accountability among regulators as well as the "sweetheart relationships and revolving door that connected the regulatory bodies and electric companies, academics, and other stakeholders in the nuclear community."[33] The report criticized the Nuclear and Industrial Safety Agency, which "lacked the philosophy, capacity, and personnel to properly fulfill its role, and it has consequently failed to train true safety regulation professionals."[34] When called to the prime minister's office during the crisis, top NISA officials could not answer questions and offered no proposals to deal with the accident. According to the RJIF, part of the blame also rests on a bureaucratic culture that regularly rotates officials through positions and cannot guarantee expertise in place during emergencies.

Finally, the report faulted poor communications, highlighting the role of the prime minister's office. As in the other reports, the RJIF noted the tension between the government's desire to inform the public and its not wanting to spark a panic. That tension was difficult to calibrate and appears to have been resolved by erring on the side of caution, resulting in a lack of communications.

Subsequent revelations about what the government did and did not know and what it chose to tell the public have fed growing skepticism about its priorities and competence.

The four reports reach similar conclusions. All but the NAIIC agreed that the earthquake was not the main cause of the nuclear disaster, although the National Diet's report merely questions the extent of the damage caused by the temblor. All agree there was insufficient preparation for an emergency of this magnitude and that the response was characterized by poor communication and a lack of cooperation among key parties. They all condemn the government's crisis management techniques, agreeing that public trust in the government was greatly damaged by incomplete information, inconsistent statements, and a widespread belief that the prime minister's office did not have a good grip on events as they unfolded.

In a shocking move, just six months later, TEPCO released the findings of an internal reform task force that conceded that it could have avoided the disaster.[35] It acknowledged the correctness of the RJIF's report and its focus on the "myth of safety," admitting that "there was a worry that if the company were to implement a severe-accident response plan, it would spur anxiety throughout the country and in the communities near where nuclear plants are sited, and lend momentum to the anti-nuclear movement."[36] The task force acknowledged that making safety improvements risked shutting down the plant and increasing costs and that it could have prompted lawsuits alleging that previous safety measures were inadequate. It also admitted that safety drills were largely a formality and that the company should have relied on international safety standards. Welcome though those admissions were, cynical observers noted that some contrition was necessary if the country was going to restart its nuclear reactors.

A Meltdown of Japan Itself

March 11 is a red-letter day in Japanese history not only for what transpired that afternoon but also for its effects and impact.[37] A 9.03-magnitude earthquake, one of the strongest of the twenty-first century, is a scientific curiosity, but the aftershocks are what make it significant. Original estimates of the number of dead and missing people on March 11 were as high as 30,000. In a report issued a year after the disaster, the government of Japan said that the number of dead exceeded 15,800, with over 3,200 still missing and another 6,100 people injured. Eleven months after the incident, more than 342,000 people were still living as evacuees.[38]

The pain was especially acute on the two ends of the age spectrum. Tohoku is one of the "grayest" parts of Japan, with a large elderly population, a fact that has particular implications for this disaster and for Japan's future. According to official estimates, 56 percent of the catastrophe's fatalities were older than sixty-five years of age.[39] In some of the hardest-hit Tohoku communities, the elderly make up one-third of the population. This alarming statistic is also a portent of Japan's demographic profile in 2030.

Children were also victims of the events of March 11. Since the earthquake and tsunami struck in the afternoon, many children were at school. While that meant that they were well prepared for disaster—Japan takes disaster preparation drills very seriously—it also meant that they were separated from their families. Some 378 school-age children lost their lives that day, more than 230 children were orphaned, and more than 1,500 children lost one or both parents. Save the Children has estimated that as many as 100,000 children were uprooted from their homes.[40] The impact of that trauma on an entire generation of young people is painful to contemplate.

The Tohoku coastline was transformed, as was to be expected from a wave that either swept away or inundated 23,600 hectares of land. Many small villages were leveled; others vanished. The areas hardest hit on March 11 are rural ones that depend on agriculture and fishing. Tohoku produces a little over 11 percent of Japan's foodstuffs and 15 percent of Japan's agriculture, forestry, and fisheries industries.[41] The tsunami damaged about 10 percent of Japan's fishing ports and left 90 percent of the fishing boats in three prefectures—Miyagi, Iwate, and Fukushima—unusable. Total damage to the country's fishing industry is estimated at ¥1.26 trillion (about $10 billion). The region generates 3–4 percent of Japan's rice, and no one knows how long it will be before the fields can be cleared of the seawater's salt, which makes replanting impossible. Fears of radioactivity are also a powerful obstacle to renewed farming. There has been concern that even if losses could be made whole—a real question given the paucity of earthquake insurance in Japan—operations would not resume. Two-thirds of farmers and one-third of fishermen are older than sixty-five, and restarting devastated businesses is a formidable challenge. By July 2011, 73 percent of farming businesses affected by March 11 had resumed operations, but less than half that amount—35.5 percent—of fishing operations had recommenced. That may be of little solace: A year after the earthquake, 76 percent of the Japanese believed that food from Fukushima was not safe despite government and scientific assurances.[42]

While the local damage was horrific, it does not capture the scale of the economic damage to Japan as a whole. The earthquake was felt throughout the country, and its impact on other industries, as well as that of the nuclear disaster, produced a tidal wave of its own. Japan's Cabinet Office estimates that the Tohoku earthquake is the most expensive disaster in human history. It puts direct damages at about ¥16.9 trillion ($210 billion), or 3.5 percent of GDP, and that estimate doesn't include losses related to the nuclear accident. Other estimates range from $100 billion to $500 billion, with the median at $275 billion. One authoritative assessment extrapolates losses from Miyagi Prefecture and came up with total direct losses of $335 billion and indirect losses of $260 billion expected with all impacts combined.[43] This number is significantly larger than the Cabinet Office's figures, but Hayashi Mompei, an economic analyst at the Osaka-based Asia Pacific Institute of Research who focuses on the economic impact of disasters, goes with the higher numbers. He dismissed government figures as "seriously underestimated" and reckoned that real losses are at least twice the official figures. He suggested that the numbers were lowballed to save money on reconstruction outlays.[44]

Whatever the correct figure is, March 11 was monumental. For comparison, consider that the entire economy of the tsunami-affected coastal municipalities was ¥2.1 trillion, and the annual budget of the Japanese national government is ¥90 trillion.[45] The 1995 Great Hanshin Earthquake did ¥9.9 trillion in damage, and the 1923 Great Kanto Earthquake did ¥16.9 trillion–¥22.5 trillion ($210 billion–$280 billion) in damage when adjusted for inflation.[46] While the government is committed to rebuilding and reconstructing the devastated regions, many losses cannot be replaced because they are intangible, with a worth and value many times their price, and because of an even more prosaic concern— a lack of insurance. Earthquake insurance is expensive, and only an estimated 14–17 percent of Japanese homeowners are covered for such incidents.[47]

A less visible, but no less important, dimension of the economic impact is supply chain disruption. Tohoku is often described as peripheral to Japan's economy, producing just 7–9 percent of GDP, but some of those businesses have critical roles. According to official figures, Tohoku is responsible for a 12.3 percent share of shipping in electronic parts, circuitry, and devices and a 14.4 percent share of information communications equipment.[48] Yet the Ministry of Economy, Trade, and Industry registered a 15.5 percent drop in total manufacturing production in Japan in March 2011, the largest decrease in the fifty-eight years since the production index was established. By comparison, the 1995 Kobe earthquake resulted in only a 2.6 percent fall in production, and the worst monthly decline in production following the 2008 global financial crisis was just 8.6 percent.[49] More than half of the decrease after March 11 reflected the plunge in transportation equipment production, which fell 46.7 percent in March.[50] In an indication of how these ripple effects work, car production fell 54.2 percent.[51]

Tohoku companies are also critical to global production. Two companies, for example, account for 25 percent of global silicon wafer production. Also hard hit were enterprises that produce materials for liquid-crystal display panel production, printed circuit boards, and other integrated circuit components.[52] While many plants are back online, infrastructure damage prevented them from reentering the global economy. The shutdown of the port of Hitachi meant the loss of 81.4 percent of Japan's dump truck exports, the closure of Onahama port resulted in the loss of 53.9 percent of Japanese exports of vinyl chloride, and the flooding of Sendai Airport saw the halt of 16.7 percent of Japanese "movement for watch" exports.[53]

As noted previously, the events at the Fukushima facilities precipitated the worst nuclear accident since Chernobyl. While the release of radioactivity was about one-tenth that of Chernobyl and the contaminated area is also about one-tenth that of Chernobyl, however, Fukushima resulted in the largest accidental release of radioactive material into the ocean in history.[54] Radioactive nuclides such as iodine, cesium, strontium, and plutonium were released either by steam venting or by water used to put out the fires leaking into the groundwater or the ocean. TEPCO's interim report on the disaster, published in June 2011, acknowledged that plutonium-238, -239, -240, and -241 were released "into the air" in the first hundred hours after the earthquake; the total amount of plutonium was put at 120 billion becquerels, which could be as much as 50 grams. An October 2011 study by the French Institute for Radiological Protection and Nuclear Safety concluded that some 2.7×10^{16} becquerels of cesium-137 (about 8.4 kilograms) entered the ocean between March 21 and mid-July. This amount, however, has been distilled in hundreds of thousands of tons of water. Soil contamination has been noted beyond evacuation zones, and radiation was detected as far away as Yokohama, but experts have cautioned against overreacting to one-off findings. While no deaths have yet been attributed to irradiation (six workers died during rescue and cleanup operations, but none were linked to radiation[55]), one study anticipates "an additional 130 (15–1,100) cancer mortalities and 180 (24–1,800) cancer morbidities" worldwide—but mostly in Japan—as a result of the Fukushima accident. Exposure to workers is expected to yield between two and twelve cancer cases.[56]

The Japanese government discovered radiation exceeding permissible minimum levels in milk, leafy vegetables, shiitake mushrooms, rice, beef, and fish. Hay and straw contaminated with cesium was found fifty miles from the reactors; experts reckon it was contaminated straw fed to cows that produced some of the high radiation levels in beef. Since natto (fermented bean curd) is often wrapped in straw, sales of it were also affected.[57] Excessive levels of radiation were discovered in freshwater salmon, smelt, and carp; a survey found high levels of radioactive cesium in twenty-three varieties of freshwater fish.[58] Radiation has meant that farmers, ranchers, and fishermen were unable to sell their products even when they got back in business. In August 2011 Tokyo was forced to develop a plan to buy beef from affected areas to offset farmers' losses. By August 2012 the Ministry of Health found that cesium levels had dropped to undetectable levels in most cultivated vegetables from the affected area, but widespread skepticism of the government meant that those findings counted for little with consumers.

Damage was done to the region's reputation and influenced thinking about investment plans. In a METI survey, 83 percent of Japanese manufacturers said they went back to their original supplier. Among those who had not returned, 58 percent were buying from an alternative supplier inside Japan, and 42 percent preferred overseas providers. Non-Japanese customers were not as committed to restoring relationships or maintaining a presence in the hardest-hit areas. Thirty-three percent of Japanese firms reported a decline in trade (e.g., requests for termination of agreements) with overseas customers as a consequence of the earthquake. About half of the respondents blamed supply problems. In a little over 40 percent of the cases, the decision reflected concern about the nuclear accident and doubts about relying on Japanese technology and products.[59] Another METI survey showed that 30 percent of firms planning to invest in Japan decided "to cancel or reduce their investment because of the earthquake disaster."[60] Abe Tadahiko, a senior executive fellow at the Fujitsu Research Institute, concluded that "trust in Japan, which is a vital mainstay of this supply chain, has been shaken in one fell swoop."[61] So, in addition to investor concerns about the future of its domestic market (the product of a shrinking and aging population), Japan must now contend with international concerns about its vulnerability to earthquakes and potential disruptions in industrial activity.

"The Limits of Government Capacity and Capability"

Any accounting for the losses of March 11 must also recognize the unquantifiable damage done to institutions and core elements of Japanese society and identity. Start with the damage to Japanese institutions. As explained in chapter 3, the DPJ government's handling of March 11 was the final nail in its coffin. In an *Asahi Shimbun* poll taken a month after the disaster, 67 percent of respondents said they did not appreciate the government's response to the nuclear accident; by September, that number had increased to 78 percent.[62] One official who worked in the prime minister's office throughout the crisis confided, "In hindsight, there is lots we could have done. . . . The Prime Minister's Office was trying to do its best, but the limits of government capacity and capability were demonstrated."[63] Not surprising, the Tohoku crisis left the DPJ "significantly discredited and its popular support eroded considerably, contributing to its landslide electoral loss in 2012."[64]

As the various investigations found, there were ample reasons to fault TEPCO, the electrical utility that ran the Fukushima facility. It badly underestimated the size of the tsunami, a failing that is hard to understand since the historical record showed waves of this size had battered the Tohoku coast frequently. The March 11 tsunami was considered a "once in a century" event even though the historical record shows the probability of large tsunamis occurring as two and a half to three times every hundred years. Only a week before the March 11 temblor, TEPCO and two other utilities urged the government's Earthquake Research Committee to play down a study—based on an 8.3-magnitude earthquake in 869—that warned of the dangers of another such incident. Their effort succeeded; the final report merely called for further study.[65]

TEPCO's insistence is inexplicable—or outrageous—given a 2008 in-house study that warned of possible flooding at the Fukushima complex. That analysis was based on an 1896 earthquake and predicted twenty-four- to thirty-one-foot waves. TEPCO officials dismissed the prospect of waves large enough to breach the seawall, and the study circulated within TEPCO for three years before being sent to NISA. In a cruel irony, it arrived at the nuclear agency four days before the March 11 temblor, but TEPCO officials said that they did not plan to take action because the estimates were only "tentative calculations."[66]

TEPCO eventually conceded that "the nuclear accident was caused by its excessively optimistic risk assessments, shortchanging of safety and training and failure to adopt appropriate countermeasures."[67] Its October 2012 analysis—which acknowledges more shortcomings than did the report issued four months earlier—points to management's "lack of vigilance" about the possible occurrence of severe accidents, its concern about "litigation risks" following an admission that severe accident measures were required, its worry that implementing such measures "would exacerbate siting community and public anxiety and add momentum to anti-nuclear movements," and its "latent fear that plant shutdown would be required until severe accident measures were put into place."[68]

The "Safety Myth" Exposed

The events of March 11 were the product of serial failures by every component of the *genpatsu mura* (nuclear village) that promoted nuclear power. Ever since Japan began its atomic energy program, that coalition used every tool at its disposal to overcome anxieties associated with nuclear power. As the only country to have ever been attacked with atomic bombs, Japan knows well the risks that can accompany the unleashing of the atom. That sensitivity was heightened in 1954, when the fallout from a US hydrogen bomb test contaminated the fishing boat *Daigo Fukuryu Maru* (Lucky Dragon No. 5). All the crew members were later diagnosed as suffering from acute radiation syndrome; radioman Kuboyama Aikichi died, becoming the first victim of the hydrogen bomb. By 1955 more than 30 million Japanese—about one-third of the population—had signed petitions calling for a ban on hydrogen bombs.

Despite public sensitivities, which were often likened to a "nuclear allergy," Japanese policymakers were eager to exploit nuclear power. Endowed with few natural resources, Japan struggled throughout the process of industrialization and modernization to secure energy supplies and to manage the demand for them. Energy security was one of the animating forces of Japanese policy in the runup to World War II and one of the most important factors in sparking the collision with the United States. Forced after the war to again confront questions about reliable supplies of raw materials and dependence on foreign sources, Japanese decision makers turned to nuclear power as the best way to secure energy for their country's postwar economic development. They wasted no time setting up a national nuclear program, and that logic continues to drive Japanese thinking.[69]

Central to Japan's commitment to nuclear power was the belief that it could be generated safely. Government, industry, and nuclear power regulators assured a skeptical and often fearful public that the risks of an accident were negligible and that such power generation posed no threat to public health and safety. Those conclusions, to unblinkered outsiders, were unfounded. One critic concluded that the history of Japan's nuclear fuel cycle efforts is marked by "failures, fabrications and perverted policy."[70] March 11 then shattered the assumptions and the assurances. In July 2011 Prime Minister Kan Naoto concluded that the country's geology and the frequency of earthquakes and tsunami—especially for the six facilities on Japan's Pacific coast—meant that he no longer believed Japan could operate nuclear power safely. (Six months later, Japan's Nuclear Regulation Authority announced that it had found active fault lines under a third nuclear reactor.[71]) Amid concern that the country's nuclear bureaucratic and regulatory structure had been compromised, all of Japan's remaining forty-eight nuclear power plants were subjected to enhanced scrutiny. Within a year every nuclear power plant in Japan had been shut down for safety inspections, triggering an intense national debate over the country's commitment to nuclear energy.

Critics charge that efforts to create a myth of absolute safety increased the risks attached to nuclear power in Japan. A "PR effort on behalf of the absolute safety of nuclear power was deemed necessary to overcome the strong anti-nuclear sentiment connected to the atomic bombings of Hiroshima and Nagasaki."[72] The group driving this campaign would go to absurd (and plainly dangerous) lengths on behalf of their cause. So, for example, bureaucrats, regulators, and industry leaders feared that even preparing for a nuclear accident would become a source of anxiety for people living near the plants. As a result, when plant operators proposed holding a nuclear accident drill that was based on an earthquake, the nuclear regulator countered that such a scenario would cause "unnecessary anxiety and misunderstanding." The drill was eventually held but premised on a heavy snowfall instead. The Rebuild Japan Initiative Foundation's 2014 report on the Fukushima accident concluded that the myth of absolute safety "implied that the mere existence of severe-accident defense would provoke public anxiety over the safety of nuclear power generation."[73] Similarly, nuclear operators and regulators made no effort to backfit systems to accommodate the latest scientific findings and innovations because "making such changes, the nuclear community felt, would be an admission that existing safety precautions and regulations were insufficient and that existing nuclear plants did not possess 'absolute security.'"[74]

Richard Samuels, whose study of the March 11 triple catastrophe is essential reading, observed that one word—*soteigai* (unimaginable)—"came to dominate the post-3.11 national discourse."[75] The word was used primarily by TEPCO officials and their backers to play down the meltdown and to imply that there was no failure since the danger was beyond reasonable expectations. What becomes clear, however, is that, in the main, the chief obstacles were ultimately more pedestrian: pursuit of profit, bureaucratic obstructionism, and groupthink. When TEPCO's planning assumptions and operating procedures were challenged, the company fought back and argued that change would force power plants offline, raising costs to businesses and damaging the company's bottom line. Regulators invariably deferred to TEPCO's expertise. This acquiescence wasn't as much an indication of regulatory capture as it was a broad concordance of the views of government and business—the regulators and the regulated—that is common throughout Japan. Dr. Kurokawa, chairman of the Nuclear Accident Independent Investigation Commission's investigation, considered it uniquely Japanese; but that sort of groupthink, without the historical and cultural roots, is evident in most countries and most bureaucracies.

Those corporate failures were exacerbated by a bureaucratic and regulatory infrastructure that had been severely compromised. The official parliamentary report on the accident lays out a long list of shortcomings and failures:

> The regulators did not monitor or supervise nuclear safety. The lack of expertise resulted in "regulatory capture," and the postponement of the implementation of relevant regulations. They avoided their direct responsibilities

by letting operators apply regulations on a voluntary basis. Their independence from the political arena, the ministries promoting nuclear energy, and the operators was a mockery. They were incapable, and lacked the expertise and the commitment to assure the safety of nuclear power. Moreover, the organization lacked transparency.[76]

As Satoh Haruko, a foreign policy researcher at the Osaka School of International Public Policy, explained, "The 'nuclear village' reflected the prevalent logic of the post-war, developmental economy state. The primary purpose of this post-war state was to pursue economic gains at all costs. In the effort to catch up and overtake the West, state and society operated like one massive corporation, the so-called 'Japan, Inc.' The country's political system, the ruling LDP allowed complacency to reign over prudence in promoting nuclear energy as part of Japan's industrial policy."[77]

March 11 didn't chasten the mythmakers. As Japan debated its postcrisis energy policy, the media exposed efforts by power utilities, regulators, and other parties to rig national hearings in favor of pronuclear views.[78] The *Japan Times* noted in an editorial that "the Agency for Natural Resources and Energy and the Nuclear and Industrial Safety Agency, both of the trade and industry ministry, asked five power companies—Hokkaido, Tohoku, Chubu, Shikoku and Kyushu—to mobilize employees and other people to express opinions favoring nuclear power generation in public meetings, symposiums, etc."[79]

The media, however, has been indicted for complicity in covering up problems and reporting only the positive side of nuclear power because of financial support from power companies; academics and other thought leaders are accused of being similarly co-opted. This steady drip of revelations about the failures of government, business, and other elites in the aftermath of March 11 has led to widespread disillusionment with the country's leadership. Opening a conference on the health effects of the Fukushima accident, Sasakawa Yohei, chairman of the Nippon Foundation, damned the government for "delayed responses, ex post facto reports and countless cover-ups." He condemned the Tokyo government and TEPCO for being "dishonest, unqualified and nontransparent," concluding that "it is no surprise that the people have become unable to trust anything."[80]

Sasakawa was right to emphasize "anything." According to the 2012 Edelman Trust Barometer, an authoritative annual twenty-five-nation survey of public trust around the world, trust in Japan's government, media, and nongovernmental organizations (NGOs) suffered double-digit declines for the first time in the survey's history. The government was especially hard hit: Official spokespersons enjoyed just 8 percent credibility, a 55-percentage point drop from the year before. Trust in government overall was cut in half, with just 25 percent of the informed public in Japan (and 24 percent of the general public) trusting the government to do what is right. A year earlier, the informed public credited the government with doing the right thing 51 percent of the time; while not a particularly impressive number, it was still twice the postaccident figure.[81] While the media (12 percent) and NGOs (21 percent) also sustained double-digit losses, trust in industry overall fell just 6 percent. Specific sectors, however, were badly hit: Energy suffered the worst blow, falling 46 points, while banks and financial services fell 20 and 17 points, respectively. The telecommunications sector also posted a 17-point decline.[82]

Rethinking the Self-Defense Forces

Two institutions redeemed themselves during those grueling times. The Self-Defense Forces and the US-Japan alliance received overwhelmingly positive appraisals for their response to the crisis. Postwar Japan has had a "strong antimilitarist sentiment, a pacifist orientation and a sort of allergic reaction" to the SDF, reports Professor Kamiya Matake of Japan's National Defense Academy.[83] That has changed, however, and Kamiya credits March 11. The Self-Defense Forces' response to the triple catastrophe was unprecedented and heroic, with the largest mobilization of SDF personnel in the organization's history. Nearly 107,000 personnel were involved, including two groups of reservists, whose services were used for the first time since the system was established in 1954. In all, 45 percent of SDF personnel were dispatched to respond to this crisis.[84] In addition, 540 aircraft and 59 vessels were deployed. The SDF performed a broad array of tasks: conducting search and rescue; leading relief efforts, including providing food, medical assistance, and health care; clearing roads and removing debris from damaged facilities such as airports and ports; transporting relief supplies; and giving watering, decontamination, and monitoring support in response to the nuclear power station accident.[85] In total, the Self-Defense Forces transported 13,906 tons of supplies and 32,985 tons of water and provided a little over 5 million meals and bathing services to over 1 million people.[86] The Ministry of Defense estimates that the SDF was responsible for 70 percent, or nineteen thousand, of the roughly twenty-seven thousand people who were rescued. Military personnel found and recovered some 60 percent of the sixteen thousand bodies recovered from the disaster. SDF water trucks and helicopters were instrumental in delivering water to help put out fires at the Fukushima nuclear plants, even though it exposed the service members to considerable danger from radiation. SDF senior personnel spoke with some awe about the commitment and dedication of the pilots and personnel who, as one former pilot explained, prepared for these missions as if they were going to war.[87]

Kamiya believes that the SDF's response transformed Japanese thinking about the military. The 2012 Cabinet Office survey showed 97.7 percent of respondents appreciated the deployment of the SDF in response to the disasters. In addition, 91.7 percent of respondents had a positive impression of the SDF, the highest percentage since the survey began and an 11 percent jump since the previous survey in 2009.[88] Even more persuasive for Kamiya is that more than 72 percent of respondents said they would approve of someone close to them (such as a relative) joining the military. Historically that has been tough for the Japanese to accept: In 1991 just 29 percent said they would support someone close to them joining the SDF, while 44 percent would oppose that career choice. Only in 2006 did more than half the respondents (51.8 percent) say they would back such a decision.

Favorable reviews of the SDF have helped to overcome long-standing domestic opposition to deploying the armed forces as an instrument of state policy (and only as a means to respond to disasters or help keep the peace, not as a means of power projection). Shortly after the disaster, analyst Kamiura Motoaki argued that March 11 provided "an ideal opportunity for the SDF to demonstrate to the Japanese public that its greatest contribution might be in the area of emergency relief," calling it a "perfect illustration of what Japanese citizens expect of their armed forces today."[89]

That appeal is not restricted to domestic audiences. Japanese politicians, military officials, and security experts have seized on the March 11 experience to make their case to the region for a larger Japanese presence and role in Asia.[90] A new appreciation for the SDF facilitates new thinking about a key instrument of state power, one that the Japanese public has been reluctant to embrace and employ. A readiness to deploy the SDF for humanitarian assistance and disaster relief (HADR) missions in Southeast Asia, which often suffers such catastrophes, would be an important contribution to regional security and burnish Japan's image. "HADR activities provide an opportunity to dispatch SDF personnel on overseas missions that do not spark controversy and that showcase tangible 'boots-on-the-ground' contributions to the global common good."[91]

March 11 had other important implications for Japanese thinking about how it engages with the world. The foreign ministry lists 163 countries and regions and 43 international organizations that reached out to Japan after the triple calamity. They extended everything from general offers of assistance to relief teams, supplies, and donations. Some of the entries are surprising: East Timor sent a hundred men to clear debris; Cambodia sent $100,000 in aid; Indonesia sent rescue workers, medical assistance, and supplies, while the Jakarta government donated $2 million; and Mongolia sent rescue teams and $1 million in donations along with supplies. Even China and South Korea, countries with mixed emotions about Japan, rose above those concerns to help. China sent a rescue team as well as 20,000 tons of fuel, 10 tons of drinking water, and nearly $5 million worth of humanitarian supplies. South Korea sent several teams of rescuers—more than a hundred people in total—and humanitarian supplies as well as boric acid to help fight the nuclear problems at the reactor units. The government of Taiwan provided more than $243 million in aid—the highest amount from any source—in public and private donations, along with two rescue teams. By September 30, 2012, Japan had received ¥8.8 billion in donations from around the world, and they helped remind the Japanese of the need to stay engaged with the outside world as they struggled to overcome the hardships that followed.[92]

A second important outcome is the boost that the US-Japan alliance received as a result of the US forces on the scene, working shoulder to shoulder with the SDF to provide relief. The day after the disaster, a joint task force of the US military in Japan (US Forces Japan) was set up to support the Japanese government's response. More than 24,000 American service personnel; 24 ships, including the USS *Ronald Reagan* and its carrier strike group; and 189 aircraft joined Operation Tomodachi, the largest joint operation ever mounted by the US and Japanese militaries. In addition to providing humanitarian assistance and helping clear infrastructure of debris, a team of American experts on chemical, biological, radioactive, and nuclear response was dispatched to Japan to help deal with the unfolding crisis at Fukushima. Surveillance assets—namely, unmanned drones—were also lent to Japan to provide real-time information at the nuclear facilities. Significantly, many of the American personnel on site were marines who had been sent from Okinawa. Marines corps personnel cause many headaches for the two countries, and the marines' response to March 11 helped polish their image among the Japanese public.[93] The US military's response was a stark contrast to that of many foreigners in Japan, and of many Japanese themselves, whose first instinct after the nuclear accident was to flee Tohoku and, in some cases, the country. The readiness of American personnel to put themselves in harm's way to help Japan put to rest the notion that the United States was not sufficiently committed to the security of Japan. Satoh Haruko concluded, "March 11 was huge for the alliance. The Japanese public for the first time saw what a military alliance was about."[94]

The Japanese public seems to have gotten the message. In a 2012 Cabinet Office survey, 79.2 percent of respondents called Operation Tomodachi a success, while 81 percent considered the US-Japan Treaty of Mutual Cooperation and Security helpful to Japan. More than 82 percent of respondents agreed that the alliance is the best way to "preserve the safety of Japan," a jump of about 5 percentage points in three years, while less than 8 percent think the treaty should be abolished and that Japan should rely only on the SDF.[95]

Asia's response to March 11 was an eye-opener for many Japanese. "Japan is within Asia, but has a mentality that isolates it from the rest of Asia," explained Doden Aiko, a senior NHK commentator who has focused on Japan's international engagement and relations with Southeast Asia in particular.[96] That mental map imploded on March 11. The outpouring of aid after the crisis, especially from recipients of Japan's own official development assistance, was "a shock to Japan," said Doden. "Some people were uncomfortable with the idea of Japan being helped by poorer countries." These countries are ready for "a more mature and equal relationship" with Japan, not one defined by the traditional roles of Japan as a donor and of their being recipients. This demands a new outlook in Japan, one in which the Japanese stop thinking of themselves as superior. Doden covered relief efforts in Tohoku by a caravan of youth volunteers from the Association of Southeast Asian Nations that was organized by the ASEAN secretariat and sponsored by a Japanese foundation. That effort was a sign of new possibilities as Japan and its neighbors carve out new roles. "The thought of Japanese being helped by Southeast Asian people is a sign that a new relationship is emerging," she explained.

Former diplomat Akashi Yasushi agreed, noting that the Japanese "were very much moved by the deep concern expressed by Asian nations."[97] Support from countries that Japan has helped in the past, said Akashi, has given the Japanese pause and forced them to reconsider their relationships in the region. "We owe so much of ourselves and what we have to non-Japanese heritages." But in referring to their cultural heritage, he confessed, the "Japanese have tended to forget the roots of these imports." The extraordinary successes of the twentieth century "blinded [the] Japanese," and this process was helped along by "arrogance born of insularity." Now Akashi sees the Japanese beginning to appreciate how much they owe to China and Korea. "There is a rediscovery by the Japanese of their cultural and intellectual roots."

Ever an optimist, Akashi hopes the events of March 11 would help reshape East Asia. He drew inspiration from the Great Lisbon Earthquake of 1755, an 8.5-magnitude temblor that triggered a tsunami and fires and produced a death toll estimated between 10,000 and 100,000 people. More significant, the internal (political, economic, and social) disruptions caused by that quake ended Portugal's colonial ambitions. While it may have awakened Portugal from its dream of empire, the quake also sparked an intellectual revolution across Europe, prompting the speculations of Voltaire, Jean-Jacques Rousseau, and Immanuel Kant.[98] Akashi argued that in the wake of the devastation, European thinkers were more inclined to think about Europe as a collective rather than just nation-states. March 11 could prove to be an equally significant moment, and "the bickering states of East Asia will enter into a new concept of being Asian." That may be ambitious. At a minimum, a Tokyo bureaucrat working in Fukuoka observed, Japan must give in "return something to Asian countries. We have to help them and co-exist peacefully with them."[99]

"Natural Disasters Reveal Us"

The events of March 11 cut deeply into the Japanese psyche.[100] Hardest hit were Tohoku residents, who lost everything. A proud and self-reliant people, historically suspicious of Tokyo, the tsunami not only stripped them of their possessions but also took their livelihoods, their history, and their ties to the land and the community. March 11 deprived them of the components of their daily lives and then robbed them of their past by erasing the monuments and reminders of their history. Compounding the damage, it forced this community into relying on the central government for its future. That day shattered lives, leaving holes—figurative, literal, and psychic—in the world. The tsunami wiped the slate clean, erasing entire villages and all that they embodied.

Not surprising, mental health professionals are concerned about the survivors. Uncertainty, isolation, and fear of radiation are daily concerns. As one psychiatric epidemiologist explained, "People are utterly fearful and deeply angry."[101]

But the psychic impact extended well beyond Tohoku. March 11 forced all Japanese to look hard at foundational beliefs about themselves and their society, about who they are and the country that they have made. In some cases, March 11 offered validation and affirmation; in others, the record is less impressive. Hayashi Toshihiko, a professor emeritus of Osaka University and the director of research at the Asia Pacific Institute of Research, explained that "natural disasters reveal us and the hidden agenda, the resilience of our society. When something big happens, a crack opens, and we see deeply into society and everyday life."[102] Immediately after March 11, Hayashi saw volunteerism, compassion, and a strong sense of solidarity among the Japanese. "Good things spring up in times of hell."

Some Japanese felt a new sense of purpose. March 11 "somehow gave us the rediscovery of the strengths of Japanese society," explained Nakanishi Hiroshi, a professor of international studies at Kyoto University's School of Law. "We talk about two lost decades politically and economically. We have a sense of decline and increasing difficulty in the present and for the future. . . . But the Japanese people took the disaster in a civilized way, and that gave us a sense of pride. The Japanese people are regaining our belief in ourselves."[103]

Young Japanese in particular discovered a sense of community and common purpose. Yamazaki Yoriko, a student at Keio University's School of Law, suggested that "before March 11, people felt vague about their identity as Japanese. Now they have this mission to contribute to Japan and the role Japanese will play in the world. It strengthened the idea of what it means to be Japanese."[104] Her friend, Igata Akira, a PhD student at Keio, agreed: "Before March 11, there was no sense of community or Japanese-ness. Now, we feel like all of us are in the same boat and have to think about the future."[105]

Agawa Naoyuki, a former lawyer and diplomat who is a vice president at Keio University, saw this phenomenon more broadly. "For the first time in Japan's recent history, something terrible happened, and young people in particular had a sense of what it means to be Japanese. For the first time, they saw that they could be of help." Agawa believes that this generation has acquired a new sense of purpose—"to work hard and be united."[106] The searing impact of March 11 may fade, but Agawa believes that spirit will remain, ready to reassert itself when needed.

For Ishinabe Hiroko, a former TV producer who grew up in Ofunato, one of the towns hardest hit by the tsunami, March 11 helped the Japanese rediscover "what they are supposed to be." While some observers were impressed by Japanese stoicism and resilience in the face of catastrophe, Ishinabe was dismissive of their applause: "Maybe the Western world thought the absence of violence and unrest was great. But from a Japanese point of view, it wasn't even a point of contention."[107] Yet for all the devastation, she saw potential benefit in March 11. It "unleashed what Japanese are supposed to be, not what Japanese are." Pressed to explain, she enumerated: "A lifestyle in harmony with nature, values that don't put yourself over others." Some dispute whether the result is the "real" Japan or an idealized version. Regardless of its accuracy, many Japanese believe in it. The reassertion of traditional Japanese values is one expression of a powerful reaction to the events of March 11.

That sense of community became a rallying point for the nation. Then prime minister Kan Naoto popularized the notion of *kizuna*, a word that means "bond" or "connection."[108] It headlined his note of thanks to the world a month after the catastrophe, as well as a similar letter to the Chinese people published the same day in the *People's Daily*.[109] It quickly became ubiquitous as the all-purpose representative word for the efforts to build ties within Japan or with Japan after March 11. It was used in official statements and exchange programs. The chief abbot of

Kiyomizu-dera Temple in Kyoto selected it in his annual designation of a kanji that best represented 2011, the Japan Kanji Aptitude Testing Foundation chose it as the kanji that best reflects the events of 2011, and it was among the top ten in the annual list of buzzwords compiled by publisher Jiyu Kokuminsha in 2011.[110] Even a center-left Kizuna Party was formed in January 2012 by former members of the Democratic Party of Japan.

Kizuna draws on the Japanese people's long-held belief that they are a single community united by blood and heritage. Scholarly debate about the validity of this construct is extensive. As one text argues, there has been an "attempt to reify images of Japan as a community united by elemental themes of race and spirit and culture. All of these interpretations emphasize the group, group effort and the ethical, cultural and class homogeneity of Japanese society."[111] While it is unlikely that Prime Minister Kan, a progressive, was deliberately propagating a conservative meme, he was giving voice to a deeply felt belief among the Japanese that they are all citizens of one country and connected to each other, and that the events of March 11 had a special relevance for all of them. And, sure enough, a 2012 public opinion poll conducted by the Cabinet Office found that almost 80 percent of the 6,059 respondents said that the 2011 disaster had impressed on them the importance of connectedness with society to a greater extent than before.[112] For this group, kizuna was a worthy means—a way to justify *doing* things—as well as an end in itself: Creating kizuna was a desirable goal.

"The Disaster Broke Us Apart"

The attention paid to kizuna—indeed, the very need to trumpet it—underscored the falsity of its most basic premise, however.[113] The Japanese did not feel tied to each other. In Japan, the farther one got from Tohoku, the less important the disaster seemed. The prevailing view in roundtables with Japanese university students was that they felt no real connection to the victims in Tohoku. For them, mentioning kizuna generated eye rolling and snorts of derision. Ohara Akane, a third-year politics student at Doshisha University in Kyoto, put it succinctly: "March 11 was news from a faraway place. It really had no impact on us. We feel sad, but nothing has really changed in our lives."[114] This was not the view of a callous, selfish student; instead, it was an honest acknowledgment that these students didn't identify with the victims and felt no more connected to them than to victims of any other disaster. For this group, the emphasis on kizuna only underscored how weak most ties are. The idea that all Japanese were connected to each other—a powerful trope in modern Japan—was revealed as fiction as many Japanese struggled to empathize with the Tohoku victims but failed.

A third group—a minority but loud—considered the use of kizuna as a cynical attempt to bamboozle people. These people called out the proponents of kizuna for perpetrating a fraud and for exploiting the crises that followed March 11 to push a fictionalized version of Japan onto a credulous and accepting population. They see kizuna not as a shock absorber, as Prime Minister Kan intended, but as a means to level expectations, to impose new obligations, and to reassert control over the community. Students at the prestigious, private Aoyama Gakuin University in Tokyo were skeptical about the period of national mourning that followed March 11, when the country halted all events that might be thought frivolous or disrespectful to the feelings of the Tohoku victims. "Moral consumerism," however, prevailed. Festivals were called off, cherry blossom viewing parties—a spring standard—were abandoned, and consumers stayed home rather than go out for dinner or indulge in shopping. Emotionally, they recognized the need to acknowledge the suffering of the Tohoku people, and they all conformed. Intellectually, they saw it as artificial and formal, with little real impact and probably even of little concern to the people of Tohoku.[115]

Commentator Tamamoto Masaru offered a scathing assessment of this thinking, dismissing it as a "village mentality" that is intended to block change. For him the picture of Japan as a village society is not a warm and fuzzy motif but is, instead, "a pathological and paralyzing condition." He charged that "the village norm is so embedded and tightly woven, there is little room for critical thought to dissolve paralyzing illusions. . . . Postwar Japan remains a village of submissive and passive peasants, bound by a smothering dosage of social cohesion, each part geared to every other part, blocking the possibility of reinvention."[116]

Cultural commentator Azuma Hiroki went further, arguing that March 11 did not just expose kizuna as a myth but also undermined the very concept of kizuna. In a powerful essay written days after the disaster, Azuma observed that the residents of Tohoku "faced truly solitary decisions. . . . Discrepancies in the sense of urgency caused by the differences in geographical area, not to mention family structure and income, further aggravate the discordance. . . . The accident at the Fukushima nuclear plant has not united the people's hearts into one. It has ripped them apart."[117] The seemingly random circumstances that separated victims from survivors meant that life had become "probabilistic . . . there was absolutely no meaning behind such selection. . . . The disaster broke us apart. We were stripped of meaning, stripped of narrative, and turned into a probabilistic existence." Azuma did not stop there, however. As he pursued his reasoning he concluded that the events of March 11 exposed a more fundamental truth about Japan. "The fantasy that all Japanese are middle-class vanished a long time ago. And postwar Japan has not produced a single principle beyond equality. Japanese people have not been able to coalesce unless 'everyone is the same.' . . . Faced with the same disaster, the gravity of the damage and the ability to respond to it differ according to each person's conditions . . . we became aware that 'everyone is not the same.'"

Kimoto Takeshi, an assistant professor of Japanese at the University of Oklahoma, agreed, noting that the entire nuclear power project rested on a bifurcation within Japan between those who would bear the risks of nuclear energy and everyone else. He reckoned that "Fukushima suffers from the consequences of the nuclear accident on behalf of the metropolitan population."[118] He added that the injustice of this "sacrificial logic" was exacerbated by cases of discrimination against evacuees because of fears of radiation.[119]

The logical extension of Kimoto's argument targets Japan's consumer culture, and many commentators were quick to make the connection. Sociologist Yoshimi Shunya argued that the nuclear accident was "a manmade disaster, the consequence of a situation created by postwar Japan's economic growth." He found the roots of the crisis in the decisions made in the aftermath of World War II: the pursuit of nuclear energy to promote an industrial revolution in Japan and the readiness to shelter under the US nuclear deterrent. The events of March 11 raised doubts about the wisdom of those choices, revealed a strong distrust among the public toward science and technology, and constituted the end of "the affluent postwar" era.[120]

The emptiness of consumerism and the fraying of ties between individuals— the erosion of the sense of community that prompted the kizuna boom—were linked in the minds of many artists who tried to make sense of March 11. Writers honed in on this sense of anomie and loss. A month after March 11, the editors of *Monkey Business*, "the leading journal of new writing in Japan," asked seventeen writers and artists to offer thoughts on "what they wish Japan had today." Novelist Shibasaki Tomoka wanted neighborhood cafeterias where people could spend time together, "get to know one another, even if they didn't necessarily chat or became close friends (although obviously it would be great if they did). Whether they talk or not, just seeing each other regularly would turn strangers into acquaintances, even if only on the level of a familiar face."[121] Critic Uchida Tatsuru wanted to build two new temples for modern Japan. In an empty field near an Osaka railroad station, he wanted to construct a Great Buddha, as "an oasis of calm in the midst of Osaka's materialistic clatter and convulsions." In Tokyo, he wanted to see a nuclear power station transformed into a Shinto shrine "for the purposes of spiritual regeneration and the pacification of angry gods." These two great offerings to the gods are intended to assuage a broader sense of unease, a feeling that the country has lost its direction and misplaced its energies.

Echoing Yoshimi, Uchida suggested that "the whole archipelago needs to quit the modern age and go cold turkey for a while."[122]

Kakuta Mitsuyo explored the emptiness of consumerism in "Pieces," the story of a middle-aged woman who is forced to take stock when she learns her husband was with another woman when the lights went out on March 11. While she enjoyed the trappings of success, the discovery of her husband's infidelity forces her to see that "to acquire was not to be happy." The flip side of that simple reality is also true: "Loss was not the root of unhappiness." It is a lesson about both the significance of the consumer impulses of modern society—"in the same way happiness could not be reduced to acquiring, neither could unhappiness be reduced to loss"—and the Buddhist truth that life is an inexorable mix of light and darkness, good and bad, having and losing. We cannot know one without the other.[123]

The loss of connection is central to Ikezawa Natsuki's "Grandma's Bible," the story of Kimura, a man who cancels a move to Arizona and returns to his hometown. Kimura is driven to do so by equal parts guilt and loss. Guilt because he sent a parcel to his brother's house that included his grandmother's Bible, and he scheduled its delivery between two and four o'clock on the afternoon of March 11, accidentally ensuring that his sibling would be at home when the tsunami struck. Loss because his return to his hometown is an attempt to reclaim his roots to that family and because the enduring image of the story is that of the Bible floating along the ocean floor. The gaping hole in his life is made plain by the mundane bureaucratic procedures of his move. He wants to transfer his place of residence to his brother's old house but wonders "whether you can change registration to a nonexistent address."[124]

"The End of Our Illusions"

A senior government official captured this spirit when he assessed the impact of March 11: "It marked the end of our illusions. We thought our economy would grow forever, that the national debt could be shouldered by future generations and the US would protect us. Now the euphoria is over."[125] The events of that day stripped away the comforts and certainties that dominated Japanese life and obliged the Japanese to acknowledge painful realities.

The pervasive sense that Japan had lost its way and the mounting dissatisfaction with the country's prospects would provide yet more reasons for the Japanese people to seize the opportunity afforded by March 11 to embrace change that had remained stubbornly out of reach. In a Pew Research Center survey shortly after the crisis, 58 percent of the Japanese thought that their country would be strengthened by the tragedy; 32 percent thought Japan would be weakened.[126]

Photographer Yoneda Tomoko gave voice to this inclination when she explained how the events of March 11 reminded her of Berlin when the wall fell in 1989. "It felt like witnessing a paradigm shift. . . . I understood that things we had believed in because they were right in front of us would not necessarily last forever and indeed had the potential to collapse or become something else entirely. . . . I think Japan is experiencing a similar paradigm shift after March 11."[127]

The status quo proved resilient, however. In his assessment of March 11, Richard Samuels concluded that "the crisis may have unstuck incremental changes," but he discerned "no shift that was not already under way."[128] The Japanese public agreed. A year after the accident, Pew Research Center polling showed just 39 percent thought Japan would be strengthened by the crisis—a nineteen-point drop from the previous poll—while 47 percent feared the country would continue to slide. Three-quarters of respondents, or 78 percent, were dissatisfied with the direction in which the country was heading.[129] Even a massive physical and economic jolt would not prove sufficient to change Japan's course, even if it did shake fundamental conceptions of Japanese identity.

Notes

1. Chaibong, "Preface," in Youngshik and Pempel, *Japan in Crisis*, 8 (see introduction, n. 1).
2. Funabashi, "Introduction," in Funabashi and Kushner, *Examining Japan's Lost Decades*, xxii (see chap. 2, n. 41).
3. Public Relations Department, "44th Opinion Survey on the General Public's Views and Behavior, January 14, 2011," English translation, Bank of Japan, February 14, 2011, https://www.boj.or.jp/en/research/o_survey/ishiki1101.pdf.
4. Author interview, Tokyo, July 10, 2012.
5. Cited in Tsunekawa Keiichi, "Toward a Balanced Assessment," in *Five Years After: Reassessing Japan's Responses to the Earthquake, Tsunami and the Nuclear Disaster*, ed. Tsunekawa Keiichi (Tokyo: University of Tokyo Press, 2016), 6n1.
6. Cited in Japan External Trade Organization, "Japan Faces Challenges of Earthquake, Tsunami, and Nuclear Disaster," *Focus Newsletter*, June 2011, 5, https://www.jetro.go.jp/ext_images/en/reports/survey/pdf/2011_06_other.pdf.
7. "Anxiety in Japan Grows as Death Toll Steadily Mounts," CNN, March 14, 2011, http://edition.cnn.com/2011/WORLD/asiapcf/03/13/japan.quake/index.html.
8. Okada Norio et al., "The 2011 Eastern Japan Great Earthquake Disaster: Overview and Comments," *International Journal of Disaster Risk Science* 2, no. 1 (2011), https://link.springer.com/content/pdf/10.1007%2Fs13753-011-0004-9.pdf.
9. Hirata Keiko and Mark Warschauer, *Japan: The Paradox of Harmony* (New Haven CT: Yale University Press, 2014), 6.

10. Lydia Smith, "Kobe Earthquake 20th Anniversary: Facts about the Devastating 1995 Great Hanshin Earthquake," *International Business Times*, January 16, 2015, https://www.ibtimes.co.uk/kobe-earthquake-20th-anniversary-facts-about -devastating-1995-great-hanshin-earthquake-1483786.

11. Videos of these scenes are available on YouTube. They are worth watching, both to try to grasp the magnitude of the devastation and to understand how surreal a catastrophe of this scale is when it unfolds in slow motion.

12. The last estimates are based on how high the wave had to be to reach as far inland as it did. While much larger than readings from most of the instruments, they are consistent with (while exceeding) historical high-water marks.

13. What follows is an overview of tumultuous events. The best synthesis I've found is Kenji Kushida, "Japan's Fukushima Nuclear Disaster: Narrative, Analysis, and Recommendations," APARC Working Papers (Stanford, CA: Walter R. Shorenstein Asia-Pacific Research Center, Stanford University, 2012). This summary draws heavily on his account. Also recommended is the report by the Independent Investigation Commission on the Fukushima Nuclear Accident, *The Fukushima Daiichi Nuclear Power Station Disaster: Investigating the Myth and Reality* (Abingdon: Routledge Earthscan, 2014). Hereafter known as RJIF (Rebuild Japan Initiative Foundation) Report.

14. What did the most damage to the plant is still disputed. Kushida, "Japan's Fukushima Nuclear Disaster," 6, points out that the Tohoku earthquake "fell exactly within the range of resonance frequencies for much of the nuclear facilities, creating massive damage even before the tsunami hit."

15. TEPCO engineers confirmed a meltdown on May 12.

16. Kurokawa Kiyoshi, "Message from the Chairman," in *The Official Report of the Fukushima Nuclear Accident Independent Investigation Commission* (Tokyo: National Diet of Japan, 2012), 9, https://www.nirs.org/fukushima/naiic_report.pdf.

17. There are also several journalistic accounts of the events, but while rich in detail, they are thin in analysis.

18. National Diet of Japan, *Official Report*.

19. Gerald Curtis, "Stop Blaming Fukushima on Japan's Culture," *Financial Times*, July 20, 2012.

20. Yuri Kageyama, "AP Interview: Japan Nuke Probe Head Defends Report," Yahoo .com, September 13, 2012, https://www.yahoo.com/news/ap-interview-japan -nuke-probe-head-defends-report-012348377-finance.html.

21. Investigation Committee on the Accident at Fukushima Nuclear Power Stations of Tokyo Electric Power Company, "Final Report" (Tokyo: Secretariat of the Investigation Committee, July 23, 2012), http://www.cas.go.jp/jp/seisaku/icanps /eng/final-report.html. Also see the executive summary, http://www.cas.go.jp/jp /seisaku/icanps/eng/finalgaiyou.pdf.

22. There is a dispute whether Prime Minister Kan countermanded the order to inject seawater or merely asked whether it might trigger recriticality.

23. TEPCO, "Release of the Fukushima Nuclear Accidents Investigation Report," press release, June 20, 2012, http://www.tepco.co.jp/en/press/corp-com/release /2012/1205638_1870.html.

24. Nagata Kazuaki, "TEPCO Lashes Prime Minister's Office," *Japan Times*, June 21, 2012, https://web.archive.org/web/20121101132556/http://www.japantimes.co .jp/text/nn20120621a3.html.

25. Nuclear Reform Special Task Force, "Fundamental Policy for the Reform of TEPCO Nuclear Power Organization" (Tokyo: TEPCO, October 12, 2012), 2, https://www7.tepco.co.jp/wp-content/uploads/hd05-01-08-000-121012e0101 .pdf.

26. RJIF Report, 3.

27. The Rebuild Japan Initiative Foundation changed its name to the Asia Pacific Initiative (https://apinitiative.org/en/about-us/) in 2017 and broadened its mission.

28. Funabashi Yochi and Kitazawa Kay, "Fukushima in Review: A Complex Disaster, a Disastrous Response," *Bulletin of the Atomic Scientists*, March 1, 2012, 1–13.

29. RJIF Report, 3.

30. Ibid., 51.

31. Funabashi and Kitazawa, "Fukushima in Review," 1–13.

32. RJIF Report, 53.

33. Funabashi and Kitazawa, "Fukushima in Review," 1–13.

34. Ibid.

35. Nuclear Reform Special Task Force, "Fundamental Policy."

36. Phred Dvorak and Rebecca Smith, "Japan Utility Says Crisis Avoidable," *Wall Street Journal*, October 12, 2012.

37. Quote in preceding subhead comes from Idogawa Katsutaka, mayor of Futaba town, interview with Associated Press, March 6, 2012.

38. Government of Japan, "Road to Recovery," March 2012, 3, https://japan.kantei .go.jp/policy/documents/2012/__icsFiles/afieldfile/2012/03/07/road_to_recovery .pdf.

39. Armand Varvaeck and James Daniell, "Japan—366 Days after the Quake," Earthquake-Report.com, March 10, 2012, http://earthquake-report.com/2012 /03/10/japan-366-days-after-the-quake-19000-lives-lost-1-2-million-buildings -damaged-574-billion/.

40. Justin McCurry, "Japan Earthquake: 100,000 Children Displaced, Says Charity," *The Guardian*, March 15, 2011, https://www.theguardian.com/world/2011/mar /15/japan-earthquake-children-displaced-charity.

41. Abe Tadahiko, "A Suggestion for Japanese Industry after the Great Tohoku Earthquake," *The Lessons of the Great Tohoku Earthquake and Its Effects on Japan's Economy*

(Tokyo: Fujitsu Research Institute, November 17, 2011), http://www.fujitsu.com /jp/group/fri/en/column/message/2011/2011-11-17.html.

42. Pew Research Center, "Japanese Wary of Nuclear Energy: Disaster 'Weakened' Nation," *Global Attitudes and Trends*, June 5, 2012, http://www.pewglobal.org /2012/06/05/japanese-wary-of-nuclear-energy/.

43. James Daniell, "CATDAT Damaging Earthquakes Database, 2010—Year in Review," Center for Disaster Management and Risk Reduction Technology Research Report (Karlsruhe: Karlsruhe Institute of Technology, 2011), https://earthquake -report.com/wp-content/uploads/2011/03/CATDAT-EQ-Data-1st-Annual-Review -2010-James-Daniell-03-03-2011.pdf.

44. Author interview, Osaka, November 9, 2012.

45. Earthquake Engineering Research Institute, "The March 11, 2011, The Great East Japan (Tohoku) Earthquake and Tsunami: Societal Dimensions," Special Earthquake Report (Oakland, CA: Earthquake Engineering Research Institute, August 2011), 11, http://www.eqclearinghouse.org/2011-03-11-sendai/files/2011/03/Japan -SocSci-Rpt-hirez-rev.pdf.

46. See, for example, James Daniell, Friedemann Wenzel, and Bijan Khazai, "The Cost of Historical Earthquakes Today—Economic Analysis since 1900 through the Use of CATDAT," Paper for Australian Earthquake Engineering Society Conference, Perth, November 14, 2010, https://www.aees.org.au/wp-content/uploads/2013 /11/07-Daniell.pdf.

47. John W. Schoen, "Insurance Industry Well-Shielded from Japan Quake," MSNBC .com, March 16, 2011, http://www.nbcnews.com/id/42095196/ns/business-world _business/t/insurance-industry-well-shielded-japan-quake/#.Ws3tdi-B2Ho.

48. Yoneyama Hidetaka, "The Effects of the Great Earthquake on Japan's Macro Economy," *The Lessons of the Great Tohoku Earthquake and Its Effects on Japan's Economy* (Tokyo: Fujitsu Research Institute, April 8, 2011), http://jp.fujitsu.com/group/fri /en/column/message/2011/2011-04-08.html.

49. Ministry of Economy, Trade, and Industry, "East Japan Great Earthquake Disaster: The World Economy, Stabilization Efforts by Coordination of Nations," *White Paper on International Economy and Trade* (Tokyo: METI, 2011), http://www.meti .go.jp/english/report/downloadfiles/2011WhitePaper/1-4.pdf.

50. Kamata Isao, "The Great East Japan Earthquake: A View on Its Implication for Japan's Economy," *La Follette Policy Report* (University of Wisconsin–Madison) 21, no. 1 (Fall 2011): 13, https://www.lafollette.wisc.edu/images/publications/policy reports/policyreport21_1.pdf#page=12.

51. METI, "East Japan Great Earthquake."

52. R. Colin Johnson, "Shuttered Japanese Chip Makers Threaten IT," *Smarter Technology .com,* March 23, 2011, https://www.flickr.com/groups/1467908@N22/discuss /72157626213375891/.

53. Ibid.

54. Murray McBride, "One Year Later, Impact of 'Great Tohoku' Quake Still Being Felt," Newswise, March 2, 2012, http://www.newswise.com/articles/one-year-later -impact-of-great-tohoku-quake-still-being-felt.

55. UN Scientific Committee on the Effects of Atomic Radiation, "Interim Findings of Fukushima-Daiichi Assessment Presented at the Annual Meeting of UNSCEAR" (Vienna: United Nations Information Service, May 23, 2012), http://www.unis .unvienna.org/unis/pressrels/2012/unisous144.html.

56. John Ten Hoeve and Mark Jacobson, "Worldwide Health Effects of the Fukushima Daiichi Nuclear Accident," *Energy and Environmental Science* 9 (June 26, 2012). This study is hotly disputed, with one critique arguing that the lead author is "an antinuclear campaigner pursuing an ideological agenda." See also Mark Lynas, "Why Fukushima Death Toll Projections Are Based on Junk Science," *Mark Lynas Environmental News and Comment* (blog), July 18, 2012, http://www.marklynas .org/2012/07/fukushima-death-tolls-junk-science/.

57. Hrabrin Bachev and Ito Fusao, "Fukushima Nuclear Disaster—Implications for Japanese Agriculture and Food Chains" (Sendai: Institute of Agricultural Economics, Tohoku University, September 3, 2013), Paper No. 49462, *Munich Personal RePEc Archive*, https://mpra.ub.uni-muenchen.de/49462/1/MPRA_paper_49462.pdf.

58. Ibid.

59. Raymond Van der Putten, "Japan: One Year after the Tohoku Earthquake," *Conjoncture*, March 2012, 16.

60. "Gaishi no Nihon banare kasoku: Tainichi toushi, 11 nen ryuusyutsu chou endaka, teiseichou de," *Nikkei Shimbun*, February 18, 2012 (in Japanese), https://www .nikkei.com/article/DGXDASFS1702G_X10C12A2MM8000/.

61. Tadahiko, "Suggestion for Japanese Industry."

62. "Naikaku no shinsai taiou 'hyouka shinai' 60%: Asahi Shimbun yoron chousa," *Asahi Shimbun*, April 18, 2011 (in Japanese), http://www.asahi.com/special/08003 /TKY201104170326.html; and "Fukkou torikumi 'hyouka suru' 18%: Asahi Shimbun yoron chousa," *Asahi Shimbun*, September 10, 2011 (in Japanese), http://www.asahi.com/special/minshu/TKY20110909617.html.

63. Author interview, Tokyo, July 10, 2012.

64. Kenji Kushida, "The Fukushima Natural Disaster and the Democratic Party of Japan: Leadership, Structures and Information Challenges during the Crisis," *Japanese Political Economy* 40, no. 1 (Spring 2014): 30.

65. Kyodo News, "Tsunami Alert Softened Days before 3/11," *Japan Times,* February 27, 2012, https://www.japantimes.co.jp/news/2012/02/27/national/tsunami-alert -softened-days-before-311/#.Wz-nii2ZOf4.

66. Japan Atomic Industrial Forum, "TEPCO Forecast 10 Meter Tsunami," Earthquake Report No. 224, October 4, 2011.

67. Jeff Kingston, "Power Politics: Japan's Resilient Nuclear Village," *Asia-Pacific Journal* 10, no. 43 (October 29, 2012).

68. Nuclear Reform Special Task Force, "Fundamental Policy."

69. A good history is Goto Kazuko, "Japan's Role as Leader for Nuclear Nonproliferation," FAS Issue Brief (Washington, DC: Federation of American Scientists, December 2012).

70. Iida Tetsunari, "What Is Required for a New Society and Politics: The Potential of Japanese Civil Society," *Asia-Pacific Journal* 10, no. 46 (November 12, 2012). For example, in 2007, TEPCO admitted to falsifying safety records at the Fukushima No. 1 reactor. Eventually the company confessed to falsification of data at thirteen of the seventeen nuclear power units it operated, with 199 incidents in total. ("TEPCO Must Probe 199 Plant Check Data Falsification Coverups," *Japan Times*, February 2, 2007; and Citizens Nuclear Information Center, "Revelation of Endless N-damage Cover-ups," *Nuke Info Tokyo* 92 (November/December 2002), www.cnic.jp/english/newsletter/nit92/nit92articles/nit92coverup.html. Seven of Japan's ten utilities admitted to falsifying nuclear repair and maintenance records. (Kingston, "Power Politics.")

71. Adam Westlake, "NRA Says Active Fault Lines under Third Nuclear Plant Most Likely Active," *Japan Daily Press*, December 12, 2012.

72. Funabashi and Kitazawa, "Fukushima in Review," 13–14.

73. RJIF Report, 181.

74. Funabashi and Kitazawa, "Fukushima in Review."

75. Richard Samuels, "Japan's Rhetoric of Crisis: Prospects for Change after 3.11," *Journal of Japanese Studies* 39, no. 1 (2013): 104.

76. National Diet of Japan, *Official Report*, executive summary, 20.

77. Satoh, "Post-3.11 Japan," 6 (see chap. 3, n. 32).

78. Linda Sieg, "Nuclear Issue Puts Increasing Pressure on Japanese Government," Reuters, July 17, 2012, https://www.reuters.com/article/us-japan-nuclear/nuclear-issue-puts-increasing-pressure-on-japan-government-idUSBRE86G09720120717?feedType=RSS&feedName=worldNews.

79. "Rigged Opinions on Nuclear Power," *Japan Times,* November 28, 2011, https://www.japantimes.co.jp/opinion/2011/11/28/editorials/rigging-opinions-on-nuclear-power/#.Wyk-YC2ZOf4. See also, Jonathan Soble, "Japan Reveals Nuclear Safety Overhaul," *Financial Times,* August 5, 2011.

80. Nippon Foundation for Social Innovation, "Chairman's Remarks," International Expert Symposium in Fukushima—Radiation and Health Risks, Fukushima, September 11, 2011, http://www.nippon-foundation.or.jp/en/who/message/speeches/2011/14.html.

81. "Post-Disaster Japan Turns Skeptical," Edelman Japan, January 2012, https://www.edelman.com/2012-edelman-trust-barometer.

82. All figures from Edelman, "Japan and the Fragility of Trust," *2012 Edleman Trust Barometer: Annual Global Study,* 5, https://sharedvaluemedia.com/wp-content /uploads/2013/04/79026497-2012-Edelman-Trust-Barometer-Executive-Summary -1.pdf.

83. Author interview, Tokyo, July 19, 2012.

84. Tsunekawa, "Toward a Balanced Assessment," in Tsunekawa, *Five Years After*, 11.

85. Japan Ministry of Defense, "Great East Japan Earthquake and SDF's Activities," *Japan Defense Focus*, March 2012, http://www.mod.go.jp/e/jdf/sp2012/sp2012_02 .html.

86. Yoshizaki Tomonori, "The Military's Role in Disaster Relief Operations: A Japanese Perspective," Paper for National Institute for Defense Studies International Symposium on Security Affairs, Tokyo, November 2011, http://www.nids.mod.go.jp /english/event/symposium/pdf/2011/e_06.pdf.

87. While the SDF effort has been the subject of particular attention and is the focus here, the contribution of other Japanese emergency responders must not be overlooked. It is estimated that 389,000 policemen were dispatched to crisis zones by June 20, 2011, as part of the Interprefectural Emergency Rescue Unit, along with 120,000 firefighters from 44 prefectures and 193 medical assistance teams. See Tsunekawa, "Toward a Balanced Assessment," in Tsunekawa, *Five Years After*, 10.

88. Cabinet Office, Government of Japan, "Public Opinion Survey on the Self-Defense Forces and Defense Issue," January 2012 (in Japanese), https://survey.gov-online .go.jp/h23/h23-bouei/index.html.

89. Kamiura Motoaki, "Self Defense Forces Gain New Cachet as Emergency Responders," *Cultural News*, May 2011, http://www.culturalnews.com/?p=4689.

90. See, for example, Sunaga Kazuo, "Japan's Experience of HADR Operations: A Case of the East Japan Great Earthquake of 2011," ASEAN Regional Forum, Phnom Penh, May 24, 2012, http://aseanregionalforum.asean.org/files/Archive/19th /ARF%20DOD,%20Phnom%20Penh,%2024May2012/Annex%20D2%20 -%20Presentation%20by%20Japan.pdf.

91. Weston Konishi, "Is Disaster Relief Revolutionising Japan's Security Affairs?," *East Asia Forum*, July 6, 2016, http://www.eastasiaforum.org/2016/07/06/is-disaster -relief-revolutionising-japans-security-affairs/. Konishi concludes that structural constraints will keep this promise from being realized, however.

92. All figures from Japan Ministry of Foreign Affairs, "List of Relief Supplies and Donations from Overseas," December 28, 2012, http://www.mofa.go.jp/j_info /visit/incidents/pdfs/r_goods.pdf.

93. The story of the marines in Okinawa is a long and unhappy tale, and it is probably the single biggest problem for the US-Japan alliance. Marines have an unsavory image among Okinawans, and a city has grown up around their air base. An accident at the facility, such as an aircraft crash that has civilian casualties, is likely

to cause a major crisis for the alliance. In many ways, however, the Okinawans' unhappiness with the marines (and the entire US military presence on their island) is a proxy for the discrimination Okinawans have felt and continue to suffer. In short, they believe that their home is the dumping ground for a military presence that most Japanese never feel.

94. Author interview, Tokyo, December 2, 2011. The US deployment and efforts to work with Japan were not without problems, as Richard Samuels explains in *3.11: Disaster and Change in Japan* (Ithaca, NY: Cornell University Press, 2013), 22–23, 94–95.

95. Public Relations Office, Cabinet Office, "Outline of 'Public Opinion Survey on the Self-Defense Forces (SDF) and Defense Issues,'" March 2012, 10, 18, http://www.mod.go.jp/e/d_act/others/pdf/public_opinion.pdf.

96. This and all subsequent quotes from author interview, Tokyo, July 22, 2012.

97. This and all subsequent quotes from author interview, Tokyo, July 12, 2012.

98. Mark Molesky, *This Gulf of Fire: The Destruction of Lisbon, or Apocalypse in the Age of Science and Reason* (New York: Random House, 2015).

99. Author interview, Fukuoka, November 26, 2012.

100. Quote in preceding subhead comes from Hayashi Toshihiko, author interview, Osaka, November 9, 2012.

101. Evelyn Bromet of State University of New York at Stony Brook, cited in Geoff Brumfiel, "Fukushima's Doses Tallied," *Nature* 485 (May 24, 2012): 423–24.

102. Author interview, Osaka, November 9, 2012.

103. Author interview, Kyoto, November 9, 2012.

104. Author interview, Tokyo, July 12, 2012. For this project, I conducted roundtables with students at universities in Tokyo, Osaka, and Kyoto. They were some of the most interesting and rewarding parts of my research.

105. Author interview, Tokyo, July 12, 2012.

106. Author interview, Tokyo, July 23, 2012.

107. Author interview, Tokyo, August 13, 2012.

108. Kan was talking about *kizuna* before March 11. Addressing the World Economic Forum's Davos conclave in January 2011, he said that he would be "reopening Japan" and using kizuna to dull the effects of that process.

109. The letter is on the prime minister's website: Kan Naoto, "Kizuna: The Bonds of Friendship," April 11, 2011, www.kantei.go.jp/foreign/kan/statement/201104/11kizuna_e.html.

110. Michael Gakuran, "Top 60 Japanese Buzzwords of 2011," *Gakuranman* (blog), December 1, 2011, http://gakuran.com/top-60-japanese-buzzwords-of-2011/#Bonds.

111. Irwin Scheiner, "The Japanese Village: Real, Imagined, Contested," in *Mirror of Modernity: Invented Traditions of Modern Japan*, ed. Stephen Vlastos (Berkeley: University of California Press, 1998), 67.

112. Cabinet Office of Japan, Shakai ishiki ni kansuru yoron chosa [Survey on the perceptions of society], *Tokyo Naifukaku*, 2012 (in Japanese), https://survey.gov -online.go.jp/h23/h23-shakai/2-2.html.

113. Quote in preceding subhead comes from Azuma Hiroki, "The Disaster Broke Us Apart," *After the Disaster* 2 (Autumn 2011): 8–17.

114. Author interview, Kyoto, November 7, 2012.

115. Author roundtable, Tokyo, July 19, 2012.

116. Tamamoto Masaru, "It Takes a Village, Alas: Japan, Land of Peasants, Embraces Conformity and Decline," Zócalo Public Square (Arizona State University), November 15, 2012, http://www.zocalopublicsquare.org/2012/11/15/it-takes-a -village-alas/ideas/nexus/#.

117. All quotes from Azuma, "Disaster Broke Us Apart."

118. Kimoto Takeshi, "Post-3/11 Literature: Two Writers from Fukushima," *World Literature Today* 86, no. 1 (January/February 2012): 14–18.

119. Ibid.

120. Yoshimi Shunya, "Radioactive Rain and the American Umbrella," *Journal of Asia Studies* 71, no. 2 (May 2012): 319.

121. Shibasaki Tomoka, quoted in "What Do You Wish We Had in Japan Today?," *Monkey Business: New Writing from Japan*, 2012, 14–15.

122. Uchida Tatsuru, quoted in ibid., 7–8.

123. Kakuta Mitsuyo, "Pieces," in *March Was Made of Yarn: Reflections on the Japanese Earthquake, Tsunami, and Nuclear Meltdown*, ed. Elmer Luke and David Karashima (New York: Vintage Books, 2012), 120, 121.

124. Ikezawa Natsuki, "Grandma's Bible," in Luke and Karashima, *March Was Made of Yarn*, 106.

125. Author interview, Tokyo, July 11, 2012.

126. Pew Research Center, "Japanese Wary of Nuclear Energy."

127. Andrew Maerkle and Natsuko Odate, "The Multiple Lives of Images," *ART-iT*, February 1, 2012, http://www.art-it.asia/u/admin_ed_feature_e/OICutqp7GDX TKQg9be5P/.

128. Samuels, *3.11*, 183–84.

129. Pew Research Center, "Japanese Wary of Nuclear Energy."

6

ABE SHINZO'S TRIUMPHANT RETURN

By December 2012 Japan had come full circle. The 2008 Lehman shock reversed the country's nascent economic recovery, paving the way for the 2009 political earthquake in which voters rejected the Liberal Democratic Party after spending decades in power and gave the Democratic Party of Japan a chance to govern. That experiment proved disastrous, however, and the 2010 Senkaku shock and the 2011 Tohoku triple catastrophe highlighted the DPJ's incompetence and the country's need for a steady, experienced government. Politically outmaneuvered, the DPJ was forced to call an election in December 2012, and headed by former prime minister Abe Shinzo, the LDP came roaring back, reversing the outcome of the 2009 ballot and claiming a mandate to lead the country. This chapter examines the second Abe interregnum through four lenses—economics, politics, foreign and security policy, and national identity—highlighting his mixed record and the way that some of his successes have contributed to subsequent failures.

Abenomics to the Rescue

Abe's ambitions have been clear. Since returning to power, Abe insisted that reports of Japan's demise were mistaken and that his country would remain in the first tier of nations and continue to play a role commensurate with both its size and its ambition to be a global leader. Within weeks of taking office, he visited the United States and put to rest any doubts about his and his country's role and purpose: "Japan is not and will never be a tier-two country. . . . I am back, . . . and so shall Japan be."[1] Japan's return required four prerequisites: stable leadership, a revitalized economy, assertive diplomacy, and a new approach to security policy. Abe intended to provide all four.

Abe insisted that he had learned from the mistakes of his first term as prime minister (2006–7) and promised voters (and the world) a laser-like focus on the economy. If nothing else, three years in the wilderness taught party strategists that their first priority in leading the government had to be a return to economic growth; social issues, no matter how integral to the vision of a "beautiful" Japan held by Abe and like-minded conservatives, should be subordinated to the bread-and-butter concerns of most voters. A recovery would restore national confidence, ensure stable leadership in Tokyo, and provide the means for a rejuvenated international presence. Abe and the LDP recognized that Japan would not be taken seriously if its economy remained stagnant or if it shrank. Without a vibrant economy, Japan would be overlooked in international councils, and the Japanese people would be more inclined to focus on domestic concerns. Neither is conducive to the international role that is demanded of a first-tier country.

Abe's blueprint for recovery bears his name, Abenomics. Six months into his tenure, Prime Minister Abe Shinzo's economic policies were touted as "the most interesting story in global economics,"[2] captivating the mainstream media, the blogosphere, and the economists who lurk in the blogosphere's depths. The prime minister graced the cover of *The Economist* in a Superman costume (with a yen symbol on his chest rather than an *S*) soaring over the Tokyo cityscape. Two years later the Abe administration was confident that Abenomics was progressing, but more objective reviews were mixed.

To advance revitalization, the new administration promoted Abenomics and its "three arrows." The first arrow is a monetary policy that aims for 2 percent inflation annually (and for ending fifteen years of deflation). It attempted to jump-start domestic demand by prodding consumers to spend, which would "pull" companies to produce more and hire more personnel. Success demanded a change in expectations (that prices will go up) and a growing money supply (to actually push prices up). The Bank of Japan (BOJ) took aim at that first objective in January 2013, less than a month after Abe took office, when it announced that it had changed its goal of 1 percent inflation to a target of 2 percent inflation. Critics argued that rhetoric alone was unlikely to have much impact, especially since the BOJ hadn't been able to hit the more modest 1 percent target. To back words with deeds, two months later, Abe forced the early retirement (by two weeks) of BOJ governor Shirakawa Masaaki and replaced him with Kuroda

Haruhiko, a monetary "dove" who was much more amenable to a loose-money policy. To give the 2 percent pledge more oomph, Kuroda and the BOJ promised an open-ended purchase of assets that would increase the base money supply about ¥5 trillion–¥7 trillion ($49 billion–$69 billion) each month. Over two years this asset purchase would grow as large as ¥270 trillion by the end of 2014.[3] The value of assets that the BOJ held reached 57 percent of GDP in 2014, or more than twice the size of both the US Federal Reserve's holdings, which are just 25 percent of GDP, and the European Central Bank's assets, which have dropped to 20 percent of GDP.[4] Shiozaki Yasuhisa, an LDP politician close to the prime minister, called this "bold monetary easing"[5]; more colorfully, it was referred to as monetary "shock and awe."[6]

The second arrow in Abenomics is fiscal policy, which includes the LDP's traditional resort to public works spending to provide domestic stimulus. In 2013 the new LDP-led Diet got to work quickly and passed a ¥10.3 trillion ($140 billion) supplemental budget that was supposed to create 600,000 jobs.[7] Abe added a second fiscal package of ¥5.5 trillion in April 2014 and a third package of ¥3.5 trillion in December 2014.[8] Fold in earthquake reconstruction-related outlays, and total spending through fiscal year 2015 rose to about ¥25 trillion (about $260 billion) from the previously anticipated ¥19 trillion ($200 billion).[9]

The third arrow consists of economic reforms to overcome structural obstacles to growth. In every assessment of Abenomics, this third arrow is its most important element. Without reform, monetary and fiscal measures are simply temporary boosts to the economy that will be swallowed up by inefficiencies that have impeded growth throughout the post–Cold War era. As Shiozaki explained, this arrow "goes to the core issues which have plagued Japan's economy for decades." They are intended to "strengthen the profitability of firms . . . by eliminating factors which block competitiveness and innovation." One prominent example is the call for more flexibility in labor regulations that will allow firms to shed unneeded workers when demand changes. If firms can't fire, then they won't hire.[10]

At first glance, the government walked the walk. The Cabinet Office established a Headquarters for Japan's Economic Revitalization, while the government-supported Industrial Competitiveness Council (chaired by the prime minister) and the Regulatory Reform Council worked on reform proposals ranging from regulatory reform to innovation and information technology policies.

In its first six months, Abenomics was a smashing success: The yen depreciated by 23 percent against the US dollar, cracking the ¥100 to the dollar mark and hitting a four-and-a-half year low; the Nikkei 225 index rose a blistering 74 percent; and Japan's GDP recorded 4.2 percent growth in the first quarter of 2013, outpacing every other developed economy and putting it on track for 3.5 percent growth for the year.[11] Over the next six months, success would be tempered, but an assessment by the Organization for Economic Cooperation and Development of Abenomics' first year was glowing.

> These initiatives helped to boost business confidence to its highest level since the 2008 crisis, while the Nikkei stock price index increased by 57 percent in 2013, its largest gain since 1972. Output growth accelerated to an annual rate of more than 3 percent in the first half of 2013, before slowing in the second half of the year. The new monetary framework has helped boost inflation expectations, with underlying inflation moving in to positive territory in late 2013. . . . The unemployment rate has also fallen gradually, reaching 3.7 percent in early 2014.[12]

Nominal GDP growth after eighteen months—a period that includes the consumption tax increase that ended the recovery for a quarter—recorded an annual pace of 2.3 percent, which was better than any equivalent period over the previous fifteen years (with the exception of the recovery from the 2008 global financial crisis). It also pushed core inflation to its highest levels for the same time frame.[13]

Four years later, however, the verdict was mixed. The Abe administration continued to tout its success in program updates titled "Abenomics Is Progressing!"[14] In January 2017 the good news included growth of ¥520 trillion between the fiscal years 2012 and 2015. During the same period, annual corporate profits increased by ¥20 trillion, unemployment had declined from 4.3 percent to 3.4 percent, and the level of dependency on government bonds decreased 12 percent.[15] A year earlier the government had proclaimed that "the deflationary situation" of the last fifteen years had been reversed: "The basic direction of prices has turned positive; both nominal and real GDP have increased." Bankruptcies reached their lowest level in twenty-five years, while the average rate of wage hikes was higher than the previous year and the highest in seventeen years.[16]

Others were not as optimistic, with an independent assessment concluding that Abenomics was a "paper tiger."[17] Japan's recovery from the global financial crisis was no better than that of the eurozone, with consumer spending continuing to fall and government spending staying largely flat for two years.[18] While the International Monetary Fund reported a 2.8 percent rise in GDP per capita from 2012 to 2015, this growth is considerably less than that of the previous three years, when Japanese GDP increased 6.4 percent.[19] Wages, including bonuses and overtime pay, adjusted for inflation fell in 2015 for the fourth consecutive decline, according to the labor ministry.[20] The 2 percent inflation target announced by BOJ governor Kuroda remained stubbornly out of reach despite nearly three years of unprecedented monetary stimulus—including a zero (and later negative) interest rate policy—and is unlikely to be met during his tenure. Fears are that slow growth, mounting debt, and limited room for monetary maneuver (courtesy of the negative interest rate policy) could produce an "Abegeddon."

The Third Arrow Misses the Mark

The third arrow of structural reform remains a source of frustration. Its failure is critical since most economists and observers believe that structural reform is key to the ultimate success of Abenomics. Here, the origin of the three arrows metaphor is worth recounting. Mori Motonari, a sixteenth-century Japanese warlord (although variants exist in most cultures), was concerned that feuding among his sons would cost them the realm he wanted to pass on to them. He called them together, gave each an arrow, and told them to break it. After easily doing so, he took another three arrows, put them together, and asked them to break them as a single group. They could not do it, thus making Mori's point: As individuals they were vulnerable; as a group they were strong. In virtually all explanations of Abenomics, the monetary and fiscal arrows are temporary stimuli intended to buy time for difficult structural reforms. The failure to make real progress on that front should undercut hopes for a sustained recovery. Shiozaki Yasuhisa, who is also one of Prime Minister Abe's confidantes, confessed, "If we miss the mark with this third arrow, I am afraid we may repeat not only 'a lost decade' or 'lost two decades,' but 'lost three decades.'"[21]

When the Abe government unveiled the third arrow in early June 2013, the response was near-universal disappointment; *The Economist* called it a "misfire" that reflected "timid attempts at reform."[22] The prime minister announced a series of ambitious targets: raising incomes by 3 percent a year so that per capita gross national income would grow more than ¥1.5 million ($14,970) in ten years, increasing power-related investment one and a half times to ¥30 trillion over the next decade, doubling the amount of inward foreign direct investment to ¥35 trillion by 2020, doubling farm exports by 2020, and tripling infrastructure exports, such as bullet trains and nuclear plants, to ¥30 trillion. In addition, the government sought to improve English-language instruction and to loosen rules that immobilize labor markets.[23] Conspicuously lacking were concrete measures to accomplish those goals, even a week later when the cabinet approved the reform plan, which included special economic zones and modest deregulation efforts, such as permitting the sales of certain drugs on the internet. Proponents explained away the lack of details, claiming that the government did not want to antagonize powerful constituencies before the July 2013 election.[24] Kicking the can down the road, the supporters assured markets that a cabinet shuffle would follow the election. Then reformers would take key positions, and real change would be evident in yet another reform package to be unveiled in the fall. The skeptics were unconvinced. History, as detailed throughout this book, gave them ample cause.

In its 2015 assessment of Abenomics, the IMF concluded that "further high-impact structural reforms are urgently needed to lift growth."[25] While acknowledging "some progress in a number of areas, the impact of reforms has yet to substantially materialize and potential growth remains far below what is required to realize the 'revitalization' scenario."[26] The IMF team wrote, "More vigorous efforts to raise labor supply and deregulate domestic markets . . . will be essential to lift growth, facilitate fiscal consolidation, and unburden monetary policy."[27]

Abenomics 2.0

The Abe administration took the IMF's advice to "reload" Abenomics and announced on September 24, 2015, that it was launching three new arrows. Declaring that "the Japanese economy is regaining its erstwhile robustness" and that "a virtuous economic cycle has been steadily in motion," the government offered up Abenomics 2.0. This new program was predicated on the belief that "Abenomics has shifted from the stage where the focus was primarily on solving the lack of demand with the aim of overcoming deflation to a new 'second stage' . . . to overcome the yoke of supply constraints due to the decreasing population."[28] The first new arrow was a pledge to create "a robust economy that gives rise to hope"; in practical terms, that meant boosting nominal GDP to ¥600 trillion by 2020 through 2 percent nominal growth and 3 percent in normal terms.[29] The second arrow highlighted support for families with children and aimed to raise Japan's fertility rate to 1.8 and to halt the slide in the population at 100 million (from the current 127 million). The third arrow vowed to create a social security program that fosters a sense of safety, so no one would need to leave a job to care for elderly parents.[30] Reaction to Abenomics 2.0 was largely negative, with some complaining that the government was moving the goalposts and others noting that the growth required to hit the first arrow's target far exceeded anything Japan had achieved during past decades.

Two years later, the Abe administration made the following claim:

Thanks to four and a half years of Abenomics, the nominal GDP and corporate profits are at a record high level. . . . The number of employed people
has risen by 1.85 million. The number of regular employees, which started
rising two years ago for the first time in eight years, has increased by 790,000
over the past two years, exceeding the increase in non-regular employees.
The active job openings-to-applicants ratio stands above 1.0 times in all
47 prefectures for the first time in history, and the unemployment rate is
2.8 %, the lowest in 22 years. Wages maintain their rising trend over the last
three years, with many firms raising their base pay for the fourth consecutive year in this spring's labor-management wage negotiations.[31]

As the summer of 2017 began, Japan's economy was enjoying the second-
longest expansion in the postwar era, posting 4.0 percent growth, and was the
fastest-growing economy in the Group of Seven.[32] This backdrop prodded the
government to adopt the "Investments for the Future Strategy 2017," which
"aims to realize Society 5.0" by increasing productivity through investments in
human resources.[33]

By the end of the summer, however, skepticism was mounting again. The
Financial Times concluded, "It will not be too long before the term 'Abenomics'
will join 'Cool Britannia', 'the end of history' and 'Brics' in the cupboard of cast-
offs: ideas that once had thrilling, zeitgeisty chic, but are now too threadbare to
be worn in public."[34] The 2017 IMF report on Japan was a little more staid but
no less critical: "After more than four years of Abenomics, inflation is still below
target, high public debt is still a concern, and structural bottlenecks remain."[35]

Revolutionary Rhetoric and Pedestrian Reality

Abenomics has been touted as a revolutionary approach to economic policy.
Making the case for Abenomics, the government highlighted the need to change
Japanese thinking. Surveying the two lost decades, the architects of the strategy
concluded that "far graver than the economic losses, however, were the losses of
confidence and future hopes among company managers as well as individuals."[36]
Addressing the country's demographic challenges, the authors of the revitalization strategy two years later noted that the country was "under a sense of crisis"
and "can afford no further delay to overcome the declining population issue."[37]
The Abe administration argued in the "Basic Concept of Revising Japan Revitalization Strategy" that "totally new ideas and . . . unconventional ideas" must be
employed "to take a decisive step to part with the past successes, and to take a
new step forward towards the unknown world."[38] Hammering the point home, it

insisted that "answers cannot be found in the ways of doing things as in the past or reliance on others." Urgency is needed: "Japan has limited time."[39]

Nevertheless, Abenomics resembles in many ways—but not all—conventional economic policy. The first arrow, monetary expansion, is a radical shift for Japan. In an open-ended commitment to add liquidity to the market, by the end of 2015 the BOJ was purchasing assets of around ¥80 trillion ($660 billion) annually and was going to start buying ¥300 billion annually of exchange-traded funds that track the JPX-Nikkei Index 400, in addition to the ¥3 trillion in exchange-traded funds it has purchased annually since late 2014.[40] This move was a historical policy change, especially for a country that has prized monetary stability and harbored a profound aversion to even the risk of inflation and the instability it could generate.

The second arrow, fiscal stimulus, has been a staple of LDP policy. By 2013 Japanese administrations had spent more than ¥75 trillion on fourteen emergency or supplementary budgets since 1999, primarily for large-scale infrastructure projects.[41] They typically provided a short-term boost for the economy, and then their effect faded. Worse, those measures added to a gross government debt that was already more than twice Japanese GDP, the worst among developed nations. Without a recovery, servicing this growing "Mount Fuji" of obligations will become even tougher and create yet more drag on what would be—because there is no recovery—a struggling economy.[42] The Bank of Japan seems more amenable to inflation, and periodic indications are that quantitative easing is contingent on a genuine commitment on the government's part to get its fiscal house in order and achieve a primary surplus by 2020 as promised.[43] Since 2015, however, the Abe administration has been less committed to that objective, and the BOJ did not seem to object.

The jury is still out on the third arrow, structural reform, but many of those suggestions have been floated for years, and the willingness of the government to make the hard choices required remains an open question. Economist Hoshi Takeo looked at the 2017 plan and concluded, "Probing beneath the borrowed and invented buzzwords sprinkled throughout the document, one finds little that is new in the latest plan. . . . [T]he same basic growth ideas have appeared year after year under a variety of labels, suggesting a fundamental lack of progress."[44] He traced the genesis of many of the Abe reforms to the Koizumi administration, noting that "the reason the government continues to tout the same deregulation initiatives over and over is that it has yet to successfully implement them."[45] When pressed, Hoshi conceded that Abe "did more than expected, but I didn't expect a lot."[46] Particularly cynical observers believe that pump-priming measures are palliatives to get the LDP through elections and that the government's real goal is a supermajority in both houses of the Diet so that it can pursue its top priority of constitutional reform.[47]

Some economists argue that the Abe proposals are not reforms at all but instead rollbacks of the liberalization agenda of his predecessors. The government's active intervention in labor markets—for example, pushing companies to increase wages, a step the companies have largely declined to take, by the way—along with setting numerical targets for corporate investment and for the number of foreign teachers in universities constitute "an attempt to build state capitalism," argued Sawa Takamitsu, president of Shiga University.[48] In many other places in the original Abenomics road map, the government is encouraged to take an active, interventionist approach to economic management. The prevailing mind-set is quite plain: "As far as the overseas activities of companies are concerned, the Government will make a dramatic shift from the existing thinking that business matters should be left solely up to the private sector. The public and private sectors will make concerted efforts to strategically acquire market share."[49] Sawa concluded,

> Abe has completely overturned the moves by former Prime Ministers Yasuhiro Nakasone and [Junichiro] Koizumi toward small government, in which economic results were to be left to the workings of free, competitive markets . . . [and] overturned Nakasone and Koizumi's attempt to turn the Liberal Democratic Party into a conservative party modeled on the Conservative Party of Britain and the Republican Party of the United States. In other words, it's as if Abe has resurrected the old LDP as well as an administration controlled by bureaucrats, both of which Koizumi set out to destroy.[50]

Sawa is not alone in this conclusion. Surveying Japan's economic landscape, a 2016 assessment argued that the Ministry of Economics, Trade, and Industry is actively working to reclaim its central position as economic manager. "Architects of Abenomics . . . have supported its resurgence. . . . Some look at surging domestic mergers and a record ¥10 trillion of outbound deals in 2015 and are convinced that the ministry has indeed recaptured some of its old magic."[51] Hoshi Takeo offered that "health care, 'Cool Japan,' agriculture, AI [artificial intelligence], robotics, etc., a substantial part or about half of the third arrow is old-fashioned industrial policy."[52] Commentator William Pesek is also in this camp, noting the real flaw of the policy: Abenomics "is trying to revive an industrial system that died even before Abe's earlier 2006–2007 stint as premier. . . . What is Abenomics, with its monetary easing, yen depreciation and corporate welfare other than a futile ploy to reanimate an economy that existed in 1985?"[53] At a corporate round-table on the future of Japan's economy in the summer of 2017, private and public sector participants agreed that reforms to stimulate innovation should include longer time horizons for corporate investments, greater government involvement in R&D, and less attention to stakeholders that were "only" shareholders. When it was pointed out that those were the features of traditional Japanese corporate decision making and were once considered obstacles to reform, the panelists were somewhat abashed, but they did not change their recommendations.

Experts aren't the only skeptics. By the summer of 2016, disapproval of Abe-nomics had reached a plurality of 45 percent in a *Yomiuri Shimbun* poll and 47 percent in an NHK survey. An *Asahi Shimbun* poll found that 69 percent of respondents said that Abenomics had made either little (50 percent) or no (19 percent) progress in boosting employment and wages.[54] In the Bank of Japan's quarterly survey conducted in the summer of 2017, only 7.6 percent said that economic conditions had improved over the last year, while 71 percent said they remained the same. Fewer anticipated improvement (7.5 percent) over the next year, and two-thirds (66.4 percent) expected conditions to stay the same. Ominously, 25 percent thought economic conditions would worsen. Finally, only 7.3 percent said that their household conditions had improved, 39.2 percent believed that their personal situation had worsened, and over half (53 percent) believed "it was difficult to say."[55] Parts of Japan were profiting from Abenomics, but ordinary citizens had their doubts.

Abe Shinzo, Ruthless Opportunist

Under Abe, the Liberal Democratic Party has racked up an impressive string of election victories since December 2012. From that ballot until the snap national election in October 2017, the LDP has won five national elections, taken control of both houses of the Diet, and claimed and held a parliamentary supermajority in the lower house. Rewarding his efforts, the LDP has changed party rules to allow Abe an unprecedented third term as party president, and, if completed, that would make him the longest-serving prime minister in Japan's postwar era.

Abe's victories include the following:

- December 2012 lower house election—The LDP came back to power after winning 294 seats, an increase of 176 over its previous perfor-mance. Its coalition partner, Komeito, won 31 seats, enlarging its presence in the Diet by ten representatives. The DPJ self-destructed in that ballot, losing 173 seats and barely besting the newly formed

Japan Restoration Party to remain the official opposition. The LDP-Komeito coalition held more than two-thirds of the seats in the legislature, allowing it to overrule the upper house and effectively ending the twisted Diet.

- July 2013 upper house ballot—The LDP won 115 of the chamber's 242 seats, an increase of 31. Komeito increased its representation to 20, while the DPJ lost 27 seats. The coalition win gave the government a comfortable majority in both houses of the Diet.
- December 2014 snap election—The LDP lost 3 seats, but Komeito compensated by picking up 4. The DPJ recouped some of its losses, and the Japan Restoration Party imploded. The biggest winner was the Communist Party, which more than doubled its representation in the Diet (to 21 seats).[56]
- July 2016 upper house election—The government continued to build its majority as the LDP won 6 more seats and Komeito claimed 5 more. The DPJ continued to shed representatives, losing 11 seats in the ballot.
- October 2017 snap election—The LDP again lost votes but benefited from a balkanized opposition that split the anti-LDP vote. The Democratic Party vanished, its members splitting between Tokyo governor Koike Yuriko's conservative Kibo no To (Party of Hope) and the progressive Constitutional Democratic Party of Japan. Significantly, the government retained its supermajority.[57]

The LDP returned to power unrepentant. An authoritative assessment of that ballot concluded that "the LDP did not engineer this great victory [in 2012] by reinventing the party that had ruled Japan from its 1955 inception to 2009. . . . [T]he LDP changed very little and those changes do not seem strongly related to its historic victory."[58] In fact, the government's agenda sometimes looks as if it was designed to antagonize the public. In December 2013 the administration passed a state secrets law, the Act on the Protection of Specially Designated Secrets, which criminalized leaking information.[59] The legislation was designed to facilitate defense cooperation with the United States—Washington has long demanded tighter controls before sharing sensitive information with Tokyo—although 80 percent of Japan's population opposed the bill amid fears that it would be used to suppress opposition to the government.[60] Abe's popularity took a hit as a result, with cabinet approval dropping about ten points to 50 percent.

That legislation was followed by the July 1, 2014, cabinet decision to reinterpret restrictions on Japan's ability to exercise its right of collective self-defense and to permit the Self-Defense Forces to use force and aid an ally under attack. This decision reversed sixty years of constitutional interpretation explicitly banning such acts.[61] The cabinet decision was followed by contentious debates in both houses of the Diet and, a year later, passage of landmark legislation to put the new interpretation into effect. Over 80 percent of the public found the government's explanations for the move insufficient and nearly 70 percent feared that the new legislation would drag Japan into conflict. Mass public protests followed the new law in 2015.[62] Opinion polls following passage of the legislation showed the cabinet's approval rating dropping below its disapproval rating.

The Abe administration also flouted public opinion when it decided to pursue membership in the Trans-Pacific Partnership (TPP) agreement, a twelve-country trade deal that was designed to yield a new "gold standard" for such negotiations. The government had several reasons for backing the TPP: It would promote trade, more strongly tie the United States to Asia, and allow Japan (and other TPP member states) to develop rules for regional integration rather than leaving them to other governments, such as China's. More controversially, the TPP would force change on some of Japan's most cosseted industries, such as agriculture, spurring reform and greater efficiencies. The public remains ambivalent, however, with pluralities opposed to or uncertain about the legislation.[63]

While Abe gets credit for pushing through the reinterpretation of collective self-defense and for joining the TPP, both initiatives were supported by DPJ prime minister Noda Yoshihiko and others in his party's leadership. Both Abe and Noda saw a compelling strategic rationale for each policy, and both would add that backing unpopular measures that nevertheless advance the national interest is the hallmark of real leadership. Still, "one of the great conundrums of Abe's second stint as prime minister is how he has managed to retain healthy levels of public support while polls consistently show a majority opposes every one of his signature policies."[64] It is harder still to reconcile the government's uneven economic performance and its electoral successes given the centrality of bread-and-butter issues to most voters.

The credit must go to Abe. The first five years of his second term demonstrated that first impressions can be mistaken and that there are second acts in Japanese politics. Abe has proven to be a genuine student of politics and a shrewd and pragmatic politician. He has played the long game, putting aside his desire to make powerful nationalist statements such as visiting the Yasukuni Shrine—an act that would infuriate governments in Seoul and Beijing (and raise hackles in Washington)—or tearing up the 1993 Kono Statement, which acknowledged the Japanese government's complicity in forcing women into sexual slavery (known as comfort women) during World War II. Abe's remarks on the seventieth anniversary of the end of World War II managed to satisfy former adversaries and victims of Japanese aggression as well as his nationalist supporters.

Abe has not abandoned his conservative goals, however. He has overcome powerful public opposition to promote a higher, more active regional and global security profile for Japan, has loosened restrictions on SDF operations, and has moved the country toward a genuine debate on constitutional revision. Abe has done so by tacking between conservative nationalist objectives (primarily in national security) and the public's preference for measures to stimulate the economy. As he depleted his political capital on the first set of policies, Abe would call an election to reestablish his mandate. All the while, the mounting threat from North Korea and concern about a rising, more confident, and assertive China validated Abe's aim to revise national security policies.

Those maneuverings would have been more difficult and likely less successful had the political opposition not been as disorganized and dispirited. The DPJ continued to struggle after it was dethroned in 2012. It managed a brief rebound in the 2014 ballot, but by 2017 the party had effectively dissolved. Other parties briefly flourished, but none showed resilience or broad appeal until the October 2017 election, when the Constitutional Democratic Party emerged from the primordial stew of opposition politics. There is hope that its identity as a progressive party—unlike Koike's Kibo no To, whose conservative policies render it almost indistinguishable from the LDP—will make it a more credible and durable opposition. That task will be made harder given Abe's ruthless opportunism and readiness to call snap elections to exploit the disorganization on the other side of the aisle.

Another factor in Abe's success deserves mention—luck. Unlike virtually every other Japanese cabinet, Abe's avoided scandal. During his first term, which lasted just one year, four ministers were forced to resign; a fifth committed suicide. This second time in office, however, has seen only minor indiscretions. His second cabinet (2012–14) was scandal free and proved to be the most stable in postwar Japanese history. In October 2014 two ministers were forced to resign for minor campaign finance violations. In the third cabinet (2014–17), two other ministers were forced to resign for finance law offenses, and a third was dismissed for inappropriate comments. That cabinet's performance was, by Japanese standards, impressive.

By 2018, however, Abe's luck appeared to have changed. In 2017 two scandals emerged that touched the prime minister. While neither at first glance appeared serious enough to trigger his downfall, they had assumed ominous proportions by the spring of 2018. The first involved Moritomo Gakuen, a Japanese preschool famous for having students recite daily the Imperial Rescript on Education, a

Meiji-era document intended to inculcate national pride and spirit. That nationalist inclination won the school the admiration of Abe and his wife, Akie, who gave a speech at the school and was later named an honorary principal.

In February 2017 reports showed that the school had purchased a parcel of government-owned land in Osaka at a steep discount—about 14 percent of its assessed value—because the land was supposedly contaminated by waste, although it was rumored that pressure from prominent patrons played a role as well.[65] The government also reportedly reimbursed expenses of the ¥120 million incurred to clean the property. The president of the school told the Diet that the prime minister and his wife donated ¥1 million to the school; Abe denied making the gift.[66] During the Diet debate, the Ministry of Finance first claimed that all records of the transaction, other than the contract itself, had been destroyed in accordance with document retention regulations. Dogged digging by opposition politicians—with some helpful leaks—forced the Ministry of Finance to retract that statement when the missing paperwork was eventually found. Then it was discovered that the documents given to the legislators had been altered; the names of prominent politicians, including "some with Cabinet experience," and that of Mrs. Abe had been removed. Prime Minister Abe has denied any involvement in or knowledge of the sale and the subsequent document alterations. The discoveries prompted the resignation of a Finance Ministry official and the suicide of another official who had worked on the deal.[67]

The second scandal concerns the decision in 2017 to grant a license to a friend of the prime minister's to open Japan's first new veterinary medicine school in half a century in a National Strategic Special Zone in Ehime Prefecture. Again, the government denied that there were any documents concerning the deal, and that statement was proved false. Subsequently, a document appeared to have been altered, removing the names of individuals who had attended a Tokyo meeting to discuss the school. It is unclear who in the prime minister's circle purportedly pressed to approve the license.[68]

Until the scandals, Abe's strong performance deterred challengers from his own party, another factor that has contributed to his longevity in office. Throughout its history, the LDP has been an agglomeration of factions that have intensely competed for cabinet posts. Prime ministerial terms and cabinet shuffles were often driven by internal party needs rather than external circumstances. But so long as Abe dominates the opposition in elections, opposition to him within his party has remain muted. Or, as one study concludes, the selection of party presidents is no longer a product of internal struggles over distributing resources but instead reflects a determination of which leader will be most likely to help the party.[69] At the end of 2017, that person was Abe, but the scandals took a toll.

A *Nikkei* poll revealed that support for the Abe cabinet had fallen to 42 percent, a fourteen-point drop in one month. (Nonsupport was 49 percent, a thirteen-point increase.) Those numbers are consistent—both in overall levels and recent changes—with other polls.[70] These developments are worrisome, prompting speculation about Abe's prospects in the fall 2018 LDP presidential election and pushing some to even question if he will remain in office that long.[71]

"Japan Is Not, and Will Never Be, a Tier-Two Country"

Nature and politics abhor a vacuum, and ultimately Abe and the LDP were sucked back into office by the DPJ's inability to provide leadership. The DPJ had proven incapable of governing, and threats both real (March 11) and potential (menacing neighbors) underscored the high costs of ineptitude. One commentator observed after the 2012 election, "If Japan has found a leader with a sense of purpose, it might have China to thank for it."[72]

Abe made his ambitions and objectives clear upon taking office. In a speech at the Center for Strategic and International Studies (CSIS) in Washington, DC, just weeks after returning to the Kantei, he pointedly rejected the assertion that Japan's best days were behind it.[73] Neither could Japan focus only on itself as it struggled with economic malaise. Instead, he argued that "the world awaits Japan," and that expectation generated three tasks for his country and his government.

> Firstly, when the Asia-Pacific or the Indo-Pacific region becomes more and more prosperous, Japan must remain a leading promoter of rules. By rules, I mean those for trade, investment, intellectual property, labor, environment and the like.
>
> Secondly, Japan must continue to be a guardian of the global commons, like the maritime commons, open enough to benefit everyone.
>
> Japan's aspirations being such, thirdly, Japan must work even more closely with the U.S., Korea, Australia and other like-minded democracies throughout the region.
>
> A rules-promoter, a commons' guardian, and an effective ally and partner to the U.S. and other democracies, are all roles that Japan MUST fulfill.[74]

That short blueprint has been a remarkably accurate guide for Japanese foreign policy under Abe. Animating his administration's engagement with the world has been Japan's desire to be a "rule maker rather than a rule taker," a country that sets the terms for institutional order rather than one that merely accepts them. This logic has been central to Abe's diplomacy, driving participation in the TPP (since renamed the Comprehensive and Progressive Agreement for Trans-Pacific Partnership, or CPTPP), despite considerable political opposition domestically (and from President Donald Trump), and in the Japan–European Union Strategic Partnership and the Japan-EU Economic Partnership Agreement.[75]

Kanehara Nobukatsu, a senior Foreign Ministry official who has been working at the National Security Council since its inception in 2013, explained Japanese thinking. "Twenty-first century Japan must become a country that believes in the universal values and makes the case not for power alone but for justice in international society. And it must become a rule maker that promotes international society's ethical maturity. Japan today must have the resolve to assume leadership and weighty responsibility in the international community of defining and achieving justice on a global scale based on conscience."[76] Thus, the language of Japan's diplomatic engagement in recent years stressed not only the government's desire to be an "architect" but also a certain rejection of Hobbesian anarchism. Asserting the need to write the rules of the international system assumes that the international order is in fact orderly and not the result of arbitrary or coercive measures by the most powerful actors. This underlies the emphasis in Japan's diplomacy on values; they reflect a respect for rules. But rules are not just a desired outcome (a structured process for arbitrating interests); they are a value in and of themselves (and thus an interest) as well.

This twofold understanding of the role of rules has inspired Tokyo to reach out to like-minded partners to help create and reinforce a rules-based order. It has manifested in Japan's pursuit since the first Abe government (2006–7) and its "values-based diplomacy."[77] It provides a ready basis for cooperation among some Asia-Pacific countries, such as the United States, Southeast Asia, Australia, and India. This effort also seeks to differentiate Japan from China and then deprives China of the opportunity to be a rule maker as Beijing does not share those values, at least insofar as it does not support democracy or rules-based dispute resolution.

The United States is Japan's preferred partner in these efforts. Its partnership with the United States has been the foundation of Japanese foreign and security policy since the end of World War II. Limitations imposed by Article 9 of the Japanese Constitution were tolerable only if the United States was prepared to assume the burden of defending Japan. The alliance that has emerged has been the core of both countries' national security strategies.[78] Every statement from every foreign or security policy meeting between the two governments has noted that the bilateral alliance is the cornerstone of regional peace and security.[79] The 2017 white paper *Defense of Japan* is explicit: "The peace and security of Japan is ensured through developing seamless defense measures by coupling Japan's own defense capabilities with the Japan-U.S. Security Arrangements."[80] Abe's approach paid dividends with President Trump. Despite concerns that the US president's views of Japan were stuck in the 1980s, an era dominated by trade frictions, Abe's courting of Trump paid off. When Trump visited Japan in November 2017, he characterized the relationship as "really extraordinary. . . . I don't think we've ever been closer to Japan than we are right now."[81]

For Abe, and fellow conservatives, Japan's partnership with the United States facilitates a second objective—the loosening of restrictions on Japan's security forces so its military can participate more fully in regional or global security affairs. Again, Abe's February 2013 CSIS speech was explicit: "As your long-standing ally and partner, Japan is a country that has benefited from, and contributed to, peace and prosperity in the Asia-Pacific for well over half a century. . . . It is high time, in this age of Asian resurgence, for Japan to bear even more responsibility to promote our shared rules and values, preserve the commons, and grow side by side with all the high achievers in the region."[82] Abe's emphasis on Japan's being a better partner has been a constant throughout his administration and should not be dismissed as a mere rhetorical flourish. Recall too the deep and abiding sense of vulnerability at the heart of Japanese thinking about the world. A more robust Japanese defense posture undercuts complaints about free or cheap riding by Japan and helps ensure continued US engagement with the region.

The second Abe government has seized the opportunities afforded by an evolving security environment, proliferating security capabilities, and mounting constraints on US security policy (fatigue from fighting wars, budget limits, and partisanship) to press a frenetic national security agenda. Since taking office, Abe has established the National Security Council, promulgated the country's first *National Security Strategy*, passed the national state secrets law (to facilitate security cooperation), rewritten the National Defense Program Guidelines (which proposes Japan's defense strategy and policies to implement it, including the structure and posture of the Self-Defense Forces), published the Mid-Term Defense Program (which translates that strategy into policy), revised principles on arms exports, revised the charter for overseas development assistance to allow a more strategic use of Japan's aid, reinterpreted constitutional provisions on the exercise of the right of collective self-defense, and passed legislation to operationalize that reinterpretation. This remarkable list of accomplishments is rendered even more impressive by the opposition that Abe had to surmount to achieve some of them.

The claim that these efforts represent radical shifts in Japanese policy is off the mark, however. These developments are part of a much longer evolution in Japan's security policy that even predates the end of the Cold War. Christopher Hughes, one of Britain's foremost Japan watchers, describes this "quest for normalcy" in considerable detail.[83] In addition to legislation passed in the early 1990s that allows the dispatch of peacekeepers, the National Diet has passed bills that better enable the government to function in a crisis and allowed Japan to participate in Operation Enduring Freedom (the US-led coalition's invasion of Afghanistan after the attacks of September 11, 2001) as well as other legislation that facilitated security and defense operations. In 2007 the first Abe government elevated the Japan Defense Agency to the status of a ministry. Beginning with the administration of Prime Minister Noda and accelerating in the second Abe government, Japan has laid the legal and institutional infrastructure to assume a higher-profile security role. Since 2011 Japan has loosened restrictions on arms exports, improved its space operations, relaxed limits on overseas development aid to permit funds to go to regional military capacity building, joined US missile defense systems, and advanced the all-important debate on exercising the right of collective self-defense.[84] Most of these moves have been driven by external events or actors, but a domestic constituency also backs the assumption of a more visible security role. Make no mistake, however: Japan's evolution is evolutionary. Changes remain incremental, and bulwarks against a radical shift remain firmly in place.[85]

A vital part of the US security agenda that Abe has also appropriated is the desire to better connect the "spokes" in the US alliance network in Asia. While the United States preferred a bilateral focus to its Asian alliances during the Cold War,[86] changes in the Asia-Pacific security environment have forced changes in Washington's thinking and encouraged the United States and its allies to seek new ways to address regional threats and challenges. For Japan, the expansion of security partners and options is an increasingly important tool of foreign policy. It facilitates coordination among partners when every country's resources are strained; it allows countries to do more with less. "Diversification in foreign policy partners . . . is designed to decrease Japan's diplomatic isolation in Asia and to increase its foreign policy maneuverability."[87] It helps undercut objections to a higher-profile security role for Tokyo by having third parties vouchsafe its credentials. Further, it insulates Japan from American caprice and serves as a hedge against radical foreign policy shifts by Washington.[88]

The "gold standard" for such cooperation is the Japan-US-Australia Trilateral Strategic Dialogue, "the most-developed cooperative relationship Washington has in the Asia-Pacific region, with a broader and more robust agenda than any other trilateral relationship."[89] While both Tokyo and Canberra have sought and built a better bilateral security relationship, the dialogue has facilitated those efforts. The Australian Foreign Ministry describes the relationship with Japan as "our closest and most mature in Asia, and [it] is fundamentally important to both countries' strategic and economic interests."[90] A Japanese defense analyst reciprocated the assessment, noting that "Australia is Japan's second, if not most important, security partner in the Asia-Pacific region. . . . [N]o other bilateral relation, excepting the Japan-U.S. alliance itself, has matched so far relations between Japan and Australia both in depth and in the range of security and defense interactions."[91]

Another key diplomatic partner for Prime Minister Abe is India. When he first served as prime minister, Abe—with the United States and Australia— reached out to Delhi as a partner with shared values. After some tentative forays, Canberra and Delhi backed away from more robust cooperation, fearing that it would look as if they were attempting to contain China and would prompt a backlash from Beijing. Nevertheless, Abe clung to a conception of Asia that includes both the Pacific and Indian Oceans, and he is often credited with the first official mention of the Indo-Pacific.[92] The two countries have sought close relations despite being frustrated by various issues, most notably Japan's objection to India's nuclear weapons program. Upon his return to power, Abe revived that vision, aided by a similar geopolitical outlook in the Obama administration. As a result, bilateral relations "witnessed a sharp upward swing," which "received an even stronger tailwind with [Narendra] Modi's election as India's Prime Minister."[93] Modi greatly admires Japan and made it his first stop outside South Asia in 2014 when he traveled as prime minister.

The Japan-India bilateral partnership is sustained by several shared beliefs and interests. The countries also share similar values: democracy, a rule of law, and a respect for human dignity. Both governments and business sectors believe mutual opportunities can be realized through closer economic cooperation.[94] Abe and Modi also maintain that their countries are undervalued in the international system. India's membership in the BRICS (Brazil, Russia, India, China, South Africa) grouping is an important vehicle for the expression of that impulse for Modi. Abe would like a reassessment of the postwar Tokyo Trials and the elimination of the Enemy State Clause in the UN Charter. Both men also seek a permanent seat for their countries on the UN Security Council. Finally, they have similar geopolitical considerations as both men are concerned about the strategic implications of China's rise and its new foreign policy and military assertiveness.[95] In 2017 Abe's determination resuscitated the "Quad"—the partnership meeting of Japan, the United States, Australia, and India—and the four governments have been working to make that cooperation real.[96]

The Association of Southeast Asian Nations also figures prominently in Abe's thinking. When the Japanese look to Southeast Asia, they see a region of more than 620 million people, with a growing, working-age middle class and a collective GDP of $2.3 trillion (in 2012, 12.5 percent of Asia's total). Japan is ASEAN's second-largest trading partner and its second-largest source of foreign direct investment. In 2015, two-way trade between ASEAN and Japan reached $239.4 billion, accounting for 10.5 percent of ASEAN's total trade. Foreign direct investment inflows from Japan to ASEAN were valued at $17.4 billion, or 14.5 percent of total FDI inflows to ASEAN.[97] The region is located at a geostrategic crossroads, astride key global sea lanes and choke points. Some $5.3 trillion of shipping transits the region annually. As one observer concluded, "A well-connected Asia-Pacific or Indo-Pacific is not possible without an open and active Southeast Asia."[98] This logic has spurred the United States and Japan, both individually and as an alliance, to deepen cooperation with (and in) Southeast Asia.[99]

Six months into his term, Abe declared that he would "attach particular importance to our relationship with ASEAN," and he implemented it vigorously.[100] In his first year back in office, he visited all ten ASEAN countries (a first for a Japanese prime minister), senior officials made numerous trips to the region, and Abe hosted the ASEAN-Japan Commemorative Summit to mark the fortieth anniversary of their relations. The meeting produced the ASEAN-Japanese statement titled "Hand in Hand, Facing Regional and Global Challenges," the vision statement on its friendship and cooperation issues, and its implementation plan. Since then engagement has continued apace. The statement from the September 2016 Japan-ASEAN summit outlines a long list of initiatives, ranging from currency swap arrangements to infrastructure investments to sustainable development projects.[101] Equally important has been engagement through ASEAN's security architecture such as the ASEAN Regional Forum and the ASEAN Defense Ministers' Meeting-Plus. Japan has also pushed bilateral outreach with capacity-building efforts for regional militaries such as the Philippines and Vietnam, regional tours by Maritime Self-Defense Force (MSDF) ships, and military exercises and drills that are open to regional observers.[102]

Central to Abe's calculations has been the recognition that many, if not most, Southeast Asian governments are increasingly uncomfortable with China's assertiveness and are eager to find diplomatic and security partners to expand their options and room for maneuver when dealing with Beijing. Those governments welcome Tokyo's outreach—along with that of Washington, Canberra, and Delhi—but they do not want to be forced to take sides in a confrontation between Beijing and those other governments. Abe has been quick to seize on that desire and has underscored the differences between Japan and China. For example, he noted that "Japan-ASEAN relations in the next 50 years would be bright if we could continue to cooperate while firmly upholding common values such as freedom, democracy, human rights, and the rule of law."[103] It is hard to miss the dig at Beijing.

Understandably, relations with China have been rocky during the Abe years. The sources of tension that predated his administration have not diminished. For one, China continues to press its claims to the disputed Senkaku Islands. In January 2013 a Chinese naval vessel directed its fire-control radar at an MSDF destroyer navigating in the East China Sea and is suspected to have also locked on its fire-control radar at a helicopter aboard an MSDF destroyer. Later that year China declared an East China Sea Air Defense Identification Zone that included the Senkakus. By 2017 a headline in the *Nikkei Asian Review* claimed, "China's Senkaku incursions are the new normal."[104] After toting up a long list of offenses, Japan's 2017 defense white paper concluded, "Japan is deeply concerned about such measures, which are profoundly dangerous acts that unilaterally change the status quo in the East China Sea, escalating the situation, and that may cause unintended consequences in the East China Sea."[105]

The dispute produced anti-Japan demonstrations in China, and views of the other country plumbed new depths in public opinion surveys. In Genron NPO's twelfth survey of Japanese and Chinese public opinion, 71.9 percent of Japanese described the relationship between the two countries as bad, while 78.2 percent of the Chinese expressed similar sentiments, an eleven-point increase from the previous survey. Despite some warming of relations at the time of the poll, 44.8 percent of Japanese and 66.8 percent of Chinese believed the bilateral relationship had worsened in the past year, and 34.3 percent of Japanese and 50.4 percent of Chinese expected a further deterioration.[106] Results from a Japanese Cabinet Office survey were even bleaker, with 80.5 percent of Japanese still saying they felt no affinity for China (although it showed an improvement of 2.7 percent from ten months earlier) and 83 percent saying relations with China are not good (again, an improvement of 2.7 percent from the previous survey).[107]

Yet economic relations remained strong. China remains Japan's biggest trading partner, and Japan is China's second-largest. "They need each other economically," explained Jiang Yuechun, a senior research fellow with China Institute of International Studies in Beijing.[108]

After two tense years, Abe and Chinese president Xi Jinping met one-on-one at the November 2014 Asia-Pacific Economic Cooperation meeting that Xi hosted.[109] Relations remained distant and perfunctory until 2017, when observers espied signs of a possible thaw. In May high-level visitors began shuttling between Tokyo and Beijing to discuss options and obstacles to bilateral cooperation on regional concerns such as North Korea or China's Belt and Road Initiative, a massive infrastructure plan for China, Asia, the Middle East, Africa, and Europe. Abe offered encouraging remarks (with caveats) about the Chinese efforts, including the initiative.[110] For the first time in thirty-seven years, no Japanese cabinet minister visited the Yasukuni Shrine on August 15, the anniversary of the end of the war. A month later, Abe made a surprise visit to the Chinese Embassy in Tokyo and attended a ceremony marking China's National Day and the forty-fifth anniversary of the normalization of bilateral relations. It was the first time in fifteen years that a Japanese prime minister joined the event. And for the first time in a decade, Abe and Chinese premier Li Keqiang also exchanged congratulatory messages on the anniversary.

Relations continued to warm in 2018. On May 9, Japan, China, and South Korea held their seventh trilateral summit, the first such encounter in three years. Afterward, Abe hosted Premier Li for a bilateral summit during which the Japanese prime minister expressed his desire "to make the 40th anniversary of the conclusion of the Treaty of Peace and Friendship between Japan and China a year that would be a new start for Japan-China relations."[111] While that sentiment is sincere, another factor is at work—the mercurial and unpredictable US president. Donald Trump's disregard for the postwar order, in particular his disdain for the rules and institutions of international trade, in theory gives them ample reason to work together.

In reality, however, the Japan-China relationship remains fraught. While both governments understand the need for a working relationship, both try to dictate its terms. Ultimately, Abe and Xi are both strong, nationalist leaders with conflicting strategic interests. Both men and their governments seek to expand their respective influence in the region and view the other as one of the most important constraints on that expansion. The Abe government regards China as a rival to its geopolitical ambitions and a threat, while Beijing believes that Japan is determined to constrain and contain its rise. Beijing sees its resurgence as normal and its policies as commensurate with its status and power, and as a righting of historical wrongs. Tokyo claims that it is defending the geopolitical status quo and the existing rules-based order. This divergence in views is most evident in the Senkaku dispute: Japan claims it is beefing up its armed forces to protect existing territorial arrangements, while China insists it is reclaiming stolen property. Tokyo backs China's rival claimants in the South China Sea to preserve freedom of navigation and an international law–based system of dispute resolution. Beijing counters that Japan is inserting itself into disputes in which it has no stake and is encouraging rival claimants to thwart China. Even the arcane and abstract arena of economic rulemaking has become a source of contention—despite the opportunities for cooperation created by President Trump's wrecking-ball approach to global trade. Japan supported the TPP (now the CPTPP) to establish a "gold standard" for regional trade relations and to undercut the Regional Comprehensive Economic Partnership that China backs; China argues (rightly) that the TPP is intended to sideline Beijing as a rule maker.

A final source of division between the two governments is North Korea, where four critical differences are evident. First, while Tokyo and Beijing agree that Pyongyang should give up its nuclear weapons, the Abe government favors a hard line toward Pyongyang to force it to the negotiating table. Beijing is reluctant to pressure North Korea, fearful that instability in that country would most impact China. Second, the Japanese are convinced that they will be the target of a North Korean nuclear weapon, imparting an urgency to their consideration of this issue that the Chinese do not share. Third, Abe has championed the cause of the abductees and has made the resolution of their fate a priority in relations with North Korea, but Beijing is indifferent. Finally, China has no desire to see North Korea reunified with South Korea. The official Japanese government position is that the country welcomes unification under Seoul.

The last piece of Japan's Asia foreign policy mosaic is South Korea. Abe inherited a relationship that was troubled and promptly made it worse. While bilateral cooperation should have been a priority as the North Korean government was ever more bellicose, belligerent, and provocative, relations between Tokyo and Seoul were instead sinking to new lows. In the summer of 2012 and under parliamentary pressure, South Korea at the last minute canceled the planned signing of a bilateral general security of military information agreement—an important but nonetheless anodyne document—thus underscoring the sense of drift, if not outright hostility, in the bilateral relationship. Shortly afterward, South Korean president Lee Myung-bak visited the disputed territory of the Dokdo/Takeshima Islands and then made disparaging remarks about the conditions for a hypothetical visit to Korea by Japan's emperor.

Abe's conservatism raised hackles in turn in Seoul, and the visits that he and his cabinet made to the Yasukuni Shrine in December 2012 confirmed the worst fears of skeptics in South Korea. Subsequent reports that Abe sought to investigate and reverse the 1993 Kono Statement was the final proof of the government's revanchist inclinations. Abe denied any intention to rewrite history, while asserting that history and security should be separated: A reassessment of the past should not preclude practical measures—bilateral security cooperation between Tokyo and Seoul, or trilateral cooperation of those two countries and Washington—to address the mounting North Korean threat.

That idea did not get a positive reception in Seoul. When Park Geun-hye succeeded Lee as president in 2013, relations remained largely frozen as Park waited for Japan to do more to demonstrate its commitment to a better relationship.

South Korean and Japanese leaders had few substantive encounters, and those meetings that did occur were notable by their coolness (especially in comparison with the cordial, if not friendly, relations between President Park and Chinese president Xi Jinping).

Park's call went largely unheeded. But by 2015 conditions had changed— North Korea had conducted a third nuclear test—and the US government's urgings and behind-the-scenes efforts had become so pronounced that in December 2015 South Korea and Japan could reach agreement on a "settlement to the comfort women issue."[112] The deal they struck was intended to "finally and irreversibly resolve" the matter.[113] The agreement was greeted with applause and jeers in both countries, and its implementation, along with the pledge to finally and irreversibly settle this issue between the two governments, is by no means certain. The election of progressive Moon Jae-in to replace President Park after her impeachment in 2017 raised fears in Tokyo (and Washington and among conservatives in Seoul) that bilateral (Japan–South Korea) and trilateral cooperation would again become a hostage of South Korean domestic politics. Moon stoked those fears when he called for a reassessment of the 2015 agreement. Ultimately, however, his government concluded that the deal should be honored, although Seoul urged Tokyo to do more to right historical wrongs.[114] The North Korean threat also straitjacketed the Moon administration, limiting his room for experimenting with a softer line of the Sunshine Policy—that is, Sunshine 2.0 or perhaps more appropriately "Moonshine."

In 2018 North Korea's diplomatic offensive created new strains in the Japan–South Korea relationship. Moon's readiness to reach out to North Korean leader Kim Jong-un exposed the yawning difference in perspectives between Tokyo and Seoul: South Korea sought engagement and rapprochement, while Japan maintained its hard line against Pyongyang. The Japanese feared that South Korea's eagerness to build relations with the North would fatally undermine the pressure campaign Tokyo felt was essential to force Pyongyang's denuclearization. Here, again, Trump was an important factor: The US president's seeming indifference to long-standing US alliances in Northeast Asia has driven home to policymakers in Tokyo and Seoul the importance of their bilateral security relations, the product of a recognition that despite their differences, both had to be ready to cooperate should US policy shift and imperil their national security.[115]

As Abe Shinzo marked five years in office, he had every reason to be confident in and proud of his foreign and security policy accomplishments. He had engineered extraordinary progress in his domestic national security agenda; consolidated and strengthened the alliance with the United States; held the line with China and put a floor on that relationship, despite challenging Beijing diplomatically and militarily; and reestablished security cooperation with Seoul to address the North Korean threat. He had also fulfilled his pledge that Japan would contribute more to security affairs and reasserted Japan's role as an important diplomatic player.

"Reform Has Another Face—Traditional Japanese Values"

Abe's victories have come with a price. The gap between his economic promises and the reality of his administration's policies, the ruthless election tactics, and his readiness to lead public opinion rather than follow it have contributed to the Japanese people's eroding faith in their institutions. The discrediting of the opposition, and its exposure as being feckless, has driven voter turnout to historical lows: Only 53.69 percent of voters cast ballots in the October 2017 election, a minor rebound from the all-time low of 52.66 percent in the 2014 lower house vote.[116]

A damaged and diminished opposition is only part of the problem, however. What Abe calls leadership—whether the issue is the TPP, the national security and defense policy, or the continued reliance on nuclear energy—has antagonized large swaths of the public. In 2017 just 50 percent of the Japanese pronounced themselves satisfied with the way that democracy works in their country, while 47 percent said they were dissatisfied.[117] In the same survey, 57 percent of Japanese said they trust the national government to do what is right for Japan, but just 6 percent have a lot of confidence in the national leadership. The government's determination to proceed on its terms has alienated large parts of the public: 34.6 percent of respondents in a Cabinet Office survey believed that their views are reflected in policy, while 62.1 percent said their views are ignored.[118] The Edelman Trust Barometer, an authoritative annual assessment of trust around the world, placed Japan among the lowest of the countries it surveyed, with just 49 percent of the informed public and 34 percent of the mass population trusting national institutions (government, business, media, and NGOs). Some 37 percent of the public trusts the government (a drop of 2 percentage points from 2016), and 42 percent believe the system is failing (45 percent are uncertain). The finding that among all the countries that Edelman surveyed, the Japanese are the most pessimistic about the future is in line with these results.[119] For a leader who believes that much of Japan's problems can be attributed to the people's lack of confidence, continuing pessimism may be the most bitter of Abe's failures.[120]

Central to the task of creating confidence is instilling a sense of pride among the Japanese. During the go-go years of the 1970s and 1980s, Japan's successes and its seemingly unstoppable rise girded the Japanese psyche. The lost decades robbed Japan of that sense of well-being and purpose, and the shocks identified in chapters 2–5—the events of March 11, in particular—kept the Japanese off balance and anxious. For some, filling that hole demanded radical solutions and bold forays into an unknown future. Their efforts bear names such as "The Strategy for a Rebirth of Japan" or "A Call for a Japanese New Deal."

For others, however, answers are to be found in Japan's past. As a former LDP politician explained, "Reform has another face—traditional Japanese values."[121] This school has adherents on both the Right and the Left, as both see hope—if not salvation—in the values of the past.

This type of thinking is easily caricatured and misunderstood. Nationalism and patriotism are loaded terms in Japanese politics. The instinctive reaction of many people, Japanese and non-Japanese alike, is to tar all proponents of the nationalist cause with the brush of reactionary, illiberal authoritarianism. Some deserve the description; the overwhelming majority does not. Many Japanese nationalists want to create a more confident nation, one that drops what they consider to be unrealistic fetters on their government and becomes a more active and better international player.

How did Japan lose its way? There are two streams of thought. One group insists its problem stems from the constitution that the Occupation forces imposed on Japan after World War II. This group maintains the document does not reflect Japan's core values and has ever since driven a wedge between the Japanese people and their idealized community. Or as Hashimoto Akiko explains, "The desire to repair a damaged reputation" animates the conservative effort to create a positive national identity; thus, constitutional revision is the cure for many of Japan's ills.[122]

Leading this fight is the Nippon Kaigi (Japan Conference), an umbrella organization for conservative groups that was formed in 1997 and whose ultimate goal is to revise the national charter. Among its reported thirty-eight thousand members are 280 lawmakers in both houses of the Diet and twelve of the twenty members of the cabinet inaugurated in October 2015 (including the prime minister—he is a "supreme adviser"—the chief cabinet secretary, and the ministers of finance, foreign affairs, defense, economy, and internal communications). Its website proclaims its objectives are to venerate the emperor and the imperial family, to revise the constitution, to change the so-called masochistic view of history and promote patriotic education, to develop national defense systems, and to oppose systems that cause the "disintegration of families," such as allowing husbands and wives to have different surnames.[123] It seeks to "restore a politics that emphasizes the importance of national interests, reputation, and sovereignty, including paying homage to Japan's war dead at Yasukuni Shrine . . . [and] Nurture young people to cultivate patriotic spirit, respect for the national anthem, flag, and history, and cherish quintessential Japaneseness."[124]

Prime Minister Abe, in a policy speech to the Diet during his first administration, referred to "values such as public service, self-discipline, morals and attachment to and affection for the community and country where we have been born and raised."[125] Articulated this way, it is hard to object to these beliefs. Others see a darker motive—the rehabilitation of the former imperial regime—and catalog a long list of particulars as proof: visits to the Yasukuni Shrine; questions about the validity of the 1993 Kono Statement, which acknowledged Japanese responsibility for the comfort women system during World War II;[126] challenges to the legitimacy of Prime Minister Murayama Tomiichi's statement in 1995 that apologized for Japanese behavior in World War II; questions about whether Japan committed "aggression" during World War II;[127] and denigrating verdicts of the postwar Tokyo Tribunals as "victor's justice." For the critics, these acts are "supporting historical revisions, the whitewashing of Japan's war crimes and brutality . . . and pledging support for a new Empire of Japan."[128]

The second group asserts that Japan's lost identity is the result of a capitalist economic model that prizes consumerism above all else. This model fragments communities by emphasizing acquisition, which creates differences, drives consumption, and erodes the traditional Japanese relationship with nature. This belief draws sustenance from Shinto beliefs, yet its modern form is largely divorced from the religion itself. While the rejection of consumption may be a product of (or reconciliation with) straitened economic circumstances, the identification with nature is widespread, and many would likely disavow the charge that it signals any conservative inclinations. Katayama Shoichi, then a researcher at the Tokyo Foundation for Policy Research, expressed this view when he noted that in Japan there is a "search for alternative values, which could be related to traditional values. We are entering a new era where people can't see the future and money can't buy everything."[129] This critique is typically articulated by the Left, which has deep suspicions of capitalism in general and the US variant in particular, but this thinking can also be found on the other end of the political spectrum, with conservatives lamenting the loss of "attachment to and affection for the community" (as Abe did in the remarks cited in the previous paragraph). This sense of community and group identity is at the core of conservative beliefs and animates much of its discourse. Nor is this a unique point of convergence for the two ends of the political spectrum. Both extremes also share an antipathy to the US-Japan military alliance: the Left because it despises US militarism and fears entanglement in its excesses, the Right because it wants more freedom of maneuver to project national power.

"Japan Needs . . . to Find Its Own Center"

Recognizing that this nostalgia animates both the Right and the Left is critical to understanding the power of the past in contemporary Japan. "For conservatives like Abe, a positive view of Japanese history is necessary to rebuild the vital link between the Japanese state and society and allow Japan to mobilize its energies for a variety of pressing tasks, including reviving the economy, addressing various social problems and defending against external threats."[130] Abe's cri di coeur *Utsukushii Kuni e* (*Toward a Beautiful Country: My Vision for Japan*) calls for a restoration of national pride through the protection and veneration of unique traditions that Japan developed through its long history. For him, the people should derive pride and identity from the state to which they belong, and patriotism (*aikokushin*) is an extension of people's love of their native place (*kyodoai*).[131] Kevin Doak, a scholar of nationalism, calls this broad conception of nationalism "civic nationalism," which promotes "healthy patriotism" and pride in one's country while being respectful of modern traditions and accomplishments.[132]

While constitutional reform is "Abe's dearest dream" and "historical mission,"[133] the changes he seeks target restrictions on Japanese participation in internationally sanctioned military missions and its ability to support its alliance partner; he does not want to resurrect a once-defeated empire.[134] In a speech at the Hudson Institute in the fall of 2013, Abe minced no words:

> Japan should not be the weak link in the regional and global security framework where the U.S. plays a leading role. Japan is one of the world's most mature democracies. Thus, we must be a net contributor to the provision of the world's welfare and security. And we will. Japan will contribute to the peace and stability of the region and the world even more proactively than before. I am determined, ladies and gentlemen, to make my beloved country a "Proactive Contributor to Peace."[135]

He then goaded his critics, "So call me, if you want, a right-wing militarist."

Even progressives such as former prime minister Kan Naoto have resorted to evoking traditional Japanese values to ease the strains of change. Addressing the World Economic Forum's Davos conclave in January 2011, Kan announced that he would be "reopening Japan" and using kizuna to dull the painful effects of that process. In his speech he attempted to articulate how Japan would shake off the torpor that had held the country in its grip for two decades and would strive to maintain the equality and order that characterized contemporary Japan. He noted that Japan's opening and the introduction of new social and economic systems would create inequality because "there will always be people who are left behind the pace of change." Since vehicles for prosperity, freedom, reform, and growth also increase disparities and isolate people, Kan called for the creation of a "new *Kizuna*, or interpersonal bonds, in order to avoid such a situation."[136] For the prime minister, an avowed liberal, kizuna harks back to a unified, undifferentiated Japanese community that was bound by ties of family or geography, in which all members are equal and no one is left out by accident or design.[137]

This idealized historical view of Japan is popular, and not just among politicians and officials. In the spring of 2007, 74 percent of Japanese respondents in a Pew poll lamented that "our traditional way of life is getting lost."[138] That loss assumed a new urgency and validity after the triple catastrophe of March 11. Ishinabe Hiroko, the driving force behind the *matsuri* (festivals) that were launched to rekindle the local spirit after those events, insisted Japan should focus its energies inward and "rebuild a society that is self-perpetuating and self-contained. We need time to rebuild. . . . Japan needs to fix the current drift and find its own center."[139] Tsuda Daisuke, a mediaist, echoed Ishinabe and credited the extraordinary power of local festivals for providing a balm for affected communities and speeding their recovery. March 11 focused attention on social resilience and the resulting appreciation of what makes and defines a community, of the traditions that should be honored and maintained, and of how they provide a purpose and objective for residents.[140]

Some Japanese have awakened to the commandeering of traditions and culture by groups with a particular agenda. Sudo Reiko, the force behind the Nuno textile collective, explained that "after March 11 we started to think about our country seriously. We look at ourselves and we feel we are Japanese and we have to think about our country, but there is no nationalism, only the right wing. The Right monopolizes the flag and the country. We started to be concerned about nationalism in a positive way; it's not just the right wing screaming in the street."[141]

Public opinion data shows that these are not isolated sentiments. According to Cabinet Office surveys, nearly half of the Japanese (47.3 percent) believe that, as citizens, more attention should be paid to their country and society (while, by contrast, 40.5 percent prefer a focus on enriching individual lives).[142] Almost 50 percent of respondents said the interests of the country should prevail over those of individuals (32.7 percent reversed those priorities). Nearly two-thirds of Japanese (65 percent) said they normally think about ways "to serve society"; they value greater community and social cohesion. Almost half the Japanese public believes that more needs to be done to tighten bonds within society—an understandable sentiment if just 41 percent of respondents said that it is desirable for all residents to help one another in times of trouble (a number that has changed little since January 2011). That last statistic also suggests that the young Japanese in chapter 5 who were cynical about kizuna and the call to unite after the events of March 11 were representative of a larger group; the emphasis on enhancing bonds among all Japanese merely spotlighted the fraying of those ties.

The Dangers of "Narrow-Minded Nationalism"

After winning the October 2017 election, Abe claimed that "we won a two-thirds majority as the ruling bloc. . . . [W]e aim to win the understanding of the people, so that we can gain a majority in a referendum [to revise the constitution]."[143] While Abe has been emboldened by his electoral success, he must still be cautious. He faces two audiences as he attempts to transform Japanese thinking about patriotism, the constitution, and the country's place in the region: One is domestic; the other is foreign. Both are skeptical of his plans.

The mass protests that greeted the passage of the national secrecy law and the security legislation were the tip of an iceberg of opposition. A Cabinet Office survey found that only 6 percent of Japanese think defense policy is moving in a positive direction after four years of Abe's reforms and a mounting external threat. More than four times as many respondents—28.2 percent—concluded it is going in the wrong direction. Only government finance and regional disparities are more worrisome to the Japanese.[144]

Regional audiences are eager to see Japan—along with other countries—engage in Asia to ensure that they have options. But the goodwill and soft power that Tokyo has accumulated are the products of a particular set of postwar policies: Japan has been a good international citizen since the end of World War II, with an exemplary record of promoting peace and the rule of law. Abe's activism raises questions about whether that past will continue to serve as precedent. His goal of reclaiming first-tier nation status—even without the explicit aim of asserting regional preeminence—may be at odds with the equality that others seek in Asia. In theory, those two positions—first-tier nation and equal partner—can be reconciled; in reality, first-tier nations have a freedom of maneuver along with a power and status that elevates them above other countries. A genuine partnership is possible only with other first-tier states. For all others, in particular those in Asia, the more likely outcome is a version of the previous relationship that locks Japan in as a mentor and leader.

A danger also lurks that a genuine, hard-edged nationalism will undercut Abe's ambitions. Tokyo's top priority is restoring political stability and economic vitality, which are prerequisites to a national recovery, and both are essential to the country's assumption of a larger international role. But non-Japanese demand another prerequisite—a historical accounting that permits the forging of an "Asian consensus" or the "shared concept of being Asian." Since status and standing are conferred by other states, the failure to reach a shared understanding of history—even if just on the boundaries of permissible statements and behavior—will undermine any Japanese leader's international ambitions.

Surveying the region, the *Mainichi Shimbun* worried about the resurgence of "narrow-minded nationalism," which, it warned, "could block international cooperation. Although patriotism is important, exclusionary nationalism only causes friction and conflicts. If Japan pursues such nationalism, it would lose out entirely the benefits to be had through international cooperation and both Japan and the rest of the world would suffer."[145]

Japanese decision makers must acknowledge and deal with these obstacles if their country is to forge a new partnership with Asia. They should not pretend that such stumbling blocks do not exist, as Finance Minister Aso Taro did when dismissing complaints about visiting the Yasukuni Shrine during Diet comments: "No country bans the government from paying respect to those who sacrificed their precious lives for their country. It is a natural duty as a citizen." Nor are decision makers able to will them away, as Abe did when he told a Diet committee that "it is wrong to think that diplomatic relations will go well" if his government stops trying to pay more respect to Japanese traditions.[146]

Abe and his supporters are right to complain that they are unfairly singled out for criticism as nationalists—the Korean and Chinese versions are much more virulent—but they must also understand that Japan has no chance of realizing its ambition to play a larger role in the region if the country's leadership deliberately antagonizes its neighbors and potential partners. The deal Abe struck with China in the fall of 2014 that put a floor on relations with China, his speech on the seventieth anniversary of the end of World War II,[147] and the December 2015 agreement with South Korea that seeks an end to the comfort women issue and allows the two countries to focus on the future—all indicate that Abe understands the stakes.[148]

Lee Chung Min, former dean of the Graduate School of International Studies at Seoul's Yonsei University and a foreign policy adviser to conservative Korean presidents, has urged Japan to shed its immobilism and speak out—and act—more aggressively in support of the values and principles that made it a twentieth-century success. In 2011 he shocked Japanese audiences during a US State

Department–supported speaking tour of Japan with his call for Tokyo to step up and assume a higher profile. But, he reminded them, Japan's strategic relevance ultimately depends on eradicating or minimizing concerns about a potential rightward shift in its security policy and strategy. He has called on Japan's leaders to "commit themselves to forging a new Asian consensus," one that makes "a bold and final break with the vestiges of World War II."[149] This not only would allow Tokyo to win the hearts and minds of Asians but also oblige other Asian states to accept it "as a vital partner and leader in the economic, political and security domains."[150]

Notes

1. "Japan is back": CSIS, "Statesmen's Forum" (see chap. 2, n. 61). The speech at CSIS was especially poignant as the think tank had a few months before issuing the third of its Nye-Armitage reports. The bipartisan assessment of the US-Japan relationship asked point blank, "Does Japan desire to continue to be a tier-one nation, or is she content to drift into tier-two status?" Armitage and Nye, *U.S.-Japan Alliance*, 1 (see chap. 2, n. 61).
2. Neil Irwin, "Why Japan Is the Most Interesting Story in Global Economics Right Now," *Washington Post*, April 4, 2013.
3. This was a somewhat arbitrary marker since Kuroda has said he would keep easing as long as it takes to meet the 2 percent goal; that is what he means by "open-ended." Edward Hugh, "The Real Experiment That Is Being Carried Out in Japan," A Fistful of Euros: European Opinion, May 14, 2013, http://fistfulofeuros.net /afoe/the-real-experiment-that-is-being-carried-out-in-japan/.
4. James McBride and Xu Beina, "Abenomics and the Japanese Economy," Backgrounder (Washington, DC: Council on Foreign Relations, March 10, 2015), http://www.cfr.org/japan/abenomics-japanese-economy/p30383. Last updated March 23, 2018.
5. Shiozaki Yasuhisa, "Japan's Economy—Can It Be Rescued and Revived by Abenomics?," remarks to the Credit Suisse 16th Asian Investment Conference, Hong Kong, March 18, 2013.
6. "Japan's Bond Market: The Wild Side," *The Economist*, Banyan Asia blog, May 24, 2013, http://www.economist.com/blogs/banyan/2013/05/japans-bond-market.
7. Shiozaki, "Japan's Economy."
8. "Japan's Economy: Pump-Priming," *The Economist*, January 3, 2015.
9. Matthew Boesler, "The Truth about Abenomics: The Japanese Economic Experiment That Is Captivating the World," *Business Insider*, March 16, 2013, www .businessinsider.com/what-is-abenomics-2013-3.
10. Jonathan Soble, "Abe's Third Arrow Aims to Pierce Labor Shield in Growth Strategy," *Financial Times*, June 4, 2013. This is a potentially double-edged sword:

Companies could opt for more part-time "irregular" workers, compounding the problems on the demand side of the economy. As one expert explains in Soble's analysis, Japan's priority is employment, while other countries prioritize wages.

11. Tom Holland, "After a Stellar Start, 'Abenomics' Faces Dim Future," *South China Morning Post*, May 17, 2013, http://www.scmp.com/business/article/1239269 /after-stellar-start-japans-abenomics-faces-dim-future.

12. Organization for Economic Cooperation and Development, *Japan 2014, Advancing the Third Arrow for a Resilient Economy and Inclusive Growth*, April 30, 2014, 2, https://www.oecd.org/japan/2014.04_JAPAN_EN.pdf.

13. Kashima Miyuki and Simon Cox, "Abenomics: What's Left in the Quiver?," Bank of New York Mellon, September 2014, https://www.bnymellon.com/_global-assets /pdf/our-thinking/business-insights/abenomics-what%27s-left-in-the-quiver.pdf.

14. "Abenomics Is Progressing!" is a regular topic on the prime minister's home page. As of this writing, the most recent assessment was June 2018 and is available at http://www.japan.go.jp/abenomics/index.html.

15. All figures from "Abenomics Is Progressing!," January 20, 2016, http://www.japan .go.jp/abenomics/index.html.

16. All figures from "Abenomics Is Progressing!," February 16, 2016, http://www.japan .go.jp/pc/abenomics/201602/.

17. Sano Hideyuki and Kihara Leika, "BOJ Launches Negative Interest Rates, Already Dubbed a Failure by Markets," Reuters, February 15, 2016, http://www.reuters .com/article/us-japan-economy-boj-idUSKCN0VP08T.

18. Richard Katz, "Why Is GDP So Flat?," *Oriental Economist*, February 15, 2016.

19. Nohara Yoshiaki and Andy Sharp, "Abenomics Losing Support with Economists and Voters Alike," *Japan Times*, March 8, 2016.

20. Ibid.

21. Shiozaki, "Japan's Economy."

22. "The Third Arrow of Abenomics: Misfire," *The Economist*, June 15, 2013.

23. Associated Press, "Japan PM Outlines Reform Strategy for Economy," *Business Insider*, June 5, 2013, https://www.business-standard.com/article/international /japan-pm-outlines-reform-strategy-for-economy-113060500169_1.html; and Kaneko Kaori and Kajimoto Tetsuji, "Japan's Abe Targets Income Gains in Growth Strategy," Reuters, June 5, 2013, https://www.reuters.com/article /us-japan-economy-arrow/japans-abe-targets-income-gains-in-growth-strategy -idUSBRE95400R20130605.

24. "Third Arrow," *The Economist*.

25. International Monetary Fund, "IMF Executive Board Concludes 2015 Article IV Consultation with Japan," Press Release No. 15/352 (Washington, DC: IMF, July 23, 2015), 1, https://www.imf.org/external/pubs/ft/scr/2015/cr15197.pdf.

26. Ibid., 9.

27. Ibid., 1.

28. Government of Japan, "Section 1 Outline: I. Basic Concept of Revising Japan Revitalization Strategy," June 30, 2015, 2, https://www.kantei.go.jp/jp/singi /keizaisaisei/pdf/dai1en.pdf.

29. Government of Japan, "Urgent Policies to Realize a Society in Which All Citizens Are Dynamically Engaged," January 22, 2016, 1, http://japan.kantei.go .jp/97_abe/Documents/2015/__icsFiles/afieldfile/2016/01/22/urgentpolicies _20151126.pdf.

30. Ibid.

31. Government of Japan, "Basic Policy on Economic and Fiscal Management and Reform 2017," Cabinet Decision, June 9, 2017, 1, http://www5.cao.go.jp/keizai -shimon/kaigi/cabinet/2017/2017_basicpolicies_en.pdf.

32. "Japan Is Now the Fastest Growing Economy in the G7," *Fortune* and Reuters, August 13, 2017, http://fortune.com/2017/08/14/japan-2q-gdp-growth-abenomics/.

33. Government of Japan, "Basic Policy," 2. "Society 5.0" is defined as "a human-centered society that balances economic advancement with the resolution of social problems by a system that highly integrates cyberspace and physical space." See Japan Cabinet Office, Council for Science, Technology, and Innovation, "Society 5.0," accessed August 15, 2018, http://www8.cao.go.jp/cstp/english/society5_0 /index.html.

34. Leo Lewis, "The End of Abenomics Will Test Japan's Appetite for M&A," *The Financial Times*, July 26, 2017.

35. International Monetary Fund, "Japan: 2017 Article IV Consultation—Press Release; Staff Report; and Statement by the Executive Director for Japan," Washington, DC, July 31, 2017, 21, https://www.imf.org/~/media/Files/Publications /CR/2017/cr17242.ashx.

36. Government of Japan, "I. Overview: 1. The Basic Concept of Growth Strategy," June 13, 2013, 1, https://www.kantei.go.jp/jp/singi/keizaisaisei/pdf/en_saikou_jpn.pdf.

37. Government of Japan, "Revising Japan Revitalization Strategy."

38. Ibid., 2.

39. Ibid., 24.

40. Nakamichi Takeshi and Fumikawa Megumi, "Bank of Japan Takes Fresh Action," *Wall Street Journal*, December 18, 2015.

41. Michiyo Nakamoto, "Japan Unveils ¥10.3tn Stimulus Package," *Financial Times*, January 11, 2013.

42. The bulk of this debt is owed to the Japanese people, making the country less susceptible to a squeeze by (foreign) creditors. But there are problems with this logic. First, at some point, those lenders—Japanese financial institutions channeling savings of the public—will need funds as depositors start consuming their savings in retirement. How the government will meet that demand without printing

lots of money is not clear. Second, it assumes that Japanese savers will be content with the abysmally low interest rates they currently receive and will continue to provide funds to the government. Third, it anticipates recovery or inflation before bond yields go up. Inflation will push yields higher as investors want to make sure their profits are not eaten by rising prices. But if bond yields rise and the economy doesn't recover, Japan is in the worst possible world with more debt and still higher servicing costs.

43. "The End of the Affair," *The Economist*, April 11, 2015.
44. Hoshi Takeo, "Two Decades of Stalled Reform: Why the Government's Growth Strategies All Look the Same" (Tokyo: Tokyo Foundation for Policy Research, June 15, 2017), http://www.tokyofoundation.org/en/articles/2017/two-decades-of-stalled-reform.
45. Ibid.
46. Author interview, Tokyo, November 2, 2017.
47. Noah Smith makes the most impassioned case in "Trust Not in Shinzo Abe, Ye Monetarists!," *Noahpinion* (blog), December 28, 2012, http://noahpinionblog.blogspot.com/2012/12/trust-not-in-shinzo-abe-ye-monetarists.html. Linda Sieg and her colleagues at Reuters support that argument in "Special Report: The Deeper Agenda behind 'Abenomics,'" May 24, 2013.
48. Sawa Takamitsu, "Abe Set to Overturn Legacies of Koizumi and Nakasone," *Japan Times*, October 13, 2013.
49. Government of Japan, "Japan Revitalization Strategy."
50. Sawa Takamitsu, "Abe Set to Overturn Legacies of Koizumi and Nakasone," *Japan Times*, October 13, 2013.
51. Leo Lewis and Kana Inagaki, "Japan Inc: Heavy Meddling," *Financial Times*, March 15, 2016. Some note that neither METI nor its predecessor, the Ministry of International Trade and Industry, was ever as powerful as advertised, but there is no missing the role afforded METI in Abenomics or the proximity of former METI officials to Prime Minister Abe (and they presumably seek more power for their former employer).
52. Author interview, Tokyo, November 2, 2017.
53. William Pesek, "Japan's Abenomics Failure Is 30 Years in the Making," *Asia Times*, August 11, 2017, http://www.atimes.com/article/japans-abenomics-failure-30-years-making/.
54. Tobias Harris, "Can Japan's Opposition Mobilise Disaffected Voters?," *East Asia Forum*, July 2, 2016, http://www.eastasiaforum.org/2016/07/02/can-japans-opposition-mobilise-disaffected-voters/.
55. Bank of Japan, "Results of the 71st Opinion Survey on the General Public's Views and Behavior (September 2017 Survey)," October 13, 2017, https://www.boj.or.jp/en/research/o_survey/ishiki1710.htm/.

56. Brad Glosserman, "An Ugly Win for Mr. Abe," *PacNet* (Pacific Forum CSIS newsletter) 89 (December 16, 2014), https://www.csis.org/analysis/pacnet-89-ugly-win-mr-abe.

57. Brad Glosserman, "Japan: Hopeless?," *PacNet* 77 (October 25, 2017), https://www.csis.org/analysis/pacnet-77-japan-hopeless.

58. Masahisa Endo, Robert Pekkanen, and Steve Reed, "The LDP's Path Back to Power," in Pekkanen, Reed, and Scheiner, *Japan Decides 2012*, 49 (see chap. 4, n. 45).

59. Linda Sieg and Takenaka Kiyoshi, "Japan Enacts Strict State Secrets Law Despite Protests," Reuters, December 6, 2013, http://www.reuters.com/article/us-japan-secrets/japan-enacts-strict-state-secrets-law-despite-protests-idUSBRE9B50JT20131206.

60. Mina Pollman, "Japan's Controversial State Secrets Law: One Year Later," *The Diplomat*, December 9, 2015, https://thediplomat.com/2015/12/japans-controversial-state-secrets-law-one-year-later/.

61. Adam Liff, "Policy by Other Means: Collective Self-Defense and the Politics of Japan's Postwar Constitutional Reinterpretation," *Asia Policy* 24 (July 2017): 139–72.

62. Robert Pekkanen and Saadia Pekkanen, "Japan in 2015: More about Abe," *Asian Survey* 56, no. 1 (2016): 44.

63. "Survey: Less Than 40 Percent of Japanese Support TPP Ratification," *Agencie EFE*, October 31, 2016, https://www.efe.com/efe/english/portada/survey-less-than-40-percent-of-japanese-support-the-tpp-ratification/50000260-3083023. Tobias Harris notes that 53 percent of respondents in an NHK poll either "greatly approved" (8 percent) or "to some extent approved" (45 percent) the agreement, while 29 percent "did not much approve" and 8 percent "did not approve at all." A *Nihon Keizai Shimbun* poll found 49 percent of respondents approved, and only 26 percent disapproved of the agreement. Tobias Harris, "The Next Steps for Japan on the Road to the Trans-Pacific Partnership" (Washington, DC: Sasakawa Peace Foundation USA, October 27, 2015), https://spfusa.org/research/the-next-steps-for-japan-on-the-road-to-the-trans-pacific-partnership/.

64. Jeff Kingston, "Abe's Faltering Efforts to Restart Japan," *Current History*, September 2016, 235.

65. "For Nonexistent High-Rise, Deeper Discount Sought for Moritomo," *Asahi Shimbun*, May 22, 2017, http://www.asahi.com/ajw/articles/AJ201705220056.html.

66. Lawrence Repeta, "Backstory to Abe's Snap Election—the Secrets of Moritomo, Kake and the 'Missing' Japan SDF Activity Logs," *Asia-Pacific Journal* 15, no. 20 (October 15, 2017), https://apjjf.org/2017/20/Repeta.html.

67. "Finance Ministry Admits Altering Moritomo Land Deal Docs: Akie Abe's Name Erased," *Mainichi Shimbun*, March 12, 2018, https://mainichi.jp/english/articles/20180312/p2g/00m/0dm/045000c.

68. Linda Sieg, "Scandal Clouds Darken for Japan's Abe ahead of Trump Summit," Reuters, April 10, 2018, https://www.reuters.com/article/us-japan-politics/scandal-clouds-darken-for-japans-abe-ahead-of-trump-summit-idUSKBN1HH0EM.

69. Ellis Krauss and Robert Pekkanen, *The Rise and Fall of Japan's LDP: Political Party Organizations as Historical Institutions* (Ithaca, NY: Cornell University Press, 2011), 141.

70. AFP, "Japan's PM Abe Not Involved in Doctoring Land-Sale Documents, Says Key Official," *Straits Times,* March 27, 2018, http://www.straitstimes.com/asia/east-asia/japans-pm-abe-not-involved-in-doctoring-land-sale-documents-says-key-official.

71. Brad Glosserman, "Why Trump Could Be the Final Nail in Abe's Coffin," *The Diplomat*, March 28, 2018, https://thediplomat.com/2018/03/why-trump-could-be-the-final-nail-in-abes-coffin/.

72. David Pilling, "China and the Post-Tsunami Spirit Have Revived Japan," *Financial Times*, May 13, 2013.

73. Abe Shinzo, "Japan Is Back" (see chap. 2, n. 61).

74. Ibid.

75. Zeeshan Aleem, "Japan and Europe's Huge New Trade Agreement Shows That US Leadership Is Already Fading," Vox.com, July 6, 2017, https://www.vox.com/world/2017/7/6/15924316/japan-europe-trade-trump.

76. Kanehara Nobukatsu, "Kokka kokueki kachi to gaikou anzenhoshou," in *Ronsyuu Nihon no gaikou to sougouteki anzenhoshou*, ed. Yachi Shotaro (Tokyo: WEDGE, 2011): 17–56.

77. Brad Glosserman, "False Choices for Tokyo," *Japan Times*, January 23, 2008.

78. To assert as some have (and do) that Japan is free or cheap riding on the United States overlooks both the substantial contributions (money, personnel, cooperative initiatives) that Tokyo makes to the alliance and the benefits the United States gains from forward positioning its forces in Asia. This forward basing is a bargain for both countries.

79. See, for example, Ministry of Foreign Affairs of Japan, "Japan-U.S. Security Consultative Committee (Japan-U.S. '2+2')," August 17, 2017, http://www.mofa.go.jp/na/st/page3e_000714.html.

80. Ministry of Defense, *Defense of Japan 2017* (Tokyo: Ministry of Defense, 2017), 211.

81. Jonathan Lemire and Jill Colvin, "In Japan, Trump Pushes New Trade Deal, Mourns Texas Shooting," *Daily Chronicle* (DeKalb, IL), November 5, 2017, http://www.daily-chronicle.com/2017/11/06/in-japan-trump-pushes-new-trade-deal-mourns-texas-shooting/avmo7vf/. By the spring of 2018, however, doubts about the wisdom of that strategy had emerged. Blindsided when Trump agreed to a one-on-one meeting with North Korean leader Kim Jong-un, Abe scrambled to ensure that Tokyo and Washington remained in lockstep. Moreover, the much-vaunted

special relationship had not earned Japan an exemption when Trump announced tariffs on steel and aluminum imports. Many observers wondered whether the relationship with Trump had become a net liability for Abe rather than an asset. See, for example, Glosserman, "Why Trump Could Be."

82. Abe, "Japan Is Back."

83. Christopher Hughes, *Japan's Re-emergence as a "Normal" Military Power* (London: International Institute for Strategic Studies, 2004). For more recent developments, see Adam Liff, "Japan's Defense Policy: Abe the Evolutionary," *Washington Quarterly* 38, no. 2 (Summer 2015): 79–99.

84. For a good summary, see Kitaoka Shinichi, "The Turnabout of Japan's Security Policy: Toward 'Proactive Pacifism,'" Nippon.com, April 2, 2014, http://www.nippon.com/en/currents/d00108/.

85. Liff, "Japan's Defense Policy," 79–99; and Brad Glosserman, "Beating Up on Tokyo: Good Fun, Bad Policy," *PacNet* 50 (August 8, 2012).

86. Victor Cha, *Powerplay: The Origins of the American Alliance System in Asia* (Princeton, NJ: Princeton University Press, 2016).

87. Thomas Wilkins, "Japan's Alliance Diversification: A Comparative Analysis of the Indian and Australian Strategic Partnerships," *International Relations of the Asia Pacific* 11, no. 1 (2011): 16.

88. For more on Japan's thinking about trilateralism, see Brad Glosserman, "(H)edging toward Trilateralism: Japanese Foreign Policy in an Uncertain World," *ISPI (Instituto per GLI Studi de Politica Internazionale) Analysis* 84 (January 2011): 116, https://www.ispionline.it/it/documents/Analysis_84_2011.pdf.

89. Yuki Tatsumi, "Introduction," in *US-Japan-Australia Security Cooperation: Prospects and Challenges*, ed. Yuki Tatsumi (Washington, DC: Stimson Center, April 2015), 16.

90. Australian Department of Foreign Ministry and Trade, "Japan Country Brief: Overview," accessed August 15, 2018, http://dfat.gov.au/geo/japan/pages/japan-country-brief.aspx.

91. Ishihara Yusuke, "Japan-Australia Security Relations and the Rise of China: Pursuing the 'Bilateral-Plus' Approaches," UNISCI Discussion Papers No. 32, May 2013, 82.

92. Ministry of Foreign Affairs of Japan, "'Confluence of the Two Seas': Speech by H. E. Mr. Shinzo Abe, Prime Minister of Japan, at the Parliament of the Republic of India," August 22, 2007, http://www.mofa.go.jp/region/asia-paci/pmv0708/speech-2.html.

93. Purnendra Jain, "Modi-Abe Love Affair Drives India and Japan Closer," *East Asia Forum*, September 21, 2017, http://www.eastasiaforum.org/2017/09/21/modi-abe-love-affair-drives-india-and-japan-closer/.

94. The Indian Embassy in Japan applauded the "vast potential for growth," noting that in September 2014, Abe pledged $35 billion in investment in India's public

and private sectors over five years, and set a target of doubling Japanese foreign direct investment and the number of Japanese firms in India by 2019. There is precedent for such hopes: Bilateral trade between the two countries more than doubled between 2006–7 and 2012–13. Embassy of India in Japan, "India-Japan Economic Relations," accessed August 15, 2018, https://www.indembassy-tokyo .gov.in/india_japan_economic_relations.html.

95. Jain, "Modi-Abe Love Affair."

96. Ankit Panda, "US, Japan, India and Australia Hold Working-Level Quadrilateral Meeting on Regional Cooperation," *The Diplomat*, November 13, 2017, https:// thediplomat.com/2017/11/us-japan-india-and-australia-hold-working-level -quadrilateral-meeting-on-regional-cooperation/.

97. Association of Southeast Asian Nations, "Overview of Japan-ASEAN Dialogue Relations," ASEAN.org, March 2017, http://asean.org/storage/2012/05/Overview -ASEAN-Japan-Relations-As-of-8-March-2017.pdf.

98. The quote and all statistics are from Aizawa Nobuhiro, "Japan's Strategy toward Southeast Asia and the Japan-U.S. Alliance," CSIS Japan Chair, Strategic Asia (Washington, DC: CSIS, April 2014), 1.

99. Satu Limaye and Kikuchi Tsutomu, *US-Japan Relations and Southeast Asia: Meeting Regional Demands Project Report* (Washington, DC: East-West Center, Japan Institute of International Affairs and Sasakawa Peace Foundation, 2016).

100. Yamamoto Daisuke, "Solid ASEAN Ties Key to Abe's Strategy," *Kyodo News*, July 13, 2013, https://www.japantimes.co.jp/news/2013/07/31/national/politics -diplomacy/solid-asean-ties-key-to-abe-strategy/#.Wf6I_raB2Ho.

101. Ministry of Foreign Affairs of Japan, "The Japan-ASEAN Summit Meeting," Prime Minister Abe's remarks, Vientiane, Laos, September 7, 2016, http://www.mofa.go .jp/a_o/rp/page3e_000590.html.

102. Tim Kelly and Kubo Nobuhiro, "Exclusive: Japan Seeks Southeast Asia Clout with Chopper Parts for Philippines Military—Sources," Reuters, August 10, 2017, https://www.reuters.com/article/us-japan-defence-philippines-exclusive/exclusive -japan-seeks-southeast-asia-clout-with-chopper-parts-for-philippines-military -sources-idUSKBN1AQ0W3.

103. Embassy of Japan in the Philippines, "Prime Minister Shinzo Abe's Congratulatory Message to the Philippines on the 50th Anniversary on the Establishment of Association of Southeast Asian Nations," August 8, 2017, http://www.ph.emb-japan.go .jp/itpr_en/00_000351.html.

104. Jibiki Koya, "China's Senkaku Incursions Are the New Normal," *Nikkei Asian Review*, September 11, 2017, https://asia.nikkei.com/Politics-Economy /International-Relations/China-s-Senkaku-incursions-are-the-new-normal.

105. Ministry of Defense, *Defense of Japan 2017*, 189.

106. Kudo Yasushi, "Polls Show Sino-Japan Public Sentiment Worsens: Direct Interaction Key to Improvement" (Tokyo: Genron NPO, September 27, 2016), http://www.genron-npo.net/en/opinion_polls/archives/5310.html.

107. Public Relations Office, Cabinet Office, "Overview of the Public Opinion Survey on Diplomacy" (Tokyo: Government of Japan, December 2016), 7–8.

108. Isabel Reynolds, "China-Japan Rivalry Deepens with Abe and Xi on Pace for More Power," Bloomberg, October 16, 2017, https://www.bloomberg.com/news/articles/2017-10-16/china-japan-rivalry-deepens-as-abe-and-xi-on-pace-for-more-power.

109. The deal would ensure that Xi had a successful APEC meeting and that there would be no distractions, such as questions about why the Japanese prime minister was not attending. The terms of the agreement have not been made public, but it is widely believed that they included a pledge by Abe to forgo visits to Yasukuni Shrine. For details of this and a regular assessment of the Japan-China relationship, see the Japan-China articles and chronologies in *Comparative Connections*, an electronic journal on Asia-Pacific relationships, at http://cc.csis.org.

110. Reynolds, "China-Japan Rivalry Deepens."

111. Ministry of Foreign Affairs of Japan, "Premier of the State Council of China Li Keqiang Visits Japan Japan-China Summit Meeting and Banquet," May 9, 2018, https://www.mofa.go.jp/a_o/c_m1/cn/page3e_000857.html.

112. Daniel Sneider, "Behind the Comfort Women Agreement," *Tokyo Business Today*, January 10, 2016, http://toyokeizai.net/articles/-/99891.

113. Ministry of Foreign Affairs of Japan, "Announcement by Foreign Ministers of Japan and the Republic of Korea at the Joint Press Occasion," December 28, 2015, http://www.mofa.go.jp/a_o/na/kr/page4e_000364.html.

114. Kim Ji-eun, "Moon Administration Will Not Renegotiate 2015 Comfort Women Agreement," *Hankyoreh*, January 10, 2018, http://english.hani.co.kr/arti/english_edition/e_international/827149.html.

115. Brad Glosserman, "Special Forum: U.S.-Japan Relations," *The Asan Forum* (Seoul) 6, no. 4 (June 29, 2018), at http://www.theasanforum.org/us-japan-relations/.

116. Jiji Press, "Election Turnout Likely Second-Lowest in Postwar Period, Estimate Says," *Japan Times*, October 23, 2017, https://www.japantimes.co.jp/news/2017/10/23/national/politics-diplomacy/election-turnout-likely-second-lowest-postwar-period-estimate-says/#.WgEveraB2Ho.

117. Bruce Stokes, "Japanese Divided on Democracy's Success at Home, but Value Voice of the People," Pew Research Center, October 17, 2017, http://www.pewglobal.org/2017/10/17/japanese-divided-on-democracys-success-at-home-but-value-voice-of-the-people/.

118. Public Relations Office, Cabinet Office, "Overview of the Public Opinion Survey on Social Awareness in Japan" (Tokyo: Government of Japan, April 2017),

15, http://survey.gov-online.go.jp/h28/h28-shakai/summary.pdf. This is a nearly 5 percentage point increase over the previous survey.

119. All data from Edleman, *2017 Edelman Trust Barometer—Japan: Annual Global Study*, February 9, 2017, https://www.slideshare.net/EdelmanJapan/2017-edelman -trust-barometer-japan.

120. Opening the Diet in 2015, Abe was blunt: "For close to 15 years, Japan has continued to suffer from deflation. I propose that the greatest issue here is the fact that the Japanese people have been robbed of their confidence." See "Policy Speech by Prime Minister Shinzo Abe to the 189th Session of the Diet" (Tokyo: Prime Minister of Japan and His Cabinet, February 12, 2015), http://japan.kantei.go.jp /97_abe/statement/201502/policy.html.

121. Author interview, Tokyo, November 22, 2007.

122. Hashimoto Akiko, *The Long Defeat: Cultural Trauma, Memory, and Identity in Japan* (New York: Oxford University Press, 2015), 5.

123. Aoki Osamu, "Abe Cabinet Has Close Ties with Rightist Political Lobby Japan Conference," *AERA,* January 25, 2016, 17–20.

124. Cited in Mizohata Sachie, "Nippon Kaigi: Empire, Contradiction, and Japan's Future," *Asia-Pacific Journal* 14, no. 21 (November 1, 2016), http://apjjf.org/2016 /21/Mizohata.html.

125. "Policy Speech by Prime Minister Shinzo Abe to the 166th Session of the Diet" (Tokyo: Prime Minister of Japan and His Cabinet, January 26, 2007), https:// japan.kantei.go.jp/abespeech/2007/01/26speech_e.html.

126. Jim Przystup, "Japan-China Relations: Treading Troubled Waters," *Comparative Connections* 15, no. 1 (May 2013): 111.

127. Yoshida Reiji, "Buoyant Abe's True Colors Emerging," *Japan Times*, April 26, 2013, http://www.japantimes.co.jp/news/2013/04/26/national/buoyant-abes-true -colors-emerging/#.UjPMAH-uqLF.

128. Song Miou, "News Analysis: What's the Difference between Abe, Yasukuni Shrine, Nippon Kaigi and the Return of Militarism? Nothing," *Xinhuanet.com*, April 22, 2015, http://news.xinhuanet.com/english/2015-04/22/c_134173141.htm. Critics note that Abe grew up at the knee of his grandfather Kishi Nobusuke, an imperial bureaucrat in charge of policy for colonized China who was arrested after the war, held on suspicion of being a Class A war criminal, and released without being charged. That relationship, they conclude, means that Abe's nationalism presages a return to those dark days.

129. Author interview, Tokyo, July 12, 2012.

130. Thomas Berger, "Abe's Perilous Patriotism: Why Japan's New Nationalism Still Creates Problems for the Region and the U.S.-Japan Alliance," CSIS Japan Chair Platform Special Ed. (Washington, DC: CSIS, October 2014), 1, https://csis-prod

.s3.amazonaws.com/s3fs-public/legacy_files/files/publication/141003_Berger _AbePerilousPatriotism_Web_0.pdf.

131. Akaha Tsuneo, "The Nationalist Discourse in Contemporary Japan: The Role of China and Korea in the Last Decade," *Pacific Focus* 23, no. 2 (August 2008): 160.

132. Kevin Doak, "Shinzo Abe's Civic Nationalism," CSIS Japan Chair Platform (Washington, DC: CSIS, May 15, 2013), https://csis-prod.s3.amazonaws.com /s3fs-public/legacy_files/files/publication/130515_Japan_Chair_Abe_Civic _Nationalism_Doak.pdf.

133. "Editorial: Abe's Game Plan for Constitutional Revision Is Dangerous," *Asahi Shimbun*, January 13, 2016. His mission is cited in Przystup, "Japan-China Relations," 116.

134. Brad Glosserman, "Dangerous Disconnects in the US-Japan Alliance," *PacNet* 26 (April 18, 2013), https://www.csis.org/analysis/pacnet-26-disturbing-disconnects -us-japan-alliance.

135. "Remarks by Prime Minister Shinzo Abe on the Occasion of Accepting Hudson Institute's 2013 Herman Kahn Award," New York City, September 25, 2013, http://www.kantei.go.jp/foreign/96_abe/statement/201309/25hudson_e.html.

136. Japanese Prime Minister Kan Naoto, "Opening Japan and Reinventing KIZUNA," speech at the World Economic Forum, Davos, Switzerland, January 29, 2011, http://www.kantei.go.jp/foreign/kan/statement/201101/29davos_e.html.

137. In *Machiavelli's Children: Leaders and Their Legacies in Italy and Japan* (Ithaca, NY: Cornell University Press, 2003), Richard Samuels called efforts to use the past "bricolage" and distinguished those changes from revolution. The revolutionary leader, he wrote, "rejects a discredited past and focuses on building the future." The *bricoleur*, by contrast, "searches for a usable past. The revolutionary focuses more on exploring new forms, while the *bricoleur* is busy exploiting old ones" (3). Those who seek to "rediscover" Japan's past are true bricoleurs, but even advocates of "re-creation" in the aftermath of March 11 have embraced old ideas to move the country forward.

138. Pew Global Attitudes Project, Pew Global Attitudes and Trends Database, "Question: Which of These Comes Closer to Your View? . . . Our Traditional Way of Life Is Getting Lost, OR Our Traditional Way of Life Remains Strong," Spring 2007, http://www.pewglobal.org/question-search/?qid=1110&cntIDs=@25-&stdIDs=.

139. Author interview, Tokyo, August 14, 2012.

140. Ibid.

141. Author interview, Tokyo, July 23, 2012.

142. All statistics from Public Relations Office, "Survey on Social Awareness."

143. Linda Sieg, "Japan's Abe to Push Pacifist Constitution Reform after Strong Election Win," Reuters, October 23, 2017, https://www.reuters.com/article/us-japan

-election/japans-abe-to-push-pacifist-constitution-reform-after-strong-election
-win-idUSKBN1CS0C3.

144. Public Relations Office, "Survey on Social Awareness," 17–18.

145. "After 60 Years of Peace, Japan's Future Lies in Global Cooperation," *The Mainichi,* April 28, 2012.

146. Both quotes are from "Japanese PM Defends Shrine Visits amid Tensions with China, S. Korea," Kyodo News International, April 13, 2013.

147. "Statement by Prime Minister Shinzo Abe" (Tokyo: Prime Minister of Japan and His Cabinet, August 14, 2015), http://japan.kantei.go.jp/97_abe/statement /201508/0814statement.html.

148. Ministry of Foreign Affairs of Japan, "Announcement by Foreign Ministers of Japan and the Republic of South Korea at the Joint Press Occasion," December 28, 2015, http://www.mofa.go.jp/a_o/na/kr/page4e_000364.html.

149. Lee Chung Min, "Has Japan Lost Its Relevance?," Paper for the 22nd Asia Pacific Roundtable, June 2008, 5, 11, http://www.isis.org.my/images/stories/isis/apr /22nd/23%20Chun%20Min%20Lee.pdf. For a summary of his thoughts during that embassy tour, see Lee Chung Min, "The Perils of a Monotone Asia," *PacNet* 69 (December 15, 2011), https://csis-prod.s3.amazonaws.com/s3fs-public/legacy _files/files/publication/pac1169.pdf.

150. Lee, "Has Japan Lost," 5.

7

PEAK JAPAN

Japan's lost decades are over. Since Abe Shinzo's return to power at the end of 2012, Japan has enjoyed political stability, an economic recovery, and an international resurgence. The celebrations have been muted, however, as Japan has experienced a similarly happy interlude before. In the five and a half years that Koizumi Junichiro was prime minister (2001–6), Japan also had stability, growth, and international stature. Unfortunately, the successes of that half decade proved temporary. When Koizumi departed the political scene, Japan slid back into bad old habits, and a series of shocks proved more than the country could absorb or use to alter the nation's trajectory.

The successes of the Abe interregnum will be equally fleeting. While it can be argued that Japan has turned the corner—a case that was made in chapter 2—a deeper look suggests otherwise. Japan faces structural challenges that elites and the public have been unable to surmount. Those obstacles are reinforced by a set of attitudes and beliefs that further inhibit Japan's capacity to adjust to changing circumstances. This chapter assesses lessons that can be gleaned from the two and a half decades since the bubble burst, their implications for Japan, and the best ways for Japan to maximize its position and sustain its place in the region and the world.

A New Dawn?

Abe Shinzo has been forthright when it comes to Japan's proper place in the world. In his 2015 New Year's address, Abe was blunt: "Our predecessors accomplished rapid economic growth, making Japan one of the greatest powers in the

213

world. . . . [A]s we mark the new year, I have renewed my determination to, together with the Japanese people, make Japan a country that once again shines on the world's center stage."[1] His strategy is twofold: "to rebuild the Japanese economy to be vibrant, and then to make Japan a dependable 'force' that works for good in the world."[2] This, he explained, heralds "a new dawn that is breaking over Japan."[3]

Neither that ambition nor the means that the prime minister and his cabinets have adopted to realize those goals are new. The twin goals of rehabilitation and reclamation of international status have animated Japanese governments since the country's defeat in World War II. Politicians have debated the timetable and the most appropriate way to reclaim that role, but the end point has rarely been disputed. A consensus emerged during the Cold War that anticipated the logic of the Abe administration: Economic success would provide the foundation for national renewal.

That plan worked, at least until 1991. When the Cold War ended, the bubble burst, and successive Japanese governments struggled to regain economic traction and restore political stability. By all appearances, the two are related, and the failure to achieve one has prevented the realization of the other. The inability to right the economy is especially troubling given Japan's previous successes and the attention—indeed, the urgency—that has been devoted to solving the problem. Previous chapters detailed a long paper trail that lays out what Japan must do to get back on track. As early as 1984, Japanese planners warned of demographic trends and their economic impact.[4] A series of programs were launched to prod women to have children—the chief initiatives go by the revealingly named Angel Plan—but they have not changed women's thinking. In 2000, after eight years of stagnation, the Prime Minister's Commission on Japan's Goals in the 21st Century, popularly known as the Kawai Commission, outlined its vision of a new Japan. The report began with an understanding of the new forces at work on countries and economies and demanded a new social contract between the government and its citizens that would unleash the creative potential of the Japanese public.[5] Six years later, the first Abe government promulgated the Asian Gateway Initiative, a package of reforms based on the premise that "for Japan to continue stable economic growth and become an attractive 'venue' to the rest of the world, it is critically important to incorporate the growth and vitality of the world, in particular Asia's growth."[6] Even at a time of "substantial economic recovery," policymakers worried about demographic problems and the need to make Japan relevant and attractive to the world, and they sought to tap external energies, especially those of Asia, to generate Japan's own growth.[7] They recognized that "the 21st century is the century of Asia" and that Japan has to find its place in the region.[8]

That initiative was followed by a Keidanren proposal and the Ministry of Economy, Trade, and Industry's "vision" (spelled out in chapter 2) that bemoaned a stagnant economy and called for liberation from "the success mythology built on growth in the postwar period." Both organizations urged Japan to link itself more closely to Asia and increase its focus on energy and environmental problems, along with service industries that would address the country's demographic ills.[9] The cabinet of Prime Minister Kan Naoto adopted the ministry's vision on June 18, 2010, and used it as the basis for a "New Growth Strategy." That was followed by the "Strategy for Rebirth of Japan" developed by the Noda administration, and Abenomics promptly replaced it when the LDP returned to power at the end of 2012.

Plainly, then, there has been consensus (among elites at least) on what had to be done, and that agreement had a pedigree that spanned Japanese governments of both stripes. One study of the lost decades concluded, "Japan has not suffered from a lack of growth strategies over the past decade and a half, although one would be hard pressed to find any impact on economic performance."[10] Another analysis tallied seven long- and medium-term growth strategies since the beginning of the twenty-first century, all of which used the same growth-rate targets (2 percent real and 3 percent nominal).[11] As economist Hoshi Takeo recounted in chapter 6, "The same basic growth ideas have appeared year after year under a variety of labels, suggesting a fundamental lack of progress."[12] Even Abenomics, the radical reform program that has marked the second Abe administration, "is not distinctively different from the reforms of Abe's predecessors."[13]

While the focus of those analyses was economic, they also offered alarming assessments of Japanese foreign policy since economic opportunities were intimately tied to diplomacy and the structure of relationships with other countries. Critics highlighted Japan's failure to adapt to changing circumstances, foreign and domestic, in ways that would facilitate economic growth and a more prominent role for the country in foreign affairs. Some efforts, such as the report by the Institute for International Policy Studies (noted in chapter 1) or the 2011 study by the Japan Institute of International Affairs (in chapter 4), focused solely on foreign policy, and they invariably decried a lack of vision and resources for diplomacy and international relations.

One constant in those assessments are warnings. The Kawai Commission noted that Japan was at a "historical turning point," adding that "we fear that as things stand, Japan is heading for decline. . . . [T]he economic bubbles of the late 1980s and then the bursting of the bubbles early in the 1990s had undermined not only the economy but also the political order and society—even the value system and ethical norms at the very core of the nation."[14] The Institute for International Policy Studies likewise concluded that Japan was facing "the dawn of a new era" and "a break with the outdated existing order."[15] The authors of the Asian Gateway Initiative worried that "it is Japan, [more] than any other Asian country, that is likely to be left out. . . . Japan's competitiveness is weakening due to delayed measures to cope with globalization."[16] In 2011 Sakurai Masamitsu, president of Keizai Doyukai, the association of Japan's top business executives, lamented that "present-day Japan is lost and moving into the future with no sense of direction."[17] His successor, Hasegawa Yasuchika, a year later argued that his country was at "a moment of truth" and "at the brink of crisis."[18]

In the intervening years, the Abe interregnum has provided a floor, but changes remain largely superficial with national trajectories largely unaltered. That is the implicit message in Prime Minister Abe's call in 2015 for "the most drastic reforms since the end of World War II."[19] His invocation of Meiji reformers Iwakura Tomomi, Okakura Tenshin, and Yoshida Shoin indicates this his ambitions are no less sweeping or urgent than theirs; his call to "press forward" with that agenda clearly indicated that the work had not yet been done.

The lack of progress, in the face of credible and increasingly sharp calls to action, is the greatest puzzle about contemporary Japan. Why has a country with an extraordinary record of mass mobilization and success in the realization of national goals failed to respond to domestic stagnation in the face of mounting external challenges? This inaction is especially inexplicable given the shocks, both internal and external, in recent years that policymakers could have used to mobilize the public to address these problems.

"People Are Getting Fed Up with Us"

There is no simple explanation for Japan's failure to act. A long list of obstacles has contributed to inertia and stagnation. The first and most visible are structural impediments to economic reform. Chapter 1 identifies some of the economic problems—a dismal demographic profile, a growing mountain of debt—while the vested interests highlighted in chapter 2 pose other restraints. An aging population will squeeze pension systems, cut productivity, drain innovation and energy, and sharpen conflicts among constituencies over dwindling government revenues. There's likely to be more intergenerational fighting for government services—guns versus butter or, more accurately, guns versus wheelchairs.

Meaningful reform threatens power alignments, and no one with power willingly relinquishes it. Some, such as economist Shibata Saori, assert that reforms adopted under the rubric of Abenomics compound uncertainty and thus undercut prospects for long-term stability. She argues that Abenomics "represents a hazard to future economic growth in Japan" for the following reasons:

Labor market reforms [have] weakened working practices that were central to the "classic" Japanese model, including the seniority wage system and stable employment system, and the transformation of those practices toward more performance-based and more competitive employment practices. . . . The liberalizing elements of Abenomics also act to create insecurity for Japanese workers, whilst at the same time relying upon an expectation that there will be increased consumption—presumably from the very same workers who are experiencing heightened income insecurity.[20]

Structural impediments also contribute to political instability.[21] Traditional bonds between voters and politicians—money and ideology—have been weakened by political reforms, and that has introduced considerable volatility into elections, as swings in the 2009 and 2012 ballots attest. In recent years, elections have produced a "twisted Diet" in which competing coalitions control different chambers of the legislature. From 2007 to 2009, the Democratic Party of Japan controlled the upper house and frustrated the LDP, which had a majority in the lower house; the LDP returned the favor from 2010 to 2012 after the DPJ won its governing majority in 2009. Voter swings assume special importance given the institutional power of Japan's upper house, which is one of the most powerful "second" chambers in the world and can block lower house and government initiatives in many situations.

Political leaders have increasing difficulty enforcing order in their parties. New selection procedures have undercut the ability of senior LDP figures to keep their juniors in line. In office, the prime minister has a limited ability to set the legislative agenda and parliamentary order; those are the province of Diet committees. As a result, concludes one incisive study, "without further changes to the political system, powerful institutional factors will continue to make it difficult for prime ministers to exercise political leadership in a sustained and effective manner."[22]

One-party rule has created other issues that are not structural per se but are related—namely, corruption and arrogance in the LDP. As noted in chapter 6, the first few years after Abe's return to power saw few of the scandals that had regularly come to stain Japanese politics. The two school-related scandals that broke in 2017—the sweetheart land deal for the Osaka kindergarten Moritomo Gakuen and the mysterious decision to grant permission to open the Kake veterinary school—indicate that old habits are reasserting themselves. The details of both scandals suggest that they are an outgrowth of the return of an entrenched political class and a phenomenon known in Japan as *sontaku*. In its original usage, the word means to "conjecture, surmise or speculate."[23] In the current political context, however, it refers to the tendency of bureaucrats or officials to anticipate their political masters' wishes and to act in ways that avoid the issuance of direct orders or that leave a paper trail. The operator of the Osaka kindergarten denied there was any influence peddling, but he conceded that sontaku may have been at work.[24]

A return to such practices will compound the unease many Japanese voters felt at the return of one-party rule (even if they continue to vote for the LDP). Voters were scarred by their experience with the DPJ government and have been reluctant since then to entrust other parties with power. Prime Minister Abe has been a merciless electoral tactician, exploiting that mistrust to engineer ever-larger political majorities, but his behavior risks breeding cynicism and indifference among voters and worse in the LDP. Anger and distrust have also been fueled by scandals that seem to reach the upper echelons of the Abe administration and the seeming dismissal of their import by that same government. Koizumi Shinjiro, a rising star in the LDP, warned after the party's October 2017 election win, "It's not just that our party has become arrogant and complacent. People are also getting increasingly fed up with us."[25]

Structural issues bedevil Japan's foreign policy as well. The limits imposed by political instability and economic stagnation are the most obvious problem. Without steady leadership, foreign leaders will not take their Japanese counterparts seriously. Why bother with the relationship building that is essential to foreign policy if Japan's prime minister, foreign minister, or defense minister will not be long in office? A stagnant economy not only deprives Japan of the resources that are essential to the conduct of foreign policy (especially one that has relied on aid and investment for influence) but also tarnishes Japan's image as a model for other countries that consequently was the source of substantial soft power.

A second and subtler structural problem for Japanese foreign policy is Tokyo's reliance on institutional platforms whose value is diminishing. Consider, for example, the alliance with the United States. The US National Intelligence Council has concluded that the relative decline of the United States vis-à-vis rising states is inevitable. While the United States will "likely remain 'first among equals' among the other great powers" for another decade or two, "the 'unipolar moment' is over and Pax Americana—the era of American ascendency in international politics that began in 1945—is fast winding down."[26] This conclusion reflects geopolitical trends, but it has been reinforced by the intense partisanship and political gridlock that has descended on Washington in the second decade of the new millennium and the uncertainty that surrounds US foreign policy in the Trump administration. This assessment has powerful implications for Tokyo as perhaps no other country has so closely tied its own future to that of the United States. The US alliance has provided a foundation on which Japanese decision makers have stood as they emerged from the destruction of World War II.[27] Since

Washington views Tokyo as a like-minded and similarly interested diplomatic partner, the United States has tightly aligned itself with Japan, providing support and backing it in regional and international forums. As the United States power and influence are reduced, so must Japan's.

A similar process is at work on the Group of Eight (G8). The Group of Seven (G7) leading industrialized countries emerged during the 1970s as the premier forum for international agenda setting and global economic management. Tokyo was the only Asian government in that exclusive club, and its "inclusion in the first of these informal summits of contemporary great powers accorded status and recognition to Japan."[28] When the Cold War ended, Russia was invited to join as the group adapted to maintain its legitimacy. A decade later, however, the G8's limits were clear. When the global financial crisis hit in 2007, the G8 recognized the rising importance of emerging powers in the global system and elevated the Group of Twenty (G20)—formerly a technical forum to address international financial issues—to a leader-level meeting to provide global guidance. Not only does the very existence of the G20 undermine the significance of the G7—the group dropped Russia after it invaded Crimea in 2014—but it also threatens Japan's "identity-defining position as Asia's representative in the mechanisms of global governance . . . as the G20 now includes China, India, Indonesia, South Korea, and even Australia as Asian members."[29] In another example of shifting global governance that disadvantages Japan, China proposed, set up, and leads the Asian Infrastructure Investment Bank, which launched in 2016. The bank competes with the Asian Development Bank, where Japan has enjoyed outsize influence. In each case, Japan's status and influence are diminished by the weakening of institutions once considered the apex of global or regional order and by the rise of new institutions of governance.

Adapting to this changing environment risks further undermining Japanese standing in Asia. Singaporean analyst See Seng Tan has warned that the Abe administration's attempts to embrace a higher regional security profile could damage Japan's "reputation as a regional leader . . . should its future participation in Asian multilateralism be shaped exclusively by the perceived need to counterbalance China."[30] This impulse could be driven either by Tokyo's aim to align more closely with or act on behalf of a US government that sees China as more of a threat than a partner or by Tokyo's purely domestic calculus that Japan should check an assertive China. This unhappy outcome does not require Japan to reject the multilateralism that has been a staple of its regional foreign policy for the last half century. However, even an "à la carte approach to multilateralism . . . risks alienating not only China but other regional countries as well. . . . Whatever contributions Japan's à la carte multilateralism might deliver to the region, they would not only be undermined by its turn to hard balancing against China, but its leadership in alternative security approaches itself could be jeopardized."[31]

"Dreams Are Shrinking in Japan"

As frustrating as these structural impediments are, a more pernicious set of restraints is attitudinal. A package of beliefs obliges the Japanese, despite increasing urgent calls for reform, to accept a troubling status quo and reject change.[32] These beliefs reflect twin strands of Japanese identity: One is expressed by a distinctive political-economic model, while the other reflects broader, more general notions of culture and appropriate behavior.

The readiness to cling to an economic model that steadily improved standards of living for over half a century is understandable. A unique variant of capitalism took Japan to unimagined heights and allowed the country "to win" the Cold War; jettisoning that proven model of success for ideas that have not been tested locally and have created alarming outcomes abroad is a tough sell. The majority of reforms that have been identified and articulated—for example, reducing state intervention and giving markets more freedom to set prices for assets—are neoliberal in nature and would reverse long-standing policies that privilege economic stability and security over growth and productivity. Ministry of Finance official Sakakibara Eisuke was speaking for the Japanese mainstream at the end of the 1990s when he denounced "market fundamentalism."[33] Even in the midst of the reformist spasm of the Koizumi years, one analyst still concluded that "no Japanese political party has ever stood unequivocally in favor of economic liberalization, and no party is likely to do so in the foreseeable future."[34] Five years later, a rejection of "market fundamentalism drove DPJ Prime Minister Hatoyama Yukio's philosophy of '*Yuai*.'" He believes market fundamentalism "results in people being treated not as an end but as a means," while *yuai* seeks "to accommodate the local economic practices that have been fostered through our traditions"[35]—an approach that also influenced the New Growth Strategy of his successor, Kan Naoto. One intellectual behind the DPJ government argued that a founding principle of that administration was a rejection of neoliberal tendencies.[36] The fitful experience of the third arrow of Abenomics is proof that ambivalence toward, if not outright hostility to, such reforms remains the norm.

This resistance is natural when 51 percent of the Japanese people disagree with the statement that a majority of people are better off in a free market society.[37] When asked "whether it is more important that individuals be free to live their lives without interference from the state or that the state play an active role in society so as to guarantee that nobody is in need," more Japanese prefer an activist state. In 2002, 50 percent of respondents selected the second option; that number increased to 55 percent nine years later.[38] Political scientist Yamaguchi Jiro insists, "The Japanese people want a welfare state. In government polls, people say they will pay more taxes if social security benefits are assured. Two-thirds agree with that direction."[39] Pew data backs him up: Its surveys show that 46 percent of Japanese respondents believe higher taxes would close the gap between rich and poor (versus 43 percent who said the answer is lower taxes).[40] In other words, a substantial and growing majority of Japanese people prefer a larger state presence in the market, at least if it means fewer "citizens in need"; employment takes precedence over expansion.

Another expression of this mentality is the relative dearth of entrepreneurial activity in Japan, especially among the young. Japan has traditionally ranked low in global entrepreneurship rankings; it is twenty-eighth in the world and sixth in the region, according to the Global Entrepreneurship and Development Institute.[41] A recent survey by the Japan Productivity Center concluded that "younger workers are the least inclined to strike out on their own in more than a decade."[42] While there are many explanations for this phenomenon, two are pertinent here—risk aversion of the younger generation in Japan and their belief that they do not or should not have to look out for themselves, as the state will. The former is a natural response for a generation that has known only stagnation. "Today's younger generation don't know what growth is. Their experience is just downsizing and recession. . . . That's why dreams are shrinking in Japan," explained one thirty-seven-year-old.[43] The result is a "fixation on working for large companies or the government," concluded Randall Jones, head of the Japan-Korea desk at the OECD.[44] The belief in the value of state activism in reducing inequality will also undercut the incentive to strike out on one's own. Why bother when the state will either protect all citizens or trim the successes of those who do take risks?

A similar mentality is at work in the business community. As R. Taggart Murphy has noted, "It's not that Japanese executives do not understand the need to streamline inefficient practices. It is that they are unwilling to do so."[45] A reluctance to pursue profit at all costs is part of this larger mind-set. "The 'let them eat cake' ethos of American industry with its mass layoffs is—so far—a nonstarter in Japan. Nor does Japan have the explicit social safety net of the European welfare states. Social welfare in Japan has long been tacitly seen as a corporate responsibility, a responsibility backed up by both formal and informal sanctions."[46] This thinking is behind Keidanren's 2009 call for a "Japanese New Deal" (in chapter 2), which emphasized the need to maintain full employment even as Japan reformed. The notion that Japanese companies work not just for their shareholders but also for their stakeholders guides boardrooms and executives and undercuts reform initiatives. That approach explains why, five years into the Abe era, Japanese companies were enjoying stratospheric profits but corporate governance was largely unchanged. The view of Matsumoto Akira, former chairman of the food group Calbee, is typical of the executive suite. His governance priorities were customers first, followed by employees, then the community, with shareholders in fourth place. Other business leaders widely share this thinking.[47] One sign of this enduring belief is the revived interest in Shibusawa Eiichi, a Meiji-era business leader who is credited with laying the foundation of Japan's modern corporate culture and is often called the father of Japanese capitalism. Shibusawa developed a corporate model that stressed moral and economic harmony, as he felt public interest should take precedence over mere monetary returns.[48]

The particulars of Japanese capitalism are part of a broader understanding of Japanese character and identity. In every statement, vision, initiative, and plan is some acknowledgment of Japanese culture and history that grounds the proposal in a larger package of beliefs and sense of national identity. Consider, for example, the Asian Gateway Initiative, which called for Japan to exploit its unique history, culture, and tradition so the world could gain a greater appreciation of Japan (and so Japan could make money). All the while it also must "create an open society while maintaining its characteristics."[49] The first words of the LDP's 2012 draft constitution acknowledges the country's past: "Japan is a nation with a long history and unique culture."[50] This sentiment is echoed in a 2017 draft constitution by the conservative *Sankei Shimbun*: "The maritime Nation of Japan developed its own unique civilization" and has a "distinctive traditional culture using . . . [its] enterprising spirit and seeking harmony with differing cultures."[51] Even the *National Security Strategy* of Japan is rooted in this cultural soil. The opening words of section 2, which explains the "principles that Japan upholds," note that "Japan is a country with rich culture and tradition."[52] There is nothing nefarious in this language—virtually all references to Japan's culture and traditions go on to highlight the vital importance of diversity and tolerance—but it is critically important to acknowledge the power of the past and the frame that it provides for Japanese thinking as the country debates reform.

Japan's culture, history, and traditions also pose powerful additional obstacles to change. For example, the Japanese are expected to endure or suffer in silence through their hardships, as Ishinabe Hiroko made clear in her comments in chapter 5. A Japanese businessman elaborated on this trait, noting that "civil coherence and a sense of community is the strength of Japanese society."[53] But as he watched the people of Tohoku accept the hardships forced on them while politicians failed to match that determination and effort, he concluded, "It's hard to argue against the idea that *gambaru* [fighting or enduring in struggle] is some obstacle to reform. If we were more upset and angry, then March 11 could have been a driving force for change." Whether one calls this "the Japanese people's normalization bias," as a researcher at the National Institute of Defense Studies explained, or "a virtuous circle of political apathy and small happiness," as one of his colleagues put it,[54] the results are the same: The people demonstrate a readiness to live with discomforts and inconveniences even though they are symptomatic of a larger problem. LDP politician Kono Taro explained the result succinctly: The "social resilience that makes Japan work is an absolute brake on change."[55]

The readiness to endure is part of a larger cultural orientation, one in which individual interests are subordinated to that of the collective. Cabinet Office surveys confirm this belief. In a 2017 poll, more Japanese believe that attention should be put on helping the country and society than on "enriching individual lives" (47.3 percent versus 40.5 percent, and the gap is widening), and a significantly larger number believe the interests of the nation should take precedence over those of individuals (49.3 percent versus 32.7 percent).[56] This emphasis blunts the impact of individual circumstances and reinforces an inclination to accept misfortune or negative outcomes by framing them within a larger social context. The call for change and the push for reform become more difficult when individual experiences are discounted. Liberalization that is based on loosening the grip of the state and empowering the individual is fundamentally alien to this outlook.

The demand for *wa* (harmony) compounds this tendency to focus on society as a whole. It is easy to caricature the role that such concepts play in Japanese society and culture, but they should not be dismissed. Kosaka Masataka, one of Japan's premier international affairs specialists during the Cold War, said that "the first article in a truly Japanese constitution would be 'Harmony must be respected.'" Scholar and Abe adviser Kitaoka Shinichi added, "Arriving at a consensus and proceeding smoothly from that consensus with as little friction and dispute as possible is a fundamental rule in Japan . . . and an important element in Japan's identity."[57]

This orientation is found on both the Left and the Right. A staple of conservative thinking is that postwar Japan has lost its way because of excessive individualism and that a rebalancing of social and individual priorities is in order. But the DPJ's "rebirth strategy" also framed economic recovery within the context of "a society of participation and mutual support"—a vague formulation that translates as more communitarian and has echoes of the traditional Japanese social ethos. Recall too that Prime Minister Kan embraced the notion of kizuna, or social bonds, first to mobilize Japan and dull the pain of reform, and then to help overcome the trauma of March 11. Kan, a progressive, was advancing the deeply felt belief among the Japanese that they are all citizens of one country and connected to each other.

For those on the Right in Japan, choices pose frustrating dilemmas. As they seek reforms to realize their dream of a more powerful and influential Japan, they must balance their impact on long-cherished social norms and idealized social structures. The most obvious example is the treatment of women. The conservative social view puts women in the household, where they provide care and support for three generations. Yet virtually every assessment of Japan's options concludes that women must be better utilized in the labor force if the country is to achieve a sustainable boost in productivity. In a 2014 analysis of "Womenomics," Goldman Sachs determined that if Japan's female employment rate were to match that of men, then the size of the workforce would increase by 7.1 million and GDP could be boosted by as much as 13 percent.[58] IMF economists reached a similar conclusion, noting that if Japan raised its female labor participation rate to the G7 level (also excluding Italy, another outlier), then its GDP per capita would be permanently higher by about 4 percent.[59] Prime Minister Abe recognizes that women are key to the rejuvenation of Japan. At the 2014 World Economic Forum Annual Meeting in Davos, he confessed that "the female labor force in Japan is the most under-utilized resource," and at the 2015 World Assembly for Women in Tokyo, he declared, "Abenomics is Womenomics."[60] Since then he has made Womenomics a pillar of his government's growth strategy.[61]

The program has had successes. In the mid-1990s Japanese female labor participation was just 56 percent; it reached 65 percent in 2015 (although the majority of jobs that Japanese women have been taking are part time).[62] The Health, Labor, and Welfare Ministry established a special fund with ¥550 billion to support municipal governments seeking to ease day care shortages.[63] An August 2015 law titled the Act on Promotion of Women's Participation and Advancement in the Workplace requires large firms and public entities with more than three hundred employees to disclose gender diversity targets and specific action plans from April 2016. But women have more part-time jobs—35 percent versus 10 percent for men—and they earn on average just 71 percent of their male counterparts' wages.[64] Japanese women also remain underrepresented in leadership positions, whether in politics, government, or business. Tellingly, the government's goal of getting women in 30 percent of all management positions by 2020 was lowered to just 7 percent by 2021.[65]

Kathy Matsui, chief Japan strategist at Goldman Sachs and one of the champions of Womenomics, concluded, "It's not just about infrastructure and hardware, it's about the psyche of the Japanese people, the morale, tradition and culture. It's what teachers think about education, what parents think about gender roles."[66] This mind-set was exemplified in 2007 by then health minister Yanagisawa Hakuo's description of women as "child-bearing machines."[67] A Cabinet Office survey at the end of 2012 reported that 51.6 percent of respondents agreed that "the husband should work and the wife should keep house," an increase of 10.3 percentage points from the 2009 survey.[68] Perhaps most alarming for proponents seeking more equality among the sexes is the rising number of Japanese people in their twenties who back this division of labor: 55.7 percent of men in the 2012 survey, a 21.4 percentage point increase from 2009, and even 43.7 percent of women, a jump of 15.9 points.

Sugimoto Mai, a young associate professor of sociology at Kansai University, articulated how many women her age feel: "The LDP really like the traditional family system. They don't like working women. Politicians say women should be at home taking care of the family. Personally, it's a very frustrating issue for me. . . . I don't like my choices. I haven't gotten married because I feel that I would have to give up my career."[69]

This tension has resulted in begrudging change that, judging from demographic trajectories, is too late. Not only is Japan's population shrinking as women opt out of their traditional roles but also preferences may have permanently shifted, making it impossible for fertility rates to reach or surpass replacement no matter what incentives are offered.[70]

A similar headache confronts conservatives as they contemplate agricultural reform, with the Trans-Pacific Partnership (finalized as the CPTPP) trade deal greatly influencing the outcome of that debate. Prime Minister Abe has repeatedly emphasized that the opening of the economy and the reform that will follow are key to restoring Japan's economic dynamism, which in turn provides the foundation for the country's international rejuvenation. Yet many conservatives also believe that Japan's cultural traditions are rooted in agriculture and are distinctive, valuable, and must be preserved. The notion that Japan is, at its core, an agricultural society in which all participants joined in the planting and the harvest has a powerful appeal. This view is, admittedly, an idealized one of Japan—and, to a large extent, manufactured—but it is effective nonetheless. It is the basis for the emphasis on the collective in Japan, or the idea that all Japanese must be part of some larger group. This belief also spurred two objections to the TPP. The first, expressed by Ito Hisaharu, a top official in the Union of Agricultural Cooperatives in Aichi Prefecture, is somewhat conventional but still compelling in a population that truly believes in the equality of its citizens. He charges that "the TPP is a battle over what kind of country we want Japan to be. Do we want to turn into a harsh society of winners and losers, or remain a gentler society where benefits are shared?"[71] This thinking isn't restricted to farmers. A medical lobby insists, "If Japan takes part in the TPP, the universality of public health care coverage may be maintained, but in name only. It is highly possible that fair and equal access to medical care, the core function of this system, will be lost. . . . Hodanren [the Japanese Medical and Dental Practitioners for Improvement of Medical Care], on behalf of 104,000 member medical and dental practitioners, firmly opposes Japan's participation in the TPP."[72]

The second objection is more powerful still and is rooted in the Japanese people's belief that they have a special tie to the environment and that farmers—rice farmers in particular—are a unique expression of Japanese cultural identity. Farmer and poet Hoshi Kanji articulated this view:

> I would like the philosophy of revering agriculture and expelling the barbarians to be the stronghold against the black ships of TPP. We need to give primary importance to agriculture for its production of food for life, and to justly appreciate its function of protecting the environment. . . . "Expel the barbarians" refers to the elimination of our disposable consumer civilization. We need to possess a set of values necessary to live simply and spiritually rich in a mature society.[73]

The power of these beliefs is widespread. The farmers and the Central Union of Agricultural Cooperatives (JA-Zenchu) collected 11.7 million signatures for a petition opposing Japan's participation in the TPP. That number is impressive for two reasons: It is nearly 10 percent of the population, and Japan has only 2.6 million commercial farmers.[74]

Yet, for all the opposition, Japan has joined the TPP and was instrumental in keeping that initiative alive—as the Comprehensive and Progressive Trans-Pacific Partnership—after the withdrawal of the United States, one of Donald Trump's very first acts when he became president. Prime Minister Abe deserves much of the credit for its survival, and Japan's commitment to the trade deal could be considered a rebuttal to my argument. But while CPTPP represents an important and positive step by Japan, Tokyo's embrace of the agreement is less than it seems. It is more accurate to say that the Abe administration *had* to push the TPP (in whatever form) if its efforts to promote a higher international profile for Japan were to have any credibility. Abe had repeatedly emphasized the need for Japan to be a rule maker rather than a rule taker, thus setting a bar for Tokyo's action and involvement as other governments contemplated a revised regional economic order. The US withdrawal from the deal required another government to step up to fill the resulting leadership vacuum. Tokyo's assumption of that role was a virtually foregone conclusion given the strategic challenge posed by China in general, its rivalry with China, and Beijing's efforts to promote alternative regional economic institutions such as the Asian Infrastructure Investment Bank and the Regional Comprehensive Economic Partnership (the direct "competitor" to the TPP). If Japan had not embraced the TPP, then Abe's tier-one aspirations would have been exposed as fantasy.

The TPP exposes another important convergence between the Left and the Right that complicates, if not undermines, debate over reform. The Japanese are grappling with principles that have guided the country since the end of World War II and provided the core of its modern national identity. As Kitaoka Shinichi, one of Japan's most important scholars of history and security policy, has explained, the national debate over the choice between Asia and the West—one that began in the Meiji era and was settled with the 1885 "Datsu-a ron" (escape from Asia) editorial—reemerged after the war. The rapid economic growth of the 1960s put an end to those discussions as Japan's trajectory once again diverged from that of the region. "From the latter half of the 1960s, questions about the essential characteristics of Japan . . . were answered with the comment that Japan had become an economic power. The economic strength of Japan was frequently cited as a key element of Japan's identity."[75] Owada Hisashi, a former diplomat who served on the UN International Court of Justice, concurred, noting that "such an orientation was only to be expected in any case because material prosperity was essential to the new Japan that had to rise from the ashes of total destruction after the war. . . . [F]or the national psyche of a whole nation affected by the disillusion of defeat, the only thing they could believe in, despite their nihilism, was material wealth."[76]

In recent years, the Japanese have felt a growing sense that this process has gone too far and has alienated them from a core component of their real identity. This concern was articulated by the Kawai Commission's report, which noted that "there is a feeling, however, that many of these elements [of Japanese identity] fell by the wayside as Japan focused single-mindedly on development through economic growth."[77] This loss is felt most acutely as the Japanese assess their relationship to the environment. They believe that they have a special relationship with nature, one that affords them unique sensitivities toward and an appreciation of the environment and the need to protect it. This long-standing identification with nature was renewed after March 11. "The Japanese people are looking at the balance of nature and business once again," argued Fukushima Akiko, a senior fellow at the Tokyo Foundation for Policy Research. "Japan learned how to live with nature in a harmonious way. We shouldn't be too arrogant. We ignored this lesson of our ancestors and this is the cost we have paid."[78] Fukushima is no doe-eyed environmentalist; she has provided counsel for several of Japan's most mainstream research institutes and is an adviser to the Ministry of Defense. Her appreciation of the new orientation suggests that it isn't a fringe view and that it has roots in the center of the political spectrum.

Nostalgia for a simpler, communal ethic in which the individual's ties to the community are strengthened and the consumerist impulse moderated is another part of this mind-set. There is a longing for a less cluttered lifestyle that emphasizes human contact rather than the mad scramble to consume. In that world, lives are slower and unmediated by large, corporatist groups. The emphasis on reconnecting with others and the environment—the kizuna mantra—in the aftermath of March 11 is the officially sanctioned version of this outlook. On this perspective the Left and Right again converge. In a phenomenon that isn't restricted to Japan, both conservatives and progressives decry the march of globalization and the leavening of national cultures. Yamaguchi Jiro explained how Japan's "conservative political forces are divided. Successful politicians emphasized globalization and a more dynamic Japan, but ordinary people aren't interested in adopting such a global culture." As a result, the "progressive political agenda is the same as the old-time conservative national agenda."[79] This should not be taken as validation of the oft-repeated fear of a nationalist resurgence. The two groups' common ground—a longing for simplicity—quickly evaporates when they try to agree on outcomes. Shared objections do not make for shared objectives.

Plainly, the debate over economic reform is part of a much larger phenomenon—national identity—that tends to be glossed over or dismissed as amorphous, indeterminate, and too elastic to be meaningful. Nevertheless, "Japan's economic crisis has been interwoven with a crisis in the understanding of what Japan's national culture is and what it entails for the economy."[80] That the Abe administration embraced the TPP and, after considerable effort, ultimately persuaded the government to adopt it is proof that these obstacles are not an absolute bar to change and that reform is possible. But Japanese beliefs, traditions, and culture and the ensuing sense of identity have produced a suite of attitudes that cumulatively creates powerful resistance to change.

The Diplomatic Deficit

Equally powerful attitudes are at work on Japan's diplomatic efforts. While Japan's leadership seeks a higher profile in Asia and the world, most Japanese have a dwindling appetite for such a role. The Japanese prefer to focus on domestic priorities, such as improving conditions at home, rather than projecting power or dealing with external issues. Representative of that thinking is a 2007 survey that asked about national policy priorities: "Assert international leadership" was ranked sixth of nine choices. This finding matched the results of a 2008 poll in which just 8.2 percent of respondents wanted Japan to "contribute to international society"; all other choices focused on domestic concerns.[81]

When in 2017 the Cabinet Office asked in its annual survey of diplomacy what Japan's main role in the international community should be, the most popular response (with 59.6 percent of respondents agreeing) was "contribute to world peace through efforts to stabilize the region and resolve conflicts peacefully, including the contribution of human resources" (although the specific nature of those resources is unspecified). Other answers included helping resolve environmental issues and global warming (53.9 percent, a reminder of the priority attached to environmental concerns), contributing to disarmament and nonproliferation efforts (46.6 percent, a 5 percentage point increase over the previous survey), cooperating to help developing countries (37.2 percent, a notable 3.2 percent decline since the last poll), and helping to keep the global economy on an even keel (31.1 percent).[82] A slight and slightly shrinking majority (50.1 percent) thought that development cooperation is best maintained at current levels and that such aid is important because it helps create international confidence in Japan. (The number of respondents who wanted the level of aid to stay the same shrank, the number of people who wanted it to increase rose from 30.2 percent to 32.4 percent, and the number of respondents who chose to reduce or eliminate aid levels declined.) A larger majority (58 percent) wanted Japan to maintain its current level of activity in the United Nations' peacekeeping operations, and those who wanted Japan to do more increased from 19.8 percent in November 2016 to 22.1 percent in October 2017. A substantial majority (77.4 percent) favored a permanent seat for Japan on the UN Security Council and for the right reasons: to contribute to world peace for Japan's national interest, to promote arms control and nonproliferation through its pacifism and nonnuclear status, and to recognize Japan's significant financial contributions to the organization.

Other surveys should give Japanese diplomats and foreign policymakers pause. The Abe administration has made reinvigorating its alliance with the United States a priority, and the public continues to show very high levels of affinity for its ally (78.4 percent) and a positive assessment of the bilateral relationship (84.4 percent).[83] Yet when Genron NPO asked in a 2017 survey about the best action and roles for Japan in the international community, the most popular response (38.1 percent) was that Japan should not rely too much on its US ally and should instead normalize relations and cooperate with a variety of major powers, including China. The second most popular answer (17 percent) was that Japan should promote norms and international cooperation, and the third most popular response (with 12.3 percent) was that Japan should strengthen cooperation with the United States.[84] When asked, "When the power disparity between the United States and China narrows, which of the following options do you think is the best?" Japanese responses were evenly split among (a) "neutrality with nuclear arms buildup"; (b) "Japan-U.S. security alliance retained as the fundamental pillar, plus friendship with China managed"; (c) "neutrality with the current level of arms buildup"; and (d) "neutrality after nonnuclear arms buildup."[85] That finding is a less than resounding vote of faith in the alliance and that pillar of foreign policy.

A priority for the Abe administration has been renewing the emphasis on national security and reversing the decline in defense spending. His government created the National Security Council, reinterpreted the constitution to allow the exercise of the right of collective self-defense (which in theory allows the dispatch of Japanese troops abroad), and steadily increased defense spending, which reached a record ¥5.1 trillion ($45 billion) in the fiscal year 2017 budget.[86] Those policies are less than they seem, however. For all the hoopla, changes in Japanese defense policy are evolutionary, not revolutionary. Defense spending is still anemic. According to the Stockholm International Peace Research Institute, Japan's defense budget actually declined between 2000 and 2016.[87]

Again, however, attitudes are even more troubling. Another Cabinet Office poll found that just 6 percent of Japanese think defense policy is moving in a positive direction after four years of Abe's policies. When asked to identify policies heading in the wrong direction, 28.2 percent said defense policy, which ranked third among the top responses.[88] Doubts about growing defense budgets will increase as Japan's population ages and as more compelling demands compete for domestic budgetary priorities. Further, it should be noted that older voters have higher turnout rates than most other age cohorts. And even though the heroic contributions of the Self-Defense Forces after the March 11 triple catastrophe awakened many Japanese to new possibilities for the armed forces in securing the nation and the region, the people continue to be deeply skeptical about the value of the military for anything other than the defense of Japan. Their suspicion will likely intensify as the number of Japanese youths shrink, for it will be difficult to send its increasingly precious young people to fight.

Seductive Comfort

To get a better sense of Japan's future, it is worth dwelling on the views of Japanese youths, and the results appear to reinforce existing predilections. For a start, there is no mistaking a general sense of happiness among Japanese youths. Sociologist Furuichi Noritoshi, author of *The Happy Youth of a Desperate Country*, notes that young Japanese today report "an unprecedented level of well-being and life satisfaction." Referencing the government's "Opinion Survey on the Life of the People" (another Cabinet Office survey), he highlighted that 79.1 percent of respondents in their twenties said that they were satisfied with the lives they were living. The finding demonstrated "the highest level of satisfaction for that age group since the survey began in 1967, far exceeding levels recorded in the late 1960s and early 1970s, during the era of rapid economic growth." The tendency is even greater among teenagers, with more than 90 percent saying in a 2012 NHK survey that they considered themselves happy.[89] As one Kyoto University student explained, "We don't feel a sense of urgency or feel pain. . . . We aren't desperate to do something new. . . . We are happy and comfortable. . . . We can sleep on trains. No one will steal our money. We go outside at midnight. We can walk home at three a.m."[90] Young Japanese are quick to contrast their lives with those of their parents. A Keio University graduate student highlighted what he called the "happiness paradox": His parents "worked very hard, got big economic growth, but they weren't very happy."[91] Miura Lully, a researcher at the Policy Alternatives Research Institute affiliated with the University of Tokyo, applied a bittersweet gloss to the experience. "I've only known lost decades," she explained. At the same time, however, she sighed, "Japan is still comfortable, rich and beautiful."[92]

Comfort leads to complacency. Nakanishi Hiroshi, a professor at Kyoto University, sees "students at good universities who are bright and serious, but they are too cocooned. . . . Their lives are reasonably comfortable, and there is less incentive to go abroad. They think the outside world is risky, messy, and we can get all the important information we need at home."[93] Statistics confirm that assessment. In 2014 the number of students studying in foreign universities had fallen to 53,197 from a peak of 82,945 in 2004—a 36 percent drop. In addition, the number of high school students studying abroad fell 15 percent from 2013 to 2015.[94] Mizuno Takaaki, a former *Asahi Shimbun* editorial writer whose work took him around the world, was forced to conclude that "young Japanese don't have the ambition compared with other Asians. They are satisfied and comfortable."[95]

Young Japanese (ages nineteen to twenty-nine) accept cultural tenets that dampen calls for reform. They are among the most fervent believers that the interests of the nation should take precedence over those of the individual and that more attention should be paid to the country rather than to individuals.[96] When asked about sources of pride in their country, younger Japanese identify "public safety" as the first item, but then they highlight historical and cultural heritage along with culture and the arts.[97] At the same time, a majority prefers a society with small individual disparities even if that means sacrificing economic growth.[98]

Some might see a worrying nationalism among younger Japanese. Fear not. An *Asahi Shimbun* poll showed that just 13 percent of twenty-year-olds and 12 percent of thirty-year-olds said that they would fight if Japan were attacked by a foreign country.[99] While 74 percent considered themselves "patriotic," their image of patriotism was tied to their "love of the land"—literally. This patriotism is a form of environmentalism that is tied to the physical territory of Japan itself.

Their interest in the world is waning. Perhaps this is because Japan's political presence in the international community has likewise declined, and "among the Japanese people today (and what is particularly troubling is that this is shared by young people), there is a tendency to accept this decline as an inevitable fact."[100] Just 24.3 percent of Japanese youths believe that they and their cohort are equipped to fulfill their role as members of the global community, and only 14.5 percent thought that their government had policies in place to help them get those tools.

Voter turnout plumbs new lows at each election. Surveys show a diminishing readiness by the Japanese to engage in political and social activities, and this tendency is especially pronounced among the young.[101] Analysts blame a belief that engagement will change nothing, that the economy is stable and therefore tolerable (even if stagnant), and that young people prefer familiarity to change. Put it all together, and this group does not appear to believe that Japan should do more in the world, that Japan needs to change, or that it is prepared to work to change the country in meaningful ways.

Mojo versus Mujo

The struggle between calls for reform and the tug of the familiar is often framed as a debate between economic principles and an idealized social order. There is another way to look at this contest, however: See it as a battle between traditional ideas of state power and a new conception of power and influence that may be better suited to twenty-first-century Japan.

Abe's thinking is old school. As do most politicians (conservative and liberal) who occupy the highest positions of national power and responsibility, he believes in a strong state and that steady and expanding state power is the foundation of a country's place in the global system. Ultimately, this power springs from a strong economy. Thus, Japan needs to recover its economic dynamism—its mojo—to reclaim its proper place on the international stage and to be in the best position to protect and assert its interests in global councils. This very traditional conception of state behavior dominates foreign policy decision making and analysis in

Tokyo and elsewhere. It relies upon conventional and concrete indices of state power, such as the size of the population, the economy, and the military, and devotes less attention to the more amorphous components of such power—the power of its ideals, the attractiveness of its values, and the effectiveness of its diplomats—primarily because they are less measurable and their impact less clear. Abe shares the views of Koda Yoji, the blunt-speaking, barrel-chested former head of the Japan Maritime Self-Defense Fleet, who argued that "Japan is declining and 20 years from now the Japanese people will lose the luxury of their security and their economy."[102]

Japan's downsizing is hard to miss. The Japanese economy constituted 14 percent and 14.6 percent of the global economy in 1990 and 2000, respectively, but its share declined to 8.7 percent in 2010 and is expected to fall further to 6.1 percent in 2016. All the East Asian economies combined—China, Hong Kong, Taiwan, South Korea, the ASEAN-5 countries (Indonesia, Malaysia, the Philippines, Singapore, and Thailand), Vietnam, and India—constituted 50 percent of Japan's GDP in 1990 and 70 percent in 2000. By 2010 China's GDP alone was already larger (108 percent) than that of Japan, and the combined East Asian economies were almost twice as large.[103] But there is no need to dig that deep into the statistics to find reasons for unease. Japan's population is declining. Its economic rank is dropping. Confidence is falling. Its international stature is diminishing. Insecurity is mounting. Igata Akira, now a visiting professor at Tama University's Center for Rule-making Strategies, ticked off a string of external factors—a rising China and other rapidly emerging powers—and internal constraints, such as energy shortages and an aging society. He concluded, "We are a global power but not a great power."[104]

A substantial number of Japanese now disavow those great power ambitions. Their disdain stems in some cases from a concern about the past and a fear that democracy may not be deeply rooted and that great power temptations will lead Japan to repeat the mistakes of the imperial era. For many Japanese, the best contribution they can make to international society is to export their good behavior and to offer to the world the solutions they have forged for problems at home. Miura Kiyoshi, a former Foreign Ministry official who works for an international consultancy, explained it well. "We are a privileged nation and people, and we should do our fair share to contribute," he said. "My wish for my country is to punch at its weight—not necessarily above its weight—but we punch way below our weight." After going through a long list of potential Japanese contributions—from mediating regional conflicts to exporting an honest business culture—he concluded, "The biggest thing we can do is to get our act together domestically, to be proud and confident and more efficient."[105]

If Japanese horizons are being reduced, it is because, among other things, increasing numbers of Japanese are ready to revisit fundamental assumptions about growth and development. This new and evolving mind-set embodies practical and philosophical considerations of Japanese identity and positive and negative assessments of the country's future and its potential, as well as a concomitant adjustment in Japanese thinking about modernization—in particular the idea that newer and bigger are not always better. Increasing numbers of Japanese people, and especially the young, see their country and its options in this light. Kato Norihiro, a literary critic at Waseda University, applauded a youth culture that is taking a more measured approach to consumerism. "'Japan is a small country,' people are saying, 'and we're OK with small.' It is, perhaps, a sort of maturity. We are coming to see the limits of our resources. . . . Japan doesn't need to be No. 2 in the world, or No. 5 or 15. It's time to look to more important things, to think more about the environment and about people less lucky than ourselves."[106]

In *Thoughts on Descent*, novelist and commentator Itsuki Hiroyuki asserted, "Japan now seems to stand at the vanguard of a new downsizing movement. . . . In a world whose limits are increasingly apparent, Japan and its youths, old beyond their years, may well reveal what it is like to outgrow growth."[107] His message caught on after the March 11 tragedy, and his book sold over 200,000 copies. For Yamaguchi Jiro, the Hokkaido University political scientist and adviser to the DPJ, this state of affairs is a call to rethink the nature of the Japanese social contract, to accept a more expansive state, and to embrace a Northern European–style social market economy. He believes that "a stable society can no longer expect growth. We can't destroy the environment and make more energy. These arguments no longer represent a stable society. Many people are tired of expansion and growth and stressful requirements caused by globalization."[108]

This thinking is often blithely dismissed as fashionable, if not naive, environmentalism or as the remnants of a leftist inclination that survived the end of the Cold War and the discrediting of socialist ideology. Critics acknowledge that frustration and opting out are natural responses to two decades of stagnation, but they counter that the shortening of horizons and the downscaling of ambitions are defeatist (to use the most inflammatory rhetoric). For them, these beliefs repudiate the basic principles of how a state should act, of how Japan has behaved since it modernized over a century ago, and of common sense. Recall the warning of Funabashi Yoichi in chapter 1: "Japan can no longer afford the delusions of 'graceful decline' or small island beautiful . . . our choice is rebirth or ruin."[109]

But this new mind-set is more than warmed-over socialism or widespread resignation. The preference for a "new and different Japan" reflects a reorientation for Japan and an evolving set of national priorities. A post-growth mentality is a complex of responses that includes identity issues, a cultural and philosophical orientation, and an adaption to Japan's particular circumstances.

Hama Noriko, the former research director at the Center for Economic and Policy Studies in the Mitsubishi Research Institute in Tokyo and dean of the Doshisha University Business School in Kyoto, calculated the price Japan has paid for economic success and the impact of two decades of slow or stagnant growth. She has concluded that "for a mature Japan, economic growth is no longer necessary."[110] She believes that Japan's "preoccupation with growth is our biggest problem as it leads to economic deadlock. Growth is for young countries. We're a refined economy and past the growing stage—except spiritually."[111]

Hama's thinking borders on heresy among most economists, but it has growing support in a country of modulated ambitions and a recalculation of what constitutes a good life. In Japan "slow growth" is another way of saying that the Japanese economy privileges security and stability over expansion, or jobs over productivity. Recall those opinion polls in which majorities preferred a more activist state if it means "less citizens in need." Employment takes precedence over expansion. The impulse to modulate ambitions is increasingly common, as was articulated in chapter 1 by Kyoto businessman Murata Daisuke and Iwase Sachiko, a senior adviser for the Japan International Cooperation Agency. More alarming for traditionalists should be the spread of such thinking among younger Japanese such as Takeuchi Hikaru, a university student who worked for Youth for 3.11, a volunteer organization set up after March 11 to harness the energies of Japan's young people. An engaged citizen, he echoed his elders to note that "Japan doesn't need to be a big country like we used to be. . . . Japan should go out and tell the world about our experience. But as a nation, we have so many problems to solve; we need to concentrate on Japanese problems."[112]

Critical to Japanese thinking is a sense of vulnerability. For some, it is the product of the "island nation mentality," and it is reinforced by the constant reminder that Japan has no resources other than its people. Writer Murakami Haruki recalled the centrality of this idea in his 2011 International Catalunya Prize speech, in which he spoke of *mujo*, a Buddhist concept in which everything is ephemeral and nothing is immutable or eternal. Murakami suggested that this concept has been "burned into the spirit of Japanese people beyond the strictly religious context, taking root in the common ethnic consciousness from ancient times." For him, acceptance of the fleeting nature of life and beauty is an integral part of the Japanese aesthetic; for us, it is another indication of the outsize role of vulnerability in the Japanese psyche.[113]

While it is easy to dismiss writers such as Murakami and accuse them of self-indulgent sentimentalism, there is no mistaking Murakami's popularity in Japan;

his writing strikes a chord. Mizuno Takaaki linked the two concepts in his reaction to the earthquake and tsunami: "We are at the mercy of forces, toyed with by nature. We are powerless in front of them."[114] Keio University's Soeya Yoshihide referred to "a sense of destiny or fate" when he described the Japanese people's casual acceptance of the inevitable "defeats" by nature. "We have to prepare for it and take it."[115] The cabinet's Investigation Committee on the Accident at Fukushima Nuclear Power Stations, which was established to review the events of March 11, reflects that same attitude in its report: "It is necessary to humbly face the reality of natural threats, diastrophism and other natural disasters."[116]

Nakanishi Hiroshi acknowledged that "*mujo* is central to Japanese identity." While Nakanishi isn't prepared to fall in behind Murakami, he conceded that Murakami "describes one potential aspect of Japan. How that element will work out depends on chances, but it is not a predetermined future."[117]

Nakanishi is foreshadowing the battle between the traditionalists such as Prime Minister Abe who are determined to help Japan regain its mojo and the many others throughout Japan, including increasing numbers of the younger generation, who are prepared to accept diminished expectations and a reduced presence. Mujo, mediated through a range of other experiences and expectations, could well prevail. The Japanese tend to see new value and benefits in accepting limits and working within them. This could become a source of strength and even a model if refined, articulated, and pursued.

This sense of acceptance, a sentiment that comes perilously close to resignation, is one of the foundations of twenty-first-century Japan. It reconciles the widespread dissatisfaction that seems to permeate the country with the readiness to continue with the status quo. Japan's future may not be as bright as its past, but the present is not bad. The Japanese have a great deal to lose, and they prefer the comforts of today, tinged by the knowledge that they are being eroded, to the uncertainty that comes with great change.

Peak Japan

If this interpretation is correct, then this era is Peak Japan. The Abe years are an interlude, a last gasp by great power traditionalists to boost their nation's standing and to secure a leading role in regional and global councils. They will be frustrated as a combination of structural constraints and attitudinal barriers conspire to limit both Japan's capacity to play that role and its desire to do so. While some will recoil at these shrinking horizons, this shift is not necessarily a bad thing.[118] Japan retains tremendous assets, prime among them its human capital. It is already grappling with some of the most acute problems of the twenty-first century and has fashioned solutions to challenges that other countries will soon face. Professor Satoh Haruko, whose work focuses on Japan's relationship with Southeast Asia, has suggested that Japan's attempts to reconcile demands for its participation in international security affairs with its legal constraints could provide a model and context for regional debates about intervention.[119] This is a potential source of considerable influence and legitimacy—soft power—in the international system. The central task for Japan is to align the expectations of its allies and friends with its own capabilities and intentions. The greatest danger for the country is unrealistic expectations of what Japan can and will do in a crisis. A failure to align the two could lead to a rupture in its alliance with the United States and diplomatic isolation.[120]

Central to any substantive vision of a new Japan is the country's relationship with Asia. Much attention has focused on Japan's military policies and how Tokyo will increase its regional security role, but this is only one facet of a larger relationship with Asia. This complex and multidimensional topic is frequently reduced to a study of history and memory, a competition for regional influence between Tokyo and Beijing, and/or a zero-sum balancing of Japan's commitments to Asia and the United States. The DPJ sought to reframe this discussion but failed. The Abe administration has made relations with Asia a priority, but its policies have been refracted through the lens of great power status and competition with China. In short, Japanese engagement with Asia has assumed its traditional outlook, even though Tokyo has more tools to use in this effort in the wake of security policy changes.

Get out of Tokyo (or stay in Tokyo and talk to businesspeople rather than foreign policy specialists), and views of Asia are clearly changing. The spread of production networks and supply chains across the region has obliged Japanese businesses to reassess their regional strategies. The dislocations that followed the shocks of March 11 reminded Japanese businesses that their future is deeply intertwined with that of the surrounding region. Aggressive energy entrepreneurs envision deep integration throughout Northeast Asia to overcome resource scarcities that have threatened the region's economies. Not only have rising skill sets forced a reevaluation of countries once thought capable of providing only cheap labor but also the emergence of a substantial and growing middle class means that these countries are increasingly viewed as markets and sources of demand themselves. This development has taken on ever-growing significance as the Japanese consumer ages and the domestic market shrinks in size.

A richer, more developed Asia obliges Japan to rethink its relationship with the region. The traditional hierarchical model no longer applies. Now the Japanese must forge genuine partnerships with Asian countries, a process that demands the reworking of fundamental assumptions about Japanese business and the retooling of basic operating practices and procedures. Professor Odaki Kazuhiko of Nihon University, for example, argues that Japan must abandon cherished theories of regional development that privilege Japan—in particular the "flying geese" theory, which argues that countries develop similar to a flock of geese, with one goose—invariably Japan—leading the way and the others following in its glide path. Odaki writes, "Preconceived notions, based on the flying geese theory, are blinding Japanese to the fact that South Korea, Taiwan and China have already overtaken Japan in many industries. The flying geese view is an obstruction for Japanese in considering how to prepare for Japan's future development."[121] Increasingly, business professionals, economic policymakers, and some politicians acknowledge this new reality and are responding to it.

The danger for Japan is that the conservatism of its current leadership risks being characterized as nostalgic and as attempting to legitimate or revive a discredited past. The pragmatism and caution Prime Minister Abe displayed throughout his campaign to advance security policy reform show that he is aware of the risks and will try to reduce both Japanese and regional anxieties. He has largely succeeded. Smartly applied, his utilization of the past could help promote Japan's reintegration with Asia. A keener understanding and appreciation of the Asian roots of Japan's culture and heritage would facilitate "a return to Asia."

Japan thus must revisit the defining element of the first Meiji moment—the decision to go "out of Asia." That choice made sense at the time but has restricted Japan's options ever since. Japan can no longer afford to be *in* Asia without being *part of* Asia. Any new relationship will depend, ultimately, on a new mentality in Japan. The region can no longer be viewed as merely the object of Japanese attentions or an assortment of countries to be led by Tokyo. Japan must pursue a less hierarchical, more egalitarian order, one that yields a genuine partnership. Critical to the success of this effort will be the forging of a new relationship with both South Korea and China. All three countries will have to work to realize that vision.

Japan has an alternative model for engaging the region—the vision of Ishibashi Tanzan and his "small Japan policy."[122] Ishibashi was a journalist and politician who in the 1920s rejected the "Big Japan" policy that endorsed expansionism in Asia to ensure economic growth and development. He feared that Japan's ventures into the Asian mainland would force the country into a more imperialist posture that would promote militarism, nationalism, and autocratic tendencies at home. Ishibashi backed international cooperation, especially in partnership with the United States, to elevate Japan's position in the world and to safeguard democracy and individual rights at home. He argued against having overseas colonies and said that Japan's rejection of such possessions would spur other colonies to demand that their overlords do the same, thus making Tokyo an international trendsetter and de facto leader of Asia. He was promoting Japan's soft power through a new relationship with Asia and the wider world. Further, the concept of mujo could guide Tokyo's policymakers both as a process—its framework promotes greater balance in Japan's external relations because it acknowledges the ultimate variability and impermanence of power—and as a principle, as it puts less emphasis on consumption and lightens Japan's impact on the environment.

It is possible, however, that Japan and the Japanese will double down on the status quo and accept increasing marginalization. Mizuno, the former *Asahi* journalist, has personal experience with the trimming of ambitions for Japan. "I wanted to see Tokyo as a new New York." But a decade of confusion, punctuated by the war on terror, the rise of China, and the intensifying frictions between it and Japan, as well as the bitter experience of the failed attempt at opposition government, left him disillusioned. Japan "will maintain its sense of uniqueness. We simply want to keep our society as it is." The cost of clinging to that ideal, however, will be high. "Japan is shrinking but that is OK. It is decaying but that is OK. Japanese want their comfortable, small village mentality, fictional communal mentality. My sense of Japan is like Europe in the 1970s—an economy that is shrinking and a sophisticated culture. We are not getting richer, but it's not bad. It is a quiet society. This is one image of Japan and the one that will prevail if current trends continue."[123] Or as Doden Aiko, an NHK commentator, said more succinctly: "We have come to the realization that our previous goals are not attainable."[124]

2020 Olympics: Turning Point or Bookend?

When historians assess the Abe era, they will use the 2020 Tokyo Olympic and Paralympic Games as their benchmark. They will note that Abe's grandfather Kishi Nobusuke championed Japan's bid for the 1964 Games. They will highlight the decisions to use the 1964 stadium as the starting point for a new, futuristic arena and to renovate other existing facilities to illustrate the continuity between the two Games. Most important, however, if Abe's vision for Japan is realized, those future historians will point out that just as the 1964 Games showcased the country's economic and political reemergence from the defeat of World War II, the 2020 Games marked a similar reemergence after two decades of economic stagnation.

Throughout his second term in the prime minister's office, no single event has weighed more heavily or glittered more brightly than the 2020 Games. The International Olympic Committee's September 2013 decision to let Tokyo host the Games was both a validation and a "fourth arrow" in Abe's quiver. He declared after Tokyo's selection: "I want to make the Olympics a trigger for sweeping away

15 years of deflation and economic decline."[125] Four years later, Abe, as well as many others, looked to the Games "to mark a significant rebirth of Japan."[126]

As have previous hosts, Japan is counting on an economic boost from the Games. The Bank of Japan has estimated that real GDP growth would increase about 0.2 to 0.3 percentage points from 2015 to 2018 because of Olympic preparations, making Japan's real GDP in 2018 about 1 percent (¥5 trillion to ¥6 trillion) higher than it would have been without the Games. Much of that growth, however, is the result of construction, which will taper off.[127] But as that building boom subsides, tourism will compensate for some of the losses. Tourism is a core component of the government's plan to boost its GDP growth target to ¥600 trillion in 2020 (from the current level of ¥500 trillion),[128] and substantial progress has been made. About 28.7 million foreign tourists visited Japan in 2017, representing a nearly 20 percent jump over the previous year and a tripling of the number of visitors in the past five years.[129] This swelling tide prompted the Japan National Tourism Organization to throw out its plan for inbound tourism. Originally, authorities aimed to host 20 million tourists by 2020, but in 2016 they announced a doubling of that goal to 40 million visitors by 2020.[130] While that target sounds ambitious, it is within reach, and the 8.5 million tourists that are anticipated to visit for the Summer Games will put an exclamation point on that effort.[131]

The Games thus have assumed an outsize role in government planning. The 2014 revisions of the National Revitalization Strategy identified the 2020 Olympics as one of two focal points for the intensification of reform efforts, noting that the preparation presents "an opportunity to accelerate reforms . . . for the purpose of vitalizing not only Tokyo but all of Japan."[132] Ministries and agencies have articulated growth plans and strategies that use the Olympics to highlight their efforts, with projects ranging from infrastructure to robotics to health care.[133] As one report explained, "We will have a great opportunity in 2020 to demonstrate the society that can be realized when problems are solved through the use of science and technology capabilities, and to show the future vision of Japan to the world. . . . [The Olympics] can give a boost to the world-wide development of Japanese industries and also encourage overseas companies to make investments in Japan."[134]

The 1964 Olympics had similar objectives. They were the first Games held in Asia—Tokyo was selected to host the 1940 Games, but they were canceled as the world marched toward war—and the government spent what some estimate as the equivalent of one year of the national budget to show the world what a country Japan had become and what it could do.[135] A *shinkansen* (bullet train) service between Tokyo and Osaka began days before the Olympic torch was lit at the opening ceremonies. Haneda Airport was transformed and a monorail constructed to link it to the city center. The cityscape saw the addition of new venues such as the National Stadium, the Nippon Budokan, the Yoyogi National Gymnasium, and the Komazawa Olympic Park Stadium, along with highways, expressways, and subway lines.[136] Trees that were planted to beautify the city are an enduring legacy of the event. High technology was on display as well: The 1964 Games were the first to use communications satellites to broadcast events and the first to use computers to keep statistics. Japan's enthusiasm for the Games sparked a boom in television sales and other consumer goods for its emerging middle class.[137] By all accounts, that coming-out party was a spectacular success.

Expectations today are equally high. The 2020 Olympics will showcase Japan's technological prowess, hospitality, and culture, all of which should boost its national confidence and domestic economy while highlighting its cutting-edge companies. Japan wants the world to come to Tokyo in the summer of 2020 and see the future. Glowing press reports detail the preparations.[138] Some of the 8.5 million spectators will arrive on jets that burn algae as fuel, a source grown on land that not only produces sixty times more oil per acre than oil made from corn but also can cut carbon dioxide emissions by 70 percent when compared to petroleum fuels. Much of the Games' energy will be provided by hydrogen, a fuel source that Japan has been especially keen to develop. The Tokyo government plans to spend ¥40 billion ($330 million) to integrate hydrogen energy into the economy with the goal of making Japan a "Hydrogen Society." The Olympic Village will be hydrogen powered, with at least a hundred fuel cell–powered buses, press lounges, and athlete dorms, and hydrogen cell–powered cars will prowl the streets.

Visitors will tackle language barriers with a real-time translation app that can be installed in phones or computers and will be available in tourist-dense areas. Other apps will allow visitors to scan and instantly translate Japanese signs. Building on Japan's reputation as one of the most automated countries in the world, the Olympic Village will become a "robot village," swarming with auto-mated assistants to help athletes and visitors with tasks ranging from carrying luggage to checking into hotels to providing information and even transportation on specific routes. Companies have announced plans to deploy fleets of driverless taxis throughout the city.

People who cannot make it into the venues will watch events on 8K (or nearly eight-thousand-pixel) high-definition screens, a transmission standard that is sixteen times the current resolution of 4K. If all goes according to plan, all of Tokyo will have become a 5G (fifth-generation) "smart city" with video streams throughout the metropolis, including 4K video in moving cars, and with "per-vasive facial recognition" used for stadium access, security, and the management of traffic, both human and vehicular.[139] People will be entertained in the evening by a manmade meteor shower, a spectacle designed to rival the extraordinary opening ceremony of the 2008 Beijing Olympic Games. As a Foreign Ministry spokesperson explained, "It's going to be a good opportunity to showcase Japanese culture, our technology, our products, our good level of service to give impetus to the Japanese economy. . . . It's exactly soft power . . . to create economic impact."[140]

The run-up to the Games has not lacked for drama, however. Some alleged the Tokyo bid committee or its representatives bought the victory in the selection process; a Japanese investigation concluded that nothing illegal transpired.[141] The original logo design for the Games was replaced after accusations of plagiarism.[142] Architect Zaha Hadid, who won the competition to redesign the stadium that will host the opening ceremony, got into a fight with the Games' organizing committee, reportedly over excessive costs (although some claim the problem was that the job should have gone—and eventually went—to a Japanese architect).[143] Cost overruns have occurred, as in virtually every other Olympics, and Tokyo has cut $1.4 billion from the budget, although accounting remains murky.[144] Plans to move the world-famous Tsukiji fish market from land needed to construct facilities for the Games have been delayed because the new site was discovered to be contaminated.[145] The water in Odaiba Bay, where the triathlon and open-water swimming events will be held, was also found to be contaminated with E. coli bacteria at levels more than twenty times higher than permitted. (Organizers say the results were due to extraordinarily high rains and can be treated. Similar problems were evident during the 2016 Rio de Janeiro Summer Olympics.) Finally, some fear that the Games will be used "to declare the end to disaster reconstruction" in the Fukushima area, suggesting things are back to normal.[146] Others, such as Ishizaka Yuji, who teaches at Nara Women's University, view the entire enterprise with suspicion. "Tokyo lacks a clear purpose for hosting the games other than city development, and that's why many people are still puzzled today."[147]

Nonetheless, organizers declare preparations to be on schedule, and supporters still look to the Games to make a turning point for Japan and to serve as the symbol of its emergence after the stagnation of the lost decades. While Ishizaka may question the design behind all that spending, for others, the focus on Tokyo is precisely the point: For them, fixing up Tokyo will fix Japan. As a Nomura Research Institute report explained, "The greater Tokyo area has a population of 36.7 million, making it the world's largest urban agglomeration. . . . [W]ith a population in excess of that of all of Canada (34.1 million), . . . Tokyo is the engine that drives the Japanese economy, [and] the rebuilding of Tokyo will lead to the re-building of Japan."[148]

Skepticism is warranted, however. It appears as if the 2020 Olympics will be like previous Olympics rather than become the transformational event that many anticipate. The reliance on generous dollops of stimulus to goose the economy is a time-tested Japanese fiscal policy. The construction boom that anticipated the Games resembles traditional Japanese development practices, not only in what money is being spent on but also where. Tokyo is benefiting, but spillover into other parts of the country has been limited. Sasaki Nobuo, a Chuo University professor of economics, argued that this approach is typical. Japan's regional development policies, he writes, "prioritized the development of hard infrastructure under the banner of shorter commutes and decentralization, while leaving fundamental soft infrastructure in its old, centralized state. . . . [S]uch policies are unlikely to create an environment that revitalizes local industry, produces jobs, and retains young people when all the central, higher-order functions of society—politics, administration, economics, information, education, culture—remain concentrated in Tokyo."[149]

Economic strategists hope that tourism will provide a compensatory boost when the construction boom subsides and that those visitors will travel beyond Tokyo. Many applaud Japanese efforts to court tourism but worry that a cheap yen is key to the success of those efforts.[150] Moreover, geopolitical uncertainties could choke the flow of tourists. Many of them are from China and South Korea, and their willingness to visit depends on good relations between their governments and the one in Tokyo. When they do arrive, there are concerns about the supply of hotel rooms, the overcrowding in highly visited locales, and the ability of non-Japanese speakers to communicate when they leave the big cities and visit lesser-known areas.

While these issues are important, they are not critical. None of the changes engendered by the 2020 Summer Olympics addresses the structural and attitudinal constraints that are the biggest obstacles to reform and renovation in Japan. The Games will open the country's doors to guests and will show off Japan's technological prowess, yet genuine revitalization demands a truly multicultural and international society and a shift in priorities. The Tokyo Olympics are intended to validate the success of Abenomics and celebrate Japan's emergence from stagnation, but they will not serve as a catalyst for the change that is needed. (To be fair, it is hard to see how a sporting event, no matter how big, could be such a catalyst.) If all goes well, and if there are no big surprises before the Games, then the 2020 Olympics will be a moment of celebration for Japan. The Games will mark not the country's reemergence, however; they will instead be a valedictory salute for Peak Japan.

Notes

1. "New Year's Reflection by Prime Minister Shinzo Abe," Prime Minister of Japan and His Cabinet, January 1, 2015, https://japan.kantei.go.jp/97_abe/statement /201501/newyear.html.

2. "Address by Prime Minister Shinzo Abe at the Sixty-Eighth Session of the General Assembly of the United Nations," New York, Prime Minister of Japan and His Cabinet, September 26, 2013, http://japan.kantei.go.jp/96_abe/statement /201309/26generaldebate_e.html.

3. "A New Vision from a New Japan: World Economic Forum 2014 Annual Meeting, Speech by Prime Minister Abe," Davos, Switzerland, Prime Minister of Japan and His Cabinet, January 22, 2014, https://japan.kantei.go.jp/96_abe/statement /201401/22speech_e.html.

4. Jonathan Last, "America's Baby Bust," *Wall Street Journal*, February 12, 2013, online .wsj.com/article/SB10001424127887323375204578270053387770718.html.

5. Prime Minister's Commission, *Frontier Within* (see chap. 1, n. 48).

6. Prime Minister of Japan and His Cabinet, "Council for Asian Gateway Initiative" (see chap. 2, n. 12).

7. Ibid.

8. Council for the Asian Gateway Initiative, "Asian Gateway Initiative," 2 (see chap. 2, n. 13).

9. Ministry of Economy, Trade, and Industry, "Industrial Structure Vision 2010" (see chap. 2, n. 17).

10. Dennis Botman, Stephan Danninger, and Jerald Schiff, "Can Abenomics Succeed? Overcoming the Legacy of Japan's Lost Decades" (Washington, DC: International Monetary Fund, 2015), 213, https://www.elibrary.imf.org/doc/IMF071/21547 -9781498324687/21547-9781498324687/Other_formats/Source_PDF/21547 -9781484352205.pdf?redirect=true.

11. Miyagawa Tsutomu, "A Growth Strategy with Renewable Energies and Human Resources Development as Its Core Is Urgently Needed" (Tokyo: Research Institute of Economy, Trade, and Industry, September 13, 2012).

12. Hoshi, "Two Decades" (see chap. 6, n. 44).

13. Shibata Saori, "Re-packaging Old Policies? 'Abenomics' and the Lack of an Alternative Growth Model for Japan's Political Economy," *Japan Forum* 29, no. 3 (2017): 400.

14. Prime Minister's Commission, *Frontier Within*, 20, 1.

15. Institute for International Policy Studies, "Vision of Japan" (see chap. 1, n. 85).

16. Council for the Asian Gateway Initiative, *Asian Gateway Initiative*, 2.

17. Sakurai Masamitsu, "Introduction," in *Vision of Japan 2020*, ed. Keizai Doyukai (Tokyo: Keizai Doyukai, January 11, 2011), 1, https://www.doyukai.or.jp/en /policyproposals/2010/pdf/110111a.pdf.

18. Hasegawa Yasuchika, "Decisive Action for Growth: Chairman's Message at the Fiscal 2012 Annual Meeting" (Tokyo: Keizai Doyukai, April 26, 2012), 1.
19. "Abe to the 189th Session of the Diet," Prime Minister of Japan and His Cabinet (see chap. 6, n. 120).
20. Shibata, "Re-packaging Old Policies?," 400, 409, 413.
21. Much of the analysis in this section is from James Gannon and Sahashi Ryo, "Japan's Way Forward: The Prospects for Political Leadership and the International Implications," in *Looking for Leadership: The Dilemma of Political Leadership in Japan*, ed. Sahashi Ryo and James Gannon (Tokyo: Japan Center for International Exchange, 2015).
22. Ibid., 181.
23. Linda Sieg, "Japan's 'Sontaku' Clouds Where the Buck Stops in School Scandal," Reuters, March 15, 2018, https://www.reuters.com/article/us-japan-politics -sontaku/japans-sontaku-clouds-where-the-buck-stops-in-school-scandal -idUSKCN1GR0T2.
24. Ibid.
25. Cited in Kihara Leika and Linda Sieg, "Abe to Push Reform of Japan's Pacifist Constitution after Election Win," Reuters, October 22, 2017, https://www.reuters .com/article/us-japan-election/abe-to-push-reform-of-japans-pacifist-constitution -after-election-win-idUSKBN1CQ0UW.
26. Office of Director of National Intelligence, *Global Trends 2030: Alternative Worlds* (Washington, DC: National Intelligence Council, December 2012), x.
27. That precise formulation was used by Prime Minister Abe in "The 13th IISS Asian Security Summit—the Shangri-La Dialogue—Keynote Address," Singapore, May 30, 2014, http://japan.kantei.go.jp/96_abe/statement/201405/0530kichokoen .html.
28. Hugo Dobson, "Is Japan Really Back? The 'Abe Doctrine' and Global Governance," *Journal of Contemporary Asia* 47, no. 2 (2017): 206.
29. Ibid.
30. See Seng Tan, "Asian Multilateralism in the Age of Japan's 'New Normal': Perils and Prospects," *Japanese Journal of Political Science* 16, no. 3 (2015): 308.
31. Ibid., 309.
32. Another attitudinal barrier to reform must be acknowledged—a belief that there is no need for change. This position has two variants. The first—that Japan has never been in really bad shape and its woes were exaggerated—is detailed in chapter 2. The second accepts that Abenomics is working; thus, there is no cause for concern. Five years into the Abe era, Pew data showed 41 percent of the Japanese said that the economy is doing well, a sharp contrast to the 7 percent that held that view in 2012 (Stokes, "Japanese Divided," 4–5 [see chap. 6, n. 117]). A cabinet office survey echoed those findings, reporting that 74 percent of the

Japanese—a record—were satisfied with their lives, and, for the first time in two decades, a majority were content with their income. This has prompted fears "that a too-easily-pleased Japan will lose its hunger for serious reform and salary increases after a couple of years of superficial tinkering. . . . That risk is now hardening, particularly after a reporting season in which companies' recurring profit rose 18 per cent year-on-year in the first quarter of the financial year but very few companies announced improved shareholder distributions" (Leo Lewis, "A Happier Japan Is a Concern for Investors," *Financial Times*, August 29, 2017). This argument has several flaws. It ignores the uneven nature of the recovery, growing signs of inequality, low productivity, and persistent structural problems. It dismisses not only the failure of the third arrow to hit its target but also the very need for a third arrow. Economists counter that successes should spur reform, not inhibit it, as change will be less painful during a recovery and costs easier to absorb. Nevertheless, it dulls the appetite for change; and if the economy is recovering and the public is content, it is hard to make a case for change whose effects are uncertain.

33. In Edward Lincoln, *Arthritic Japan: The Slow Pace of Economic Reform* (Washington, DC: Brookings Institution Press, 2004), 51.
34. Derek Hall, "Japanese Spirit, Western Economics: The Continuing Salience of Economic Nationalism in Japan," *New Political Economy* 9, no. 1 (March 2004): 84.
35. Hatoyama, "My Political Philosophy" (see chap. 4, n. 72).
36. Yamaguchi Jiro, "Neoliberalism no Shuen to Seiken Sentaku," *Sekai*, November 2008, 118, cited in Hashimoto Tsutomu, "Discourses on Neoliberalism in Japan," *Eurasia Border Review* 5, no. 2 (2014): 106, http://src-h.slav.hokudai.ac.jp/publictn/eurasia_border_review/ebr_v5n2/EBR_v5n2_99.pdf.
37. Pew Research Center, "Emerging and Developing Economies Much More Optimistic Than Rich Countries about the Future," *Global Attitudes and Trends*, October 9, 2014, 16, http://www.pewglobal.org/2014/10/09/emerging-and-developing-economies-much-more-optimistic-than-rich-countries-about-the-future/.
38. Pew Research Center, Question Database, *Global Attitudes and Trends*, Spring 2011 and Summer 2002, http://www.pewglobal.org/question-search/?qid=1030&cntIDs=@25-&stdIDs=.
39. Author interview, Sapporo, December 5, 2011.
40. Pew Research Center, "Emerging and Developing Economies," 14.
41. Global Entrepreneurship and Development Institute, "Japan," accessed August 15, 2018, https://thegedi.org/countries/Japan.
42. Ujikane Keiko, "In Japan, World's Gloomiest Millennials See a Future of Struggle," *Financial Times*, November 24, 2016.
43. David Pilling, "Youth of the Ice Age," *Financial Times*, June 6, 2012.
44. Cited in Ujikane, "In Japan."
45. Murphy, *Japan and the Shackles*, 209 (see chap. 2, n. 80).

46. Ibid., 211.
47. John Plender, "Cash Hoarding Companies Are Still a Problem for Japan," *Financial Times*, November 12, 2017.
48. "Shibusawa Eiichi: Japan's Moral Capitalist," Nippon.com, October 23, 2017, https://www.nippon.com/en/tag/shibusawa-eiichi/.
49. Council for the Asian Gateway Initiative, *Asian Gateway Initiative*, 3.
50. Liberal Democratic Party of Japan, "Draft for the Amendment of the Constitution of Japan (in Contrast to the Current Constitution)," April 27, 2012, https://www.voyce-jpn.com/ldp-draft-constitution.
51. *Sankei Shimbun*, "A Proposed 'National Constitution of Japan' by Sankei Shimbun," in Japan Forward, May 3, 2017, https://japan-forward.com/a-proposed-national-constitution-of-japan-by-sankei-shimbun/.
52. *National Security Strategy* (Tokyo: Prime Minister of Japan and His Cabinet, December 17, 2013), 2, http://japan.kantei.go.jp/96_abe/documents/2013/__ics Files/afieldfile/2013/12/17/NSS.pdf.
53. Author interview, Washington, DC, September 25, 2012.
54. Author interview, Tokyo, July 13, 2012.
55. Author interview, Tokyo, July 17, 2012.
56. Public Relations Office, "Survey on Social Awareness," 4, 7 (see chap. 6, n. 118).
57. Kosaka quote and Kitaoka comment are from Kitaoka, "III. Japan's Identity" (see chap. 1, n. 86).
58. Goldman Sachs, "Womenomics 4.0: Time to Walk the Talk," Portfolio Strategy Research, May 30, 2014, http://www.goldmansachs.com/our-thinking/pages/macroeconomic-insights-folder/womenomics4-folder/womenomics4-time-to-walk-the-talk.pdf.
59. Chad Steinberg and Nakane Masato, "Can Women Save Japan?," IMF Working Paper 12/248 (Washington, DC: International Monetary Fund, October 2012).
60. Emily Chen, "When Womenomics Meets Reality," *The Diplomat*, October 6, 2015.
61. Several key performance indicators measure progress: increasing female representation in leadership positions across Japanese society to 30 percent by 2020; lifting the labor participation rate of women between the ages of twenty-five and forty-four from 68 percent in 2012 to 73 percent by 2020; raising the percentage of women returning to work after their first child from 38 percent in 2010 to 55 percent by 2020; increasing the supply of childcare facilities with the goal of eliminating children on day care wait lists by 2017 (22,741 children were wait-listed as of April 2013); and raising the percentage of fathers who take paternity leave from 2.6 percent in 2011 to 13 percent by 2020. Goldman Sachs, "Womenomics 4.0," 7.
62. Annabelle Landry, "Kathy Matsui Takes Stock of Abe's 'Womenomics' Reforms," *Japan Today*, February 3, 2016, http://www.japantoday.com/category/lifestyle/view/kathy-matsui-takes-stock-of-abes-womenomics-reforms.

63. Ito Masami, "Assemblyman's Rebuke of Moms Seeking Day Care Draws Outrage," *Japan Times*, February 28, 2013.

64. Goldman Sachs, "Womenomics 4.0," 14.

65. Steve Mollman, "Japan Cuts Its Target for Women in Leadership Positions from 30% to 7%," *Quartz*, December 6, 2015, http://qz.com/567026/japan-cut-its-target-for-women-in-leadership-positions-from-30-to-7/.

66. Sekiguchi Toko, "Q&A: Goldman's Matsui Says Survival Instinct Driving 'Womenomics,'" *Japan Real Time*, April 23, 2015, http://blogs.wsj.com/japanrealtime/2015/04/23/qa-goldmans-matsui-says-survival-instinct-driving-womenomics/.

67. "Yanagisawa Calls Women Child-Bearing Machines," *Japan Times*, January 28, 2007.

68. Kyodo News, "51% Want Wives to Stay Home: Poll," *Japan Times*, December 17, 2012, https://www.japantimes.co.jp/news/2012/12/17/national/51-want-wives-to-stay-home-poll/#.WsttUy-B2Ho. See also Gender Equality Bureau, "Women and Men in Japan 2013," cited in Helen Macnaughtan, "Womenomics for Japan: Is the Abe Policy for Gendered Employment Viable in an Era of Precarity?," *Asia-Pacific Journal* 13, no. 12 (March 30, 2015), https://apjjf.org/2015/13/12/Helen-Macnaughtan/4302.html.

69. Author interview, Kyoto, November 7, 2012.

70. Ironically, most studies show a positive correlation between women in the workforce and higher fertility rates. See, for example, Ministry of Economy, Trade, and Industry and Japan Small Business Research Institute (JSBRI), *2012 White Paper on Small and Medium Enterprises in Japan* (Tokyo: METI and JSBRI), 130.

71. Martin Fackler, "Japan's New Leader Takes on Old Order to Jolt Economy," *New York Times*, March 7, 2013.

72. Japanese Medical and Dental Practitioners for Improvement of Medical Care, "We Oppose Participation in TPP, Which Would Render Japan's Public Health Care System Dysfunctional," accessed August 15, 2018, https://hodanren.doc-net.or.jp/tpp/130624tpp-e.html.

73. Cited in Yamada Takao, "Fighting TPP with 'Reverence' for Farming and 'Expulsion' of Consumer Culture," *The Mainichi*, October 31, 2011.

74. Ulli Jamitzky, "The TPP Debate in Japan: Reasons for a Failed Protest Campaign," *Asia Pacific Perspectives* 13 (Spring/Summer 2015).

75. Kitaoka, "III. Japan's Identity," in Kenichi et al., *Japan's Identity* (see chap. 1, n. 86).

76. Owada Hisashi, "In Search of a New National Identity: An Analysis of the National Psyche of Post-War Japan," in *A New Japan for the Twenty-First Century: An Inside Overview of Current Fundamental Changes and Problems*, ed. Rien Segers (Abingdon: Routledge, 2008), 240.

77. Prime Minister's Commission, "A Beautiful Country and a Safe Society," in *The Frontier Within*, sec. 2, http://www.kantei.go.jp/jp/21century/report/htmls/5chap4.html (see chap. 1, n. 48).

78. Author interview, Tokyo, July 19, 2012.

79. Author interview, Sapporo, December 5, 2011.
80. Derek Hall, "Japanese Spirit, Western Economics: The Continuing Salience of Economic Nationalism in Japan," *New Political Economy* 9, no. 1 (March 2004): 94.
81. "Nenkan renzoku chousa 'nihon jin' kokkakan dentou ya bunka ni hokori kyouiku to keizai jishin usinau: tokusyuu," *Yomiuri Shimbun*, January 25, 2008 (in Japanese).
82. All data in this paragraph from Public Relations Office, Cabinet Office, "Overview of the Public Opinion Survey on Diplomacy" (Tokyo: Cabinet Office of Japan, December 2017), https://survey.gov-online.go.jp/h29/h29-gaiko/summary.pdf.
83. Ibid.
84. Genron NPO, "Japanese Public Opinion on US Leadership and the Role of Japan" (Tokyo: Genron NPO, July 13, 2017), http://www.genron-npo.net/en/opinion_polls/archives/5359.html.
85. Cited in Inoguchi Takashi, "Shinzo Abe's Leadership and the Legacy of Japan's Defeat," *Georgetown Journal of Asian Affairs* 2, no. 2 (Winter 2016): 23–24.
86. Kaneko Kaori, "Japan PM Abe Says No Defense Budget Ceiling as 1 Percent to GDP," Reuters, March 2, 2017, https://www.reuters.com/article/us-japan-defence-budget/japan-pm-abe-says-no-defense-budget-ceiling-as-1-percent-to-gdp-idUSKBN1690EZ.
87. SIPRI Military Expenditure Database, "Data for All Countries from 1988–2016 in Constant (2015) US$" (Solna: Stockholm International Peace Research Institute, 2017), accessed October 15, 2017, https://www.sipri.org/databases/milex.
88. Public Relations Office, "Survey on Social Awareness," 17–18.
89. All data from Furuichi Noritoshi, "When Will the 'Postwar' End? Japanese Youth in Search of a Future," Nippon.com, February 10, 2015, https://www.nippon.com/en/in-depth/a04002/.
90. Author interview, Kyoto, November 7, 2012.
91. Author interview, Tokyo, July 12, 2012.
92. Author interview, Tokyo, July 21, 2012.
93. Author interview, Kyoto, November 9, 2012.
94. James McCrostie, "More Japanese May Be Studying Abroad, but Not for Long," *Japan Times*, August 10, 2017.
95. Author interview, Tokyo, July 20, 2012.
96. Public Relations Office, "Survey on Social Awareness," 17–18.
97. All data from Cabinet Office of Japan, "International Survey of Youth Attitude 2013," June 2014, chap. 2, http://www8.cao.go.jp/youth/english/survey/2013/pdf/part2-2.pdf.
98. "Poll of Young People in Their 20s," *Asahi Shimbun*, December 29, 2013, 30–31.
99. Ibid.
100. Yamauchi and Nakayama, "Why Do We Need?," in Yamauchi and Nakayama, *The World*, 3 (see chap. 4, n. 75).

101. Kobayashi Toshiyuki, "Lower Willingness for Political and Social Activities of the Japanese and Its Background," *NHK Monthly Report on Broadcast Research,* January 2015, www.nhk.or.jp/bunken/english/reports/summary/201501/02.html.
102. Author interview, Tokyo, July 10, 2012.
103. Shiraishi Takashi, "Japan's Asia/Asia Pacific Policy in Flux," in Funabashi and Kushner, *Examining Japan's Lost Decades,* 207 (see chap. 1, n. 33).
104. Author interview, Tokyo, July 12, 2012.
105. Author interview, Tokyo, July 21, 2012.
106. Kato Norihiro, "Japan and the Ancient Art of Shrugging," *New York Times,* August 21, 2010.
107. Cited in Bae Myung-bok, "Japan's Path to a Graceful Descent," *Joongang Daily,* March 19, 2012.
108. Author interview, Sapporo, December 5, 2011.
109. Funabashi, "March 11," in Chandler, Chhor, and Salsberg, *Reimagining Japan,* 8 (see chap. 1, n. 93).
110. Cited in Bae, "Japan's Path."
111. Judit Kawaguchi, "Words to Live By: Hama Noriko," *Japan Times,* July 24, 2012.
112. Author interview, Tokyo, March 26, 2013.
113. Murakami Haruki, "Speaking as an Unrealistic Dreamer," speech on receiving the International Catalunya Prize, *Asia-Pacific Journal* 9, no. 29 (July 19, 2011), https://apjjf.org/2011/9/29/Murakami-Haruki/3571/article.html.
114. Author interview, Tokyo, July 20, 2012.
115. Author interview, Tokyo, July 12, 2012.
116. Investigation Committee, "Final Report," 28 (see chap. 5, n. 21).
117. Author interview, Kyoto, November 9, 2012.
118. I make no judgments about these choices. The point is to be clear about the implications of such decisions for Japan so that there are no misunderstandings about what the country is or is not capable of doing.
119. Author interview, Tokyo, March 23, 2013.
120. For suggestions on what other countries can do and how they should respond to Peak Japan, see Brad Glosserman, "Peak Japan and Its Implications for Regional Security," Special Report (Barton: Australian Strategic Policy Institute, March 2016), 23–24, https://s3-ap-southeast-2.amazonaws.com/ad-aspi/import/SR86_Peak_Japan.pdf?PadQZtTBAG1kn3OoM9rqk3H7vDRXH_sm.
121. Odaki Kazuhiko, "Release the Geese," *Japan Journal,* May 2012, 24.
122. This analysis relies on Suzumura Yusuke, "Logical Structure of Ishibashi Tanzan's 'Small Japan Policy,'" accessed August 15, 2018, https://researchmap.jp/muxwut1b6-18603/?action=multidatabase_action_main_filedownload&download_flag=1&upload_id=7604&metadata_id=10756.
123. Author interview, Tokyo, July 20, 2012.
124. Author interview, Tokyo, July 22, 2012.

125. Jonathan Soble, "Shinzo Abe to Write Revival Story for Japan with Olympics," *Financial Times*, September 10, 2013.

126. Osaki Tomohiro, "Shinzo Abe Calls for Japan's 'Rebirth' by 2020 along with Constitutional Revision," *Japan Times*, December 19, 2017, https://www.japantimes.co .jp/news/2017/12/19/national/politics-diplomacy/shinzo-abe-calls-japans-rebirth -2020-along-constitutional-revision/#.WtF_Jy-B2Ho.

127. Richard Smith, "Tokyo 2020 Olympics Is a Winner for Japanese Economy," *The National*, June 25, 2017, https://www.thenational.ae/business/tokyo-2020 -olympics-is-a-winner-for-japanese-economy-1.93228.

128. "To achieve the economic target of JPY 600 trillion": Cabinet of Japan, Council on Economic and Fiscal Policy Working Paper, April 2016, cited in André Andonian et al., "The Future of Japan's Tourism: Path for Sustainable Growth towards 2020" (Tokyo: McKinsey & Company, October 2016), 7, https://www.mckinsey .com/~/media/mckinsey/industries/travel%20transport%20and%20logistics /our%20insights/can%20inbound%20tourism%20fuel%20japans%20economic %20growth/the%20future%20of%20japans%20tourism%20full%20report .ashx.

129. AFP, "Japan Breaks Tourism Record as It Gears Up for 2020 Olympics," *Straits Times*, January 12, 2018, http://www.straitstimes.com/asia/east-asia/japan-breaks -tourism-record-as-it-gears-up-for-2020-olympics.

130. Kato Fumiko, "Asia's Rediscovery of Japan: The Boom in Inbound Tourism," in *Reinventing Japan: New Directions in Global Leadership*, ed. Martin Fackler and Funabashi Yoichi (Santa Barbara: Praeger, 2018), 59.

131. Jones Lang Lasalle, Hotel and Hospitality Group, "Tokyo 2020 Olympics: Expectations for the Hotel Industry," November 2014, 4, http://www.joneslanglasalle .co.jp/japan/ja-jp/Documents/Hotel%20Intelligence/201411%20JLL_HH _OlympicReport_EN.pdf.

132. Government of Japan, "Japan Revitalization Strategy: Japan's Challenge for the Future," rev. ed. (Tokyo: Government of Japan, June 24, 2014), 17–18, https:// www.kantei.go.jp/jp/singi/keizaisaisei/pdf/honbunEN.pdf.

133. See, for example, Cabinet Secretariat, "Japan Revitalization Strategy (Growth Strategy), Revised in 2015: Major Achievements to Date and Further Reforms" (Tokyo: Government of Japan, April 2016), 11, https://www.kantei.go.jp/jp/singi /keizaisaisei/pdf/new_seika_torikumien.pdf.

134. Ministry of Education, Culture, Sports, Science and Technology, "Feature 2: Science and Technology Development toward the Tokyo Olympic and Paralympic Games in 2020," January 8, 2015, 21, http://www.mext.go.jp/component/english /__icsFiles/afieldfile/2015/01/08/1354397_005.pdf.

135. Alexander Martin, "The 1964 Tokyo Olympics: A Turning Point for Japan," *Wall Street Journal*, September 5, 2013, https://blogs.wsj.com/japanrealtime/2013/09 /05/the-1964-tokyo-olympics-a-turning-point-for-japan/.

136. Nakabushi Tatsuya, "Tokyo 2020: Building a Positive Legacy," Nippon.com, November 14, 2017, https://www.nippon.com/en/currents/d00359/.

137. Martin, "1964 Tokyo Olympics."

138. The items in the rest of the paragraph are from Bryan Lufkin, "8 Reasons Why the Tokyo Olympics Will Be the Most Futuristic We've Ever Seen," Gizmodo, September 24, 2015, https://gizmodo.com/8-reasons-why-the-tokyo-olympics-will-be -the-most-futur-1728007440.

139. Joon Ian Wong, "The Olympics' 2020 Tech Sponsors Plan to Turn Tokyo into a 5G 'Smart City,'" Quartz, February 25, 2018, https://qz.com/1215328/mwc-2018 -5gs-coming-out-party-will-be-the-tokyo-2020-olympics-according-to-intel/.

140. Cited in Stephen Wade and Mari Yamaguchi, "Tokyo Returns with Summer Games with Something New to Prove," *Chicago Tribune*, February 24, 2018, http://www .chicagotribune.com/sports/international/ct-olympics-tokyo-2020-20180224 -story.html.

141. Ibid.

142. Hiyama Hiroshi and Richard Carter, "Tokyo 2020 Olympics 'Back on Track' after Rocky Start," *Japan Today*, April 4, 2018, https://japantoday.com/category/sports /tokyo-2020-olympics-'back-on-track'-after-rocky-start.

143. Jessica Mairs, "Construction Work Starts on Kengo Kuma's Tokyo 2020 Olympics Stadium," *Dezeen*, December 14, 2016, https://www.dezeen.com/2016/12 /14/ground-breaking-construction-kengo-kuma-tokyo-2020-olympics-japan -national-stadium/.

144. Hiroshi and Carter, "Tokyo 2020 Olympics."

145. Consumers Union of Japan, "Moving Tokyo's Fish Market: Tsukiji in Trouble," March 25, 2009, http://www.nishoren.org/en/?p=236.

146. Wade and Yamaguchi, "Tokyo Returns."

147. Cited in ibid.

148. Kobayashi Koji, "The Need for 'Rebuilding Tokyo' with the 2020 Olympics as Impetus," NRI Papers No. 200 (Tokyo: Nomura Research Institute, June 1, 2015), 2, https://www.nri.com/~/media/PDF/global/opinion/papers/2015/np2015200.pdf.

149. Sasaki Nobuo, "Regional Revitalization: Another Perspective," *Japan News*, February 23, 2015, http://www.yomiuri.co.jp/adv/chuo/dy/opinion/20150223.html.

150. Leo Lewis, "Strong Yen Adds Uncertainty to Japan Tourism Surge," *Financial Times*, August 22, 2017, https://www.ft.com/content/e11a2a42-8727-11e7-bf50 -e1c239b45787.

INDEX

Abenomics, 170–74, 215; and Abenomics
2.0, 175–76; fiscal policy of, 172, 177; as
hazard for future, 216–17; initial success
of, 172–74; labor policy of, 172, 178,
201–2n10; monetary policy of, 171–72;
rhetoric vs. reality of, 176–79; and structural economic reform, 172, 174–75,
177–78, 220

Abe Shinzo: and Asia, 41–42, 188–89; "a
beautiful country" as goal of, 2, 24;
and China, 189–92, 200; as conservative and nationalist, 24, 182; economic
policies of, 48, 53, 170–78; first term
in office, 70–71; foreign policy of, 24,
184–94; and Japanese military, 180–81,
197–98; on Japanese values and pride,
194, 196, 197, 200; "Japan Is Back"
speech of, 64–65n61, 170–71, 184, 186,
201n1; on Japan's global role, 24, 184,
186, 199–200, 213–14, 232, 233; and
LDP, 25, 38; national security agenda
of, 24, 180, 186–87, 193–94, 199, 230;
and North Korean abductees, 35n59; as
opportunist, 179–84; as political tactician, 181–82, 218; public opinion about,
25, 180–81, 184; reform call by, 216;
return to power of, 72, 170; and scandals,

25, 70, 71, 182–83; and state secrecy law,
186, 199; and Trans-Pacific Partnership,
181, 185, 226–27, 228; and Trump, 186;
and "Womenomics," 224; and Yasukuni
Shrine, 24, 181, 191, 192, 209n109
Abe Tadahiko, 146
Abu Sayyaf, 116
Act of Special Measures Concerning Nuclear
Emergency Preparedness, 135
Act on Promotion of Women's Participation
and Advancement in the Workplace, 224
Act on the Protection of Specially Desig-
nated Secrets, 180, 199
Afghanistan, 26, 187
Agawa Naoyuki, 156
Akashi Yasushi, 154, 155
Allison, Anne, 104
anti-nuclear sentiment, 141, 148
Aoshima Yukio, 83
Aoyama Gakuin University, 158
Aoyama Shachu, 88–89, 91
APEC (Asia-Pacific Economic Cooperation),
111–12, 190–91, 209n109
Asahina Ichiro, 88, 90–91
Asahi Shimbun, 23, 82, 129, 146, 179
ASEAN. *See* Association of Southeast Asian
Nations (ASEAN)

253

ABOUT THE AUTHOR

Brad Glosserman is the deputy director of and a visiting professor at the Tama University Center for Rule-making Strategies and a senior adviser at Pacific Forum International, a Honolulu-based think tank. Prior to his October 2017 return to Tokyo, he served for sixteen years at Pacific Forum, briefly as the director of research and then as the executive director. From 1991 to 2001, he was a member of the *Japan Times'* editorial board and continues to serve as a contributing editor. He is the coauthor (with Scott A. Snyder) of *The Japan–South Korea Identity Clash: East Asian Security and the United States* (Columbia University Press, 2015).

Brad earned a BA from Reed College, an MA from the Johns Hopkins School of Advanced International Studies, and a JD from the George Washington University National Law Center, and he briefly was a member of the Washington, DC, bar. He now lives in Tokyo with his wife, Fan, and his son, Reed.